'You Are Gods'

Prosveta S.A – B.P.12 – 83601 Fréjus CEDEX (France)
ISBN 2-85566-827-1
Original edition: ISBN 2-85566-716-X

Omraam Mikhaël Aïvanhov

'You Are Gods'

Psalm 82: 6
Gospel of St John 10: 34

PROSVETA

Table of contents

The teaching of Master Omraam Mikhaël Aïvanhov was exclusively oral. This book is the first part of a synthesis compiled from his impromptu talks. His works are published in two collections: 'Complete Works' and 'Izvor Collection'. In the notes to each chapter, these are referred to respectively as 'C.W.' and 'Izvor', followed by the appropriate number.

The editor

Omraam Mikhaël Aïvanhov

Part I

_____

'You
are
Gods'

_____

Part I ~ 'You are Gods'

1

'Be perfect as
your heavenly Father is perfect'

Human beings are weak, wretched sinners. This is what the Church has been telling Christians continually for centuries. Original sin, the fault committed by their first parents, has condemned them for ever to a life steeped in darkness, error and misery. Human beings are conceived in sin, born in sin, and are not able to break away from this sinful state. Well, let me tell you, by continuing to stress and propagate such an idea, a person's hope and desire to cast off the shackles of his limitations is diminished. We should dismiss these ideas that keep human beings deeply mired in their weaknesses. Human beings are sinners... human beings are malicious... that is understood, but nowhere is it written that they should remain so for all eternity. You will say: 'But what about original sin? No human being can escape the consequences of original sin.' Where did you find such an idea? Not in the Gospels, that is certain. Did Jesus speak of original sin? No. And not only did he not speak of it, he spoke these unprecedented words: *Be perfect therefore as your heavenly Father is perfect.* How can fallen beings achieve this ideal of divine perfection?

By affirming the reality of one God, Moses brought something fundamental to religious consciousness, and in a wider sense also to the understanding of man and the universe. But this God was an implacable master, an all-consuming fire. Human beings were mere timid creatures who trembled before him, slaves who had to fulfil his commandments on pain of being annihilated. And then came Jesus saying this one God is a Father and we, his children. This notion reduces the distance separating us from God: family ties unite us to him. Everything is changed. And where exactly does that change lie? In our perception. But how many Christians have really understood what it means to be the child of God? How do they picture their heavenly Father? As an old man with a long beard, watching them, noting the good and bad things they do? Or as a kindly indulgent old man, on whose knees they climb to pull his beard and hair? Even if Christians have been saying for centuries: *Our Father who art in Heaven*[1] they have not yet understood in depth the consequences of this divine filiation. If we are children of God it means that we are of the same nature as God (a child cannot possess a nature different from that of its father) and original sin should no longer be invoked to explain the pitiful state in which we find ourselves... and in which we would necessarily remain.

You will say that this idea of an original sin, which led our first parents, Adam and Eve, to be banished from Paradise, is in the Old Testament, the Church did not invent it. Yes, indeed, and their punishment was coupled with these terrible words, which God addressed to Adam: *Cursed is the ground because of you; in toil you shall eat of it all the days of your life; thorns and thistles it shall bring forth for you; and you shall eat the plants of the field. By the sweat of your face you shall eat bread until you return to the ground, for out of it you were taken; you are dust, and to dust you shall return.* Then, at the entrance to the garden, the Lord God placed angels armed with a flaming sword to guard the way in.

Does this mean that humankind was rejected for ever? No, the conception of divine punishment inflicted on human beings because of the disobedience of their first parents corresponds to the image of the merciless vengeful God of the Old Testament. By teaching us that God is a Father, Jesus not only brought us to a better understanding of the Deity, he also helped develop our understanding of man and of his predestination. Even if he did not openly talk about original sin, he alluded to it in the parable of the prodigal son, in which he showed that the son who had left his father's house was also able to return. If he understood the fault he had committed, his father would welcome him, and not only welcome him, but would lay on a feast to celebrate his return and reinstate him in his previous dignity.

Those who are not aware of their dignity as children of God expose themselves to losing their way and falling into despair because they will never find that which, deep within themselves, they are really looking for. How can human beings really blossom if they ignore their true nature, that divine nature with which they must identify? This is what Jesus brought to light when he said: *The Father and I are one.*

Of course you will say: 'Yes, but Jesus is Jesus, not us. He is truly the son of God, whereas we ...' Well, listen to me carefully. If the Church made Jesus equal to God himself, the second person of the Trinity, Christ – a cosmic principle – that was its business, but in doing so it committed a grave error, for this put an infinite distance between God and us. And this error has had appalling results.[2] Jesus, for his part, never said any such thing. He never claimed to be different in essence from other human beings. When he said he was the son of God, he was not implying that he was by nature superior to the rest of humankind. On the contrary, while saying he was the son of God he also emphasized the divine nature of all human

beings. Otherwise, what would be the meaning of his words in the Sermon on the Mount: *Be perfect therefore as your heavenly Father is perfect,* and, *the one who believes in me will also do the works that I do and, in fact, will do greater works than these?* To interpret these words correctly, however, you have first to recognize the reality of reincarnation.*

If Jesus said that we can accomplish the same works as he, it must be that we possess the same nature, the same quintessence as he. Why do Christians neglect this aspect of his teaching? First of all, because they are lazy. They are not prepared to make an effort to follow in Jesus' footsteps. They say: 'He was the son of God, so he was perfect and there is nothing extraordinary about him having exceptional knowledge, virtues and powers. Whereas for us poor sinners it is normal to be weak, selfish and malicious, and we shall therefore remain so.' Well no, it is not normal, not normal at all! We are children of God just as Jesus was the son of God. The only difference is that Jesus was aware of his divine nature and predestination and he had already worked towards this in his previous incarnations. He came to earth with immense possibilities and a very clear idea of his mission, but he too had to work hard on his inner self, he too had to resist temptation, fast, and pray. Have you had a look at the Gospels? Why did he have to wait until he was thirty before receiving the Holy Spirit? And why did the devil try to tempt him?

Both in his words and by the way he lived Jesus never ceased to accentuate his divine filiation and his divine filiation is also ours. As long as we do not realize this we cannot know who we are, neither can we manifest ourselves as truly free beings. Yes, because the worst kind of slavery human beings

* On the subject of reincarnation, see Part IV, Chap. 2: 'Reincarnation: the teaching of the Gospels'.

15

can be subject to is to be kept in ignorance, unaware of their dignity as children of God. It is because Jesus wanted to reveal this great truth to the people that he was crucified, for to say that all human beings are children of God was to say that they are all equal. And this would have been to deprive a small minority of privileged people the right to consider themselves superior to others and so strip them of their powers and prerogatives. This, of course, the Pharisees and Sadducees could not accept.

Jesus was the most revolutionary of God's messengers. He was the first to defy all the ancient customs, and his audacity in proclaiming that he was the son of God and that all human beings are equally sons and daughters of God was expiated on the cross. The insistence with which Jesus accentuated man's divine filiation offended and irritated the Scribes and the Pharisees to the point that they attempted one day to stone him. But Jesus said to them: *I have shown you many good works from the Father. For which of these are you going to stone me?* Then they answered, *It is not for a good work that we are going to stone you, but for blasphemy, because you, though only a human being, are making yourself God.* And then Jesus reminded them of the verse in the Psalms: *Is it not written in your law, 'I said, you are gods'?*

So by insisting on man's divinity, Jesus was only restating a truth already written in the Old Testament. This truth had been intentionally disregarded, and to some extent continues to be so today. Even the Church, whose task it is to pass on the teaching of Jesus, does not concern itself greatly with promulgating this knowledge, which would enable human beings to understand and feel that they are brothers and sisters sharing the same divine origins. Yes, indeed, all men and women are brothers and sisters because they all share the same divine origins. And Jesus not only disclosed this through words, but through deeds as well. He did not frequent the rich, eminent, and educated, but sought out the humble, the poor, and the uneducated, even those who led ungodly lives. He welcomed them, talked to them, ate with them – and this exasperated the Pharisees.

You know the story of the Samaritan in St John's Gospel: *He left Judea and started back to Galilee. But he had to go through Samaria. So he came to a Samaritan city called Sychar, near the plot of ground that Jacob had given to his son Joseph. Jacob's well was there, and Jesus, tired out by his journey, was sitting by the well. It was about noon. A Samaritan woman came to draw water, and Jesus said to her, 'Give me a drink.' (His disciples had gone to the city to buy food.) The Samaritan woman said to him, 'How is it that you, a Jew, ask a drink of me, a woman of Samaria?' (Jews do not share things in common with Samaritans.) Jesus answered her, 'If you knew the gift of God, and who it is that is saying to you, "Give me a drink", you would have asked him, and he would have given you living water.' The woman said to him, 'Sir, you have no bucket, and the well is deep. Where do you get that living water? Are you greater than our ancestor Jacob, who gave us the well, and with his sons and his flocks drank from it?' Jesus said to her, 'Everyone who drinks of this water will be thirsty again, but those who drink of the water that I will give them will never be thirsty. The water that I will give will become in them a spring of water gushing up to eternal life.' The woman said to him, 'Sir, give me this water, so that I may never be thirsty or have to keep coming here to draw water.' Jesus said to her, 'Go, call your husband, and come back.' The woman answered him, 'I have no husband.' Jesus said to her, 'You are right in saying, "I have no husband"; for you have had five husbands, and the one you have now is not your husband. What you have said is true!' The woman said to him, 'Sir, I*

17

see that you are a prophet. Our ancestors worshipped on this mountain, but you say that the place where people must worship is in Jerusalem.' Jesus said to her, 'Woman, believe me, the hour is coming when you will worship the Father neither on this mountain nor in Jerusalem. You worship what you do not know; we worship what we know, for salvation is from the Jews. But the hour is coming, and is now here, when the true worshippers will worship the Father in spirit and truth, for the Father seeks such as these to worship him. God is spirit, and those who worship him must worship in spirit and truth.' The woman said to him, 'I know that Messiah is coming' (who is called Christ). 'When he comes, he will proclaim all things to us.' Jesus said to her, 'I am he, the one who is speaking to you.'

So Jesus did not make these revelations – which give us the key to spiritual life – to an important man, not even to an educated man. He made them to a woman, a simple woman who asked him simple questions, a woman who, judging from common moral principles, led a dissolute life, and furthermore, a woman who belonged to a people hostile towards the Jews: the Samaritans. It was to her that Jesus spoke of the water that gives eternal life. It was to her that he said that the place of worship did not matter, be it mountain or temple, because God could only be worshipped beyond all material form: in spirit and in truth,[3] that is, in the most sacred and most secret depths of human beings. And it was to her that he disclosed that he was the Messiah: *I am he, the one who is speaking to you.*

Why did Jesus adopt this attitude? Because the truths he brought did not concern only a few doctors of the law or a few powerful individuals. They concerned all human beings. They concerned the very essence of human beings, the essence that can be touched by those truths whatever their education, social class, sex or nationality. Jesus provoked the anger of the political and religious authorities of his time with this attitude, because with it he undermined the very basis of their power.

Be perfect therefore as your heavenly Father is perfect. What was Jesus thinking of when he spoke these words? Was his knowledge of human nature so inadequate? Why did he give human beings an ideal that is seemingly so unattainable? Because he knew that a person's true nature is his divine nature, and in every person he saw that which is eternal and all-powerful: their spirit, a spark from the bosom of the Creator.

But then why is the Christianity community such a sorry sight? Two thousand years ago Jesus said: *Be perfect therefore as your heavenly Father is perfect,* and yet, all over the world Christians fight and annihilate each other in all manner of ways as if they were animals. They continue to be weak, wretched, selfish, and evil. This proves that the knowledge and methods they have been given are inadequate and ineffective; they need something more. Everything is in the Gospels. The Gospels contain treasures, but treasures which they have not yet discovered, let alone put into practice. Yes, the Gospels contain everything; but the heads of Christians contain very little.

No book can teach us more essential truths than the Gospels.[4] You say you have read them and they did not reveal a great deal; that is why you are now turning to Eastern religions and philosophies in an attempt to find your way. Well, you simply have not understood anything about the boundless wisdom contained in the Gospels. Yes, of course I realize that you are fed up with well-known texts and feel like a change of diet. But it is dangerous to seek out teachings you do not understand, because they are not suited to your make-up and your mentality. Some Westerners have studied and practised them to good effect, but they are rare. We Westerners have the Gospels. You have neither read them seriously nor thought about them in depth, but you are looking for something else.

For what purpose? Very often people follow an Eastern teaching in order to boast about it to others or simply to feel themselves different. But there is no point in that. It only proves that you like the exotic, and not the simple, straightforward truth. People turn their backs on Jesus, but in order to follow whom?[5]

Be perfect therefore as your heavenly Father is perfect. The teaching of Christ leads human beings towards the realization of the highest ideal there is: to resemble that divine model they carry within themselves. What more is there?

Notes

1 See *The True Meaning of Christ's Teaching*, Izvor 215, Chap. 1: 'Our Father Which Art in Heaven.'
2 See *The Splendour of Tiphareth*, C.W. 10, Chap. 16: 'Christ and the Solar Religion'.
3 See *'In Spirit and in Truth'*, Izvor 235, Chaps. 11 to 14.
4 See the commentaries on the Gospels, in C.W. 1 and 2.
5 See *Life and Work in an Initiatic School*, C.W. 30, Chap. 5: 'The Spirit of the Teaching', p.152-160.

2

'The Father and I are one'

By presenting Yahweh as the one and only God, Moses was introducing a truly revolutionary idea. But this Master of the universe was formidable and could only inspire fear in human beings. Hence the words: *the fear of the Lord, that is wisdom*. Fear, however, is a negative emotion. If you live in the grip of fear you can never truly blossom, and with time this fear slowly destroys your psychic life, in other words, your intellectual, moral, and spiritual life. With love on the other hand, human beings blossom, and this is why Jesus came to earth and said God was a Father. Of course a child also fears his father a little, and that is a good thing, because he must realize there are rules that should not be broken, and if he breaks them, he will be punished. But a father is mainly loved by his children, not only because he has given them life but also because he shares all his riches with them, and this is how his children blossom.

But Jesus showed us that we can go further still. As long as we continue to keep God somewhere far away, in a region of the universe we call Heaven, with its angels and archangels, we admit there is a separation, a break, even if we think of ourselves as his children. If we believe that God is outside of

us and we are outside of him, then we must be subject to all
that lies in the space separating us; we are outside his light,
his peace and his love. This is why we must reach the
consciousness in which we feel we are in him and he is in us.
And this is what Jesus meant when he said: *The Father and I
are one.*

You will say: 'But even if God is our Father, is it not more
respectful to consider him as a king, whose throne is in heaven
and whom we must venerate and worship? That is what we
have been taught.' Well, if you like. But there are an infinite
number of degrees of truth, and the truth about God must
evolve within us as we evolve, in other words, as we become
aware of the wealth and complexity of our inner life. Do not
be shocked if I tell you there is no one, absolute truth about
God. We discover God as we progressively discover ourselves.
This is why the Initiations of ancient Greece taught: 'Know
yourself, and you will know the universe and the gods'.

People who have not yet developed a consciousness of
their psychic life are mainly sensitive to the phenomena of the
physical world – light and darkness, warmth and cold, well-
being and pain – and can only conceive of a God whose
manifestations are similar to those of the natural forces to
which they are subject. But now that people have gained a
greater awareness and knowledge of their inner self, it is possible
for them to discover that this God, whom they always felt to
be outside of them, is actually inside them. God is infinity,
immensity, he impregnates the entire universe with his presence,
and we are part of him, an infinitesimal particle of him, and
at the same time he is in us. Two thousand years ago Jesus
said: *The Father and I are one,* but human beings have not yet
really learned to understand God in this way, to feel him within
them like a living entity, a force, a light, from which nothing
can separate them. From time to time we hear a mystic, a poet

or a philosopher express this idea, and we say: 'Oh, how poetic, how profound!' But we do not then set to work on this idea, in order to live it. We continue to think of God as being outside of us, and this is why we shall continue to feel restricted, unsatisfied. So many obstacles separate us from him! It is impossible to reach him.

It comes as no surprise, therefore, to see that so many people today claim no longer to believe in God and even deny his existence. It is really quite understandable. Since they can no longer accept the 'external', stilted image they have been given, and since they do not know where to look for him, they ask themselves pointless questions about his existence. But asking questions will not provide them with answers. They will only find answers by working to deepen their awareness of a divine life, a divine presence within themselves. Only within ourselves can we discover the reality of God, until the day when, like Jesus, we are able to say: *The Father and I are one.*

People's religious conceptions will soon change. There is no doubt about that. We have had the Old and the New Testaments and now there will be a Third Testament, which will complement the two that have gone before.[1] In the Third Testament this truth that human beings must get so close to God that they sense his living presence within them, will be accentuated, stressed, and held as quintessential. Then they will no longer question his existence and will cease to feel abandoned by him.

Many mystics have complained of being abandoned by God. But God did not abandon them; it is they who were not able to maintain their awareness of his presence within them. God never abandons us. The changes occur in our consciousness. Sometimes our soul is more receptive and we feel penetrated by divine light and warmth, at other times it closes up and we are deprived of this light and warmth. And whose fault is that?

Imagine that the day is fine and sunny, but suddenly clouds begin to gather in the sky. They hide the sun, the sky darkens and you start to feel cold. You are at the mercy of the clouds. So, what can you do? You can wait, and while waiting, complain that the sun has abandoned you. But you would be wrong, because the sun never abandons anyone. All that has happened is that you are below the clouds. So you need to rise above them until there is nothing between you and the sun. The sun is there, it is shining, it has not abandoned you. If you feel abandoned it simply means you are too far below the clouds. For those who have inwardly risen above the clouds, the sun shines continuously. They feel penetrated by its light and warmth, and nothing conceals it from them.

The same applies to God. If we remain too low, there will always be clouds separating us from him. We must rise higher, ever higher, so that we may come closer to him. Indeed, we must get so close that we are able to bear him within us, to hold him so deeply within us that we are continuously bathed in his presence. As long as we continue to think of God as being outside of us, we will remain outside of him. And if we are outside of him, we will be like objects to him.

What does it mean to be an 'object'? An object is something in front of you, outside of you. Take, for example, a farmer, a craftsman or a factory worker: they need objects, their tools, which are obviously separate from them. They use their tools, for a while and then when they have finished their work they put them away and bring them out again the next day. And it is the same for us: if we think of ourselves as existing outside of God, we have the feeling that he picks us up and then puts us aside like objects. Indeed, just look at a potter and his pots or a cook with her saucepans. If saucepans could think they would moan: 'Why does our mistress abandon us? When she uses us we are warm, the food makes music as it is

25

cooking and she scrapes us gently with a spoon. But she always ends by abandoning us. How cruel!' Yes, it is the fate of pots and pans to be put away in a cupboard and forgotten for a time. And if we behave like pots and pans towards God, it is not surprising that he forgets us from time to time. Who could blame him? What would you say to one of your saucepans if it started to complain about being abandoned?

As long as you think of God as existing outside of you, you must expect to be left aside from time to time. You have no right to complain. And if you pray to him thinking he is somewhere beyond the stars, how do you expect your prayer to reach him? Whereas if you feel he is there, close by, within you, immediately you enter into communication with him and are filled with his presence. As long as you have not learned to find God within yourself, you will continue to have ups and downs. Sometimes you will feel joyful and inspired, and then suddenly you will feel a terrible dryness within you, the aridity of the desert, and you will say: 'God has abandoned me.' No, you are mistaken. God is within us and he cannot abandon us. It is of course very difficult to keep this awareness of God's presence alive within us. At one time or another even the greatest saints, despite their love, despite their elevation, have experienced this feeling of being abandoned by God. Even Saint Theresa complained, asking the Lord why he toyed with her as with a ball, sometimes picking her up, and then dropping her.

If we feel abandoned by the Lord it is because we too abandon him. Are we always with him? No, so why should *he* always be with us, always thinking of us? Who are we, what do we represent for him, that he should have to look after us all the time? In truth, however, the Lord is always thinking of us, but in a different way than we imagine.

When a child is born, cosmic Intelligence gives him everything he needs to live on earth. Nothing is missing: he has a head, arms, legs, organs; everything is there. He has been sent to earth fully equipped, just as soldiers are given a uniform, boots, a helmet, a gun and ammunition – and after that it is up to them. We too are given all the elements we need to live and flourish spiritually. The Creator has given them to us together with all the physical and spiritual organs we need to attract them and retain them within us.[2] And it is our fault if we are not able to use these elements to transform our entire being into a temple of the Deity. Yes, better than a palace, a temple. Of course we would already be doing quite well if we were able to transform our inner self into a palace. But a palace lacks the element of sanctification found in a temple. If you succeed in making a temple of yourself, God will enter you and never leave you. The Deity does not leave a sanctuary that has been dedicated to him and in which we continue to worship him in purity and light.[3]

Christians must decide to follow the path Jesus has laid out for them, the only one that allows human beings to grow as spiritual beings and to do good all around them. Because their real potential, their real riches stem from the awareness that God is within them. When Jesus was working miracles he said: 'It is not I, but my Father who acts through me.' If you efface yourself, if you melt into the Deity so as to become one with him, you will become a formidable power. Yes, by shrinking yourself down until you melt into God, you become great. Whereas if you stand before him as a separate being, opposing him to the point of denying his existence, you will become ever weaker. If you reject your true self, which is God himself, you deprive yourself of his riches, because he is not able to give them to you. You and he form two separate worlds, unable to communicate with each other because they do not vibrate in unison. But the day you learn to enter the divine vibrations, there will be no more separation.

The aim of all spiritual disciplines is to bring people to recognize themselves as being God himself. Every step you are able to take towards this recognition, towards this identification, will bring you closer to your true self. When you succeed in developing this divine awareness it will affect everything you do. You will begin to feel like a different person and God himself will manifest in you. This is what Jesus meant when he said: *The Father and I are one*. The initiates of India have summarized this work of identification with the formula: 'I am That.' In other words only That exists, I only exist insofar as I manage to identify with That. And the disciples learn to meditate on this formula, which they repeat until it becomes an integral part of them.

People for whom this identification truly becomes a reality live in fulfilment. Of course, not everyone can reach the summit, but all those who are prepared to make the effort are capable of escaping certain limitations, provided they learn to use the means God has made available to them. God has given everyone the possibility of coming closer to him and becoming like him.[4] Even those with great limitations and disabilities have the means to surpass, to outstrip themselves. If they accept to turn their thoughts and their attention towards those inner regions where the divine spark shines, they will understand where their true predestination lies.

So you too can meditate on these formulas: *The Father and I are one,* and 'I am That'; repeating them, whilst never forgetting that this is merely an exercise. Do not begin to imagine that you are already God himself! Otherwise you will become unbearable – you will even risk losing your reason. The closer you come to these divine realities inwardly, the more you must remain simple and humble, and not try to crush others with your superiority. Quite to the contrary, in fact: you must become increasingly generous and loving. Because God is love. If you are going to poleaxe others to show that you are a deity, then you have understood nothing. That would be hypertrophy of the personality and not identification with the Deity. So, I am warning you, although this exercise is the best, it can also be very dangerous. You must be vigilant and take precautions, in other words, start by recognizing that others, like yourself, are a part of the Deity. And as they are a part of the Deity, like the Deity, they are within you, they are you. All of humankind lives within you and you within it. When you think like this you cease to be in opposition to the people around you, you begin to feel their needs, their worries, their suffering, and you are driven to help them. Otherwise you will become a monster, to whom others are mere insects that can be squashed. When I give you certain methods, I must also warn you of the precautions to take to ensure that these methods do not cause you any harm.[5]

Always keep in mind that all the creatures around you are a part of you. When we walk along this path of true philosophy, we see that all creatures are one. In reality there is only one Being and that is the Creator. All creatures everywhere around us are but the cells of his immense body. Learn, therefore, to unite with all these cells through thought. This is how you will achieve full identification with the Creator.

The true transformation of human beings lies in this consciousness, this realization of unity. We do not exist as separate individuals. Each one of us represents a cell in the immense cosmic organism, and our consciousness must melt into this universal consciousness, which embraces man completely.

Notes

1 See *A Philosophy of Universality*, Izvor 206, Chap. 2: 'No Church is Eternal'; Chap. 3: 'The Spirit Behind the Form'.
2 See *Harmony*, C.W. 6, Chap. 4: 'A Disciple Must Develop his Spiritual Senses'.
3 See *Love and Sexuality*, C.W. 15, Chap. 17: 'Emptiness and Fullness: the Holy Grail'; *The Fruits of the Tree of Life*, C.W. 32, Chap. 24: 'The Holy Grail'; Chap. 25: 'Building the Inner Sanctuary'.
4 See *'Know Thyself'* Jnana Yoga, C.W. 18, Chap. 6 (v): 'Concentration, Meditation, Contemplation and Identification'.
5 Ibid., Chap. 2: 'Spiritual Work'; *The Mysteries of Fire and Water*, Izvor 232, Chap. 12: 'The Cycle of Water: Love and Wisdom'.

3

The return
to the house of the Father

The story of original sin as it is told at the beginning of The Book of Genesis is one of the most difficult to interpret.[1] You know this story: on the sixth day of creation God created man and woman and put them in the garden of Eden. He allowed them to eat the fruit of all of the trees except the tree of the knowledge of good and evil, saying: *in the day that you eat of it you shall die.* But the serpent convinced Eve to disobey God, and Eve in turn persuaded Adam. They ate the fruit of the tree of the knowledge of good and evil, and to punish them for their disobedience, God banished them from Paradise. Many people have concluded from this story that the situation resulting from their act of disobedience did not figure in God's plans. Well, this is not at all certain.

Who was this serpent who could speak so well and who knew so much? And why had God allowed such creatures to live in Paradise? (For just as Adam and Eve represent not only one man and one woman but the whole of humankind, the serpent represents a category of beings.) No one could enter without God's permission. And if God created the serpent before human beings, it must have been for a purpose, for nothing could happen independently of his will.

The serpent, which slithers along the ground, is a symbol of matter. And the story of original sin is the story of the descent of man into matter. The question then is whether by choosing to make this descent, human beings acted absolutely in contradiction to the divine will, or whether God, who left them free, had envisaged this possibility for them.

When Adam and Eve had eaten the forbidden fruit, God said: *See, the man has become like one of us, knowing good and evil; and now, he might reach out his hand and take also from the tree of life, and eat, and live forever.* Does this mean that there were two trees or only one? What is important, is this image of the tree, and if we can interpret it, it will help us to understand what theologians have called 'the fall'.

One could say that when the first human beings lived in Paradise they were at the top of the cosmic Tree. Symbolically the top represents the flowers. So Adam and Eve lived amidst the flowers, in other words, in light, warmth, beauty, and freedom. But gradually they began to ask themselves questions: 'What is this tree we live in? Where does the energy that feeds it come from? We see branches and a trunk, but down below there is something else we cannot see. What is it? We would like to find out.' And of course, when we want to find out about things we have to go and explore them. So they left their magnificent home that touched heaven, descended the length of the trunk and ended in the roots, underground. But as it is dark and cold underground, and they did not have the same freedom of movement, they ended by feeling crushed. The roots represent a state of consciousness. God had said to Adam and Eve: *but of the tree of the knowledge of good and evil you shall not eat, for in the day that you eat of it you shall die.* But they did not die. They ate of it and yet they continued to live. True! But they continued to live somewhere else, because the death God spoke of was simply a change of state. Death is always

33

simply a change of state. Inwardly the first human beings left the region of flowers for the region of roots.

What tradition calls 'the fall', then, is simply this choice the first human beings made to go and explore the world in order to acquire knowledge. They were free and they decided to go down below so as to get to know the whole tree. Well, that is all right, but when you change places you also change conditions. And since the conditions of earth are not those of heaven, they became subject to the cold, to darkness, disease, and death. They had wanted the knowledge that the serpent had, in other words, they wanted to explore matter, and they did so. In fact, as we can see, they were very successful. You will say: 'And God punished them for it.' No, he merely let them suffer the consequences of their decision. He did not reject humankind; on the contrary. If they want to leave the roots in order to return to the top of the tree, to the light and warmth, amidst the flowers and the colourful, fragrant fruit, they can do so. But they must first complete the experience they started.

You must not think that God is angry with human beings. No, he is generous and understanding. He allows them to have their experiences. The day they wish to return, they will return, and he is always ready to welcome them. He is waiting to receive them, to embrace them. He has given them eternity, incarnation after incarnation. He says: 'They will suffer for a while – a few million years, of course, but what are a few million years compared with eternity? They are my children; their spirit is immortal and one day when they return to me, they will be so happy they will forget all their suffering.' This is God's reasoning. And while they are waiting to return to him, human beings continue to learn.

As long as man lived in Paradise, he could stay there, but since the downward move was initiated, he now has to go all the way, passing through all the stages, to the end. And if he wants to go back, he will have to travel a long and difficult route. Suppose you are at the top of a mountain. If you are sensible and take care not to slip, you will not fall. You can stay up there as long as you like. But as soon as you allow yourself to slip, you will be forced to follow a certain path, across rocks, through the undergrowth and the brambles, and you could even fall into a ravine. Nothing depends on you any longer, because once you have initiated the movement, you are no longer free. And then what a problem to return to the top!

As soon as we leave the top we are subject to the laws of a world over which we have no hold. It is we who are dependent on it. To remain free we should have stayed near God. There, all the space was ours, everything depended on us, because the divine world is made of a material so subtle, so malleable, that we had complete power over it. That is where we were truly free. The mistake the first human beings made, indeed the mistake of humankind as a whole, was to confuse freedom with the right to do as they pleased. Well no, our freedom is the freedom of choice, but once we have made our choice, we can no longer escape the consequences of that choice.[2]

Do not think that the history of man could unfold without God's consent, or that nothing – neither man's disobedience nor the events marking his destiny – was planned in advance. Human beings moved away from God, but God was not completely opposed to this, otherwise they would not have been able to move away. Everything we do is, in a sense, possible only with the consent of God. And if we want to return to him, God will welcome us.

To show you that this idea is not contrary to the philosophy of Jesus, I shall read you the parable of the prodigal son. *There was a man who had two sons. The younger of them said to his father, 'Father, give me the share of the property that will belong to me.' So he divided his property between them. A few days later the younger son gathered all he had and traveled to a distant country, and there he squandered his property in dissolute living. When he had spent everything, a severe famine took place throughout that country, and he began to be in need. So he went and hired himself out to one of the citizens of that country, who sent him to his fields to feed the pigs. He would gladly have filled himself with the pods that the pigs were eating; and no one gave him anything. But when he came to himself he said, 'How many of my father's hired hands have bread enough and to spare, but here I am dying of hunger! I will get up and go to my father, and I will say to him, "Father, I have sinned against heaven and before you; I am no longer worthy to be called your son; treat me like one of your hired hands."' So he set off and went to his father. But while he was still far off, his father saw him and was filled with compassion; he ran and put his arms around him and kissed him. Then the son said to him, 'Father, I have sinned against heaven and before you; I am no longer worthy to be called your son.' But the father said to his slaves, 'Quickly, bring out a robe – the best one – and put it on him; put a ring on his finger and sandals on his feet. And get the fatted calf and kill it, and let us eat and celebrate; for this son of mine was dead and is alive again; he was lost and is found!' And they began to celebrate.*

Jesus summarized the entire human adventure with this story. Human beings wanted to travel, why stop them? God knew that they would be hungry and thirsty, that they would suffer, but that one day they would understand that no one could love them as much as their Father, and then they would return and all would be well. God is always said to have been furious about man's fault, but this is not so, not in the least. He let man do as he wished. God had his plans and he is patient. He said: 'Sooner or later my children will return. After a great deal of suffering, they will return. They will be covered in dust, dressed in rags, starving, but this doesn't really matter. They will be wiser and this is what is most important. I am preparing a feast to welcome them.' In the meantime, however, since human beings chose to descend, they cannot immediately return to the house of their Father, they must continue the experience to the end, far away from Paradise.

But the image of the Paradise they lost remains embedded deep within them. The life they lived in the world above is imprinted upon them like an indelible memory. This is why they sometimes yearn for it. Sometimes, in their prayers, their meditations, through something they read, after admiring a view, seeing a work of art, hearing a piece of music, something inside them, a memory, awakens. They relive a few moments of Paradise, they feel encouraged, appeased, enlightened. Yes, but unfortunately, some time later, they go back to their mundane preoccupations and everything fades away. They forget what they experienced. Sometimes they think it was an illusion, and tell themselves not to dwell on it. No, these states are not illusory, they reflect reality, the most essential reality, and you should try to retain them, to dwell on them in order to be able to relive them.[3] This is what is taught in an initiatic school: how to return to paradise, to our father's house.

The aim of all religions, all initiations, is to help human beings return to the primordial state of beauty and light they enjoyed when they dwelt in the bosom of the Eternal Lord. Religions do not concern themselves so much with recounting the different moments of creation, and Moses for instance, wrote no more than a page to describe how God created the world. On the other hand the instructions given to the Jewish people to meet the demands of Yahweh fill several books. Of course, there have been philosophers, theologians, and high initiates who have studied the question of creation, of manifestation, that is, of the descent of the spirit into matter. But on the whole they have not found it really useful to teach human beings about this. They have been more concerned with giving them methods to allow them to return to their celestial fatherland.[4]

The psychic life of human beings – that is, their intellectual, moral, and spiritual life – can be summarized in two words: ascent and descent. To ascend means to adopt the viewpoint of the spirit, and to descend means to adopt the viewpoint of matter. Now that we have descended into matter we cannot live like pure spirits. To live in matter involves all kinds of needs, and nature gives us all necessary means to provide for those needs. Someone will say: 'Since I have to return to God I shall rid myself of everything and go to him directly.' Well no, that is not possible. Now that we have left Paradise we cannot behave as if we had stayed there. As long as we make every effort to use all we have at our disposal to return to God and not to distance ourselves even further from him, that is enough. What counts is the goal, the direction we take; in other words, the reason why we do things. Whether we meet the different needs of our physical body, whether we study, choose a profession, or decide to have a family, all this is fine, as long as we do everything in our power to return to God, because this return takes place first and foremost in our consciousness. We have all descended into matter – since we have incarnated – and matter imposes limitations on us. But we are not obliged to let ourselves be swallowed up by it. On the contrary, we must learn to work with it and to work on it.

The story of the prodigal son is that of every human being, who, instead of living according to the divine laws, decides to do as he pleases, because he supposedly needs freedom and adventure. Initially, this new situation seems quite pleasant, because he thinks he is free from all constraints, but little by little things become difficult. Even if he happens to be rich and live an opulent life, spiritually he begins to feel deprived – he feels hunger, thirst, cold, because he no longer has shelter. Far from God we have no shelter and are exposed to all kinds of hardship.

The moment people begin to distance themselves from light and warmth, in other words from divine wisdom and love, things become more complicated for them. Imagine the following: it is summer, the sun is shining, it is warm. Life is very straightforward. But then comes winter. You need wood, coal, fuel oil, heating appliances, etc., and you have to get in stores of food, you need extra clothing, and more lighting. And then come fog, snow, and ice. Communications are more difficult, there is a greater risk of accidents. There is less light, less warmth and everything becomes more complicated. In the same way, every time people distance themselves in their thoughts and feelings from the spiritual sun, from God, they gradually lose their ability to manifest in light, love, or peace. And then of course a different ability appears, the ability to suffer, to weep, to scream, to become malicious and destroy everything. The poet Dante, who was versed in esoteric philosophy, described hell as an inverted cone. The greater the guilt of a person, the deeper he had to descend into the cone to suffer limitations. This is of course merely an image, but it corresponds to reality. The deeper you descend into matter, the more you distance yourself from the spirit, from the Source, from God, the more you are crushed, limited, and unhappy.

This is why, every day, morning and evening, we must get closer to the light, the warmth and the life of this spiritual sun, which is God. Of course, we are obliged to live on earth and therefore to be involved in a multitude of activities, but we should always maintain the desire to get closer to the Source. And if, inadvertently, we distance ourselves from it, we must stop immediately and redress the situation. You cannot be blamed for making a mistake, but you can be blamed if you persist in that mistake.

You feel restricted, tied down, enslaved, and you ask yourself: 'Where have I ended up? How do I get out of here?' Well, there is only one answer, and that is to get back on the upward path.[5] It is not enough to belong to a religion or a spiritual teaching, you must set yourself a definite task, a programme to be carried out. If you have a programme, even if you do not manage to complete it fully, there will at least be something written down somewhere to remind you that you took the right decisions, and the furrows you will have dug out will be ready to be filled with beneficial forces.[6]

When you dig out a furrow, it channels the rainwater. When you set yourself a programme, it is as if you were digging out furrows in which celestial currents will flow. If you do not set yourself a programme, time will pass and you will have achieved nothing. Then it will be no use to you to belong to a religion or a spiritual teaching. And not only will it be no use, I would even go so far as to say it will be detrimental. Because the truths given to you in a religion or a spiritual teaching are true forces, and those who do not decide to make good use of these forces will one day be swept away by them. The truths of religion, the truths of initiatic science are like matches. If you are careless with matches you risk burning yourself and burning others. Just think of all the damage caused by the followers of religions and members of spiritual communities who have not been able to do constructive work with the truths they have been taught.[7]

All the sacred books contain symbolic accounts illustrating the two processes of distancing and return. And the aim of an initiatic school is to bring people back to the house of their Father, the high retreat referred to in Psalm 91: *My refuge and my fortress; my God, in whom I trust.* Each time you succeed in rising to this high retreat you will feel safe, the forces of evil will not be able to come and catch you unawares.[8] You must realize that you all have this region within you. But to find it you must devote at least a few minutes every day to enter into yourself, to meditate, to pray. This is how you elevate yourself to the peak of your being, the place where God lives within you. God does not live in a region where enemies can get to him, so look for him within yourself and take refuge in him.

Notes

1 See *Les deux arbres du Paradis*, Œuvres Complètes, t. 3, chap. IX (1) : «Les deux axes Bélier-Balance et Taureau-Scorpion» et chap. IX (2) : «Le serpent de la Genèse» ; – *Le langage symbolique*, Œuvres Complètes, t. 8, chap. IX : «Pourquoi l'homme a entraîné les animaux dans la chute».
2 See *Truth: Fruit of Wisdom and Love*, Izvor 234, Chap. 18: 'The Truth Shall Make You Free'.
3 See *Le devoir d'être heureux*, Fascicule n° 3 : «Retrouvez les moments de bonheur», p. 30-32.
4 See *'Know Thyself' Jnana Yoga*, C.W. 17, Chap. 9 (II): 'Truth – Unity and Multiplicity'; *The Fruits of the Tree of Life*, C.W. 32, Chap. 6: 'The Fall and Redemption of Man'.
5 See *The Seeds of Happiness*, Izvor 231, Chap. 11: 'The Land of Canaan'.
6 See *A New Earth*, C.W. 13, Chap. 2: 'A Daily Programme'; *Golden Rules for Everyday Life*, Izvor 227.
7 See *La pédagogie initiatique*, Œuvres Complètes, t. 28, chap. II : «Le sens de la vie, l'évolution».
8 See *«Au commencement était le Verbe»*, Œuvres Complètes, t. 9, chap. VIII : «La haute retraite».

Part II

What is
human
nature?

1

Lower nature
and higher nature

However thorough and discerning an analysis we make of human nature, it is impossible to find a system that fully accounts for its huge complexity. This is why it is not surprising that all known religions and philosophical systems have described the human psychic structure in different ways.

Hindus divide human beings into seven divisions, each division corresponding to one of the seven bodies – physical, etheric, astral, mental, causal, buddhic, and atmic. Astrologers divide them into twelve, corresponding to the twelve signs of the zodiac, and alchemists into four, corresponding to the four elements – earth, water, air, and fire. Cabbalists have chosen four and ten, corresponding to the four worlds and the ten Sephiroth. Chinese and Persian philosophies use two – spirit and matter, masculine and feminine, positive and negative, heaven and earth, good and evil. As for Christians, they divide human beings into two – body and soul, but also into three – body, soul, and spirit – corresponding to the three persons of the Trinity – Father, Son, and Holy Spirit, which in turn correspond to the triad of the will, the heart, and the intellect. Some esoterics prefer to divide human beings either into six, because this expresses the triad in the two worlds – world above and below – or into nine, which expresses the triad in the three worlds – physical, psychic, and spiritual. The variations are endless and they are all justified. What is more, each one completes the others to some degree.[1]

The truth is that it all depends on how you look at human beings. Each of these divisions is merely a convenient way of presenting certain aspects of the make-up of a human being. None of them contradicts the others because each is true from a particular point of view. We make it easier to understand the anatomy of the human body by using different charts showing the different systems – skeletal, muscular, circulatory, and nervous. In geography too, to ensure as complete a coverage as possible of the region we are studying, we use different maps – geological, physical, political, economic, industrial and so on. And initiates, just like anatomists and geographers, use different diagrams or divisions, depending on the aspects of human beings they want to study or the questions they want to examine.

You have no doubt noticed that when I talk about human beings, I often use a division into two; I talk of their lower nature and their higher nature. Why? Because if there is one question that is not clear to people it is this. We talk of 'human nature', but what is 'human nature' really? Why do people not react to the same situation in the same way? Why does one person who has suffered an injustice think of nothing but revenge, while another, having suffered the same injustice, not only does not seek revenge, but forgives and repays with good instead of evil? Which of these approaches is 'human', the first or the second? A woman meets a man and falls head over heels in love with him. But the man is married. He is happy with his wife and children, but that does not stop her. She pursues him, and using guile and manipulation she finally manages to get him in her grip and destroys his home and family. Another woman in the same circumstances is able to control her feelings and desires, and even if it means she has to suffer, she thinks it is more important to keep the family together and happy. So here again, which attitude is 'human', the first or the second?

The truth is that both are human, but the first person's behaviour is inspired by her lower nature, and the second by her higher nature, because human beings contain both of these natures. To talk of human nature in itself, therefore, is not very meaningful. So often you hear people justify selfish, aggressive, or cowardly behaviour by saying: 'It's only human.' And if you think about it carefully, this 'it's only human' actually means 'it's animal'. Why do we have to give in to such weaknesses?[2]

People are very confused about this, and this is why they need to become aware of another nature within them, a higher nature, which manifests differently from that which they are accustomed to thinking of as 'human nature'. For what they call human nature is in fact only their lower nature, a legacy of the animal kingdom of which they still bear the mark. No one is free of this legacy. The difference between people is that some feel the need to control these animal tendencies, and others do not.[3]

Animals are fine as they are. All that matters to them is survival – to find food and shelter, to reproduce, and to defend themselves – so it is normal that they be completely guided by their instincts. But the same does not apply to human beings. They have a different vocation. And even if we still have to drag our animal nature around with us, it is not our true nature. Our true nature is our divine nature, the flame that burns inside us and that we must keep alight and continue to feed. We have to recognize that whereas our instincts are always ready to manifest without having to be encouraged, our divine nature needs to be protected and upheld. When people are in a situation where they have to fight for survival or defend their belongings, they do not need to be reminded to do so. They act spontaneously. But when they need to show wisdom, generosity, and selflessness, it is more difficult. It requires effort. And even if we possess these qualities, they will not express themselves if we are not vigilant.

When we speak of a human being, therefore, we must remember that we are speaking of a single creature with a dual nature. These two natures manifest in opposite directions, but they share the same structure, because God is at the origin of both. Yes indeed, within us, as in the universe, is the cosmic Spirit that we call God. But what is God? Even the religions which proclaim the existence of one God present him as a trinity. Christian theology teaches the mystery of one God in three persons – the Father, Son, and Holy Spirit – which is referred to as the Trinity. In fact the Trinity is not a mystery to those who know how to use the law of analogy.

If you want to understand what this divine Trinity is,[4] you must turn to the sun. The sun is a formidable life-creating force, which manifests as light and heat. If you are capable of understanding these manifestations in depth, you will discover the relations that exist between the life, light, and heat emitted by the sun and the three persons of the Trinity. And these three principles – life, light, and heat – exist on all levels of creation, from the physical plane to the divine plane. On the spiritual plane, life – in other words creative omnipotence – manifests as wisdom (light) and as love (heat). These three principles – power, wisdom, and love – exist in the Trinity. Father, Son, and Holy Spirit cannot be isolated from each other, neither can the life, light, and heat emitted by the sun be isolated from each other. You see, the mystery of one God in three persons is not so difficult to understand. What will always remain a mystery, however, is the immensity, the splendour of this primordial Essence from which stems all that exists. Though we study it all our lives, we shall never come to the end of it.

God, the Master of Life, is infinite power, infinite wisdom, and infinite love. And we have been created in his image. Through our will we seek power, through our intellect we seek wisdom, and through our heart we seek love. Every human being is a trinity that thinks, feels, and acts. Jesus referred to this trinity when he said: *So I say to you, 'Ask, and it will be given you; search, and you will find; knock, and the door will be opened for you'*. This surprises you? Well, these words can be understood only through the knowledge of this trinity of the intellect, the heart, and the will, which forms our psychic make-up. *Ask, and it will be given you*. But ask for what? And what is it within us that asks? And what searches? What knocks? It is the heart that asks. It is the intellect that searches. And it is the will that knocks. The heart asks, and what it asks for is love, warmth, and tenderness. The intellect, on the other hand, does not ask, it searches, but it searches neither for warmth nor love, because the intellect cannot function properly in the warmth; warmth puts it to sleep. The intellect searches for light, it searches for wisdom, above all it searches for methods to find wisdom. And the will knocks, because it is imprisoned and it wants space and freedom to assert its creative power.

Ask, and it will be given you; search, and you will find; knock, and the door will be opened for you. For two thousand years Christians have been repeating these words from the Gospel, but have they understood that when Jesus gave us these precepts, he was giving us a concept of a human being, which he defined as heart, intellect, and will? The heart strives for its ideal, which is divine love; the intellect strives for its ideal, which is divine wisdom; and the will strives for its ideal, which is divine power.[5]

Unfortunately, the trinity represented in human beings by the three faculties of thought, feeling, and action is more often inspired by their lower nature than by their divine nature. This is why it produces thoughts, feelings, and actions that are totally ordinary, prosaic, sometimes even criminal. It can be compared to Cerberus, the three-headed watch-dog of Greek mythology, which guarded the entrance to the underworld. And opposite this Cerberus stands our divine nature, our higher self, reflecting the three cosmic principles of the Holy Trinity. Our higher self stems from these three principles of Father, Son, and Holy Spirit and partakes of the same qualities. We all bear within us this self, which is of the same quintessence as the divine Trinity. It lives within us, and we must enable it to take possession of our entire being so that it may be fully manifested.

You understand now why we cannot talk of 'human nature', as if it were one. We should talk of the two natures, the lower and the higher nature, which have the same faculties of thought, feeling, and action, but which are orientated in opposite directions.

The diagram overleaf will help to explain this concept of the two natures, each of which is divided into three according to the three functions of man – intellect, heart, and will, or thought, feeling, and action. Each of these functions has its own seat – or vehicle, or body – through which it expresses itself. Our lower nature comprises the physical body (the will), the astral body (the heart), and the mental body (the intellect), and our higher nature comprises the causal body (higher intellect or reason), the buddhic body (higher heart or soul), and the atmic body (higher will or spirit).

The three concentric circles show the relationship between the higher and the lower bodies. The atmic body, representing divine strength, power, and will, is reflected through the physical body, representing will-power and strength on the physical

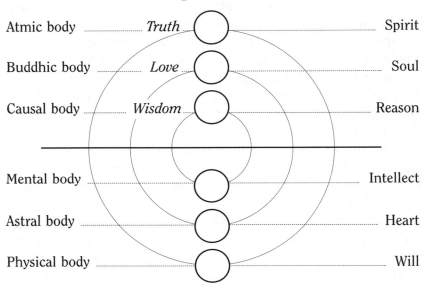

plane. The buddhic body, which represents the soul with all the most elevated feelings of love, sacrifice, and goodness, manifests through the heart or the astral body. The causal body, which is the vehicle of the most far-reaching and luminous thoughts, manifests through the intellect or the mental body.

Much time, study, and work is still necessary and many experiences still need to be undergone before the bodies constituting our lower nature are capable of revealing the qualities and virtues of our higher nature. But the day human beings succeed in developing these virtues, their mental bodies will become so insightful that they will finally understand divine wisdom, their astral bodies will nourish the most noble feelings, their physical bodies will have the power to do anything, and they will become divinities.[6] This is why the only truly important activity we have in life is to identify and understand the manifestations of our two natures.

I call these two natures 'personality' and 'individuality'. These two words are used arbitrarily in everyday language. People say someone has a strong personality or a strong individuality, by which they mean exactly the same thing, and this leads to much confusion. To understand what I mean about our higher and lower natures, we first need to examine the word 'personality', which comes from the Latin *persona*. The persona was the masks actors in the theatre in Rome wore when they acted in a play. This use of masks is found in many different cultures; the actor puts on a mask, which immediately reveals to the audience the role he is about to play; and he changes masks as and when his role changes. Thus the theatre gives us an idea of what personality is. Personality is the role that the incarnated spirit assumes during a lifetime. Today it is that of a man or woman, with a certain temperament, certain faculties and certain shortcomings, certain qualities and faults. In another incarnation the spirit will return with a different appearance, a different personality. But the being that appears in different masks and costumes from one incarnation to another is inhabited by an entity that does not change, because it is the person's true self, the divine self, the individuality.

The gravest error of human beings is that they always tend to identify with their lower self. When people say: 'I want... (money, a car, a wife), I am... (unwell, in good health, sad, joyful), I have... (this wish, or taste, or point of view)', they think it is their true self speaking. No, it is not! This is where they are mistaken. It is their lower nature that is wishing, thinking, suffering, and they, in their ignorance, rush to satisfy this lower nature. They have never stopped to analyse themselves and try to get to know their true nature and the different planes on which it evolves, so they constantly identify with their personality, and more particularly, with their physical body. It is time they realized that the manifestations of their body, heart, and mind are not an expression of their true self, and that by rushing to satisfy their demands, they are putting themselves at the service of something other than their true self.

Jnana yoga is what the Indians call the yoga of self-knowledge. Those who practise this yoga begin by analysing themselves. They become aware that even if they lose an arm or a leg, they retain their self; they can continue to say 'I'. The self, therefore, is not their arm or their leg, or indeed any other organ. And since their limbs or organs are not them, it means they are something more than just their body. Then they study their feelings and find that these never cease to change, from one day to the next, from one moment to the next. Moreover, since they are able to observe and analyse these feelings, it means their true self is elsewhere, beyond these feelings. Then, when they study their thoughts they come to the same conclusion. Their self is other than their opinions and their thoughts. And so they discover that this self they are looking for, this true self, is the higher self. They discover that this self is great, powerful, luminous, omniscient, a part of God himself, and they do everything in their power to find this self and unite with it.[7]

It is now up to each and every one of you to understand that what you normally call your self, is but a fleeting, partial reflection of your true self, a mirage, an illusion. This is the illusion that Hindus call 'maya'.

The divine nature dwells in every human being. Its home is in the celestial regions, where it enjoys the greatest freedom, the greatest light, and the greatest powers. But it can only express itself in the denser regions of matter to the extent that the three lower bodies allow it to do so. A person who, on the physical plane, is ignorant, malicious, and weak is at the same time, on a higher plane, an entity possessing wisdom, love, and strength. This is why the same person is so limited here below and has such riches and perfection up above.

You must know that you are all divinities. Yes, you are divinities and you live in a very elevated place where there is neither limitation nor darkness nor suffering. There you live in plenitude, in fulfilment. But you are not yet able to bring this life you live on high down to this plane. You are not yet able to feel it, to understand it, to reveal it, because your personality does not allow you to do so. Your personality is obtuse, opaque, ill-adapted, or ill-adjusted, like a radio that cannot receive a broadcast properly. Occasionally you experience a revelation, you have an intuition, because you have succeeded in reaching your divine self. But this does not last long. After a short while the clouds re-appear. And then again, some time later, while reading a book, listening to music, looking at a view, seeing a face, or while praying or meditating, once again you feel something like a flash of lightning, bright and dazzling. But again this does not last. And so human life alternates between light and darkness. You will experience this every day until one day, at last, thanks to all your prayer, meditation and work on yourself, you become the expression of the Deity and begin to live a new life. You are totally reborn.

So try to take this question of personality and individuality seriously. I really believe this is the fundamental question. Over the years, many thinkers, philosophers, and mystics have shed light on all kinds of subjects related to the inner life. I, on the other hand, have simply tried to explain one single question, that of the lower nature and the higher nature, the personality and the individuality. Every being comes to earth with a temperament which drives them in a certain direction. From a very early age I sensed that this question of two natures was important.

I was about sixteen years old when I had an experience which would mark me for the rest of my life. One night, in a kind of half-sleep, I had a vision: two people stood before me, one of impressive stature, emanated strength and power, but his face was hard, his eyes dark and fearsome. The second was radiantly beautiful and his eyes, like those of Christ, spoke of the immensity of divine love. They both stood before me and I had a feeling I should make a choice between the two. I was impressed by the power of the first, but in my heart, in my soul, I was frightened by something merciless and even cruel that I sensed in him. So I chose the one with the visage of Christ; the one who was the image of goodness, of sacrifice. And I did everything in my power to resemble him.

This is how this question of two natures first presented itself to me. And I have not ceased to study it since, because it is the key that enables us to solve all problems. I have read many books, I have visited many countries, I have met many people, and unfortunately, I have found that the greatest minds, the people in the highest places, rarely know when they are acting according to their lower nature and when they are acting according to their higher nature. They have no clear knowledge or understanding of this question, no standard by which to judge their actions. They see nothing wrong with any of their thoughts, feelings, opinions, tastes, or desires, simply because they are *their* thoughts, *their* feelings, *their* opinions, *their* tastes, *their* desires. They always feel they are justified in holding them. They are incapable of recognising all the elements of darkness and dishonesty that have infiltrated them, and even if they realize it, they do very little to remedy the situation.

It is difficult, of course, to see all this clearly, because the two natures are intertwined and entangled, and human beings – who are not always enlightened enough to distinguish the influences they are subject to – often allow themselves to be carried away by their personality. The difficulty, of course, lies in the coexistence of these two natures within us. This is how some people, whom we thought of as reasonable, sensitive, good, honest creatures, commit acts of great cruelty or folly. Nothing can stop them, and we are surprised because nothing led us to foresee such actions. Everyone exclaims: 'But how can this be? He was a good husband; she was a good wife; they were good parents. We don't understand.' Well, it is perfectly understandable. It *can* be explained. These people's lower nature had had no previous opportunity to manifest, but the day the conditions were right, it awoke, and since they had not worked on their higher nature to enable it to intervene, their lower nature gained the upper hand. In time of peace, for instance, people generally behave fairly reasonably and with a certain degree of goodness, but in times of trouble, in time of war, they are capable of committing the most horrendous deeds. We see this all too often. Is it they who have changed? No, it is their lower nature manifesting itself, because conditions were right for it to do so.

Until human beings become aware of the coexistence of two natures within them and the need to give pre-eminence to their higher nature, they will be capable of the worst atrocities. And it is no use asking ourselves: 'But how can this be? How is it possible?' Everything is possible. Yes, everything. But the opposite can also happen: seemingly ordinary people may suddenly show heroism, a strength of character of which no one thought them capable. In some circumstances, even criminals can show kindness, altruism, or self-sacrifice, because suddenly their higher nature has come into play.

When people are in a negative frame of mind they tend to think it is their lower nature that has worsened, and when they go through a good phase, they think it has improved a little. But they are mistaken. The lower nature never improves.

57

It continues to be what it is. It is their higher nature that has found better conditions for its manifestation. And then once again, their personality gets the upper hand, confusing everything and dragging them back into a deplorable state. And so it goes on. You must understand that it is not the self that changes its nature and becomes worse or better. No, it is not the self that changes. It is two totally different natures which alternately make their appearance on this stage we call 'the self'.

Our individuality never allows itself to drift into negative thoughts, feelings or deeds. If human beings show signs of such things, it is not their individuality but their personality that is the cause. The converse is also true. It is not the same nature that changes from one state to another. No, good cannot become evil, neither can evil become good. Each retains its own individual nature for eternity. Evil does not change into good and vice versa. When good manifests, we lose sight of evil, it is rejected. But when the good weakens we see that evil is still there, it was not dead.

If you make a very noble, very generous gesture it means you have momentarily risen above your personality. But as soon as you return, you will find it is just as you left it, and then of course your actions will not be so commendable. So you complain: 'But I haven't changed at all. I am still the same.' Yes, to the extent that you allow your personality to manifest you are still the same. But allow your individuality to manifest and you will again be able to achieve great things. Your mistake was to descend to the level of your lower self so quickly and to say: 'But I haven't changed at all. I am still the same.' But then who was it who just did these marvellous things? It was certainly not your lower nature.

What a great step forward it would be if human beings were taught about personality and individuality. To understand this question of personality and individuality everyone should begin by analysing their actions and seeing how things unfold: 'I had this thought; I had that feeling; I acted in this way... why? And this is what ensued...' Yes, instead of always looking outwards for knowledge that is not very useful, it would be far better if human beings looked inwards and consciously sought experiences that would enlighten them about this question of two natures. Most of the time they go forward blindly, thinking they are behaving correctly, and all the time they are being guided by their lower nature. And then occasionally – they do not even know why – their higher nature bursts out and incites them to act with goodness, generosity, and disregard for their self-interest. Well, it would be far better for them if they acted consciously, if they could say to themselves at every moment of the day: 'Let's see... this thought, this feeling, this desire, this act... was it inspired by my lower nature or by my higher nature?'

Let us go back now to the diagram of the six bodies. You will see that the three lower bodies – physical, astral, and mental – are separated from the three higher bodies – causal, buddhic, and atmic – by a line of demarcation. This line represents our consciousness.[8] It is their consciousness that places human beings between the lower world and the higher world. If you are not vigilant, if your consciousness is not awakened, the dark forces of your personality will begin to take control.

This idea of humans existing on the border between the higher and the lower worlds was expressed by the Ancients with the image of the guardian angel standing on their right and the devil on their left. The angel advises and enlightens, while the devil seeks to make them his victims by leading them into error. You might wonder why the angel and the devil do not

Higher nature

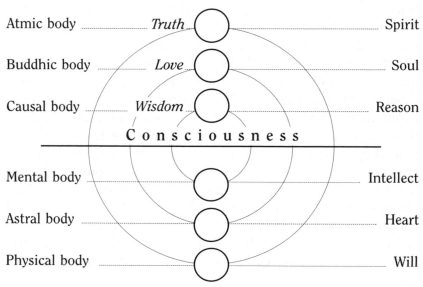

Atmic body .... *Truth*	Spirit
Buddhic body .... *Love*	Soul
Causal body .... *Wisdom*	Reason

C o n s c i o u s n e s s

Mental body	Intellect
Astral body	Heart
Physical body	Will

Lower nature

just go for each other's throats. That would be far simpler. The winner would get the poor wretch for himself! But no. They respect and appreciate each other, they greet each other: 'Hello there. How are you?' The devil does not lash out against the angel of light, and the angel does not strike the devil. Why? Because the guardian angel and the devil are images expressing the two realities of a higher world and a lower world within a human being.

We could use yet another image and say that what is below us, tempting us, is the moon, which represents our instincts, our belly and our genitals. Whereas above us is the sun, representing our soul, our spirit, God. It is always the same idea: the higher and the lower, and we are placed between the two, with the option of either soaring up to the heights or allowing ourselves to fall into the abyss. It is we who have to decide which way to go. If we have understood where our interests lie we will make great efforts every day to reach out toward our higher self, because it is there that we shall find light, peace, freedom, and all true riches.

So be forewarned: when you come and listen to me, you will always hear about this tedious, unexciting subject of the lower nature and the higher nature, personality and individuality, because this is the knowledge that will allow you to transform your existence. I know you would prefer to hear me talk about other things, to reveal the mysteries of alchemy, magic, or the Cabbalah. Well no, here you have someone who is here precisely to bother you by asking you to work on yourselves. I know this does not please you, but try to understand and accept it. Of course, if I wanted to I could talk about all kinds of topics. There is plenty to talk about! But would that really change your existence? No. Whereas if you succeed in doing this work on yourselves by applying the rules I give you, all learning, all knowledge will follow naturally.

For me, this question of personality and individuality is vital. As I have said, I have never stopped studying it, because once we are clear on this subject, we hold the key that will allow us to solve all the problems of existence.[9] So make up your minds to take this question seriously. And to take it seriously means first of all to study yourselves, to observe yourselves, so that you know at every moment of the day whether it is your individuality or your personality that is manifesting. Whatever you are doing, whatever you are thinking, an automatic mechanism in your mind – a kind of internal computer – should tell you which of the two natures is at work. Your whole future hangs on this practice. Nothing should pass through you without your having clearly identified it. Whether or not you subsequently succeed in following the correct path is another matter. You will still be swept along by your personality, this is inevitable. People do not change that quickly. But what is important is to be able, before you act, to identify which of the two natures is inspiring your actions and then to make sure you have not allowed yourself to be led astray. Yes, we first need to know what we truly want to do and then to check whether that is what we actually did.

I may be taking things too far by going over this again and again, but if there is no one who repeats and stresses these vital truths, you will stop making an effort. If I stop, you will not continue by yourselves. This is why I go on insisting. By talking as I do about this subject, I am giving you my most precious legacy.

Notes

1 See *Man's Psychic Life: Elements and Structure*, Izvor. 222.
2 See *Man's Two Natures: Human and Divine*, Izvor. 213, Chap. 1: 'Human nature or animal nature?'
3 See *True Alchemy or the Quest for Perfection*, Izvor. 221, Chap. 4: 'Our heritage from the animal kingdom'.
4 See *The Splendour of Tiphareth*, C.W. 10, Chap. 4: 'The Creator Sows Seeds in us and the Sun Makes them Grow', p. 59-63.
5 See *The Second birth*, C.W. 1, Chap. 2: 'Ask and it will be given to you', p. 61-62.
6 See *The Splendour of Tiphareth*, C.W. 10, Chap. 9: 'Some Prayers to say at Sunrise', p. 117.
7 See *A New Dawn*, C.W. 26, Chap. 2 (IV): 'The True Religion of Christ'.
8 See *'Know thyself' – Jnana Yoga*, C.W. 17, Chap. 7: 'Consciousness'.
9 See *The Key to the Problems of Existence*, C.W. 11.

2

'No one
can serve two masters'

I

It is all too clear that we possess two natures and that we are constantly torn between the two. This is quite easy to comprehend. But the question is: how should we react toward them? Jesus touched on this issue in the parable of the disloyal manager, but no doubt very few people have recognized this because you cannot interpret this parable if you have not already thought a good deal about this question of the two natures.

Then Jesus said to the disciples, 'There was a rich man who had a manager, and charges were brought to him that this man was squandering his property. So he summoned him and said to him, "What is this that I hear about you? Give me an accounting of your management, because you cannot be my manager any longer." Then the manager said to himself, "What will I do, now that my master is taking the position away from me? I am not strong enough to dig, and I am ashamed to beg. I have decided what to do so that, when I am dismissed as manager, people may welcome me into their homes." So, summoning his master's debtors one by one, he asked the first, "How much do you owe my master?" He answered, "A hundred jugs of olive oil." He said to him, "Take your bill, sit down quickly, and make it fifty." Then he asked another, "And how much do you owe?" He replied, "A hundred containers of wheat." He said to him, "Take your bill and make *it eighty." And his master commended the dishonest manager because he had acted shrewdly; for the children of this age are more shrewd in dealing with their own generation than are the children of light. And I tell you, make friends for yourselves by means of dishonest wealth so that when it is gone, they may welcome you into the eternal homes. Whoever is faithful in a very little is faithful also in much; and whoever is dishonest in a very little is dishonest also in much. If then you have not been faithful with the dishonest wealth, who will entrust to you the true riches? And if you have not been faithful with what belongs to another, who will give you what is your own? No slave can serve two masters; for a slave will either hate the one and love the other, or be devoted to the one and despise the other. You cannot serve God and wealth."**

At first glance, this parable is almost incomprehensible. Jesus talks about a manager who is disloyal to his master, but instead of reprimanding him, his master praises him. And Jesus appears to approve of this attitude since he says, *make friends for yourselves by means of dishonest wealth.* Immediately afterwards, however, he also approves of loyalty: *Whoever is faithful in a very little is faithful also in much... If then you have not been faithful with the dishonest wealth, who will entrust to you the true riches?* Does this mean that Jesus encourages both loyalty and disloyalty? What is dishonest wealth and what are true riches?

When people descend to earth they enter the service of one master, their personality, which is represented by their physical, astral and mental bodies. But sooner or later they are sent back. And 'to be sent back' means to die. If we are intelligent

* Luke 16: 1-13

65

we should think in the same way as the manager of the parable: *What will I do, now that my master is taking the position away from me? I am not strong enough to dig, and I am ashamed to beg.* All reasonable beings knows they will one day be turned out of their physical body – this exceedingly demanding master – but that does not mean that they will have learned to renounce all the desires they were able to satisfy when they inhabited this body. Since they are no longer able to work, they will be tempted to beg; in other words, to descend among the living in order to satisfy themselves through them. This is what happens to those who are too loyal to their personality: once they have left their physical body, they become beggars on the astral plane and seek out the places where human beings indulge in all kinds of unsavoury behaviour and unhealthy pleasures so as to feed on their emanations.

In order not to fall into the category of the beggar spirits, the manager in the parable decided to be disloyal to his master – his personality – by using dishonest wealth to make friends. So he reduced the debts owed by his master's debtors. What does this mean? Well, instead of giving full satisfaction to his physical, astral, and mental bodies, he gave them smaller doses. In other words, he put his personality on a strict diet by depriving it of the time and the physical, emotional, and mental energies which he would otherwise have devoted to this insatiable master – who would have devoured them – and secretly gave them to the *invisible friends of the eternal homes*. In other words, he saved some capital and deposited it in the celestial bank, so that the day he went to ask for it from the bank, he would be recognized and welcomed. He devoted some of his time and some of his physical, emotional, and mental energies to his individuality instead of keeping them exclusively for his personality. He was disloyal to his personality in order to make friends by means of the riches he had 'unjustly' put aside.

This is how we must interpret this parable if we are to understand why the manager was praised by his master. Who is this master who praised him? Not his personality, that is certain! It could not congratulate him since it was wronged by him. No, it was his individuality who said: 'You are very clever. You did well.' So this is not the same master. If we are to interpret this parable correctly, we must understand there are two masters. Indeed, Jesus talks of two masters at the end of this parable. *No slave can serve two masters; for a slave will either hate the one and love the other, or be devoted to the one and despise the other. You cannot serve God and wealth.* The 'wealth' mentioned here is material wealth, as opposed to all the spiritual riches represented by God. Human beings cannot serve both their higher nature and their lower nature at the same time. Only one kind of disloyalty, one kind of injustice is allowed: those that we commit toward our personality, that is, toward the material, the perishable.

You are probably wondering what is represented by the debtors whose debt was remitted, and what kind of debt this was. The debtors are the lower entities from the physical, astral, and mental planes, who, having taken certain spiritual elements from a human being for their own nourishment, must pay them back in the form of less subtle energies. If we remit their debt, it means that we relinquish the less subtle energies they owe us, in other words, we are embarking upon the path of abstinence, silence, prayer, and meditation. These restrictive measures cut down on the energy our personality would otherwise need. When our lower nature partially gives up the attempt to satisfy all its appetites, then our higher nature is able to gain strength, because it no longer has so many materials to supply. If on the other hand, our lower nature spends a great deal of time eating and enjoying itself, our higher nature is weakened because it has to supply energy to the lower nature. It is always the spirit that supplies energy to matter.

You will notice, however, that Jesus did not say in the parable that the dishonest manager remitted the entire debt owed by each of the debtors, but only a part of it. This means we should not exaggerate with these restrictions. Jesus shows that we must work for our first master – our individuality – but we do not have the right to abandon the second – our personality – completely. In other words, we should not forego everything and allow ourselves to die from our self-imposed abstinence. We must be disloyal to our second master, but only up to a point. If until now we have felt obliged to bestow upon that master – our stomach – dozens of oysters, kilos of caviar, several chickens, turkeys, and more, all washed down with several bottles of the best wines and followed by a number of liqueurs and cigars, we should try to cut down on this menu a little. We shall still be well nourished and will have remitted the debts of the entities that supply us with the energy needed to digest such repasts, thus making friends of the higher entities who will later welcome us into the eternal homes.

Of course, this regimen of restrictions imposed on the stomach is just an image. It is meant to represent not only the satisfactions of the physical body, but also those of the astral and mental bodies, the three bodies that constitute the personality.

When Jesus said: *Whoever is faithful in a very little is faithful also in much... If then you have not been faithful with the dishonest wealth, who will entrust to you the true riches?*, he meant that if you are not faithful to your individuality when it comes to benefits of little significance, you will not be entrusted with the immense riches of the spirit.

Jesus also referred to this issue of material wealth and spiritual riches in another passage of the Gospels, when he said: *Do not store up for yourselves treasures on earth, where moth and rust consume and where thieves break in and steal; but store up for yourselves treasures in heaven, where neither moth nor rust consumes and where thieves do not break in and steal. For where your treasure is, there your heart will be also… No one can serve two masters; for a slave will either hate the one and love the other, or be devoted to the one and despise the other. You cannot serve God and wealth.* You will notice that both passages are followed by the same comment on the two masters: *No one can serve two masters… You cannot serve God and wealth.*

Now, let us try and see what else this passage teaches us. Where do we generally keep our treasures? In a safety deposit box in an earthly bank. But Jesus advises us to keep our treasures in the heavenly bank. And just as the two masters of the dishonest manager – his personality and his individuality – are within him, the two banks are also within him, and they too represent his personality and his individuality.

Generally speaking, earthly banks offer three different services. The first provides safety deposit boxes in which we keep our reserves. The second handles the movement of capital and loans. The third involves financial dealings and speculations. Well, these same three functions have their parallel in the structure of the personality. The safety deposit boxes correspond to the reserves of the physical body. The department dealing with the movement of capital corresponds to our feelings – the astral plane, the realm of the heart, which constantly establishes relations based on interest. The department that handles financial dealings and speculations, corresponds to the mental plane, the intellect, which constantly calculates how to get the most out of every situation, even though this may be to the detriment of others. Earthly banks always become richer at the expense of others, while trying to convince everybody that their

activities and actions are inspired only by the desire to benefit
their fellow man. Jesus wants to make us understand that these
banks are not secure, that our treasures are not safe there,
because they are threatened by rust, moth, and thieves. And
what are rust, moths, and thieves?

Rust can be seen to symbolize that which attacks metals
and the mineral kingdom in general. But in the hierarchy of
nature's kingdoms, the mineral kingdom corresponds to the
physical plane, to the will. Rust therefore symbolizes everything
that paralyses our will and prevents us from acting.

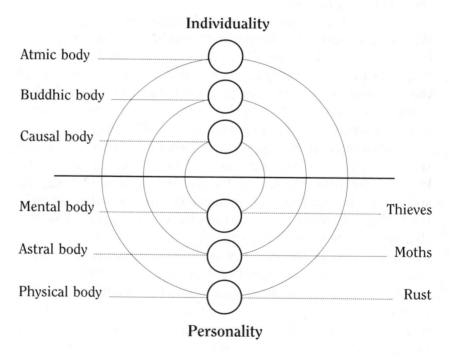

Moths thrive in certain conditions. With moths we enter
the astral world, the world of desires and feelings. Human
beings whose hearts are filled with selfish desires, jealousy, and

spite, are eaten up by moths. Indeed, do we not say about a person who is plagued by bad feelings that these feelings 'gnaw' at him?

A thief waits for people to leave their house or to be asleep before he breaks in to steal. Thieves symbolize enemies of the mental plane. If your intellect is clouded or half asleep, you will be attacked by the thieves of doubt, distrust, and worry. All these thoughts that despoil, weaken, and exhaust human beings, are they not thieves who come and take away their riches?

Rust, moths, and thieves are the enemies of the will, the heart, and the intellect, and Jesus warns us about them when he says: *Do not store up for yourselves treasures on earth.* The earth he refers to is our personality, which is constantly exposed to rust (inertia of the will), to moths (passions of the heart), and to thieves (darkness of the intellect). And if we have faith in the earthy bank, the personality, we will end by losing everything.

Jesus himself explains this advice: *For where your treasure is, there your heart will be also.* Yes, human beings always attach their heart to what they consider most precious, and if this eludes them in some way, their heart suffers. This is what happens to people who amass treasures on earth, in other words who use their will, their heart, and their intellect in order to satisfy their personality, because everything that satisfies the personality is ephemeral, perishable. The true treasures Jesus speaks of can only be acquired through a higher work of the will, the heart, and the intellect, because activity prevents the ravages of rust, love kills moths, and wisdom keeps us safe from thieves.

Jesus says: *Store up for yourselves treasures in heaven.* But what is the heaven within us? Where is it? In another passage in the Gospels, Jesus says: *I will show you what someone is like who comes to me, hears my words, and acts on them. That one is like a man building a house, who dug deeply and laid the foundation on rock; when a flood arose, the river burst against that house but could not shake it, because it had been well built. But the one who hears and does not act is like a man who built a house on the ground without a foundation. When the river burst against it, immediately it fell, and great was the ruin of that house.*

The house Jesus talks about is not, of course, the building that shelters us with our families and belongings, but our inner self, which we must build on solid foundations – rock – and not on sand, where bad weather will always be a threat. And 'bad weather' represents, of course, our own disorganised thoughts and feelings, and also the events in our lives for which we are unprepared. If we are to defend ourselves and master the situation, we must free ourselves from the astral and mental planes – the realms of the personality – and rise to the causal plane – the realm of the individuality. That is what is meant by building our house on rock.[1]

You cannot do without your heart and your intellect, that is understood, but you should at least refrain from dwelling on their level. Go to the higher levels. Go and set up house on the causal plane. Of course it is not so easy to relocate, because, for generation after generation, human beings have built their houses in the lower regions of the astral and mental planes. In other words, they have been living amidst intrigue, passion, and confrontation for centuries. This is why they never succeed in truly resolving their problems. The regions in which they stagnate are too exposed to winds and storms. They must move upwards, to the regions where true understanding and love reign, because only there will they have at their disposal all the means to act. They will of course continue to have to face up to the trials and tribulations of life, but because their house – their true house – will no longer be in the lower regions, they will end by conquering the elements.

If you are now wondering why your life is so fraught with distress, I will tell you that it is to teach you how to think, what to rely on, and where to focus your work. Everything must serve to steer you toward a far wider, far greater, far truer understanding. You must understand that every event is an opportunity to rise much higher, to become more noble, to become stronger, above all to liberate yourself. Then, instead of complaining, you will thank heaven and say: 'Oh Lord God, if it had been left to me to decide to rise toward you, I don't think I would have managed in this incarnation, or even in the next. My God, you are so good. You want to free me from the quagmire I am in. I thank you.' And you will embrace all the opportunities that present themselves so as to understand them from this new point of view.

Instead of always exaggerating the things that cause you to complain and rebel, get into the habit of thinking, reasoning, studying. This is how you move up to the higher region, the causal plane, the rock of which Jesus speaks. You will say: 'All right, let's move. Let's take our car and fill it with our belongings.' No, wait. It seems to me that it would be better not to take anything. All that baggage is too heavy. You would do far better to acquire other furniture, other objects, in a lighter, purer, more luminous material, because it will wear better.

In the Sephirotic Tree, the causal plane is represented by the Sephirah Binah, the region of the twenty-four Elders referred to by St John in the Apocalypse: *Around the throne are twenty-four thrones, and seated on the thrones are twenty-four elders, dressed in white robes, with golden crowns on their heads.*[2] The twenty-four Elders are seated on these immovable rocks, the thrones, which symbolize stability. Binah is the region of Understanding, and this is where you must bring your little caravan – or pitch your tent, if you prefer. Binah is also the high dwelling place referred to in Psalm 91: *Because you have made the Lord your refuge, the Most High your dwelling place.*

Yes, I know, it is difficult. It is not enough merely to decide to move home. It is when we try to do so that we see how much we are still attached to the lower regions of the astral and mental planes. We are like a fish that decides to leave the sea or the river to go and grow some lungs. To move to the causal plane you too must develop the appropriate organs, because even if you managed to elevate yourself to the higher regions for a moment, you would not be able to remain there if you do not have the necessary faculties. You will have only just arrived and already you will want to go back to earth. You will say: 'But this place is like the desert. I'm bored. There are no cigarettes here, no pubs, no clubs. I want to smoke; I feel like drinking; I feel like kissing pretty women. I want to go back down.' To be able to live in the sublime regions, you must have other needs. This is why not everyone is able to move; they do not yet have those needs. It is no use moving some people up there by force, because they will decamp immediately.

You, at least, must prepare to move; you must practise getting closer to the divine world. Once this becomes a habit you will progress ever further, you will have a more vast, broader, clearer and more profound view... until you succeed in dwelling permanently in these blessed regions. Every day, in your meditations, in your prayers, try to rise high, very high, as high as possible.[3] Imagine that you are ascending a mountain. This image will lead you to another mountain within you and you will reach the summit, the causal plane, the home of your higher self. In the Cabbalah, God is always referred to as the Most High because symbolically the home of power is on high.

'No one can serve two masters'

So, never forget: it is on high that you will find true strength and true security.

Notes

1 See *'Know thyself'* – *Jnana yoga,* C.W. 18, Chapter 5: 'The causal plane'.
2 See *The Book of Revelations: a commentary,* Izvor. 230, Chapter 7: 'The Twenty-four Elders and the Four Holy Living Creatures'; *Angels and other Mysteries of the Tree of Life,* Izvor. 236, Chapter 15: 'Binah'.
3 See *'In Spirit and in Truth',* Izvor. 235, Chapter 3: 'The link with the centre' and Chapter 4: 'Reaching for the top'; *The symbolic Language of Geometrical Figures,* Izvor. 218, Chapter 5: 'The pyramid'.

II

'No one can serve two masters'. It is clear, therefore, that we must put ourselves at the service of our individuality. We must feed our individuality by reducing the time and energy we have been in the habit of devoting to our personality. But we must not totally neglect our personality either. Indeed, as you saw in the previous chapter, Jesus did not say that we should no longer give anything to our personality. He said we should simply reduce its rations. We should not let it die of hunger, because our personality is extremely useful – indispensable in fact – as a servant. And do we leave a servant without food and lodgings? No, but neither do we allow a servant to rule the house.

When it comes to our personality, however, we are dealing with a very particular kind of servant. One that is very skilful, cunning, and stubborn. One whose only desire is to be mistress in your house and who knows just what to do to control you. How? By telling you lies. You have no doubt observed how people in everyday life behave when they want to control others. They tell them what they want to hear; they promise them that all their desires will be fulfilled; and they approve of their behaviour, for which they can always find a justification. Well, this is exactly what the personality does to have us eating out of its hand. Yes, it is truly unbeatable in the art of finding

76

arguments to justify all our bad tendencies. Do you get angry? That is fine, you have to stand up for what you believe in. Do you always criticize other people's decisions and attitudes? Quite right, because you are more capable of seeing the truth of the matter. Are things never good enough for you? Well, this proves that you are a perfectionist. Do you envy other people's material privileges? This is not envy; just an objective judgement, because those people enjoy privileges that they do not deserve. Do you drink or take drugs? Well, you do this to find inspiration or because others make your life unbearable. And then, of course, there are all the reasons you invent to escape your responsibilities, to deceive or desert your husband or wife, to exploit others, to reject or massacre them. Oh yes, the cunning of the personality is quite extraordinary. But once we realize what it is like, and understand all its scheming and trickery, we cannot go wrong again. First, however, we must make the effort to observe and analyse its methods.

You must be on your guard. Your personality will lead you to believe that by listening to its reasoning, by following its advice, you will find happiness. And this is true. To begin with, you will experience some minor satisfactions, but after a while things will begin to turn sour. The personality is very good at putting on an act and leading us astray. It is very knowledgeable, so knowledgeable that it can bring stars down to earth to persuade you with irrefutable arguments to give in to all your bad tendencies. And it will succeed in convincing you, because there are scientists and artists in the personality. It is not alone; it represents a whole world. It can go to great lengths of charm and seduction. It knows how to sing, dance, write verse, look at you lovingly. But its only aim is to enslave and devour you. Why is the personality so attractive? So that it can better get its claws into you. Did you not know this? It is like the devil, who, as we saw, is one of the ways in which the personality expresses itself. The devil too has very seductive ways. If he seemed frightening, he would tempt nobody. Of course the individuality too is full of poetry, music, dance, and wonderful fragrance, but that is different. The individuality does not use its talents to limit and enslave us, but to free us and to beautify and revive us.

As I have said before, human beings possess a lower nature and a higher nature and they are continually torn between the two. This is quite easy to comprehend, but in practice it is not so simple. In everyday life, we have to analyse each and every situation, and this means that we need the knowledge that will enable us to distinguish the manifestations of each of our two natures and then to place our lower nature under the authority of our higher nature. This requires years of study and effort. So study your personality well, weigh up its advice, and you will find that it cannot conceal itself. Its way of asking, demanding, snatching things is easily recognizable. Even when it has taken everything for itself, it is still not satisfied. The merest trifle upsets and offends it, and it thinks only of revenge. Yes, nothing is more sensitive or vindictive than our personality. It is a bottomless pit, a shrew, a monster of incredible cruelty. We can never find words strong enough to describe it. Do not delude yourselves therefore; it is not simply because you have decided to make your personality your servant that it will obey you.

Have you never heard rich people complaining about their servants? They do this despite all the precautions they took when hiring them. You will say they exaggerate... Sometimes, yes, but not always. There have been cases where servants have brought their masters nothing but unhappiness. Well, be aware it is the same with the personality. It is not because you have decided to make it your servant, that it will actually serve you.

Be careful, it is more likely to use you than to serve you. Nothing stops it. It is tireless. Indeed, if there is one enviable aspect of the personality, it is this: its tireless energy. None of its other characteristics are worth anything. Only this one quality: its tirelessness. Just look at thieves, killers, and crooks: how active and energetic they are! That is because they are being manipulated by their personality, which never leaves them in peace. Whereas, honest people tire immediately. Since they are not driven by any particular desire to steal someone's property or avenge themselves, they lead peaceful lives. They earn their living, they take care of their families, and they are content. To do no wrong is enough for them. Well no, it is not enough. Once they decide to put themselves at the service of their higher nature, they will understand what true work is, work in the service of the highest ideal.[1] Then they too will become tireless. But in the meantime, only their personality is tireless.

In any case, how could we expect our personality to be at peace when we see how everything in life is designed to inflame its desires? The world is full of advertisements, sales catalogues, and so on, telling us to 'buy this, or taste that'. Innumerable appliances and products exist to make houses and cars more comfortable, our material lives easier, our bodies more appealing. It is the same with novels, films, plays, and shows of every kind... Almost all of them seek only to please the personality. And people – saturated with all the goods and pleasures put before them – are not only no happier, they are becoming unbearable, and quite understandably so, since only their lower nature is being fed.

So, let it be quite clear: to stop feeding our personality exclusively does not mean we should annihilate it. Our personality is part of us and we must live with it. Without it we can do nothing on earth, because it is the storehouse of all our qualities and gifts. It is our personality that possesses all our hidden riches and raw materials, that is, all our instincts and appetites, all that enables us to cling to our life on earth. It is the personality that cares for, preserves, and increases our possessions. It is like an old grandmother, who keeps the keys to the safes and cupboards. It arouses, of course, all our desires, and this is why, ultimately, it usually succeeds in gaining the upper hand. You must learn to be more intelligent than your personality before you can subjugate it and make use of all its riches. Do not delude yourselves; if you are unable to enslave it, it will enslave you; it will devour you and there will be nothing left of you. And even when you succeed in reducing your personality to the role of servant, you cannot rely on it, because it is disloyal, cunning, and rebellious. It only pretends to accept your authority. In reality, it is continually trying to overthrow your power.

When two countries are at war with each other, one of them ends by winning, and the loser has to submit, give up territory and be subject to occupation, taxes, and so on. But this situation is never definitive, because the people who were the losers do not accept defeat so easily. They grumble and work behind the scenes for their liberation. Then one fine day, when the conqueror, feeling proud and triumphant, is resting on his laurels, the underdog counter-attacks and the situation is reversed. This has happened repeatedly in one form or another throughout political, economic, and social history, but it also happens in our inner lives. We cannot enslave our lower nature once and for all. It never surrenders. It doggedly continues its underground work. If we want to keep it in submission, we must arm ourselves to the teeth and never for one moment relax our vigilance. And that is exhausting.

Even saints, initiates, and great masters are sometimes overcome by fatigue. They are forced to let go, and then the personality rears its head again. But unlike the majority of human beings, initiates, and great masters know how to remedy the situation. Since our lower nature possesses an incredible arsenal before which we are powerless, we must find allies to help us in this uneven struggle. This is what a country does in time of war; it forms pacts with allies. Humankind has the age-old wisdom to look to allies for help, because alone we are too vulnerable. In the same way, in this struggle with the personality, we must realize that we cannot triumph alone over the dark and mysterious forces within us.[2] The only solution is to unite with the Deity, with celestial entities, with archangels and divinities, and enable them to make war in our stead. Then we become spectators, we can watch the battle and see how heaven – the higher nature within us – is gaining the victory.

So do not try to annihilate your personality because not only will you not succeed, but it is you who will be annihilated. Begin by uniting yourself with heaven and then turn to your personality with the absolute conviction that you truly are the master, and it will be forced to obey. Be sure, of course, to show conviction and audacity, otherwise it is you who will be floored. Suppose someone wants to ride a horse, but is afraid. As soon as he mounts, the horse will throw him because it senses it is dealing with a coward, so to teach him a lesson it bucks, and down he goes. You must be like Alexander the Great who was capable of riding Bucephalus. No one could break in this horse, but Alexander managed to ride it. The horse did not throw him because it sensed who Alexander was.

Our personality is a wild horse, which only the truly bold can tame and very few people are capable of true audacity. When it comes to harming others, cheating, hurting, and annihilating them, then yes, nothing stops them. As for harming themselves, there too... no holds barred! Look at the recklessness with which people throw themselves into adventures from which they emerge completely shattered. It is only when it comes to subjugating their lower nature that they become timid, they do not dare.

But this too must be very clear: to tame your personality and replace its manifestations with those of your individuality does not mean to annihilate it, as so many mystics and ascetics have done in the belief that to ensure their salvation they had to live in squalor and deprivation, flagellate themselves, wear hair shirts, and so on. With such treatment their poor personality was annihilated and was no longer capable of anything. In reality, our personality will always maintain some roots in the physical body, because the physical body is its first refuge. Even when there are no more selfish feelings in the astral body, even when there are no more dark thoughts in the mental body, the personality continues to retain its footing on the physical plane. It is there, in the physical body, that it continues to survive. And this is necessary, because if it were to disappear from the physical plane as well, our higher nature, God himself, would not be able to manifest in us. This replacement I am talking about is, in reality, neither complete nor permanent. In the psychic sphere the personality may be replaced once and for all, but it will continue to exist on the physical plane, and we must, therefore, give it something to live on.

The following image may help you understand better the relationship between the personality and the individuality. Imagine a tree: when you study the different parts of a tree and their functions, you could say that by analogy the roots, the trunk, and the branches correspond to the personality, and the leaves, flowers, and fruits correspond to the individuality.[3] Our personality is the material support, the receptacle, the conductor, and our individuality is the spiritual element that lies at the origin of all manifestations.

Let us now look at the correspondences between a tree and our different bodies. The roots correspond to our physical body, the trunk to the astral body, and the branches to the mental body. These three bodies – the physical, astral, and mental – form the trinity of our personality. It is they that allow us to act, to have feelings and thoughts, but in the lower regions. The leaves correspond to the causal body, the flowers to the buddhic body, and the fruits to the atmic body. They form the trinity of our individuality, and it is thanks to them that we are able to think, feel, and act in the higher regions.

The roots, the trunk, and the branches remain throughout the seasons, whereas the leaves, the flowers, and the fruits appear and then disappear. Similarly, our personality – our

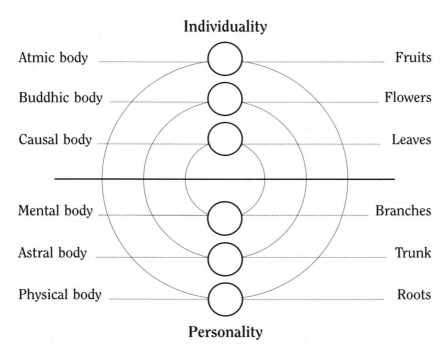

physical, astral, and mental bodies – remains in place as a permanent support, while our individuality – the inspirations given to us by our causal, buddhic, and atmic bodies – visits us for a while and then leaves us again.

In the spring the tree begins to manifest by producing leaves, flowers, and fruits. This is our individuality. Why do the leaves, flowers, and fruits not remain? They go away, and then they return, like all those poetic inspirations that visit us for a few minutes from time to time, whereas the roots, the trunk, and the branches are always there. Of course, just as a tree grows, our personality can grow and spread, but basically it remains the same: the roots (our genitals and our belly), the trunk (our lungs and our chest), and the branches (our brain). If the forces of the spirit do not flow through it, it remains naked and sterile, like a tree in winter. So we must work at letting the spirit enter us. Like the tree that becomes covered in leaves, flowers, and fruits for everyone to enjoy, people who open themselves up to the spirit become a blessing to all who approach them.[4]

Just as the roots, the trunk, and the branches represent the foundations of the tree, the personality represents the foundations of a human being, and there must be no question of destroying these foundations. We must give our personality food and water and keep it alive. At the same time we must devote most of our time and efforts to nourishing our individuality, until it becomes so wonderfully powerful that it will seize our personality and make its home within it, as in conquered territory. It is then, like Saint Paul, that we shall be able to say: *It is no longer I who live, but it is Christ who lives in me.* In the meantime, however, while feeding our individuality we must not allow our personality to die of hunger, otherwise we will die with it.

You will say: 'All right, that's fine, we understand. But how do we know how much to give to each one?' To answer this question I will again use a passage from the Gospels. One day the Pharisees asked Jesus a question about the taxes owed to the emperor, hoping that his answer would give them reason to accuse him. They asked him if it was lawful to pay taxes to Caesar. And the Gospel says that Jesus, who was aware of their malice, said: *'Why are you putting me to the test, you hypocrites? Show me the coin used for the tax.'* So they brought him a coin, and he said, *'Whose head is this, and whose title?'* They answered, *'The emperor's.'* And Jesus answered: *'Give therefore to the emperor the things that are the emperor's, and to God the things that are God's.'*

Who is the emperor and what does he represent? The emperor represents the powers of the earth as opposed to God, the celestial King. Thus the emperor could be interpreted as one of the forms of the personality which lays claim to our resources, just as the emperor Caesar levied taxes. Indeed, we all carry within us an emperor who is constantly making demands on us, and since he has to live, we are forced to give him something. But not everything. And now you will ask: 'Yes, but how much should we give him?'

And to answer this I shall use yet another image. You want to make a fire, and you burn a few branches. What do you see? You see flames, a mass of flames shooting up, then a smaller amount of gasses, then even less water vapour, and in the end, all that remains is a small amount of ashes. So, where have all the different elements gone? The fire, the gasses, and the water vapour have risen heavenwards. Only the ashes remain on earth. And this shows how much you must give to your personality: the same share as that of earth, let us say a quarter... and that is being generous. And the remaining three-quarters must be given to your individuality. Yes, one quarter is enough for your personality, for Caesar, but all the rest must go to your individuality, to God. Of course, most people do exactly the opposite. They give one quarter to God – perhaps not even that much – and three-quarters to Caesar. Well, you must realize that this is in contradiction to celestial mathematics.

Notes

1 See *Life force*, C.W. 5, Chapter 10: 'A high ideal'; *A New Dawn*, C.W. 26, Chapter 5 (2): 'The Kingdom of God and His Righteousness'.
2 See *The Key to the Problems of Existence*, C.W. 11, Chapter 17: 'Call on your allies'.
3 Ibid. Chapter 15: 'The new philosophy'.
4 See *The Symbolic Language of Geometrical Figures*, Izvor. 218, Chapter 7: 'The quadrature of the circle'.

3

The three
great temptations

One can always debate the reality of heaven and hell, of angels and devils, but one thing is certain and not debatable, and it is that human beings possess two natures with opposing tendencies. However, at a time when it would have been impossible to speak about psychological concepts because no one or almost no one would have understood, the initiates presented higher nature and lower nature in the form of an angel and a devil. The angel stands on man's right-hand side and the devil on his left; the devil seeks to lead man astray so that he becomes his victim, while the angel enlightens him with good advice. This is the meaning of the episode in the Gospels where the devil leads Jesus into temptation in the desert.

Then Jesus was led up by the Spirit into the wilderness to be tempted by the devil. He fasted forty days and forty nights, and afterwards he was famished. The tempter came and said to him, 'If you are the Son of God, command these stones to become loaves of bread.' But he answered, 'It is written, "One does not live by bread alone, but by every word that comes from the mouth of God."' Then the devil took him to the holy city and placed him on the pinnacle of the temple, saying to him, 'If you are the Son of God, throw yourself down; for it is written, "He will command his angels concerning you," and "On their hands they will bear you up, so that you will not dash your foot against a stone."' Jesus said to him, 'Again it is written, "Do not put the Lord your God to the test."' Again, the devil took him to a very high mountain and showed him all the kingdoms of the world and their splendour; and he said to him, 'All these I will give you, if you will fall down and worship me.' Jesus said to him, 'Away with you, Satan! for it is written, "Worship the Lord your God, and serve only him."' Then the devil left him, and suddenly angels came and waited on him.

Matthew 4: 1-11

Jesus was led up by the Spirit into the wilderness to be tempted by the devil. There is the first point requiring interpretation. If the Spirit himself led Jesus into the desert to tempt him, it is proof that the 'evil' spirits – who tempt us and subject us to trials – are in fact workers of God, charged with fulfilling the will of entities who are more evolved than they.

We shall not ask ourselves whether the devil really did appear before Jesus to make the propositions related in the text. One thing is certain, however; the person who wrote about this episode from the life of Jesus possessed great initiatic knowledge. The very nature of the temptations, the way in which the devil presents them to Jesus, and the replies Jesus gives each time, have great significance. This is why we should consider this text carefully.

'If you are the Son of God'... This is what the devil says to Jesus each time to provoke him. And then he incites Jesus:
– to change some stones into bread;

89

– to throw himself from the pinnacle of the temple in the belief that God, in his everlasting love, will save him by sending angels to protect him;

– to fall down and worship him in exchange for all the kingdoms of the world, which he shows him from a very high mountain.

Since this scene takes place in the desert, we can imagine that the ground is littered with stones, and it is these stones the devil asks Jesus to change into bread. But after that, did the devil really take Jesus from the desert to the holy city – Jerusalem – to place him on the pinnacle of the temple? And finally, did he also take Jesus from the temple in Jerusalem to the summit of a very high mountain? There were no high mountains in Palestine. This means we must look at this story from a symbolic point of view. Then we will discover that these three temptations concern the three spheres of our physical, affective, and intellectual lives, in other words our physical, astral, and mental bodies, which make up our lower nature, our personality.

'If you are the Son of God, command these stones to become loaves of bread,' says the devil to Jesus. Here bread symbolizes earthly food and, in the general sense, everything that allows us to live on the physical plane. But Jesus sets spiritual food and possessions against earthly food and possessions: *'One does not live by bread alone, but by every word that comes from the mouth of God.'*

When the devil takes Jesus to the pinnacle of the temple – and here, the temple symbolizes religion, in other words the heart – he asks Jesus to throw himself down, telling him that there is nothing to fear, he will be protected. What is meant by 'throwing down'? It means the attitude of those who believe they can challenge God. Whatever they do, whatever insane adventures they embark upon, they think they risk nothing.

They believe God will send an army of servants to protect them. And this is what people do when they yield to the enticements of the astral plane without thinking. They feel so sure of themselves, of the validity of their desires, of their claims, that they believe they can put God to the test. And look at the cunning of astral entities: in order to persuade Jesus, the devil quotes Psalm 91: *'he will command his angels concerning you'*. This is very revealing: it shows that in seeking to lead us astray, our lower nature, hypocritical and cunning as it is, does not hesitate to use religion to convince us. But God does not protect unreasonable beings who justify their actions and behaviour by quoting holy texts. This is why Jesus replies to the devil's second suggestion saying: *'Do not put the Lord your God to the test'*, meaning, do not put his love and faith to the test. Only those who do not 'throw' themselves down are protected; for those who do 'throw' themselves down, the law of gravity goes into effect.[1] For this law governs the psychic as well as the physical plane.

Last, the devil takes Jesus to the summit of a very high mountain. The high mountain represents the head, the mental plane. People who believe themselves to be knowledgeable always tend to believe they are superior to others, and demand that others recognize them as a leader or a master, whom they should obey. From the summit they have reached they feel they are capable of dominating the world and laying hold of all its riches. They believe themselves to be equal to God. By offering Jesus all the kingdoms of the world and their splendour, the devil tries to awaken in Jesus this spirit of pride which led some of the angels to rebel against God and incited the first man and woman to eat from the forbidden fruit so that they might become his equal. But what Satan, in the form of the serpent, succeeded in obtaining from Adam and Eve, he was unable to obtain from Jesus. Jesus did not want the kingdoms of the world that the devil would have given him if he fell down and worshipped him, and he replied: *'Away with you, Satan! for it is written, "Worship the Lord your God, and serve only him."'*

The devil wanted Jesus to fall down and worship him, he wanted to make Jesus his servant. Yes, our lower nature wants us to put ourselves at its service and makes us all kinds of promises provided we serve it. But it is up to us to know who to serve, our higher nature or our lower nature, God or Mammon. Jesus chose God. With this final defeat, the devil realized there was nothing for it: once someone has succeeded in conquering their pride, he is incorruptible, for pride is the weakness that is hardest to overcome. So many remarkable people have fallen on account of pride, because they were vain of their knowledge, their virtues, and their abilities.

These three temptations to which the Spirit subjected Jesus are temptations that we too must confront daily. Every day our lower nature importunes us, and with great skill paints in glowing colours what we stand to gain from following its advice. Our material life will be secured, Providence will favour the fulfilment of all our desires, and we will have all the power and the glory in the world. Our higher nature also talks to us and warns us that we are moving in the wrong direction and it advises us to correct our course. But since we lack judgement, we rarely notice that our higher nature is giving us good advice, and even if we do notice, we do not listen. The suggestions of our lower nature are so much more appealing!

Temptations are trials to which heaven subjects human beings. Every day we all undergo tests, both big and small. At the time we may not realize it. Only later do we know whether we have passed or failed. These tests lead people to know themselves better, because the truth is they do not yet know themselves. They think they are just and faultless, that they understand everything perfectly. And so to make them aware of their shortcomings and inadequacies, heaven subjects them to certain trials, and that is why temptations are useful: they lead human beings to an awareness of what they truly are.

There is a great deal one could say about this text from the Gospels. Why did Jesus not strike the devil? Why did he not drive him away with abuse? Because Jesus knew the laws and understood that to react to evil with violence only reinforces it. But most of all, he understood that this entity that represents evil in the universe has a purpose, that it is part of the cosmic order. So what did Jesus do? He responded to each of the tempter's suggestions in turn and his words forced the tempter back. The devil placed certain benefits on one side of the scales, and in reply, Jesus placed others on the other side. On the cosmic scales of light and darkness, the devil placed material possessions and Jesus placed spiritual possessions. When faced with Jesus' answers the devil understood there was no point in persisting. The Gospel says: *'Then the devil left him.'* Because he identified with his higher nature, Jesus' response was right, in that he tipped the balance toward his celestial Father. He said no to the devil and then angels came to wait on him.

So, what lesson should we learn from this episode in the Gospels? It is that we too must learn to say no to the devil. You protest: 'But we are not Jesus. We are weak. It is difficult for us to resist evil.' Well, you are mistaken. You are not weak, only ignorant. You do not know where your strength lies. So I will tell you: your strength lies in your ability to say no. Human beings, who have been created in the image of God, are as powerful as God, but only in their ability to say no. This means that no one in the world can force you to do what you do not want to do. In this you are as powerful as God. Even if all the powers of darkness teamed up against you to force you to act according to their will, as long as you opposed them, they could not compel you. Even God cannot compel you. If human beings knew their true power, they would be above all temptation or seduction, above all crime. If a person commits a crime it means he consented to it – he did not say no. The spirits of the invisible world have the right and the means to tempt us, but they have no right to force us. Only through ignorance of their divine origin and spiritual power do human beings succumb to the attacks of evil.

This question of our two natures must become gradually clearer to you, because depending on whether you identify with one or the other you will draw nearer either to heaven or to hell. A person's personality is like a door leading to hell and it is through this door that hell is able to reach him. But every time you succeed in overcoming temptation, you receive additional strength and light. After every victory that has been won and every problem that has been resolved, the angels come to serve those who have triumphed. But they only come afterwards, not before. When human beings admire the rich, the well-educated, and the powerful, they are merely imitating the celestial spirits. These spirits on high are obliged to salute and respect people who are rich in virtue, who possess spiritual powers and knowledge. They bow before them and put themselves at their service.

So, if you want to attract the attention of the luminous entities and forces of nature you must become rich. You will say: 'But how do I become rich?' By learning to work on the qualities and virtues of your higher nature. These qualities and virtues manifest through projections of light and colour, which the spirits perceive from afar. It may be that human beings do not see these, but that is a different issue. The spirits on high immediately see the light emanating from you and are attracted to it.[2]

Each time you elevate yourself, in other words, each time you succeed in overcoming a weakness, a temptation, a vice, orders concerning you are automatically given in heaven, without any intervention from you: a certain spirit is ordered to obey you; a certain ability will be granted you; certain conditions in your life must be changed. But it is not up to you to concern yourself with this. All you have to do is to continue your inner work: surmounting and defeating this problem, that obstacle. All the rest will be given to you automatically.

You must also be aware, however, that this victory over your temptations is an undertaking that never ends, because in the inner life nothing is ever acquired definitively. Every day, at every moment, we have choices to make. Life never ceases to offer us opportunities to satisfy our personality. And if we manage to resist, we sense that we have moved up a step on the path of light and we are happy. It is as if, after a difficult climb, we had reached the top of the mountain. We take a deep breath, we are happy.[3]

But as long as we are on earth we will not be able to remain for any length of time on the summits we sometimes manage to reach. We must constantly fight to reconquer them. Once we have left the earth for another world, we shall no longer need to fight, because we shall no longer be subjected to temptation. But as long as we remain on earth, we must be vigilant to the very last minute. The psychic life follows the same pattern as breathing and eating. We have barely taken a breath before we have to breathe again. We have eaten today, but we will have to eat again tomorrow. A certain experience has led us to understand the meaning of life, but the meaning of life is not given to us once and for all. We must undergo another experience, and then another, and still others. We may

95

have overcome a temptation, but we will be tempted again, and so once again we will have to try to be victorious.[4]

Notes

1 cf. *True Alchemy or the Quest for Perfection*, Izvor. 221, Chapter 11: 'Pride and humility'.
2 cf. *Light is a Living Spirit*, Izvor. 212, Chapter 5: 'How to work with light'.
3 cf. *The Powers of Thought*, Izvor. 224, Chapter 13: 'Reaching for the unattainable'.
4 cf. *On the Art of Teaching from the Initiatic Point of View*, C.W. 29, Chapter 1: 'On the spiritual work'.

4

Taking and giving

Take a quick look at how human beings behave and you will see that, be it in the emotional, social, political or economic sphere, their problems arise from the fact that most of them are driven by purely personal, selfish motives. The standard, the rule, the ideal to which they aspire is always that of taking. And there are thousands of different ways of taking. If they were better educated, if they had the advice of wise and lucid guides who pointed out the harmful aspect of such an attitude, they would be able to escape the darkness in which they are floundering, unhappy and dissatisfied, ready to destroy themselves and others.

You only have to look at society to see that everything in it is organized to satisfy a person's lower nature, with its primitive, untamed instincts. All the rules and criteria of society, the whole of education even, are all based on this mentality of taking everything for yourself, of winning, making a profit, taking advantage of every possibility. Why think of others? If they stand in your way, you can simply push them aside or even crush them. Why hesitate?

And this attitude prevails, as I have said before, despite the fact that when man was created in God's workshops, cosmic Intelligence sowed in him seeds that were destined to develop into qualities, virtues, and sublime gestures of self-denial and renunciation. Occasionally you see these qualities manifested in certain people, but only very rarely. Evidence of the personality on the other hand, can be seen everywhere. It never stops spreading its influence like tentacles. And it is so resourceful and capable of all kinds of intrigue, all kinds of trickery. How busy and how skilful it is! Yes, and despite its miserliness, it even urges people to give, but only so as to be better able to take. Are most gifts not simply bait to allow the giver to attract and despoil others?

The personality shows no restraint, no mercy. It wants to own everything, to swallow up everything, and since it is never satisfied, it is not only ungrateful, it is also angry that we do not give it more. The personality is insatiable – it is a bottomless pit. And this is how the need to take leads to people developing all kinds of harmful tendencies such as envy, rebellion, cruelty, and vengeance.

The individuality, which knows only how to give, can be compared to the sun, whereas the personality, which knows only how to take, can be compared to the moon or the earth. The sun sends what it produces far into infinite space so that many other creatures may benefit from it, while earth is content merely to take, to absorb. Of course earth cannot be said to give nothing. Indeed, it uses what it receives to produce minerals, plants, and so on. But it does so for itself. The other planets do not benefit from any of these. So, the earth does something with what it takes, but it keeps it for itself – or its children, which amounts to the same thing. And our personality also makes something of what it takes, but it too keeps it all for itself.

Now if we want to examine the difference between the earth and the moon from the point of view of our personality, we must refer to the language of symbols in which the earth corresponds to the physical world and the moon corresponds to the astral world. Obviously, our physical body has needs, but these are easily satisfied. What is insatiable in us is our astral body, the body of desires.

Let us take the fundamental example of food. If we only wanted to satisfy the real needs of our physical body, would we have any use for all these recipes that fill so many cookery books? No. Would we need all these drinks that are stacked on the shelves in our shops? No, we would not. All we need to survive is two litres of water a day. Our physical body needs very little and only very simple things. It is our astral body, the body of desires that needs a whole variety of foods and goods, ever more complicated and more sophisticated, because its appetite is insatiable. This is not a bad thing in itself. Indeed, quite to the contrary; cultures and civilisations are the result of this need to taste more elaborate foods, to possess objects that are more aesthetically pleasing and made of more precious materials. Living in caves, wearing animal skins, eating wild fruits and raw meat, drinking water from the rivers, getting about on foot, these are the conditions in which primeval man lived, and I am not saying that human beings should have been content with that. But if all these desires that well up in people and that lie at the origin of civilisations are not controlled, purified, made luminous, they may also be the cause of their ruin.[1]

The body of desire or the astral body, which is symbolized by the moon, is the centre of our personality and this is where all our covetousness comes from. The astral body gives the impetus and the mental body builds plans to satisfy it. Understand this well: it is our desires that determine our behaviour, and although the intellect has the capacity to override them, more often than not it puts itself at their service. Isn't this true? Just look at how everyone puts their intelligence at the service of their appetites and passions. All the knowledge, all the cultural riches human beings possess are used to satisfy something obscure that comes from deep within them. Even people considered to be the most enlightened, the most developed mentally, are often at the service of questionable, dubious forces and impulses.

This is why it is important that everyone should decide to re-examine this crucial question of ends and means. If you are honest with yourself you will realize that most of the time your goal is to please your personality, to satisfy your instincts and desires. And the means? Well, these are everything heaven has put at your disposal, all your physical and mental faculties, all the forces of nature. Yes, people tend to place all these divine means at the service of wretched, pitiful goals. Science, philosophy, art, heaven itself... they all exist only to serve the most mundane interests, appetites, and whims. From now on you should do the opposite. Everything you have been taking as an goal must become a means. All the impulses of your lower nature must serve only to reach the sublime world, the light.[2] This is what it means to make your personality your servant. And if you succeed in making this radical change in your way of thinking, your entire life will be transformed.

I remember, years and years ago, in Bulgaria, during one of the meetings of the Brotherhood of Sofia, Master Peter Deunov[3] asked us: 'What is the difference between the old teaching and the new teaching?' A few people offered answers with all kinds of long-winded and complicated explanations. In the end the Master spoke, saying simply this: 'The old teaching shows us how to take, and with the new teaching we learn to give.' The answer was short and clear, although of course it needs a great deal of explanation truly to understand what taking and giving mean in every area of life.

To give is not merely to give alms, a few coins, a few pieces of bread, some old clothes, or anything material. There are so many ways of giving. In everything we do there is an opportunity to give, in other words, to show greater understanding and less self-interest in our relations with others. Kindness, generosity, tolerance, self-denial, all these qualities are included in 'giving'. And selfishness, jealousy, intolerance, all these faults are included in 'taking'. 'Taking' is what our personality does. It is always alert to the need to monopolize, to assert itself. And if obstacles stand in the way of the fulfilment of its desires, it mobilizes all the resources of the intellect, emotions, and will in order to achieve its aims. Our individuality, on the other hand, never ceases to give, to pour forth, to radiate. It seeks to enlighten, help, and support. All it wants is to give something of itself. It does not seek to keep hold of what it possesses and it does not object to someone coming to take it away. On the contrary, the individuality is happy to see that it helps others to nourish themselves and become more luminous.

The fundamental quality of our higher nature is to shine, to radiate like the sun.[4] Indeed, all virtues are nothing other than a radiation, a projection of light from the centre to the periphery. You will say that the moon also sends us rays. Yes, but even if we see it shining in space and lighting up the night, this light is not its own. Egoists cannot project light. Light is something we must detach, tear from ourselves. It can only be a manifestation of impersonality, of self-denial.

So many people complain saying: 'I embarked on the path of spirituality years ago. I have been making an effort for years but I feel I am making no progress.' Well, this is simply because you have not yet understood what true disinterestedness, true selflessness, is. Everything you do is still for your own benefit. Try to analyse your actions and you will find that in the majority of cases the motives of your lower nature have crept into what you had thought to be a disinterested act. You work, you care for others, but you do so for yourself, to satisfy your lower nature, which gradually becomes a tumour in your psyche.

Jesus touched on this aspect of the issue of the two natures when the rich young man came to him, asking: *'Teacher, what good deed must I do to have eternal life?' – And he said to him... 'If you wish to enter into life, keep the commandments.' He said to him, 'Which ones?' And Jesus said, 'You shall not murder; You shall not commit adultery; You shall not steal; You shall not bear false witness; Honour your father and mother; also, You shall love your neighbour as yourself.' The young man said to him, 'I have kept all these; what do I still lack?' Jesus said to him, 'If you wish to be perfect, go, sell your possessions, and give the money to the poor, and you will have treasure in heaven; then come, follow me.' When the young man heard this word, he went away grieving, for he had many possessions. Then Jesus said to his disciples, 'Truly I tell you, it will be hard for a rich person to enter the kingdom of heaven. Again I tell you, it is easier for a camel to go through the eye of a needle than for someone who is rich to enter the kingdom of God.'*

Most commentators felt this image of the camel was so exaggerated, even ridiculous, that they never really took it seriously. The truth is, they were unable to interpret what Jesus said, because they did not know the make-up of human beings. They knew nothing about the astral body, about its nature and its manifestations.

Desire and greed are manifestations of the astral body and if the astral body is not controlled or educated, it swells up more and more and becomes a monstrous tumour within us. This is the case of the rich, who, in their desire to amass always more things than they need, end by having a gigantic astral body which prevents them from entering the kingdom of God. For entry to the kingdom of God is difficult. You only gain access through the 'narrow door' Jesus refers to in another passage of the Gospels: *'Strive to enter through the narrow door; for many, I tell you, will try to enter and will not be able.'* Only those who have learned to give, to divest themselves, are welcomed into the kingdom of God.

Let us now take a closer look at the nature of the camel. The camel has adapted itself perfectly to the desert, where hardly any vegetation grows. The little it finds is enough, and with the reserves it stores up it can walk for days without food or water. The camel, therefore, has a minute astral body and this is why it symbolizes the true spiritualist, who makes do with very little and who is capable of overcoming life's difficult conditions. When Jesus said the camel could go through the eye of a needle, he was not referring to the physical body – that would be ridiculous – he was referring to the astral body. You see, his words are now clear. The body of desires is a bottomless pit. So, it is this body of desires that you must work on, because true evolution only begins the day you succeed in acting in an impersonal and disinterested manner.

'Taking' is the old teaching, and 'giving' is the new teaching. You will say: 'But if we are to give surely we must already possess something, so that means we have to take from somewhere.' Well, that is not so certain. Initiates will tell you that, on the contrary, you must give in order to have. This needs some explanation of course. It is true that you cannot give if you do not yourself possess something, and you cannot have anything if you have not received anything. But the question is from where and from whom we receive. Most people draw from others, and this is how they gradually take everything they have: their money, their possessions, their strength, their ideas, their feelings... everything. Just look at the way people understand love. They take; they never stop taking. You could even say that lovers are the greatest thieves. And since poetry, fiction, theatre, and film are full of love stories, all we are ever told are stories about thieves. It is all about who will manage to steal, to lay claim to the other person's time, feelings, and thoughts.[5]

And on the psychic plane, just as on the physical plane, all you see is stealing. You will say: 'But how do we stop being thieves?' You must learn to be like the sun. In the morning, when the sun rises, what you see before you is the most sublime manifestation of individuality. Such pouring out, such generosity, such self-giving! Of course, if no one explains to you what is happening and how to interpret it, you can look at the sunrise all your life and continue to adhere to the law of your personality, continue to take. But when you come to understand what the sunrise is, you will feel the power, the magnitude, the immensity of this act of giving, you will work to change everything in you and you will rejoice as you succeed more and more each day.[6]

Every morning the sun says to you: 'Leave your selfish thoughts and feelings behind and learn to open yourself up, to radiate, to illuminate, and to warm all creatures.' And do not worry that you will become increasingly poor, because there is a cosmic law which says that the more you give, the more you receive. A void does not exist in the universe. As soon as a void develops, something comes to fill it. This law works on all planes, and if what you give is luminous, radiant, and beneficial, the law of affinity will also see to it that from the other side you receive elements of the same quality, of the same luminous and radiant quintessence.

The sun cannot be exhausted, because thanks to its desire to give it is constantly replenished. The sun sends us its rays, but at the same time it never ceases to receive new energies from the immensity of creation. While radiating outwards, it absorbs into its centre the riches and energies of God himself. Indeed, if you questioned it, this is what it would explain:[7] 'When I send my light and love through space, I attract the purest, the most vivifying elements in return. Learn to work as I do and you will find that when you spend your energies to benefit others, very shortly afterwards you will feel replenished with new energies...' How can this be? Well, mysterious as it seems, it is still absolutely true.

From now on – if you have absorbed what I have been saying – you will begin to look at the sun in a new light, and major changes will take place within you. Everything depends on our understanding, on the way we see things. It is through in-depth and true understanding that people become able to trigger the celestial currents within themselves. And then they are transformed and become like the sun. They begin to give and to discover they have never felt so rich, so lucid or so powerful.

When we become truly rich and powerful inwardly we feel protected from all the different kinds of fear that might besiege us. It is the personality that is afraid. It is afraid because it feels poor, defenceless, exposed to all kinds of danger. This is why its sole concern is to safeguard its subsistence, its security by taking and accumulating as much as possible, and by trying to eliminate those who appear to threaten this security. If you are afraid you cannot show generosity. You cannot even be sincere or honest. You become false and hypocritical, and try to exploit every situation, even if it is to the detriment of others.[8] Indeed, because our personality is afraid it is capable of the most ignominious behaviour.

So, there is no higher ideal than to become like the sun. Try to nurture this ideal, so that it grows within you and your whole being becomes inflamed and illuminated by it. Only with this high ideal can all that is best in your heart and soul begin to germinate. Without having to make a great effort, without even having to think about it, you will begin to show the best tendencies. The only truth worth searching for is the spiritual sun, which brings out all our qualities as soon as it begins to shine, just as the physical sun makes all of nature come to life.

The sun symbolizes generosity and this is why we must take it as an example. Some of you will say: 'But the sun is not a human being.' Of course not, but it does more than any human being can do. It is certainly better to form a bond with a creature – which, although it is not human is able to influence us with its light and its warmth – than with human beings who are weak, selfish and without light. Suppose even that the sun is no more than molten metal or rock – that is fine by me – as long as it manifests qualities that are superior to those of human beings I shall go toward it, because when I am near it I feel elated, when I am near it I grow, when I am near it I become more intelligent, when I am near it I am healed. Why do you not want to do the same?

Once you have been with the sun for a long time and have learned to identify with it you can turn to human beings without injuring or cheating anyone. You will greet them, look at them, smile at them, shake their hand, talk to them or work with them, but you will never cease to give them something good, something luminous. And in doing so you will blossom, grow, progress, elevate yourself higher and higher, because you will be obeying the law of love, the true law of love, the law of giving. And while you are giving you will also be receiving, because divine light will be descending on you like a river of clear pure water.

You will say: 'But Jesus never spoke of the sun as you do. He never said we should be like the sun.' No, it is true that he never spoke these words, but he did say *the righteous will shine like the sun*. And the righteous in the Old and New

Testaments are those who, in their thoughts, feelings, and deeds, behave according to God's will. So, you see, the idea is the same.[9]

The sun shows us the way. It shows us that we should give, that is, we should warm, illuminate, and vivify. But who will let themselves be persuaded? Most people will find this image pretty or poetic, but as with everything poetic, they will rank it with what is unachievable, with castles in the air, and they will continue to take and to want to be the centre of the world around which all else must revolve and which all else must serve.

Well no, it is we who must be servants. To give is to be a servant. Of course, if you do not understand the profound meaning of the word 'servant' you will have no desire to be one. You would see it as a position of inferiority and would feel humiliated. Well, do you think the sun feels humiliated? Jesus said: *'The greatest among you will be your servant.'* Why the greatest? Because in order to be a servant in the initiatic sense of the word you must possess exceptional qualities. You must be like the sun and work with disinterestedness, the utmost selflessness, giving light, warmth, and life. Is that humiliating?

Now, if you really carry through your analysis you will see that, in reality, absolute disinterestedness does not exist. Behind each and every physical and mental manifestation lies a degree of self-interest. Be it a material, crude interest or a more subtle interest such as progressing, becoming enlightened, perfecting oneself. The difference is that in the second case the interest is spiritual and pure and causes no harm to anyone – it is even beneficial to the entire world – whereas in the first case it can only be satisfied to the detriment of others. So there are two kinds of self-interest. One that only concerns individuals and their personality, and this is rarely beneficial to those around them. And the other which is so vast that it encompasses the whole collectivity.

You must get into the habit of analysing your thoughts, feelings, and actions. You must subject everything you do to close scrutiny and discover what kind of self-interest lies behind it. You will see that very little will pass the test and reveal itself to be truly impersonal. But I repeat, total absence of self-interest does not exist. There are simply varying degrees which are more or less spiritual. Even if your only desire is to make human beings happier, more luminous, warmer, and more alive, you are still pursuing an interest, that of becoming like the sun. Although this interest is so disinterested that it enters a different category altogether and becomes divine, by pursuing it you are still pursuing your self-interest. And I too have an interest, the greatest of all, which is to leave indelible traces of the divine world within you, so that later on, when you are far away from me, you will remember them.[10] So you see, I too am pursuing an interest.

Notes

1 See *The Yoga of Nutrition*, Izvor. 204, Chap. 6: 'The Ethics of Eating'.
2 See *Golden Rules for Everyday Life*, Izvor. 227, #25, 'Choosing the Means to Fit the End'.
3 See *Hommage au Maître Peter Deunov*, Coll. Izvor n° 200.
4 See *'In Spirit and in Truth'*, Izvor. 235, Chap. 16: 'The Truth of the Sun is in Giving'.
5 See *Love and Sexuality*, C.W. 14, Chap. 7: 'Jealousy'; Chap. 15: 'Wealth and Poverty'; Chaps. 18 and 21: 'A Wider Concept of Marriage'; Chap. 26: 'The Bonds of Love'; *Love and Sexuality*, C.W. 15, Chap. 3: 'The sun is the Source of Love'; Chap. 11: 'Restoring Love to its Pristine Purity'; Chap. 21: 'A Broader Concept of Marriage'; Chap. 25: 'Love God so as to Love Your Neighbour Better'.

6 See *The Splendour of Tiphareth*, C.W. 10, Chap. 8: 'Love as the sun Loves'.

7 Ibid., Chap. 20: 'The Sun Teaches by Example – The Sun, Heart of our Universe'; *A New Dawn: Society and Politics in the Light of Initiatic Science*, C.W. 25, Chap. 4 (v): 'Communism and Capitalism', p. 132-133.

8 See *Vie et travail à l'École divine*, «Le disciple aux prises avec sa nature inférieure».

9 See *Toward a Solar Civilisation*, Izvor. 201, Chap. 2: 'Surya Yoga'; Chap. 3: 'The Search for the Centre'.

10 See *What is a Spiritual Master?*, Izvor. 207, Chap. 6: 'A Master is a Mirror Reflecting the Truth'; Chap. 7: 'A Master is There Only to Give Light'.

5

The voice
of
our higher nature

Every day our divine nature speaks to us. It tries to make itself heard to advise and enlighten us. But it does not shout, it does not resort to violence. It whispers its advice once, twice, three times, and then it stops talking. Our lower nature, on the other hand, having other plans and needs, insists, repeats, and makes a din. Its aim is to deafen us poor human beings so that we give in and say: 'If it is so insistent, it must mean it is right.' This is why our personality fears nothing more than silence. It flees silence. It senses that silence would hinder it, inhibit its trickery, curb its whims, thwart its arrogance and that it would end by being paralysed, repressed, unable to find the right conditions to realize its plans.

Silence is like a door opening onto the celestial regions, and our personality senses that this silence represents the end of its reign, that it will be forced to resign. At the slightest offence, instead of keeping quiet, it hammers away in our heads: 'Retaliate, get your own back.' It never stops nagging. As for our individuality, it advises: 'Stay calm, wait a while. There is no need to worry, because no one can really hurt you. Try to have a little more light in the future, a little more love.' This is the advice of our individuality. But in the meantime the personality does everything in its power to drown out this voice with trumpets and big base drums, and it is so persistent, day in, day out, that – simply because human beings are rather silly creatures – we end by saying to ourselves: 'All right then, let's do it!'

All the practices of a spiritual teaching – meditation, prayer and so on – have only one purpose, and that is to give less space to the personality so as to give the individuality more opportunity to express itself.[1] That is what true silence is. To achieve silence on the physical plane is easy, all you have to do is close the doors and windows or stop up your ears. But to achieve silence in your thoughts and feelings, that is much more difficult. Because a person's inner self is an open house, where crowds of people arrive all at once to express themselves and make their demands.

If you come to an initiatic school it is to learn things that are essential, otherwise there is no point. And one of these essential things is just this: to achieve inner silence, to hush all the discussion and rebellion, the quarrels stirred up by thoughts, desires, and feelings that are out of control, and to receive at last true answers to the questions you are asking yourself, the answers from your divine self.[2]

Silence should be understood to be a prerequisite, a state of consciousness in which something mysterious and profound begins to reveal itself. This 'something' is sometimes called the voice of silence. Once you succeed in calming everything within you, and even stopping your thoughts – because the movement of thought also makes a noise – you will hear this voice of silence, which is the voice of your divine nature.

In order to escape inner noise you should stop living superficially, on the surface, because there you are exposed to bustle and turmoil. Seek instead to free yourself from worries and prosaic preoccupations, and especially to change the nature of your needs. Because every need, every desire, every wish leads you onto a particular path, and, depending on the nature of your need, wish or desire, you will end up either in a jungle full of marauding wild animals or in a realm of celestial creatures who welcome you with harmonious concerts.

Even when you try consciously to create silence within yourself to meditate, you often feel you are not succeeding. You close your eyes, but all your problems, worries, and resentments resurface. You continue inwardly to bicker with your wife or husband, you smack your children, you settle scores with the neighbour who offended you, you demand a pay-rise from your boss, you picture an object you want, and so on. And you still call this 'creating silence'. Well no, it is a hullabaloo. And this hullabaloo is audible. Indeed, we sometimes have the impression we can hear the inner noise of certain people. They may be completely motionless, they may not open their mouths, but they make a deafening noise. And then there are some people – unfortunately these are all too rare – who seem steeped in silence. Even when they speak, something silent emanates from them, because silence is a quality of the inner life.

Inner silence develops when the physical, astral, and mental planes of your being coexist in harmony. So, if you wish to create silence within, you must begin by creating harmony between your body, heart, and intellect. Harmony is the key that unlocks the doors to the realm of silence.[3] There have no doubt been times when you have suddenly felt a deep silence come over you, as if the inner noise you had not noticed until then – because you are continuously drowned in it – stopped abruptly. You then feel as if a weight had been lifted from your shoulders: obstacles vanish, shackles fall away, doors open, and your soul, finally freed from its prison, can escape and expand in space.

And this experience of silence, which you have had the good fortune to receive as a gift from heaven – whether or not you have done anything to deserve it – can be renewed: you can try consciously to repeat it. Little by little you will sense that all the discordant voices that never stop demanding and threatening begin to quieten down. Only one soft voice, a mere murmur will remain: the voice of your higher nature, the voice of God.

In reality this inner voice never stops speaking inside each one of us, but it takes a great deal of effort to be able to distinguish it from all the other noises, whether internal or external. It is like trying to follow the melody of a flute amidst the sounds of drums, and trumpets. We need to learn to perceive this very gentle voice talking to us. We have no trouble hearing the booming voice of our stomach shouting out its hunger or that of our genitals clamouring for a victim. But when the divine voice urges us to be more patient, to learn to control ourselves, to make an effort, we tell it to be quiet. It is very easy to turn a deaf ear to this little voice. It is so gentle, it never insists.

You will say: 'But how can this be? God is strength, power, he has all the means he needs to make himself heard.' Yes, but look at the story of Elijah in the *Book of Kings*. In order to escape the wrath of Queen Jezebel, Elijah fled into the desert where he walked for forty days and forty nights, until he reached Horeb the mount of God. God finally passed by him. First there was a great wind which split mountains and shattered rocks. But God was not in the wind. After the wind there was an earthquake, but God was not in the earthquake. After the earthquake there was a fire, but God was not in the fire. Last, after the fire came a soft, gentle murmur... and God was in this murmur. So remember this: God was not in the gusts of wind, nor in the earthquake, nor in the fire. He was in the murmur. The voice of God does not make much noise, and to hear it we need to be very attentive and to have silenced all the other voices within us.

The prophet Jonah also heard the voice of God telling him to go to Nineveh to urge its citizens to repent. But Jonah was afraid and did not want to obey, so he embarked on a ship going to Tarshish, at the other end of the world. Once at sea, a mighty storm came up. The sailors were terrified and decided to consult heaven by casting lots to find out who had attracted this storm. The lot fell on Jonah. Then the sailors threw Jonah into the sea, but he was swallowed by a whale and stayed in its belly for three days and three nights. There he thought and finally understood, asked God for forgiveness, and promised to do as he wished. Then the whale spewed Jonah out upon the dry land, and he was saved. Well, those who are prevented by the din of their whims and fears from hearing the voice of God will also come across whales, as did Jonah, and will remain in their bellies for several days, until the uproar dies down and they hear the voice of God and obey him. And what about you? Think of all the whales you have already encountered in your life! Yes, whales of all shapes and sizes!

If you were more attentive and more discerning, you would sense that before every major undertaking in your life – a journey, a job, a decision to make – a voice is advising you. But you do not pay attention, you are too busy listening to the uproar of your desires and whims. A voice needs to make a lot of noise before you hear it. If it speaks softly, you do not hear it. But when by your own fault something unfortunate happens to you, you sometimes say to yourself: 'Yes, of course, something did warn me, but it was so faint, so very faint.' You did not listen because you preferred to follow the voices that insisted and spoke very loudly to mislead you.

God speaks to us quietly and without insisting. Intuition speaks no louder. If you are not attentive, you will not make out this voice and will always end by losing your way. What are the signs by which we recognize this voice from heaven if it is so soft, melodious, and brief? Well, it manifests in three ways. First, by generating light within us; second, by giving us a sense of dilatation, warmth and love in our heart; last by stimulating the will within us to accomplish noble, disinterested deeds and giving us the inner freedom to realize them. So, clearly, you need to be attentive, for these are the criteria, the signs to look for.

Of course there are many people who claim that God speaks to them and that they hear his voice. And what does this voice tell them? They say it gives them the mission to bring order to the world, to hunt down traitors, to exterminate heretics or unbelievers. And off they go to war! There is no doubt, they do hear a voice, because everything that exists has a voice. But a voice that tells them to re-establish order and justice with threats and violence cannot be the voice of God. Let us be quite clear about that. This is the voice of their lower nature.

So, next time you have an important decision to make, try to bear in mind these criteria. If you feel troubled because there are too many contradictions whirling around inside you, pushing you this way and that, decide nothing and wait. You cannot see clearly amidst such turmoil, indeed all the conditions are right for you to make mistakes. It is far better to take your time and begin by composing yourself, because only when you have created silence in your thoughts and feelings will you receive the answer from your higher self. From this silence clarity, lucidity, and certainty will emerge and you need it in order to make the right decisions.[4]

There is no point in aspiring to great spiritual achievements if you fail to stop the noise and disorder in your psychic life. Silence, the true silence which finally gives your higher nature the opportunity to make its voice heard, cannot establish itself within you because of all this disorder. You must devote a few minutes each day, several times a day, to instilling this silence within you. Close your eyes, try to free yourself from your everyday worries and direct your thoughts toward the summits, toward the sources of life that feed the entire universe. And when you sense that you have stopped the flood of images, feelings, and thoughts, say the words 'thank you' inwardly.[5] These are the simplest words of all, but they release all tension, because by saying thank you, you bring yourself into harmony with heaven, you escape the narrow circle of your limited self to enter the peace of cosmic conscience. And as breathing also has a significant calming and harmonizing effect, try to regulate your breathing as you say the words 'thank you'. Breathe in deeply and breathe out slowly, until there is no air left in your lungs.[6]

So, get into the habit of restoring silence within you several times a day. Even if you only have a minute or two in which to do so, that is fine, do it. Even if you are in the street, stop in front of a shop window and pretend to be looking in – so that no one notices what you are doing – close your eyes for a few seconds and try to isolate yourself with your mind and unite with the world of harmony and light. Then you can go on your way again.

Of course, once you have succeeded in creating this silence within you through prayer and meditation, you must also learn to maintain it. You must be careful not to let it slip away, for what good are your efforts if you immediately lose all the benefits you gained from it?

Understand this well, spiritual life is not a question of trying occasionally to re-establish the link with the world of silence and light and then forgetting all about it and allowing yourself to be drawn back into the disorder and noise of life, only to start all over again the next day. There is no point in that. On the contrary, this silence you have succeeded in establishing within must be with you all day and must imperceptibly communicate a rhythm, a grace to everything you do. With every move you make, with every touch, this harmonious movement will be passed on to all the cells of your organism. It will be as though everything within you were music and dance.

The achievement of inner silence is an indication of your evolution. And not only will this silence open up the doors of enlightenment for you, but you will become a source of blessing to everyone around you. So, even when the hustle and bustle of everyday life surrounds you, try to maintain the silence within. Do you understand me? Yes, well it is not enough simply to understand. You must also apply it. For so many people there is a huge chasm between understanding and applying. They understand, they understand... but when it comes to doing something about it, they are unable to. But in initiatic science understanding and application go hand in hand. To an initiate, to know is to be able to do, and those who do not succeed in applying what they claim to have understood, have not truly understood.[7] If you have really understood what true silence is, you will achieve it. And then you will discover that it is never empty or mute; that it is inhabited, alive and vibrant, that it talks and sings.[8]

Through meditation, prayer, and contemplation we will one day succeed in silencing the big base drums, all these chaotic forces whirling around inside us. Then silence will come and spread out to enfold us in its marvellous mantle. A new light will appear, and the Deity within us will make its voice heard.

25

Notes

1 See *The Powers of Thought*, Izvor 224, Chap. 10: 'The Power of Concentrated Thought'; Chap. 11: 'Meditation'; Chap. 12: 'Creative Prayer'.
2 See *The Path of Silence*, Izvor 229, Chap. 2: 'Achieving Inner Silence'; Chap. 7: 'Harmony, the Essential Condition for Inner Silence'; Chap. 8: 'Silence, the Essential Condition for Thought'; Chap. 9: 'The Quest for Silence is the Quest for the Centre'; Chap. 12: 'The Voice of Silence is the Voice of God'.
3 See *Harmony and Health*, Izvor 225, Chap. 2: 'The World of Harmony'.
4 See *The Path of Silence*, Izvor 229, Chap. 13: 'The Revelations of a Starry Sky''; Chap. 14: 'A Silent Room'.
5 See *Love and Sexuality*, C.W. 15, Chap. 26 (I): 'Live Lovingly'.
6 See *Harmony and Health*, Izvor 225, Chap. 6 (II): 'How to Melt into the Harmony of the Cosmos'.
7 See *Education Begins before Birth*, Izvor 203, Chap. 11: 'Education versus Instruction'; Truth: Fruit of Wisdom and Love, Izvor 234, Chap. 2: 'Truth, the Child of Wisdom and Love'.
8 See *The Path of Silence*, Izvor 229, Chap. 6: 'The Inhabitants of Silence'.

6

Sensitivity
to the divine world

It is often said that simple, primitive, ignorant people find happiness more easily than people who are educated and cultivated. And it is true that as our intelligence and taste develop, we also develop greater sensibility, we become more sensitive, and therefore also more vulnerable to the changes in the material and psychological conditions in which we live. So, what can we deduce from this? That to be happy we should remain primitive, we should remain savages? Well, why not in that case go even further and descend to the level of the animal kingdom? Animals are happy; they do not have our problems. And it could be that plants are even happier still because they do not suffer. And what about stones? Stones feel nothing, so that is even better. How is that for logic!

The main difference between the various realms in nature – mineral, vegetable, animal, and human – is understanding, sensibility, because evolution is proportional to sensibility. Plants have greater sensibility than stones, animals are more sensitive than plants, and human beings are more sensitive than animals. But the chain of creatures does not end there. Above human beings are the angels, the archangels, and all the angelic orders. Indeed, there is a whole gradation of creatures, each more sensitive than the last, ascending all the way to God himself.

God is omniscient, he feels everything, he sees everything, he knows everything, precisely because he alone is truly sensitive. This is the true scope of sensitivity: the only truly sensitive being is God. As for human beings, of course, by becoming more sensitive, they become more vulnerable and their suffering increases. But it is nevertheless preferable for them to develop their sensibility, because this is what makes us evolve.[1]

But if we want to understand this clearly, we must return to the issue of the two natures within us, the lower nature and the higher nature. As long as humans have not started to work on themselves so as to control the selfish tendencies of their lower nature, the development of their sensitivity will obviously be fraught with problems and suffering of all kinds. Unfortunately, the education given in schools and universities only accentuates these tendencies. By this undue emphasis on the acquisition of knowledge to the detriment of character formation, young people are given excuses to become increasingly selfish, difficult, and demanding. Nothing is done to teach the students to use the knowledge they have acquired by applying it to more noble, more generous ends. On the contrary; in every field they learn to use their knowledge to further their own social success, their prestige, and their material well-being. And when they become responsible adults in society all they think of is taking as big a share of everything as they can, and this of course breeds dissatisfaction, aggressiveness and quarrels. Each one feels threatened and cheated by the selfish behaviour of others.

You would expect educated and cultivated people to react in a measured and reasonable manner when faced with difficulties. More often than not, however, this is not so. The merest trifle reduces them to a pitiful state of anger or depression, and they have neither the power nor even the will to remedy the situation. All their knowledge, all their erudition cannot help them. So, even if we feel it is good for people to continue their schooling to an advanced age, we have to admit that even more important than learning is character formation.[2]

What is essential is to live, not to accumulate knowledge. And in order to live, to be able to face up to all the conditions of life, we must strengthen our character. Otherwise, what use are people who are incapable of facing the realities of life? The neuralgic sensibility that is fed by our lower nature, the personality, makes life very difficult, and this is why people have come to the conclusion that in order to be happy, it is better not to be sensitive.

In fact, a clear distinction should be made between true sensitivity and this pathological sensibility, which might more correctly be called touchiness or a sickly sentimentality. True sensitivity is a faculty that enables us to ascend very high, very far, and to gain access to the realities of an increasingly subtle world. Sentimentality, on the other hand, is a manifestation of our lower nature, which, believing itself to be the centre of the world, feels that it is not given sufficient consideration, and so it always feels frustrated, hurt, and becomes aggressive. Once you make this distinction, it becomes clear that a good deal of work needs to be done to control and dominate your lower nature. Only then can true sensibility flourish and grow richer.

Sensibility is not simply a faculty that stirs our emotions and fills us with wonder for the people we love, for the beauty of nature or works of art. Sensibility is the prerequisite for evolution. It is a higher faculty that opens the doors to immensity to us and allows us to understand the divine order of things. It is this that allows us to get in touch with the regions, entities, and currents of heaven and to vibrate in unison with them.[3] This is the sensibility we must all cultivate, otherwise humankind will regress. There are so many people who seem to be returning to the animal, vegetable, or even the mineral stage. They make no effort to train their sensibility. Either they allow themselves to give in to sadness, disappointment or rebellion, or they try to harden themselves, or even to lose touch with reality. Well, this is not the way to evolve.

If we want to evolve we must work on our sensibility so as to refine our psychic matter and make it more flexible and purer so that it vibrates differently. Thus, while making us better able to perceive the divine world, true sensibility shields us from stupidity, wickedness, and offence to the point where we no longer notice them. Before developing this spiritual sensibility we reacted to the slightest aggression, whereas now it no longer affects us. True sensibility, that of the soul and the spirit, protects us from sentimentality, the unreasonable sensibility of our lower nature. And this brings two benefits: we allow the light, beauty, and bliss of the divine world in, and we escape the darkness, ugliness, and suffering of earth. So this is worth some thought.

Truly sensitive creatures are not vulnerable. It is exactly because they have sensibility that they escape malevolence, rudeness, and ugliness. It is not so easy to get at them because they are elsewhere, higher up. They have identified with their higher nature and they feel things differently. When you are sensitive to the divine world, you are shielded, as if you were wrapped in a protective covering. You are only open to what is good, beautiful, and luminous, and you are shielded from all that is negative. The day you decide to develop true sensitivity, you will feel that something inside you responds only to messages from heaven, and you will be able to bear humiliation, loss, and injustice more easily. You will say: 'Oh, that is nothing compared to the riches I possess,' and you will carry on regardless.

Nothing is worse than the means people use to protect themselves from suffering... wine, alcohol, drugs, and so on.[4] If you want to protect yourself, if you want to be shielded, you must endeavour to go higher and further. As soon as you succeed in elevating yourself, in uniting with your higher self, your heart, intellect, and soul will no longer be affected, no longer vibrate in response to baseness and vileness. People can criticize and offend you, sully, humiliate and denigrate you, but you will not collapse like so many – artists in particular – who have died of sorrow or committed suicide because they were too vulnerable, too sensitive. But this was the sensitivity of their lower nature, which becomes unsettled at the merest trifle. Why not develop the attitude: 'It's unfair, but I don't care, because I live elsewhere, in a different world'?

Sages, initiates, or even artists in the initiatic sense of the word have such sensitivity to beauty that sometimes they cry when they come into contact with it. And when people offend them, they do not cry. They merely shrug their shoulders. Whereas others end up in floods of tears at the merest humiliation, but never shed a tear before the splendour of nature or works of art. There, where the Deity himself manifests, they remain dry-eyed. They feel it is dignified to show no emotion, they would think it beneath them to shed tears. Well, I tell you, on the contrary, that you should show yourself unperturbed by humiliation and impassive to grief, but you can succumb to tears before beauty. Because the tears you shed before beauty are like dew, like celestial rain, like magnificent currents that purify you, that water the flowers in your divine garden and give you the impetus to continue your work. Tears shed through disappointment and bitterness may bring some relief, but that is all. Whereas tears of wonder are impregnated with such divine strength that – and this may come as a surprise – Master Deunov advised us to take a clean handkerchief to catch them, saying that this handkerchief would be like a talisman, because each tear shed in this way contains something of the Deity.

People who prefer not to be sensitive so as not to suffer are making a grave error in their reasoning. Why? Because if you have understood what spiritual work truly entails, you will discover that, on the contrary, it is your sensibility that protects you from suffering by placing you out of reach, whereas insensitivity turns you to stone. If you are a stone you may no longer feel anything, but there is always a chance that you may shatter into pieces. Whereas if you are sensitive, of course you may suffer, but this suffering will spur you on to develop your perception of the higher planes, and there you will be out of reach. As you know, it is so much easier to catch a four-legged animal than to catch a bird. Try to shoot an eagle in full flight, and it soars up so high into the sky that you lose sight of it.

So, like the eagle, try to make yourself invisible to those who attack you. There are still countless steps to climb before you are protected. But there have been a few beings who succeeded in refining their sensibility to such an extent that they were able to melt into the light, to identify with it, and through the light they were able to become invisible and move in space. Of course, those who have succeeded in reaching that point are still very rare, but since some have succeeded, it proves it can be done.

Therefore, whatever happens to you, do not try to deaden your mind with drink or pills under the misconception that by numbing your thoughts and feelings you will ease the suffering. No, you will be able to bear the suffering better if you are awake and lucid, and if you think about how to extricate yourself from the unbearable pressures of the astral and mental planes.

Otherwise you will lose your soul.[5] You have first to accept suffering in order to use it. The Creator has given suffering the specific function of awakening the divine world in human beings. But human beings seem to do everything in their power to oppose this awakening of divine aspirations. But now you, at least, must realize that it is for your own good that you must try to understand the spiritual language of certain kinds of suffering. Learn to welcome them by telling yourself: 'This is a message from heaven. It is asking me to start working to develop this quality, or that virtue.' While you are busy uniting with heaven, with light, and with beauty, you will forget the suffering and when you return it will have disappeared. Even if you think back later to the cause of this suffering, you will feel no more pain, because you will have risen above it.

True sensitivity is open only to the world of light; it is closed to the world of darkness. Sentimentality, on the other hand, is exactly the opposite. So, we need to have greater sensitivity even though it means we shall have to suffer. A person whose sensitivity has been dulled regresses to the mineral world, whereas true evolution, which is a forward movement, is associated with an increase in sensitivity.

I am not saying that you should not feel suffering any longer. That is not possible. Everyday life is full of occasions to suffer. I am saying that we must learn to transform our suffering. Someone has offended or hurt you, and you are distressed? Well, this is normal. But if you really want to progress, you must tell yourself: 'This person has hurt me, but there are so many others who love me, who are thinking of me.' For some so-called 'sensitive' people, it is as though heaven, the angels, friends, and the beauty of art and nature had suddenly disappeared. All they have left is sorrow, ugliness, malicious and unjust people. But it is stupid to react like this... it is just too stupid! All that these poor wretches think is left for them is to kill themselves – and this, of course, is what some end by doing. Why were these unfortunate creatures never taught to open their eyes, so that they could say to themselves: 'It's all right. What have I lost? Very little. And what can I gain? Everything.'

Let us say you have thrown some dead leaves into a spring. If this spring is pathologically sensitive, in other words, if it is feeble or dried up, the leaves will rot and smell bad. But if this particular spring is alive, it will flow vigorously and continue to gush forth without even realizing you have thrown dirt into it, and the dead leaves will be washed away. This is how a living spring resolves the problem. So, if you are a dried-up spring, you will rot and make yourself ill, but if you are a vigorous spring, in other words if you love all that is beautiful and good in human beings and in the universe, your love will protect you.[6] It will reject all that is negative so that you will always be pure, alive, and radiant. As soon as you start to complain: 'Oh, he said this... she did that', it is finished; you are no longer a living spring. Become a living spring and you will be protected.

Our only protection is our love for the things of heaven, for celestial creatures. But as most people do not understand this, they resort to having a few drinks or swallowing some tranquillizers. And then, after a brief moment of respite, their suffering returns and is often worse than before. Thus these people will always be unhappy, always be victims, and not so much victims of other people as victims of themselves, of their own laziness and stupidity.

You must understand once and for all that human beings and life's events will always be what they are. They will not change to spare your sensibility. It is you who must change. You who must extricate yourself from the claws of your personality and develop your sensitivity to the divine world. You will say: 'But how? It is such a difficult thing to do.' No, it is not difficult. Simply start by becoming increasingly aware of the value of some of the moments you live, of those moments of silence and contemplation during which you receive a light, a blessing from heaven. Your weakness and vulnerability stem from your lack of this awareness. You are not able to make these moments of grace last. You lose them very quickly simply because you do not realize how precious they are. You are always preoccupied with other trifles that seems more important at the time – some little job that needs to be done, some discussion about an insignificant matter. You think heaven should always be there, always pouring out its blessings. And you, well, when it suits you and you have nothing more interesting to do, you will stop a few minutes to receive them. Well no, this is not the way. Heaven is not at the disposal of fickle, heedless people. Heaven pours out its blessings at a given moment, under certain conditions, and if you are not sufficiently aware to receive them or if you are not able to preserve them, well that is too bad, because they will leave you.

So try to be careful: when you feel you have had a revelation, a blessing from heaven, try to treasure it, because happiness lies in a constant attention to all that is beautiful, in a sensitivity to all that is divine. When you sense that the spirit, that light has visited you, do not let these impressions fade away by immediately thinking about something else. Ponder them for a long time so that they may penetrate you deeply, and so leave traces within you for eternity. You must make this a habit. Instead of always dwelling on the negative, on your disappointment and resentments, thereby feeding and strengthening them, put them aside, get rid of them, and concentrate on all that is good, pure, and luminous in your life. This is the only effective way to silence the moaning and groaning of your lower nature, which is always offended and hypersensitive.

I can even give you a method for this. Try to remember the most luminous moments of your existence and examine who instigated them and how they arose. Recall them often, just as you play a song you like over and over again. You will then relive the same feelings of purity, freedom, and light. We have a huge store of records inside us. Indeed, every event in our life, however minor, is recorded. Psychologists call these recordings 'memory' or 'the subconscious'. But it does not matter what we call them. What matters is to be able to use them. Once you have managed to experience a divine second, it means that eternity has crept into that second. You have taken a picture and the negative will live eternally. It is inside you and it is indelible. So, when you are in a black mood, when you feel troubled or lost, find your inner recordings and try to retrieve those marvellous states of consciousness which allowed you to understand, for a few seconds at least, that life can mean light, peace, beauty, love, and fulfilment. Even if for the moment you find yourself in a situation and a state of mind far removed from those divine moments, they have not been wiped out. You can retrieve them and feel their beneficial vibrations flowing through you.

Unfortunately, most people tend to do the opposite. They remember the things that made them suffer and they carry them about with them, look at them, turn them over in all directions, chew them over. And this is very dangerous: you should never go back to what has been bad in your life. You should draw your conclusion from it once and for all and then not go back to it. Continually going over negative events or states of mind is harmful. Put them behind you, and instead try to retrieve all the moments in which you came to understand and sense the meaning and the beauty of life. Return to those moments often, because in doing so you will amplify and vivify them, and, unlike ordinary music records which end by wearing out, the more often you play the records of your heart and soul, the stronger and more durable they become. So whether they be beneficial or harmful, the same law applies: the more you use them, the stronger they become.

Do you understand? If you want to develop true sensitivity, the sensitivity that will protect you from the unhealthy manifestations of your lower nature, try to go back as often as possible to those moments in which you felt the reality of divine life. Remember that at some point in your life you heard a magical voice singing celestial songs. Go to your inner collection of records, put on the record, and once again you will be captivated, spellbound. And in this way you will continue to progress along the path of light.

Notes

1 See *'Know Thyself' Jnana Yoga,* C.W. 17, Chap. 3 (III): 'Spirit and Matter'.
2 See *Youth: Creators of the Future,* Izvor 233, Chap. 6: 'Knowledge Cannot Give Meaning to Life'; Chap. 7: 'Character Counts for More than Knowledge'.
3 See *La pédagogie initiatique,* Œuvres Complètes, t. 29, chap. IV : «Le savoir vivant : vivez dans la poésie».
4 See *Réponses à quelques questions actuelles,* «La drogue, une maladie de l'âme», Fascicule n°1, p. 13-14.
5 See *The Tree of the Knowledge of Good and Evil,* Izvor 210, Chap. 8: 'Suicide is not the Answer'.
6 See *The Mysteries of Yesod,* C.W. 7, Chap. 14: 'A Spring of Fresh Water'; *Cosmic Moral Law,* C.W. 12, Chap. 12: 'The Moral Law Exemplified in a Spring'; *On the Art of Teaching from the Initiatic Point of View,* C.W. 29, Chap. 4 (I): 'On the Living Knowledge'.

7

'Blessed
are the peacemakers'

Blessed are the peacemakers, for they will be called children of God.

For Jesus to link peace to the elevated status of children of God in this way, he had to have deemed it to be extremely precious. Indeed, we see from the Gospels that he used the word 'peace' very often: *'Peace be with you'; 'Go in peace';* and at the end, as he left his disciples, he said to them: *'Peace I leave with you; my peace I give to you.'* What did he mean by this and how did he understand the word 'peace'?

All over the world people seek peace, but it remains out of their reach because they do not really know what it is or how to find it. If we want to know what peace is we must look at it from the esoteric point of view, but even if we succeed in knowing and understanding peace, it is still one of the most difficult things to achieve.

People seem to believe that by eliminating something or someone outside of them they will be able to find peace. But they are mistaken. Even if we did away with weapons and armies, people would still find a way to destroy each other. People may advocate peace, and it may even be imposed by force, but this peace will not last if we continue to support the causes of war. Peace is first and foremost an inner state, and this inner state will never be achieved by eliminating anything on the outside. So it is within ourselves that we must begin to work at peace. Let me give you an example. Suppose someone has accumulated huge debts in order to satisfy his desires and is unable to repay them as he had promised. He now has a pack of creditors chasing after him. How can he have peace? 'By running away' you may say. All right, but what about the creditors within him, and by this I mean the worries, the uneasiness, that pursue him? How will he escape these? No, no! This kind of reasoning comes from a lack of true knowledge. Do not delude yourselves, conscience always catches up with us in the end.

At first sight, it may seem easy for people to find peace. You only need to go somewhere where there is no one else – in a forest, a desert or a mountain – wherever solitude and silence reign. There you can be quiet and peaceful, no one will bother you. But this does not necessarily mean that you are at peace. Why? Because you will have taken your 'transistor' with you. Yes, human beings always carry a transistor in their heads. They are never without it, and it is almost always switched on. Even when they are in solitude and surrounded by silence, they are still inwardly tuned in to their husband, their wife, their mother-in-law, their children, their neighbours, their boss, their rivals, or whoever. And the arguments that go on...! They never stop ruminating the ambitions, the demands, the grudges, the disappointments of their lower nature, so even if on the outside everything is calm, storms and hurricanes continue to rage inwardly. And sooner or later all this inner unrest ends by having repercussions on the outside.

In our physical body every organ fulfils the specific function assigned by nature. But that is not the end of it, because these organs are interlinked and they must work in harmony with each other, otherwise there will be what musicians call discord and what we generally know as illness. We can be in good health only if all our organs work for the good of our organism as a whole.[1] And health brings a certain peace, but this is still only a purely physical stage. To find inner peace we have to go much higher, so that all the elements of our psychic organism vibrate in unison, in other words without selfishness, without conflict, without prejudice, just like the organs of a healthy physical organism. Peace is a higher state of consciousness, but this state also depends on the proper functioning of the physical organism, because even if peace of the soul and the spirit is what is most important, it is difficult to enjoy that peace if the body is suffering. We must, therefore, be vigilant and endeavour to keep our physical bodies in good health.

If you are to achieve peace, you must have a thorough knowledge of human beings, of the different bodies that constitute them and which all have their own needs and aspirations. When the instruments of an orchestra are perfectly tuned and all the musicians obey the conductor, there is perfect harmony. In human beings peace is also a harmony between all our physical, psychic, and spiritual elements, and this harmony can be achieved only if all these elements accept the authority of our divine nature.

Just as health is the result of harmony between the different parts of the physical organism, peace is the result of harmony between the different elements of the psychic organism, in other words the spirit, the soul, the intellect, the heart, and the will. And if peace is so difficult to achieve it is because they so rarely work in harmony. A person may have lucid and wise thoughts, but then his heart, invaded by some impassioned feelings, pushes him to do something stupid. Or he may be motivated by the best desires, but his will is paralysed, and so on. How can anyone feel at peace in the midst of all these contradictions?

You will never understand what peace is – what is more you will never succeed in achieving it – if you do not understand that it is a result, a consequence. Yes, peace is first and foremost a state of consciousness which presupposes that all our functions, all our physical and psychic activities exist in perfect balance and harmony.[2] From the moment you allow yourself to harbour wishes and desires inspired by your personality, you can no longer be at peace, whatever you do, because you will have already sown within you the seeds of disorder – and hence of war – simply by having those wishes and desires.

Before we can find peace we must know the nature and properties of all our thoughts, feelings, and desires, so that we never allow anything to enter us which might disrupt our inner harmony. At the same time, we must work to eliminate from our organism anything that does not vibrate in unison with the world of light.

If you eat and drink without moderation or discernment you introduce indigestible elements into your organism and they will give you nausea, colic, stomach cramp, and so on. And the same applies on the psychic plane. If you do not concern yourself with the quality of the feelings, thoughts, and desires with which you nourish yourself, you expose yourself to 'indigestion' and you cannot be at peace. Peace is also the fruit, therefore, of a profound knowledge of the nature of the elements with which we nourish ourselves on every plane. And as we acquire this knowledge we must develop vigilance and a strong will so that we never allow impurities to enter us. Sages and initiates, who attach such importance to purity, are not fanatical puritans. They have simply learned from their own experience that all the impurities that slip into their feelings or thoughts take away their peace. And if you too observe yourselves, you will find the same.[3] As I have said, peace is the result of harmony, absolute consonance between all the factors and elements that make up human beings, and this harmony can exist only when all these elements have been purified. If they are not in harmony it means that they have been contaminated by impurities.

When disorder finds its way into your heart or your intellect, it is because you have absorbed something impure, and by impure I mean simply something that you cannot assimilate, something that is too alien. Impurities are harmful because they cannot be assimilated. They may not be impure in themselves, but they are considered impure because their presence in the psychic organism causes disruption. They are therefore undesirable and you must rid yourself of them. If you are unwell or troubled, it is because you have allowed an impurity to invade you in the form of a thought, a feeling or a desire.

Every impurity, be it on the mental, astral, or physical plane, brings turmoil – in fact, 'turmoil' is the least that can be said, because on the psychic and physical planes impurities can cause poisoning and even death. It is therefore vital to purify yourself on all planes; on the physical and especially on the psychic plane. But as soon as the word purity is mentioned, most people no longer understand anything. When they hear the word purity, they immediately associate it with sexuality, when in fact that is only a very limited aspect of it.

If we want to understand purity it is not even necessary to consider it in the moral context, where it leads to interminable discussions which only serve to make it less clear. Purity belongs in all areas of our lives, but it will be clearer to you if we began by studying it in the human organism, with nutrition.

As you know, it is not enough for food-stuffs to be considered edible; they also have to be prepared before they are fit to eat. Most of the time we have to wash them... but this is often not enough. Some vegetables and fruits need to have stones, pips, skins or shells removed. We cut the rind off the cheese we eat. Fish have to be gutted and then, before we eat them, we remove the bones, and so on. Think about it for a moment, and you will find that there are hardly any food products that can be absorbed as they are. Even milk is sterilized... and not all water is fit to drink. You must always be very careful about what you eat and drink. And even if you take all the precautionary measures necessary, you must be aware that no food is ever perfectly pure. So, what does our organism do? Well, it has installed a monitoring system.

Just as customs officers are stationed at the borders of a country to inspect cars and luggage and make sure that people do not smuggle anything in, human beings have their own kinds of customs officers who examine their food and discard anything that cannot enter the organism's make-up. Despite this, people often interfere unconsciously with the work of these entities charged with this task of triage so that harmful elements are allowed in and begin to accumulate. In truth I tell you: people influence the creatures, the cells charged with their protection (in more scientific terms this is referred to as the immune system) simply by the way they think and feel. If they are not careful they introduce disorder and a lack of discernment into these workers, who then begin to lose their ability to see clearly and allow harmful elements through.

Thoughts and feelings are also food and we absorb and digest them well or less well depending on their degree of purity. This is why we must sort our psychic food just as we sort our physical food, because in doing so we eliminate the indigestible and harmful elements from it. We eat bread, fruit, vegetables, fish, and meat, and so on. Well, in the realm of thoughts and feelings the same variety and the same qualities of food exist as on the physical plane, ranging from fruit fresh off the tree to game that has gone high. There are also wines and pastries, but, even if they are of the best quality, we have to be careful not to overindulge.

In the Emerald Tablet, Hermes Trismegistus says: 'You shall separate the subtle from the gross gently and with great diligence.' To separate the subtle from the gross is to separate the pure from the impure, just as we extract gold or precious stones from the gangue. The whole of life is based on this principle of separation, of sorting. Sorting happens everywhere in industry (refining, distilling, purification) and in commerce (first class, second class, and so on). And exams, competitions, and contests are equally nothing more than a way of sorting people. Be it the nomination of a general or the election of Miss Universe, there is always some sorting involved. Everyone knows this. We have all experienced it. But when it comes to the inner life, where there are harmful thoughts and feelings that could engender disease or disintegration, people do not think to do any separating, discarding, or sorting. To most people, all thoughts and feelings are pretty much the same. Well no, here too you should make a distinction, as with food or fuels, which are classified according to quality: grade 1, grade 2, and so on.

Take the example of fuels. In the past, people used materials of such poor quality for heating and lighting that they produced smoke, irritated the eyes, and smelt badly... enough to suffocate you! Today, on the other hand, we have electricity, which leaves no waste and produces no smoke. As for coal, we know it comes in different grades, ranging from that which produces very little heat and a great deal of clinker to that which produces a great deal of heat and very little clinker. All combustible materials – coal, wood, paraffin, or petrol – contain some non-combustible elements, (although in different proportions, and it is this that is important). Every material is therefore of a certain quality, good or inferior; this is why we always have to make a choice.

Well, thoughts and feelings are also combustible materials, but since they are not all of excellent quality, they cannot all produce the best light, or the best heat, or the best energy for movement. Just as with food, we can accept some but we must reject others, so that the astral and mental stomach can digest them more easily. Suppose you are harbouring thoughts and feelings of jealousy, hatred, vengeance; what will they produce? A great deal of heat, that is for sure, but also a lot of smoke, which will obscure your inner view, as well as a great deal of waste, which will poison you. Of course, science as we know it has no branch in which thoughts and feelings are studied in depth and classified. Any kind of thoughts, any kind of feelings... they are all the same. We swallow them, we feast on them, without any concern for the results this may have. We make no distinction between them.

People always have passions and desires bubbling away inside. There is no shortage of passion and desire... the world is full of them. What is rarely or never present, however, is the wisdom that makes it possible to establish a scale of values so as to be capable of choosing only the best. And yet you need to be aware that you are building your entire being with the materials you absorb. If these materials are not pure, therefore, you will become ill. This is an absolute law, not only on the physical plane, but on the psychic plane as well. Just as you must be careful to eat only food that has been properly cleaned and washed, you must also be alert, night and day, to all that enters you in the way of thoughts and feelings. Set up customs officers at your borders, and whenever a thought, feeling, or desire presents itself, say: 'Wait a minute, where do you come from? Show me your true colours. What will you bring me if I let you in?' Watch them carefully and if you feel there is something not quite right, simply drive them away.

You will say: 'But how can I choose my thoughts and feelings? How can I know whether they are pure or impure?' Well, it is very easy. Personal, selfish thoughts and feelings inspired by our lower nature cannot be pure. All thoughts and feelings that involve only our own self-interest without bringing anything useful or good to the world as a whole, are impure. So it is easy to classify things: concupiscence, jealousy, anger, sensuality, the lust for power, and so on, all bring impurities. Whereas thoughts and feelings which are inspired by your higher nature and urge you to do only what is good and useful to others – generosity, patience, self-denial, sacrifice, and so on – these thoughts and feelings are pure. So now you have a criterion and it is a very simple one. Of course I know that although the criterion is simple such purity is not necessarily easy to achieve. But you must at least begin by understanding what purity consists of, and then you must love it, desire it with every fibre of your being, and finally endeavour to achieve it.[4]

Be quite clear on this; you will know peace only when you have introduced purity into your cells, into your entire being, through unselfish thoughts and feelings. You need look no further than generosity, self-denial, mercy, pardon... Only thoughts and feelings of this kind will bring you peace, because they are pure. Someone has behaved badly toward you? How will you find peace if all you can think about is finding a way to tell him or to avenge yourself? But is it not ruminations of this kind that take up part of our time every day? Life is full of misunderstandings, clashes, the settling of scores! And even if the resulting confrontation does not occur on the physical plane, it occurs in the heart and in the mind. But all this is too personal, too selfish, and although people may feel more at ease for a few hours or a few days after engaging in a confrontation, they cannot be said to have found peace. That ease is merely a respite, a lull (and even the wicked can have this kind of peace), and disorder and torment return. To be free from inner agitation and disquiet for a few hours is not peace. Peace, true peace, is an enduring state. Once you have succeeded in establishing it within you, you can never lose it again.

You have to suffer and suffer, and experience disappointment – sometimes even complete despair – before you understand that what you have been looking for brought you only problems and worries. But when, after all the suffering and struggling, failures and victories, you finally succeed in allowing your divine nature to triumph over the rebellion and tumult of your lower nature, then and only then will you find peace. Until then you may manage to experience a few delicious moments, but how ephemeral they are.

Many people say: 'I have lost my peace.' But peace, true peace, cannot be lost. We may sometimes become agitated, but such agitation is merely a superficial motion. Inwardly, deep down inside, there is peace. It is like the ocean: its surface roils with the constant swell of the waves, but in the depths below the surface peace reigns. Once you have succeeded in establishing true peace within you, any disruption that may arise on the outside will no longer trouble you. You will feel protected, sheltered, as if in a fortress. Psalm 91 says: *'Because you have made the Lord your refuge, the Most High your dwelling place...'* This high dwelling-place is your higher self. If you succeed in reaching this point, the summit of your being, then you will know peace.

This peace is a divine, inexpressible sensation, and once you have succeeded in tasting it, it will follow you everywhere. You felt it yesterday; today it is still with you, all day, and the next day it is waiting for you from the moment you wake up.

To your amazement you will find you do not even have to make an effort to find this peace again, whereas before, you needed to concentrate for a long time in order to calm down, you had to pray, or sing, or maybe even take some tranquillizers. Now, there is no need for this. Peace is already there, within you.

You will say: 'But life is a succession of changes, from success to failure, plenty to poverty, health to illness, joy to sorrow. People have to live with these changes.' True, but you can fall ill, suddenly lose all your wealth, be imprisoned, persecuted, see the ones you love disappear, and still not lose your peace. Of course you will suffer – I am not saying you will not suffer – but to suffer does not mean to lose your peace. As long as your consciousness does not stagnate at the level of events, for every difficulty and every trial, you will find an explanation, a truth which will calm and console you. Having risen very high, you will understand that these states are transient, that your true self is immortal and that nothing can affect you. You already carry this peace within you. If you are not aware of it, it is because you remain on the periphery of yourself, and when you are on the periphery you are always exposed to change. Just as you begin to feel some respite, your troubles return, as if to punish you for having stolen those few moments of peace.

So always keep hold of this ideal of working for what is good, of helping others, of loving and forgiving them, until it becomes very strong and impregnates all your cells, and they begin to vibrate in unison with it. Then peace will never leave you again. Even if some outside events come to trouble you, when you look within yourself you will see peace is still there, despite everything. And it will no longer be, as before, an imposed or artificial calm which lasted only as long as the efforts you made to maintain it, but a state that has become a part of you.

Only those who succeed in maintaining the integrity of this kingdom they represent achieve constant and enduring peace, a peace that is like an uninterrupted symphony that brings them bliss. They feel they have reached a sublime state of consciousness, in which all their cells bathe in an ocean of light, swim in living waters, and feed on ambrosia. They live in such harmony that all of heaven is reflected in them and they begin to perceive splendours they had never noticed before. Splendours, both visible and invisible, they had never discovered because they had been too troubled and agitated to focus on them. Just think for a moment about what happens to you the moment you receive some bad news or when you are sad or annoyed. You notice nothing of what is going on around you. You are overwhelmed by your inner agitation. And even if your eyes come to dwell on people or objects, you see nothing. Only peace, like the mirror of a still expanse of water, allows you to see and understand the presence of the subtle realities.[5] This is why the initiates, who have succeeded in tasting true peace, discover the wonders of the universe.

There, that was just a few remarks about peace...

Now do not start imagining that you will find peace by changing your husband or wife, your apartments, friends, jobs, countries, religion, or whatever. Peace does not depend on changes of that kind. They may bring some tranquillity, some respite, that is true, but other problems will soon beset you again, because you will still not have understood that peace depends solely on a change in your inner life. Implement this change and you will find peace, even though you remain with the same people, in the same place, in the same difficulties. True peace comes from within. It gushes forth, it floods into you despite the trials and anxieties of the outside world. It is like a river flowing down from the heights. Once you possess this peace you will be capable of pouring it out, of spreading it as something real, something alive. And you will benefit the whole world by bringing this peace to others.

Many people today are working for peace in the world. They meet, they talk, they write, they set up associations for peace, but this is not enough, because the lives these people lead are not lives for peace. One way or another they continue to foster war within themselves. The day they come to understand that all the cells in their body, all the particles of their physical and psychic being must live in accordance with the laws of peace and harmony, that day they will truly be working for peace. Because this peace will emanate from them like beneficial waves and have an impact on all creatures around them. These were the people Jesus referred to when he said: *'Blessed are the peacemakers, for they will be called children of God.'*

Notes

1 See *Harmony and Health*, Izvor 225, Chap. 3: 'Harmony and Health', Chap. 4: 'The Spiritual Foundations of Medicine'.
2 See *'Know Thyself'- Jnana Yoga*, C.W. 17, Chap. 2: 'The Synoptic Table'.
3 See *The Mysteries of Yesod*, C.W. 7, Chap 7: 'Purity and Peace'.
4 Ibid.: Chap. 5: 'Purity in the Three Worlds'.
5 See *Looking into the Invisible*, Izvor 228, Chap. 9: 'The Higher Degrees of Clairvoyance'; Chap. 10: 'The Spiritual Eye'; Chap. 11: 'To See God'.

Part III

'So God created humankind in his image'

Part III - 'So God created humankind in his image'

1

God, nature, and humankind

In Genesis it is written: *'God created humankind in his image.'*

Since the beginning of time the initiates, guardians of the Mysteries, have taught that a human being is a synthesis of the universe, of nature. Everything that exists in the universe exists in a human being, but on a smaller scale. This is why the universe is called the 'macrocosm' (great world) and a human being is referred to as a 'microcosm' (little world). And God is the name of the supreme Spirit who created both the great world (nature) and the little world (a human being), which he animates and sustains, because he is the only source, the only giver of life.

God, nature, and humankind. God is the Father, the Creator; nature is his spouse, the matter on which he works, the Mother who brings into the world all that exists. And humankind was created in their image. Humankind is the fruit, the child of the heavenly Father and Mother Nature. And just as children inherit their father's and mother's characteristics, humankind is a synthesis of all the materials and elements of Mother Nature and all the powers and energies of the heavenly Father.

It is not enough, therefore, to say that a human being is a microcosm created in the image of the macrocosm, because that correspondence applies only to the physical, material plane, whereas a parallel correspondence exists on the spiritual plane between the human spirit and the cosmic Spirit. Through the spirit, human beings are in the image of God, just as, on the physical plane, the microcosm is in the image of the macrocosm, nature. And just as the spirit of God animates the universe, the human spirit animates the physical body, the microcosm. Once we know this, we can understand what it really means to say that humankind was created in the image of God. Both in spirit and in body, a human being is the repetition of these two great cosmic principles: the universal Spirit and Nature, the heavenly Father and the divine Mother.[1]

Human beings therefore have a father and a mother in heaven. Some of you will say: 'So what are you telling us; that God has a wife? That's outrageous.' Well, you find this outrageous because you have never made the effort to understand this on the level of principles. Whatever name you give them, it is the two great principles, the masculine and the feminine, that are responsible for creation. No creation of any kind is possible with one principle alone. The two must be together and united. God has a spouse whom cabbalists call Shekinah. This being that we call God – and which Christianity represents as a masculine force – is in fact masculine and feminine. For creation or manifestation to occur, there must be polarization, in other words there must be a masculine principle and a feminine principle: God must be both masculine and feminine in order to manifest. As was taught in the Orphic initiations, 'God is both male and female'.[2]

Why did the Fathers of the Church represent the Deity as a confirmed bachelor? Were they so puritanical that the idea of God having a spouse offended them? God's spouse is not a woman, she is the subtlest virgin matter, the extraordinarily alive, pure, and luminous substance he uses in order to create.

Just as a man needs a woman to give a body to the energies that emanate from him; just as an artist needs materials to give form to his ideas and aspirations, the heavenly Father, the cosmic Spirit needs the divine Mother, the universal Soul, and together they continue to create worlds populated with myriads of creatures.[3]

Through both our spirit and our body we are children of the heavenly Father and the divine Mother. This means that if we want to understand human beings, we must understand their Father and Mother. And if we want to understand their Father and Mother, we must understand human beings, because within each one, God and nature are inextricably linked. If we say that a human being represents a microcosm created in the image of the macrocosm, it means that the four elements[4] and all the realms of nature are present in a human being. The mineral realm is represented by the skeletal system, the vegetable realm by the muscular system, the animal realm by the circulatory system, and the human realm by the nervous system.

In nature, the mineral realm represents the foundation, the base, and in human beings it is the skeletal system that forms the base, the solid framework supporting the structure that is our body.

The vegetable realm – the trees, flowers, and all species of plants – is more flexible, more active than the mineral realm, but it has not been given the ability to move from place to place. Vegetation can spread in all directions, but it cannot actually move about. It stays where it was initially sown or planted and where it has started to grow. In a human being, it is the muscles which correspond to vegetation in that they have a certain flexibility: we can relax or contract them, but they remain fixed to our bones just like plants to the earth.

What is it that moves and runs about? Animals. Animals move around freely – and some eat others. So animals correspond to the circulatory system, the blood, in which all kinds of microscopic organisms mill around (microbes, bacteria, viruses, etc.). The good eat the bad and the bad eat the good... a whole army of sentries and soldiers.

And finally, the human realm, which is characterized by thought, understanding, and reason, corresponds to the nervous system. You will say: 'What do you mean? That human beings are represented in human beings?' Yes indeed, the human being as such represents a specific level in the ladder of evolution. It is in human beings that we see the first manifestation of thought. But it is easy to see that people are not always governed by thought. They can sometimes be as inert as stone, or abandon themselves to a vegetative life like plants, or fall prey to their instincts like animals. In spite of this they remain human beings. And yet, how often, when we see how some people behave, we exclaim: 'It is not worthy of a human being.'

And then there are others who seem to belong to a different species altogether, one that is far more evolved than human beings. These are the very great artists, great creators, saints, and initiates. Yes, for over and above the nervous system is that of the aura, which is far more subtle than the nervous system and represents the boundary between the human and the angelic worlds. This system corresponds to our spiritual centres – the aura, the chakras*, etc. – which we all possess. But most human beings have not yet awakened these centres. They are unaware of their existence.

So, when we say that the different realms of nature are represented in human beings, we are not referring only to a physical reality (stone corresponds to the skeletal system, plants to the muscular system, and so on), but also and especially to a psychic reality. The mineral, vegetable, animal, human, and

* See Part VII, Chaps. 1 and 4.

angelic realms correspond to the different states of consciousness we experience. The mineral realm is represented by the unconscious, the vegetable realm by the subconscious, the animal realm by the consciousness, the human realm by the consciousness of self, and the angelic realm – which is also that of the great masters and initiates – by the super-consciousness.

If this human microcosm is to live and develop, it needs to remain in touch with the macrocosm, nature. The microcosm must continually maintain a relationship of exchange with the macrocosm, and it is this symbiotic exchange that makes up 'life'. Life is nothing but a continual exchange between human beings and the universe.[5] From the atom to the stars, nothing exists in the universe that is not brought to life, animated, by the cosmic Spirit, and human beings must strive to keep this spark alive within them.

Notes

1 See *The Book of Revelations: a Commentary*, Izvor 230, Chap. 3: 'Melchizedek and Initiation into the Mystery of the Two Principles'.

2 See *«Au commencement était le Verbe»*, Œuvres Complètes, t. 9, chap. X : «Le péché contre le Saint-Esprit est le péché contre l'amour», p. 170-173.

3 See *Angels and other Mysteries of The Tree of Life*, Izvor 236, Chap. 10: 'The Cosmic Family and the Mystery of the Trinity'.

4 See *The Fruits of the Tree of Life – The Cabbalistic Tradition*, C.W. 32, Chap. 7: 'The Four Elements'.

5 See *Spiritual Alchemy*, C.W. 2, Chap. 3: 'Living in Conscious Reciprocity with Nature'.

2

The Tree of Life

God, Nature, and man – that is, the Creator, creation, and the creature – and the bonds that exist between them are the essential questions at the heart of all religions. In whatever form the different religions present these questions, they all basically revolve around them. I personally feel that the Cabbalah, the Jewish esoteric tradition, best expresses the links that exist between the Creator, creation, and human beings. Having studied the great religions of the world, I find that this is the best, most extensive and also the most precise system of explanation of the world. The cabbalistic system is symbolically represented by the Sephirotic Tree, the Tree of Life. I am not saying that the other doctrines are bad or incorrect. No, of course not. But the view they give is not as structured, nor as profound and comprehensive. The Sephirotic Tree truly synthesizes God, the universe, and human beings. To me it is the key that enables us to unlock all mysteries.

In reality no one can give an exact, objective explanation of what the universe is or how it was created, even less of who this God is who created it. The Sephirotic Tree represents a system of explanation of the world, which is by nature mystical. Its foundations go back thousands of years and the exceptional spirits that conceived it obviously did not have astronomical telescopes with which to study the universe. But they had understood that the words spoken by God when he created human beings, *'Let us make humankind in our image'*, mean that the key to all knowledge is the science of man himself. They had understood that the study of human beings, their nature, the different functions of their physical and psychic organisms, leads to the knowledge of God and the universe. Yes, because God and the universe are reflected in a human being. As the initiates of ancient Greece taught: 'Know thyself, and thou shalt know the universe and the gods.'

By means of meditation and an intense inner life, the cabbalists achieved a grasp of cosmic reality, which can only be translated through symbolic stories and images. It is the essential core of this tradition, continually repeated and meditated over the course of the centuries, that has reached us.

The Tree of Life comprises ten regions or sephiroth, which correspond to the first ten numbers. Indeed, the Hebrew word 'sephirah' (sephiroth in the plural) means 'numeration'.

The ten sephiroth are:
- Kether: the Crown
- Chokmah: Wisdom
- Binah: Intelligence
- Chesed: Mercy
- Geburah: Force
- Tiphareth: Beauty
- Netzach: Victory
- Hod: Glory
- Yesod: the Foundation
- Malkuth: the Kingdom

You will no doubt ask: 'But why ten sephiroth? Is the universe really divided into ten regions?' No, and you must understand that the Sephirotic Tree is not intended to teach us astronomy. The number ten is symbolic. It represents a totality, a finite whole, and, as I have said, the word 'sephirah' means numeration. With the first ten numbers all numerical

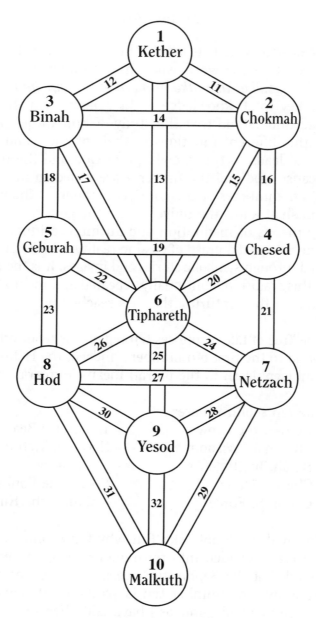

The Sephirotic Tree

combinations are possible. God first created ten numbers, the ten sephiroth, and with these ten numbers he is able to create other numbers, that is, an infinite number of other existences.[1]

Cabbalists also recognize an eleventh sephirah, *Daath* (Knowledge) – although they rarely mention it – which they place between Kether and Tiphareth.[2] And above the sephirah Kether, they speak of a region they call Ain Soph Aur, limitless light, the region of the Absolute, of the unmanifest God.

According to the account in Genesis, creation began at the moment God pronounced the words: *'Let there be light'*. Does this mean no light existed before that? No, before God said: *'Let there be light'* the reality we call light already existed but in a form we cannot even conceive and which the cabbalists call *Ain Soph Aur*: Unlimited Light. *Ain Soph Aur* is the Absolute, the unmanifest. So the Deity, as the cabbalists understand it, is located above and beyond light and darkness, above and beyond the created worlds. And to express this mystery of the Deity even better, the cabbalists have conceived of a region beyond *Ain Soph Aur*, which they call *Ain Soph*: Unlimited, and even beyond *Ain Soph*, *Ain*: Un, or negation.

So, at the origin of the universe there is a negation. But the 'Un' which means an absence, a lack, does not mean non-existence. Ain is not absolute nothingness, but a life beyond manifestation, beyond creation. So far beyond that it seems to be a non-existence. The cabbalists use Ain, Ain Soph, and Ain Soph Aur in an attempt to translate these realities that escape our comprehension.

Then God said, *'Let there be light'*. So God 'spoke'. But there is, of course, no possible comparison between this 'word' of God and what we call a word. It is simply a way of expressing the idea that, in order to create, God projected something from himself. And this projection – which was himself, a new form of himself – we call light. To say that God spoke means that

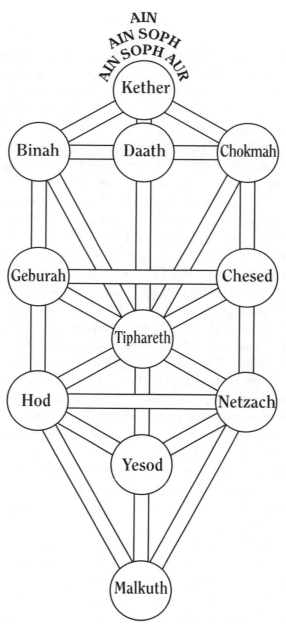

AIN
AIN SOPH
AIN SOPH AUR

Kether

Binah   Daath   Chokmah

Geburah   Chesed

Tiphareth

Hod   Netzach

Yesod

Malkuth

The Sephirotic Tree

he willed to manifest. And if you find this difficult to understand, just let us take an example from everyday life. You have an idea, but where exactly is this idea? We can neither see it nor find it anywhere in your brain. Also, we have to admit that we do not know what it is made of. But as soon as you express this idea in words, we can perceive its existence. And then, when you put it into effect, it incarnates in matter and becomes visible. Words are the intermediary between the plane of pure thought, of non-manifestation, and that of their realization in matter. This is an image of the process of creation.

If we then compare the sentence in Genesis: *Then God said, 'Let there be light.'* to the first words of St John's Gospel: *In the beginning was the Word, and the Word was with God, and the Word was God... All things came into being through him, and without him not one thing came into being,* we get an even better understanding of this relationship between the divine Word and light. Light is the substance produced by the divine Word so that it might become the substance of creation. The physical world as we know it is only a condensation of primordial light.[3] God, the active principle, projected light and then he worked on this light – which was already a substance – to create the universe.

Theologians and philosophers have said that God created the world from nothing. From nothing outside of himself, yes, that is correct, and this is what is difficult for us to understand, because for us it is only possible to build something if we have materials and tools outside of us. This 'nothing' is the 'Ain' of Ain Soph Aur, but Ain, as I have said, is not non-existence. In reality it is impossible to create something out of nothing, and this idea of a creation out of nothing only means that in order to create the universe, God drew a substance from himself. The universe is nothing more than this substance which he drew from himself, which thus came to be outside of him, but which is still him.[4]

161

Even science will one day discover that light is the primordial substance from which the universe was created. You will say that when you look at rocks, plants, animals, or human beings you do not see that they are made of light. Well, this is because in physical matter, primordial light is condensed to such a degree that it has become opaque. We persist in thinking that matter and light have nothing in common, because we do not realize that what we call matter is in fact condensed light. Also, of course, because our physical eyes are not capable of perceiving this primordial light. Thus light is the subtlest state of matter, and what we call matter is only the most condensed form of light. The whole universe is made of the same matter – or of the same light – more or less subtle, more or less condensed.[5]

There have been exceptional instances of mystics and clairvoyants who claimed to have seen everything around them suddenly come to life and become radiant. Objects and the whole of nature, the trees, the flowers, the grass, the stones, all radiated light and seemed to speak through this light. This can be explained quite simply by the fact that those who saw these things had been allowed to see the true nature of matter, which is light. When a human being is truly inhabited by spiritual light, this light may burst out to the point of becoming visible, then the person's face and body are illuminated, just as the face and the body of Jesus were illuminated at the Transfiguration on Mount Tabor.

But let us return to the ten sephiroth. Each sephirah is defined by five names: the name of God, the name of the sephirah itself, the name of the chief archangel of an angelic order, the name of the angelic order, and finally the name of a planet or a cosmic body representing the material support of the sephirah.

So there are five distinct aspects and you will better understand the nature of these if you know that there is a correspondence between these different aspects and the five principles in a human being: the spirit, the soul, the intellect, the heart, and the physical body. God corresponds to the spirit, the sephirah to the soul, the chief of the angelic order to the intellect, the angelic order to the heart, and the planet to the physical body.

Each sephirah is a region inhabited by an order of luminous spirits headed by an archangel, who in turn is subject to God. So it is God who governs these ten regions, but each time under a different name. This is why the Cabbalah has ten names for God. These ten names correspond to different attributes. God is One, but he manifests differently depending on the region. It is always the same one God, but presented under ten different aspects, and none of these aspects is inferior or superior to the others.

The ten names of God are:
– in Kether: Ehieh
– in Chokmah: Yah
– in Binah: Jehovah
– in Chesed: El
– in Geburah: Elohim Gibor
– in Tiphareth: Eloha va Daath
– in Netzach: Jehovah Tzebaoth
– in Hod: Elohim Tzebaoth
– in Yesod: Shaddai El Hai
– in Malkuth: Adonai-Melek.[6]

The chiefs of the angelic orders are:
– Metatron: He who stands by the Throne
– Raziel: Secret of God

– Tzaphkiel: Contemplation of God
– Tzadkiel: Justice of God
– Kamaël: Desire of God
– Mikhaël: Who is like God
– Haniel: Grace of God
– Raphaël: Healing of God
– Gabriel: Power of God
– Uriel: God is my Light (or Sandalfon, who is seen as the power that unites matter and form).

The angelic orders are:
– the Hayoth HaKadesh: Holy Living Creatures, or as they are known to Christianity, the Seraphim
– the Ophanim: Wheels, or Cherubim
– the Aralim: Lions, or Thrones
– the Hashmalim: Shining Ones, or Dominations
– the Seraphim: Fiery Ones, or Powers
– the Malakhim: Kings, or Virtues
– the Elohim: Gods, or Principalities
– the Bnei-Elohim: Sons of the Gods, or Archangels
– the Kerubim: Strong Ones, or Angels
– the Ishim: Men, or the Communion of Saints.[7]

And finally the cosmic bodies or planets which correspond to the physical plane are:
– Rashith HaGalgalim: First Swirlings
– Mazloth: the Zodiac
– Shabbathai: Saturn
– Tzedek: Jupiter
– Maadim: Mars
– Shemesh: the Sun
– Noga: Venus
– Kokab: Mercury

– Levanah: the Moon
– Aretz: the Earth (or Olem HaYesodoth, that is, the world
of foundations).

The Ancients, who worked with only seven planets, did
not assign a place on the Sephirotic Tree to Uranus, Neptune,
or Pluto. For them Kether represented the nebulae or the First
Swirlings: Rashith HaGalgalim, and Chokmah represented the
Zodiac: Mazloth. We can keep this order, but we can also place
Uranus on the level of Chokmah, Neptune on the level of Kether,
and Pluto on the level of Daath.

Since the cabbalists represented creation in the form of
a tree, this table of the sephiroth can only be understood if we
bear in mind the image of a tree. A tree has roots, a trunk,
branches, leaves, flowers, and fruits, which all work together
in harmony. And the sephiroth are interlinked by paths of
communication, which are simply referred to as 'paths'. These
paths, twenty-two in all, are named after the twenty-two letters
of the Hebrew alphabet.

א	Aleph	ל	Lamed
ב	Bet	מ	Mem
ג	Gimmel	נ	Nun
ד	Dalet	ס	Samekh
ה	Heh	ע	Ayin
ו	Vav	פ	Peh
ז	Zayin	צ	Tzadi
ח	Chet	ק	Qof
ט	Tet	ר	Resh
י	Yod	ש	Shin
כ	Kaph	ת	Tav

Now, how does a tree develop? The kingdom of God, said Jesus, *is like a mustard seed that someone took and sowed in the garden; it grew and became a tree, and the birds of the air made nests in its branches.* As long as a seed has not been planted we cannot know anything about it, because life is trapped inside. But as soon as you put a seed into the ground, it divides, it sprouts, a shoot appears and begins to grow, then you can begin to see what it is.

The seed that has been planted corresponds to the first sephirah, Kether, the Crown. Until the seed has been planted the process of life cannot begin.

Once in the ground, the seed divides and polarizes and the result is Chokmah, Wisdom, the binary, the opposition of masculine and feminine, negative and positive. The forces contained in the Crown begin to divide, to oppose each other. And this is why those who do not understand duality, opposites, cannot understand wisdom.

In reality, however, these forces are not completely divided. They remain closely linked through the Crown, which tells them: 'You are masculine and feminine, positive and negative, so unite and go into the world and work.' They unite and Binah, Understanding, creates harmony between them. In obedience to the Crown's command, Binah reconciles opposites and the shoot appears.

Kether, Chokmah, and Binah are the roots embedded in the ground of the world above. You will say: 'But surely plants dig their roots down, into the earth.' Yes, but this is because in plants it is the roots that represent the head through which they feed. But with people, the roots are at the top, in their head. A human being is a tree, whose roots are planted up above, in heaven. Like the three sephiroth Kether, Chokmah, and Binah, our head breathes and finds its nourishment in the soil of the divine world.

Now, for the plant to appear above ground, the fourth sephirah needs to step in. This is Chesed, Mercy. Chesed represents the trunk of the tree, the force that seeks to stand up to all adversity.

The fifth sephirah, Geburah, Force, corresponds to the branches, which begin to spread in all directions. When a human being, a society, or a people becomes powerful, they spread in all directions.

The sixth sephirah, Tiphareth, Beauty, represents the leaves, which are not only the tree's finery, but which also enable it to breathe and nourish itself with light.

And after the leaves come the buds. This is the seventh sephirah, Netzach, Victory. If the tree has reached the budding stage, it means it has been able to conquer all difficulties, and it will bear fruit.

Then a great work begins in the buds in order to bring forth flowers. This is the eighth sephirah, Hod, Glory, Praise. The tree is covered in flowers and offers up its fragrance, like incense, to celebrate the glory of the Everlasting God.

Finally, the fruit forms within the flower, and the sun ripens it and gives it colour. This is the formation of the child, the ninth sephirah, Yesod, the Foundation. This fruit will be the starting point of another life, a new tree. This is because the fruit produced by Kether, the original seed, itself contains seeds, and this is Malkuth, the tenth sephirah. From the original One, the seed has become Ten, symbol of a multitude. Every seed produced by the fruit represents Malkuth, the Kingdom of God. How do we know it really is the Kingdom of God? Put the seed into the earth and all the other attributes will soon appear. So, Malkuth and Kether come together again. The beginning and the end of things are analogous. This is why Jesus compared the Kingdom of God (Malkuth) with the mustard seed. *'It grew and became a tree, and the birds of the air made*

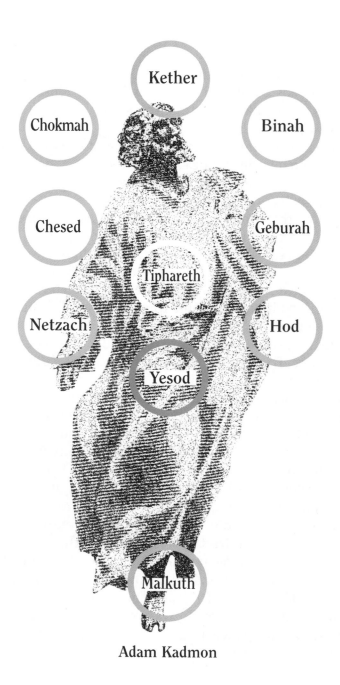

Adam Kadmon

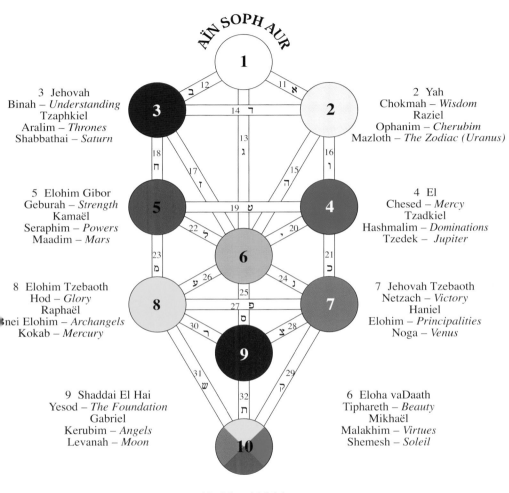

1 Ehieh
Kether – *The Crown*
Metatron
Hayot haKadesh – *Seraphim*
Rashith haGalgalim – *First Swirlings (Neptune)*

AÏN SOPH AUR

3 Jehovah
Binah – *Understanding*
Tzaphkiel
Aralim – *Thrones*
Shabbathai – *Saturn*

2 Yah
Chokmah – *Wisdom*
Raziel
Ophanim – *Cherubim*
Mazloth – *The Zodiac (Uranus)*

5 Elohim Gibor
Geburah – *Strength*
Kamaël
Seraphim – *Powers*
Maadim – *Mars*

4 El
Chesed – *Mercy*
Tzadkiel
Hashmalim – *Dominations*
Tzedek – *Jupiter*

8 Elohim Tzebaoth
Hod – *Glory*
Raphaël
Bnei Elohim – *Archangels*
Kokab – *Mercury*

7 Jehovah Tzebaoth
Netzach – *Victory*
Haniel
Elohim – *Principalities*
Noga – *Venus*

9 Shaddai El Hai
Yesod – *The Foundation*
Gabriel
Kerubim – *Angels*
Levanah – *Moon*

6 Eloha vaDaath
Tiphareth – *Beauty*
Mikhaël
Malakhim – *Virtues*
Shemesh – *Soleil*

10 Adonai-Melek
Malkuth – *The Kingdom*
Sandalfon (Uriel)
Ishim – *Beatified Souls*
Olem HaYesodoth – *Earth*

Sephirotic Tree

nests in its branches.' Who are these birds? All the angelic hierarchies that inhabit the universe created by God.

The Tree of Life therefore represents the universe which God inhabits and impregnates with his quintessence and it also represents a human being created in the image of God, in other words, in the image of the universe. When the Cabbalah speaks about the creation of man, it is not speaking of human beings as they are today. It is speaking of Adam Kadmon, primordial Man, cosmic Man, whose body is formed by the constellations and the worlds.[8] Kether is his head, Chokmah is his right eye and the right-hand side of his face, Binah is his left eye and the left-hand side of his face, Chesed is his right arm, Geburah his left arm, Tiphareth his heart and solar plexus, Netzach his right leg, Hod his left leg, Yesod his genitals, and Malkuth his feet.

You must understand the meaning of these correspondences correctly, however. You must not imagine that the universe has organs like ours or expect to find the exact equivalent of what exists in the universe in us. It is in their essence that our organs and those of the universe have something in common which creates an affinity between them. And it is this law of affinity which allows us to contact in space the forces, centres, and worlds that have their correspondences within us. The knowledge of these correspondences opens infinite opportunities for us.

Every human creature is a repetition of the cosmic Tree, but on a smaller scale. In the branches of this tree all the birds of the air can find shelter. If we are aware of this and if we work towards our divine predestination, the birds of the air – the angels – will come and shelter in our branches. The angels are always attracted to people who embrace the spiritual life. They find a home in them and fill them with their light and their grace.

Let us now examine the different divisions we find in the Sephirotic Tree.

To the cabbalists the universe created by God is a whole, which is perfectly expressed by the Sephirotic Tree. But within this whole they distinguish several planes.

Horizontally, there are four planes. These are, from top to bottom:

– Olam Atziluth, the world of emanations – comprising the sephiroth Kether, Chokmah, and Binah – which corresponds to the element fire.

– Olam Briah, the world of creation – comprising the sephiroth Chesed, Geburah, and Tiphareth – which corresponds to the element air.

– Olam Yetzirah, the world of formation – comprising the sephiroth Netzach, Hod, and Yesod – which corresponds to the element water.

– Olam Assiah, the world of action – formed of the one sephirah Malkuth – which corresponds to the element earth.

The world above and the world below are linked in one hierarchical structure, and this hierarchy is also reflected in a human being.

– Neshamah, which corresponds to Olam Atziluth, the divine plane of soul and spirit, represents fire within us.

– Ruah, which corresponds to Olam Briah, the spiritual world, the mental plane, represents air within us.

– Nephesh, which corresponds to Olam Yetzirah, the psychic world, the astral plane, represents water within us.

– Guph, which corresponds to Olam Assiah, the physical plane, represents earth within us.

You will say: 'But when you presented the structure of each sephirah, you spoke of five divisions. The spirit and the soul were not together, they were separate.' Yes, they can be presented either separately or together.

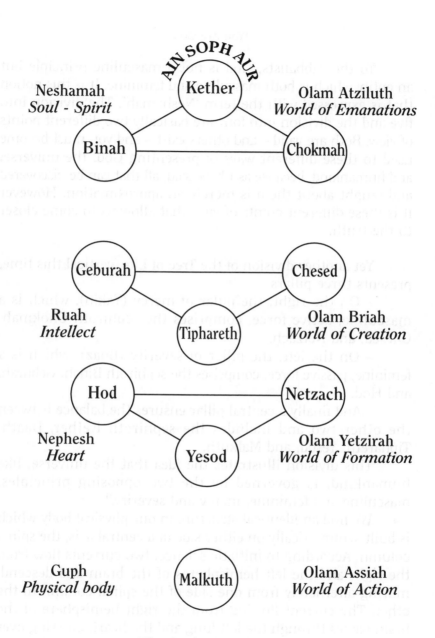

AIN SOPH AUR

Neshamah *Soul - Spirit*	Kether	Olam Atziluth *World of Emanations*
Binah		Chokmah

Geburah		Chesed
Ruah *Intellect*	Tiphareth	Olam Briah *World of Creation*

Hod		Netzach
Nephesh *Heart*	Yesod	Olam Yetzirah *World of Formation*

Guph *Physical body*	Malkuth	Olam Assiah *World of Action*

The Sephirotic Tree

To the cabbalists, God is not a masculine principle but an entity which is both masculine and feminine. It is this notion that is expressed with the term 'Neshamah'. The division into five and the division into four are basically two different points of view. Both are valid – and others exist – and you must become used to these different ways of presenting God, the universe, and humankind, because as I have said, all that can be discovered and taught about them is merely an approximation. However it is these different points of view that allow us to come closer to the truth.

Yet another division of the Tree of Life, vertical this time, presents three pillars:
– On the right, the pillar of mercy (Yakin), which is a masculine, active force, comprises the sephiroth Chokmah, Chesed, and Netzach.
– On the left, the pillar of severity (Boaz), which is a feminine, passive force, comprises the sephiroth Binah, Geburah, and Hod.
– And finally a central pillar ensures the balance between the other two and includes the sephiroth Kether, Daath, Tiphareth, Yesod, and Malkuth.
This division illustrates the idea that the universe, like humankind, is governed by the two opposing principles, masculine and feminine, mercy and severity.[9]
We find an identical structure in our physical body which is built symmetrically on either side of a central axis, the spinal column. According to initiatic science, two currents flow from the right and the left hemispheres of the brain and descend, moving alternately from one side of the spinal column to the other. The current flowing from the right hemisphere of the brain passes through the left lung and the heart, crossing over to the liver, and then back again, passing through the left kidney

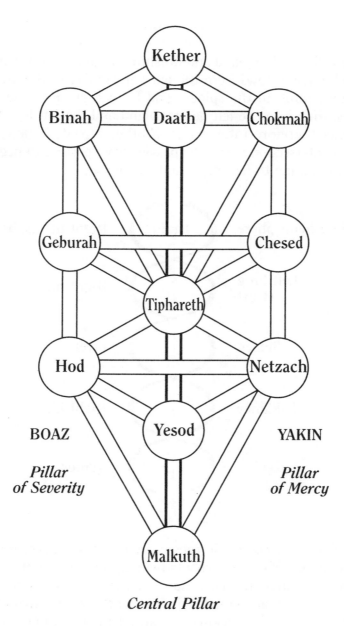

Kether

Binah   Daath   Chokmah

Geburah   Chesed

Tiphareth

Hod   Netzach

BOAZ   Yesod   YAKIN

*Pillar
of Severity*   *Pillar
of Mercy*

Malkuth

Central Pillar

The Sephirotic Tree

to the right genital gland and finishing up in the right leg. The second current flows from the left hemisphere of the brain to the right lung, to the spleen, and from there into the right kidney, then into the left genital gland and the left leg. These currents therefore intersect each other repeatedly and each point of intersection marks the passage from positive to negative, from masculine to feminine, and *vice versa*.

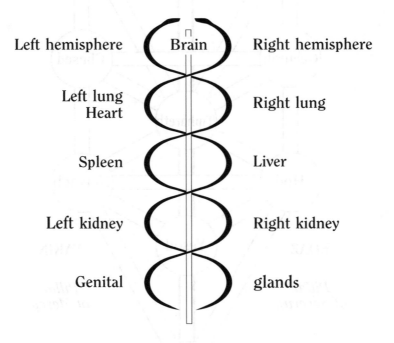

Left hemisphere	Brain	Right hemisphere
Left lung Heart		Right lung
Spleen		Liver
Left kidney		Right kidney
Genital		glands

The Caduceus of Hermes is another way of representing this structure. The two serpents twined round the central wand are the two currents that wind their way from one side to the other of the spinal column. Hindus call these two currents Ida and Pingala, and the central channel in the spine is called Sushumna.[10] The breathing exercises we do every day are linked to the polarity of these two currents. Closing the left nostril, we breathe in through the right nostril, and then closing the right nostril, we breathe out through the left. And then we repeat the exercise, but in reverse, breathing in through the left nostril with the right nostril closed, and breathing out through the right nostril with the left nostril closed. These breathing exercises help these two currents to flow properly.[11]

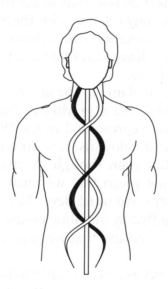

The sephiroth can be superimposed on the symbol of the Caduceus. In human beings the sephiroth are the chakras, the subtle centres situated in our etheric and astral bodies. By moving up and down, the two currents Ida and Pingala animate the chakras. Those who develop the ten sephiroth within themselves hold the magic wand on the spiritual plane – the magic wand that can transform everything within them.

As you see, this table of the sephiroth shows only the forces of good. If you seek to perfect yourself, these are the only ones you should study, the only ones you need to concentrate on. The truth is, however, the Cabbalah also speaks of ten dark sephiroth, the kliphot. These regions correspond to what Christians call Hell. They represent the inverted reflection of the divine sephiroth, just as the Devil is the inverted reflection of God. The cabbalists have also given names to these evil regions and to the spirits that inhabit them, but I shall not go into detail on this. I do not want to say their names because I do not want to have any relation with these regions.[12] All you need to know is that these infernal regions exist and that they also exist within us. Heaven and hell exist outside of us, and they also exist within us.

From stones and plants to the archangels and to God, all that exists in creation exists also within a human being. All the realms of nature are represented in us. We contain all that exists both above and below us: heaven and hell, the angels and the demons. But even though we may be inhabited by demons that does not mean that we must allow ourselves to be consumed by them. We must never forget that heaven also dwells within us and that by initiating certain inner movements, the law of affinity will ensure that we manage to reach heaven.

You may not yet see very clearly what you can do with all this new knowledge or how everything is connected. This is only to be expected. But if you learn to approach it with great patience, humility, and respect it will gradually become much clearer.[13]

The Sephirotic Tree, if it is to become the basis of true spiritual work, must be a permanent subject of meditation. So, try to assimilate these concepts slowly, in the realization that this Tree of Life exists within you and that the only worthwhile activity is to make it grow, flower, and bear fruit.[14] Do not concern yourself with how many years, or even how many reincarnations it will take before you truly become this Tree of Life. You may have to come back thousands of times before these ten sephiroth engraved within you begin to vibrate and your inner being is illuminated by all the lights of the Tree of Life.

Notes

1 See *Cosmic Balance – The Secret of Polarity*, Izvor 237, Chap. 3: 'One and Zero'.
2 See *Angels and other Mysteries of The Tree of Life*, Izvor 236, Chap. 5: 'The Sephiroth of the Central Pillar'.
3 Ibid., Chap. 8: 'When God Drew a Circle on the Face of the Deep'.
4 See *The Fruits of the Tree of Life – The Cabbalistic Tradition,* C.W. 32, Chap. 5: 'The Creation of the World and the Theory of Emanation'.
5 See *Life and Work in an Initiatic School – Training for the Divine*, C.W. 30, Chap. 6 'Matter and Light'; - *Angels and other Mysteries of The Tree of Life*, Izvor 236, Chap. 7: Light, the Substance of the Universe'.
6 Ibid., Chap. 4: 'The Names of God'.
7 Ibid., Chap. 3: 'The Angelic Hierarchies'.
8 Ibid., Chap. 11: 'The Body of Adam Kadmon'.
9 See *Cosmic Balance – The Secret of Polarity*, Izvor 237, Chap. 1: 'Cosmic Balance and the Number Two'.
10 Ibid., Chap. 9: 'The Caduceus of Hermes – The Astral Serpent'.
11 See *A New Earth – Methods, Exercises, Formulas and Prayers,* C.W. 13: 'Breathing exercises', p. 28-30; - *The Fruits of the Tree of Life – The Cabbalistic Tradition*, C.W. 32, Chap. 16: 'Human and Cosmic Respiration'.
12 See *The Book of Revelations: a Commentary,* Izvor 230, Chap. 10: 'The Woman and the Dragon'.
13 See *The Fruits of the Tree of Life*, C.W. 32, Chap. 1: 'How to Approach the Study of the Cabbalah'.
14 See *Angels and other Mysteries of The Tree of Life*, Izvor 236, Chap. 1: 'From Man to God, the Notion of Hierarchy'.

3

From seed to tree

Be perfect as your heavenly Father is perfect. If Jesus was able to advocate such an ideal to his disciples it is because he knew that human beings carry within them the image of perfection of the heavenly Father. If you compare this image to a seed, you will see that it is by feeding and watering this seed, by bringing it to life, that human beings gradually move closer to that perfection. But it is important to understand how this seed, on the face of it so minuscule, can be of such immeasurable significance.

What exactly is a seed? It is a living creature which continuously calls on the forces and materials of the universe so that it may accomplish its task. And its task is to resemble the tree that produced it. The Creator has given the seed the vocation of resembling its father, the tree, and this is why, once planted, all its work will be in harmony with this vocation. It takes from the earth and the atmosphere only the elements it needs to grow, leaving the others. This is how it gives expression to the tendencies written into the blueprint it carries inside. Well, you should be aware that this applies to human beings as well as to seeds.

We read in Genesis: *'Let us make humankind in our image, according to our likeness; and let them have dominion over the fish of the sea, and over the birds of the air, and over the cattle, and over all the wild animals of the earth, and over every creeping thing that creeps upon the earth.' So God created humankind in his image, in the image of God he created them.* Why did Moses repeat the word 'image' in the second sentence but not the word 'likeness'? This gives us some food for thought. By repeating the word 'image' and omitting the word 'likeness' Moses implies that God intended to create humankind according to his likeness, in other words, perfect like himself, but that he did not do so. He created humankind only in his image. You will say: 'But isn't that almost the same thing?' No, image and likeness are two different things. Look at a seed, it does not look like the tree from which it came, but it is in the tree's image, in that it contains its image. Once you plant it in the ground, it will begin to resemble the tree. Likeness is the ultimate, perfect development of the image. If you did not know that the acorn was the fruit of the oak, would you ever imagine the two could be related? No, because the acorn is still only in the image of the oak. But plant an acorn in the ground and years later it will become a magnificent tree and end by resembling its father, the oak-tree.

What does a seed contain? If you open it up and examine it under a microscope you will not find the image of a tree. How can such a minuscule and seemingly insignificant creature ever become an enormous plant with roots, a trunk, branches, leaves, flowers, and fruits? Well, it bears within it a blueprint which is of an etheric nature, and therefore invisible. You would have to be able to see into the etheric world to discover the whole structure of the tree as it will develop in accordance with pre-determined lines of force. In the same way, the microscopic study of the seed a man implants in a woman will not show you what the child will be. But once implanted in the woman's womb and nourished by her blood, it slowly develops, and one

181

day the child comes into the world possessing all its own physical and psychic characteristics.

Every seed you find in nature carries within it an original blueprint and once a seed is planted it begins to grow, and its entire development will progress in accordance with this blueprint, as it gradually acquires the same characteristics – shape, size, colour, flavour, scent, and attributes – as the plant that produced it. We see this natural phenomenon ceaselessly repeating itself before our eyes, and this process of growth of a seed reveals the mystery of a human being, the mystery of our own psychic and spiritual life. Human beings also carry within them a blueprint which determines and directs the growth of the forces within them.

Just as a seed is predestined to become like its father the tree, it is the vocation of human beings to attain the perfection of the heavenly Father, to which Jesus refers. It is imprinted in our make-up. Of course this process of evolution takes centuries and even millennia, which is why we can say that Jesus' precept: *Be perfect as your heavenly Father is perfect,* infers reincarnation. Otherwise, what are we to think of these words? Either Jesus spoke rashly when he enjoined human beings, who are so imperfect, to attain the perfection of the heavenly Father within a few years, or he thought it was easy to become like him. Neither interpretation speaks in his favour. In reality, Jesus could not have believed human beings are capable of becoming perfect within a single lifetime. What he did know is that by seeking this perfection and by working to attain it, after many reincarnations human beings would reach their objective.

We can now more easily understand why Moses repeated the word 'image' twice in the story of Creation, but did not mention 'likeness' again. The divine virtues are potentially present in all human beings created in the image of God, and although they are sometimes able to manifest them, these manifestations are still very faint. One day, however, as time goes on, humankind will develop and human beings will resemble their Creator and possess the fullness of his virtues. So you see, the omission of the word 'likeness' and the repetition of 'image' implies the concept of reincarnation. The entire human evolutionary process is contained in this transition from image to likeness.

It is in fact possible for people to reach perfection much more rapidly, provided they are able to find this image of God within them and devote all their efforts to nurturing it. Some western travellers have recounted seeing fakirs in India plant the stone of a mango, for instance, in the ground and then, by their powers of concentration, make it grow into a tree and produce fruits which they then distribute to the crowd. I have been to India and I saw nothing like this, but although at first it appears implausible, in theory the phenomenon is not impossible. It can be explained by the fact that the fakir has learnt to work with the etheric substance called 'Akasha' in Sanskrit. This substance, which is everywhere in the atmosphere, can be used to speed up the growth process in plants, because by acting on the blueprint in the seed, it brings the fruit to maturity much more rapidly. Those who are able to concentrate on the akashic force – this quintessence comprising all the elements plants need, i.e. warmth, light, magnetism, electricity, and so on – are able to make a plant grow in a very short time, whereas it would normally take years to complete its growth.

We can give the fakirs in India credit for making a tree grow and bear fruit within a few minutes, but what should interest us more is the realization that the equivalent process exists on the spiritual plane in relation to human beings. The Creator has deposited seeds within us, the seeds of all the divine virtues, and if they have not yet come to the surface it is because they have not received sufficient light, warmth, and water. Of course, even if we do nothing, these qualities will develop simply by force of circumstance, but only after several millions of years. And it would be a shame to have to wait that long, when in fact we all have the ability to make them grow far more quickly.

We must learn to work at getting closer each day to divine perfection, a blueprint of which we already carry within us, just like a seed. A seed does not resemble the tree, but the image of the tree is inscribed in it. Before materializing on the physical plane, a seed exists somewhere up above, on the subtle planes, and if it is given favourable conditions, it will germinate and become a tree. And the vocation of the seed we represent is to come increasingly closer to the image of our heavenly Father we carry within us, to vibrate in unison with him so as to resemble him.

What a magnificent tree the oak is! And yet, initially it was just an acorn that had fallen to the ground and could have been eaten by a stray pig. And the same goes for us; we too are almost nothing, but if we are able to utilize this fantastic force, the akashic force, to work on the divine image within us, we will become what God intended us to be. This force is 'the strength of all strengths' to which Hermes Trismegistus refers in the Emerald Tablet and which he calls Telesma.[1] About it he says: 'its father is the Sun.' Whatever name we give it, it is always the same force that comes from the sun. The sun is its distributor and its inexhaustible source.[2] One of the manifestations of this force is love. Not the emotion that often causes human beings more torment than joy, but the cosmic energy that drives the worlds.

God created us in his image and it is now up to us to endeavour to attain this likeness. But of all the billions of people on this earth, how many actually concern themselves with resembling the Deity? To become a physicist, a doctor, a lawyer, a banker, a minister, an actor, a pop star or an Olympic champion, yes, there is no lack of candidates. And of course, from an earthly point of view these are all worthwhile. But what about the heavenly point of view? From the heavenly point of view the only thing that is worthwhile is to work to resemble our heavenly Father, to make at least an effort in that direction, to go ever further, ever higher so as to see things differently, in their immensity and their splendour.

Yes, God created humankind in his image and this image is imprinted in the seed of the atmic body, in other words, in the spirit, where absolute perfection reigns. And if it is impossible to see this perfection, it is because the other bodies obscure it, acting like screens of opaque and distorting glass. But by concentrating on this sublime seed that embodies perfect wisdom, perfect love, human beings gradually begin to bring to life the divine blueprint within, and this blueprint will not only change the vibrations of their psychic bodies, but also those of their physical body.

You will say: 'But how can I enliven this seed? How can I feed it?' Well, just take a look at the way the forces of nature work. During the winter nothing grows, despite the fact the earth is full of all kinds of seeds. There is neither sufficient heat nor light, so the seeds wait. And then with the return of spring, the heat and light from the sun intensify and all those seeds that had remained hidden and invisible up until then begin to germinate. I can hear you thinking: 'Well, that is something we have known for a long time.' I have no doubt you do, but I say it anyway, to show you that you might not have understood it very well. People say they know, they know, but without understanding anything. Knowing and understanding are two very different things. You know, but what good has this amazing knowledge done as yet? None. If you had understood you would have sensed that you too possess seeds, which you must allow the sun's light and heat to reach so that they may grow.

Now, when I speak of the sun in this way, I am referring, of course, to the spiritual sun of which our physical sun is but a reflection. The sun of the physical world is a door which gives us access to the sun of the spiritual world, and we must therefore learn to work with it. If you adopt the habit of watching the sun rise during the spring and the summer you will make it possible for the akashic force, Telesma, which the sun propagates throughout space, to vivify the sublime seed within you that bears the perfect blueprint of the Deity.

Learn to cultivate your own soil. Nothing can grow without the sun, so you must consciously put yourself in its presence, expose yourself to its rays every day so that it may awaken the divine seed God has deposited in your soul. You will gradually feel very tiny shoots sprout within you, and these shoots are the qualities and virtues of your heavenly Father, which seek only to grow and flourish. These shoots also need watering of course. The sun sends its light and warmth, but it cannot water the plants. Water thus becomes the sun's partner; and within us that partner is love. The sun does part of the work and our love does the other part. This is why, when we are in the sun's rays, we too must be active like it and water all these seeds with our love, our gratitude, and our enthusiasm so that every day we may come closer to our high ideal.[3]

Starting today, therefore, make up your minds to begin this work, the only work worth undertaking, because every achievement, every success will stay with you throughout your life and even beyond, throughout all your successive incarnations, until you reach the perfection of the heavenly Father you bear within you.

From seed to tree

Notes

1 See *The Splendour of Tiphareth*, C.W. 10, Chap. 14: 'The Sun Has the Solution to the Problem of Love – Telesma'.
2 See *Light is a Living Spirit*, Izvor 212, Chap. 2: 'The Rays of the Sun: their Nature and Activity'.
3 See *The Splendour of Tiphareth*, C.W. 10, Chap. 12: 'The Prism, Symbol of Man'.

4

The sun, image of God
and image of humankind

The intellect, the heart, and the will are the three principles that make up the psychic structure of human beings. Our intellects enable us to think, our hearts to experience emotions, and our wills to act. In this sense, humankind is in the image of God. Only in his image, however, because God is all-knowing, all-loving, and all-powerful, and humankind still has a long way to go before it reaches this divine perfection. It is our predestination to resemble our Creator, to come closer and closer to the holy Trinity of Father, Son, and Holy Spirit. And one of the ways to achieve this is to gaze at the sun, to meditate on it and seek to identify with it.

The sun is light, heat, and life. If we consider the light to be intelligence, heat to be love, and life to be power, we begin to understand that the sun too was created in God's image, and not just in his image but also in his likeness.[1] Unlike human beings, who are so limited, the sun illuminates, heats, and vivifies the entire universe with its light, heat, and life. And if we are able to interpret its manifestations, we understand that only the sun can reveal the mystery of the holy Trinity to us. The Father is the source of life that manifests in the form of light (the Son) and heat (the Holy Spirit). But you could also say that the Son represents love, because it is the Son who sacrifices himself eternally so that creation may live on. And the Holy Spirit represents light, since he illuminates our intelligence and bestows the power to penetrate mysteries, to prophesy, to speak in tongues. Whether we identify the Son with light and the Holy Spirit with love, or *vice versa*, makes no difference to the essence of the holy Trinity. What is important for us is to understand that through its life, its light, and its heat, the sun is the best symbol of the holy Trinity.

God created us in his image, and by saying: *'Be perfect as your heavenly Father is perfect'*, Jesus asks us to achieve this likeness. But God is so exalted, so far away! How can we have any idea of his perfection? If the Deity is relegated to some distant, unknown place, if we can neither see, nor contemplate, nor move closer to him, it is not surprising human beings gradually lose touch with him, showing contempt for the divine image within them by committing the most senseless and immoral acts. How can we fail to realize that the power, wisdom, and love of God are best manifested by the sun? This is where we should look for the holy Trinity: in the sun.

Instead of treating the Deity as an abstract notion which no one – or almost no one – understands, our starting point should be that which is tangible, concrete, in other words, the sun. You will say: 'But surely temples, statues, candles, and the host are tangible.' Yes, of course, but all these things are limited, cold, and dead.[2] What temple or church can be compared with nature, and what man-made host can be compared with the sun? If you reach toward the sun, this immense host, if you commune with it every day, you will sense that nowhere else does God manifest with such splendour. Why do human beings prefer to pray to an abstract God in cold, dark churches? They should begin by turning to the sun to be warmed, enlightened, and vivified. Then, if they have the mental capacity to do so, they will be able to turn to an abstract God.

The sun shows us the way. Every day as we look at it, we see a reflection, an image of the holy Trinity, and if we learn to work with this model, our own small trinity can also become holy. Even if we repeat Jesus' words: *'Be perfect as your heavenly Father is perfect'*, it all remains theoretical since we have never seen the Father and do not know how he manifests. But through the sun we are at least able to gain some insight into what the heavenly Father is. The sun also reveals to us that the Father, the Son, and the Holy Spirit are one, because they are inseparable. And if we do differentiate between them, it is because we seek to gain a more precise idea of them, but in reality they are one; the three are one. And the same is true of a human being.

The human intellect, heart, and will are not separated from each other. They work together. The intellect makes plans and the heart lends a hand and encourages it: 'Go on, I'm with you all the way.' And then the will rushes to realize the plans and we see the three running along together. Sometimes, of course, the will leads the heart, and then a person can be in real trouble, because the intellect has been overtaken by the other two and is lagging behind. And although the intellect shouts: 'Wait for me, you are making a mistake!', they reply: 'Oh be quiet, you know nothing about it.' Yes, those three really do have some heated arguments, because this particular trinity is still far from holy.

If we want our trinity to become holy we must take the sun as our model and strive to be like it so as to become luminous, warm, and vivifying like it. To become like the sun is, of course, an impossible goal, but reaching the goal is not what is most important. What is important is to advance, to progress. Instead of continuing to mark time in old, ineffective conceptions, it is far better to go in search of the sun each morning and to adopt the ideal of resembling it. There is a law of mimicry in nature by which creatures begin to resemble what they look at. So, if we look at the sun often and for long periods of time, if we understand it, if we love it, if we let its rays penetrate us, we will gradually become like it. In fact, if we know how to condense those rays and store them up in our solar plexus, we will be able to draw on our reserves later and become indefatigable. There is a whole science to be learned, a long training to be undergone, but those who take it seriously will receive blessings every day.

If religion is to be truly meaningful and useful it must bring human beings closer to the spiritual truths so that they may understand them, live them, feel them, unite with them, and commune with them every day. By nourishing themselves every day with food so pure and luminous, they will be forced to transform themselves. Only by absorbing top quality food on the psychic and spiritual planes can human beings truly progress on the path of evolution. And only the sun can give them this food, which consists of light (wisdom) for their intellect, heat (love) for their heart, and life (power) for their will.

By meditating on the relationships that exist between God, the sun, and human beings, we begin to understand how the three persons of the holy Trinity, Father, Son, and Holy Spirit, can be found in the sun's life, light, and heat. And since we human beings are ourselves a trinity, we can enter into a relationship with the divine Trinity, through the intermediary of the sun. If the only thing you understand in your entire life is that through the sun you can commune with the holy Trinity so that it may give you all its blessings... to understand this is in itself a huge step forward. In this way, in time, you will have the arms to triumph over all your enemies. Not your external enemies – who are not really so dangerous – but those that

193

dwell within you. You will turn them out and the holy Trinity will come and make its home within you. This is the best promise of resurrection and life.

Everything that appears on earth ends by disappearing. Only the sun overhead remains, unchanging, eternal. And it is to it that we must look. Unfortunately people either neglect the sun or exaggerate its role. Either they think it has nothing to do with religion or they believe it to be a divinity. Well, they are mistaken on both counts. By not giving the sun a place in their inner lives, people deprive themselves of a vital element. But to think of it as a divinity is to revert to the mentality of primitive peoples who worshipped the forces of nature.

The sun should be seen only as an intermediary, which paves the way toward finding God, our inner sun. Herein lies the fundamental difference between our teaching and that of most of the forms of sun-worship which have existed throughout the history of humankind – and which certainly exist still in a few places in the world. Some people seem to be concerned that we take the sun for God himself. Well, let them rest assured. There is no question of confusing God with the sun. God is inconceivable, inexpressible, and we can never fully understand what he is.

We do not worship the sun, we worship only God. But if we look more closely at the image of the sun as a symbol, it becomes clear that for human beings it is the best image of God. That is all. This is our absolute conviction. And this means you must learn to find the sun inwardly. Yes, because you could look at it for years, imagining all kinds of things about it, but so long as you do not feel it vibrate, radiate, pulsate within you, it will remain distant, unfamiliar, it will not speak to you, and you will gain nothing from going to watch it. You may feel slightly warmer, slightly more full of life; you may receive some energies or vitamins, but you will not discover the essential. And the essential is to find the inner sun, the sign that God dwells within you.

If the sun is not yet able to help you very much in your spiritual life it is because you think you know it simply because you see it every day. Well no, it is not enough to see in order to know. True knowledge is a realignment, a fusion with what we want to know. You cannot say: 'I have seen, I have touched, therefore I know.' If only it were that easy! Do we know the earth simply because we touch it? No. Do we know water simply because we drink it? Do we know air simply because we breathe it and feel the wind blowing? No. Neither do we know the light, heat, and life of the sun, even though we feel them and see them. If you truly want to know the sun, you must vibrate in unison with the light, the heat, and the life that emanate from it.

The only true religion, therefore, is the solar, the religion of the sun. Understand me correctly, however. I am not saying the other religions are wrong or bad. No, but they are true only to the extent that they approach the solar religion. There are so many religions in the world and we know almost nothing about them. So many have disappeared and others will do so in the future. Even the Christian religion may disappear. But it will come back in a different form insofar as it is inspired by the solar religion, for the religion brought by Jesus was a solar religion. This is something Christians have never understood.[3] Christ said: *'Be perfect as your heavenly Father is perfect'*, but how can we have any idea of this perfection if we do not take the sun as our model?

The sun is a servant of God, one of God's best servants. It has existed for billions of years, forever indefatigable, generous, faithful, and true. So many of those who have claimed to be servants of God have become discouraged, so many have backed

195

down and betrayed their faith. Human beings cannot really be trusted. You will say: 'But if you do not trust human beings, why do you talk to them? Why do you teach them?' I trust what is divine in human beings, but not what is human in them. This is because I know in advance that the human in them will weaken one day or another. What is human is not durable, it melts like wax and tarnishes like lead. I know what to expect in that respect. I know that human beings bear within themselves something that is unchanging, eternal, and divine like the sun, but as in all creatures who live on earth, there is another part of them which eventually loses its light, which weakens and dies.

If you want to advance with confidence on the path of perfection you must model yourself on no one but the sun, not even on saints or initiates. They can, of course, provide you with examples of great virtues, but they know that compared with the sun they are nothing. And this is why they show such humility. They bow before the sun. They know that whatever they do, their light, their heat, and their life cannot compare with the light, heat, and life of the sun.[4]

You wonder, perhaps, how we should understand Jesus' words: *'I am the light of the world'*. When Jesus spoke those words he was identifying with Christ. Christ is a cosmic spirit, who illuminates not only the earth, but the entire universe and all the entities that inhabit it. Christ is the true cosmic sun; he is the spirit of the sun. And in this sense we could say that the physical sun we see is the clue that leads us to Christ, the cosmic sun. Because it is the spirit of the sun we must find, and not, like astronomers, look only at its physical body.

This is why, every year with the return of spring, we prepare ourselves to watch the sunrise, in the knowledge that only it is able to bring to life the image of God within us. What a privilege it is to be able to watch the sun rise every morning!

There is nothing more beautiful. It is the source that vibrates, gushes forth, and flows. It is impossible to tear yourself away! Especially when you arrive very early, before the actual sunrise, and see that first light of dawn breaking, a sacred sensation grips you. It is as though the whole of nature were celebrating a mystery, and you are compelled to adopt a different attitude so as not to disrupt that sacred moment. This is true poetry, and we should pray that all human beings may one day be able to drink from this overflowing abundance of life.

The sunrise is a symbol and this symbol can be found in every manifestation of life. Everything that progresses, elevates itself, and flourishes is linked to the sunrise. And it is up to you to feel it. It all depends on the faith, the conviction with which you concentrate on the sun.[5] Depending on your attitude, the sun will become a real, living, powerful presence, or it will simply remain a physical object, which gives you light and warmth of course, but no more than an electric light bulb or a stove.

By moving a little closer each day to the truth the sun represents, the sun which is in the image and likeness of God, we begin to sense it is showing us the path of life, light, and warmth, so that we wish for nothing more than to become like it. Of course, we will not become like the sun, that is impossible. But that does not matter. Let us print its image in our heads as an ideal, because, in fact, it is the impossible, the unachievable that works, that gives us strength and transforms us. Yes, it is not that which you hold or possess, it is not that which you have achieved that makes you evolve. It is that which is impossible, unachievable, that you must seek, because only that will stimulate you to keep going forward.

Notes

1 See *The Splendour of Tiphareth*, C.W. 10, Chap. 15: 'The Sun is in the Image and Likeness of God – 'In Spirit and in Truth'.

2 See *In Spirit and in Truth*, Izvor 235, Chap. 12: 'An Image Can Be a Support for Prayer'.

3 See The *Splendour of Tiphareth*, C.W. 10, Chap. 16: 'Christ and the Solar Religion'.

4 Ibid., Chap. 20: 'The Sun Teaches by Example – The Sun, Heart of our Universe'.

5 See *A New Earth*, Volume 13, Chap. 9: 'The Sun and the Stars'.

5

'You shall love the Lord your God'

One of the best known passages in the Gospels is the one in which a scribe asks Jesus: *'Which commandment is the first of all?'* and Jesus answers, *'You shall love the Lord your God with all your heart, and with all your soul, and with all your mind, and with all your strength. The second is this, You shall love your neighbour as yourself.'*

You shall love the Lord your God with all your heart, and with all your soul, and with all your mind, and with all your strength. With this reply Jesus defines a human being as being made up of four psychic principles: the heart, the soul, the mind (the faculty of thought), and the spirit (strength), because only the spirit has true strength. But in order to grasp the full scope of these words we must first understand the difference between the heart and the soul, and between the mind and the spirit.

The heart and the soul are the vehicles of our emotions, feelings, and desires, but whereas the heart is the seat of feelings, emotions, and desires associated with the satisfactions or frustrations of everyday life, the soul is the seat of spiritual, divine emotions and impulses. And the same relationship exists between the mind or intellect and the spirit as between the heart and the soul. The mind is the seat of thought and reasoning aimed at satisfying personal interests and material needs, and the spirit is the principle of purely disinterested thoughts and activities.

The heart and the soul are two expressions of the feminine principle, and the mind and the spirit are both expressions of the masculine principle. In the lower regions the feminine principle manifests through the heart, and in the higher regions through the soul. In the lower regions the masculine principle manifests through the mind, and in the higher regions through the spirit. The masculine and feminine principles therefore use four vehicles: the heart, the mind, the soul, and the spirit. The two principles and the four vehicles all dwell in the same 'house', the physical body.

Let me tell you a story, which might shed more light on this issue, for it is still too abstract for many of you. Imagine a beautiful house in which live the two proprietors. They are husband and wife and they have two servants, a live-in couple. The master of the house has to be away from home from time to time, and the wife stays behind, somewhat sad and listless, waiting for her husband to return while continuing to oversee the running of the household. When the husband returns, laden with gifts, there is great rejoicing. But sometimes the master of the house takes his wife with him on a long journey, and the manservant and the maid, finding themselves with no one to supervise them, decide to enjoy their freedom to the full. They begin to go through the cupboards and find all kinds of food and drink. And since a feast is much more entertaining if it is shared with others, they invite the neighbours to join them. After a few hours, of course, a table has been knocked over and some bottles – and even a few heads – have been broken. When the master and his wife return they are horrified by what they see. Naturally they take disciplinary action and demand the house be put back in order. And after a while everything returns to normal.

Let us now interpret this story. The house is the physical body. The maid is the heart and the manservant is the mind. The mistress of the house is the soul and the master the spirit. Often the spirit leaves us and our soul feels rather abandoned, but when the spirit returns it brings with it inspiration and an abundance of light. When the soul and the spirit go away together the heart and the mind, left to their own devices, rush into all kinds of foolishness in the company of other hearts and other minds.

If we stay with this image a while longer, we discover the respective roles of the heart, the mind, the soul, and the spirit. You know that a maid is usually more attached to the mistress of the house, and the manservant to the master. What differentiates the masters from the servants is their way of life, their behaviour, their activities and concerns, and the employers do not always tell their servants the secrets of their work or their plans. In the same way, the soul and spirit act without revealing their intentions to the heart and the mind.

But if the maid, through her impeccable behaviour, wins the trust of her mistress, the latter will sometimes talk to her about her activities, about her happiness and about the love she feels for her husband, the spirit. And then the maid (the heart) is delighted to have been taken into her mistress's confidence. And equally, when the manservant, through his loyalty, wins the trust of his master, the latter begins to tell him things and the manservant (the mind) becomes more enlightened and more lucid. However, this can only happen if the servant couple – heart and mind – live in perfect harmony in the service of their masters. If there is conflict between them and the desires of one contradict the wishes of the other, they hinder the work of the soul and the spirit. You should meditate on the many combinations and applications of this image, because all our inner states and even our physical health are determined by the relationships formed between these four inhabitants of our house.

So it is clear, the heart-mind couple is a repetition on the lower plane of the soul-spirit couple. And children are born from the union of each of these couples. The union of the mind and the heart produces actions on the physical plane,[1] whereas the union of the soul and the spirit produces actions on the spiritual plane.

The interrelation between these four principles explains why the heart and the mind can only err when they are not subject to the soul (which represents divine love) and to the spirit (which represents divine wisdom). But once they have grown in the way of love and wisdom, the heart and mind will become the son and daughter of God. For the time being, however, they are not even very good servants. A true son is one who endeavours to reflect the perfection of his heavenly Father, and a true daughter, one who endeavours to reflect the perfection of the divine Mother. So, when the heart and the mind have learned to act with love and wisdom, they will be the son and daughter of God in the image of whom they were created.[2] Until then, they are not the son and daughter of God, only of humankind.

Humankind's greatest error was to break off communications between the lower regions of heart and mind and the sublime regions of soul and spirit. Deprived of this interrelation, the heart and the mind are harrowed and tormented. Only one thing can save them: to find their masters and place themselves at their service again. Then the heart will become the conductor of the soul and divine love will begin to flow through it; and the mind will become the receptacle of divine wisdom and the spirit will begin to manifest through it.

You shall love the Lord your God with all your heart, and with all your soul, and with all your mind, and with all your strength. By saying this Jesus implied that we should place all our faculties at the service of God. But how? Master Peter Deunov said: 'Let your heart be as pure as crystal, your mind as luminous as the sun, your soul as vast as the universe, and your spirit as powerful as God and one with God.' This means we must love God with the purity of our heart, with the light of our mind, with the immensity of our soul, and with the strength of our spirit. This is what loving truly entails.

Our heart must be pure, that is, free from selfish feelings, from all the wishes and desires that make of it a bog, because the cloudy waters of a bog cannot reflect the splendour of heaven. Our mind must be luminous, in other words, free from the dust picked up along the way and which now prevent it from seeing clearly.[3] Our soul must be vast, and it is love that makes it dilate. Indeed when you are filled with love you feel capable of embracing the entire universe. And lastly our spirit must become powerful by uniting with the Creator, because true strength comes from the divine source.

Unfortunately, all these faculties which we should place at the service of our heavenly Father and Mother so that we may begin to resemble them, are more often put at the service of other human beings, and this is our downfall. Someone comes to you and says: 'My friend, give me your heart, I need it.' Initially you may refuse, but he begs you, he implores you, and so a day, a week, a month go by and finally you give in and give him your heart. But since we cannot walk around with two hearts, he will soon drop yours... and you will have a broken heart. So now it is your turn to cry: 'What have you done with my heart?' Someone else may ask for your mind, saying he needs it to carry his affairs through to a successful conclusion. When he has been insisting for a few weeks, again you give it to him... and with that you lose your independence, your freedom of thought. And once your heart and your intellect have been taken from you, it is as if you had also given away your soul and your spirit, because the heart and the intellect are the intermediaries which enable you to make contact with your soul and spirit. Once these bridges are down, you have lost everything. In reality, the soul and the spirit can never be enslaved because they are divine in essence. They are free and invulnerable. So, if it is also true to say that they can be subjugated, it is because of their bond with the heart and the mind. For your heart and your mind can be enslaved, and when this happens, the path to the soul and the spirit also becomes closed to you.

Many people have given or sold their hearts and minds in return for pleasure, glory, money or power. You will say: 'But what should we do if someone asks us for them?' Suppose you possess a violin; it is tuned to your vibrations and each day you delight in the marvellous tones it produces. And then someone comes along and demands you give it to him. Will you hand it over? No, you must tell him: 'My friend, you are welcome to come and listen to the airs I play on my violin, but the violin is mine. I shall keep it. It was not made for you.' Or suppose you have some capital in a bank. If someone asks you for it, you will say: 'My friend, I will give you the interest from this money, but I shall keep the capital so that it continues to earn interest.' Or perhaps you have a fruit tree growing in your garden, a peach tree that produces delicious peaches, and someone comes along and wants to transplant it to his garden. You will tell him: 'My dear friend, I shall keep this tree in my garden, but you are quite welcome to eat as much fruit from it as you wish. I'll even give you a cutting, which you can plant in front of your house, but that is all.' Or suppose you possess an extremely rare and precious book, and again you are asked to give it away. You will say: 'No, I will not give you this book, but come to my house every day if you like, and you can read it there or even copy it.'

It is now up to you to find the correspondence between these examples and what you should give of your heart, your mind, your soul, and your spirit. Do not give your heart, give only your feelings and emotions. Do not give your mind, give your thoughts. Do not give your soul, but the love emanating from it. Do not give your spirit, only the beneficial forces that flow from it.

You can be safe only if you give everything to God, and 'everything' means your spirit, your soul, your mind, your heart, and even your body, as well as your house and the money you possess. Of course, God will not come and take your money to put it in his coffers for safekeeping, but the mere gesture, the mere thought of giving him everything will make your money safe. And then you can wait for him to tell you what to do with it. You are the banker, the cashier, and God, who is the owner, will give you the right advice to ensure this money will never be lost. Yes, because money belongs to God! If so many rich people lose their money or fail in business, it is because they did not previously dedicate their money to God, the only one who is able to advise on how to make good use of it.

But above all it is your heart you must give to God. Why? Because it is first and foremost into your heart that the devil worms his way. The heart corresponds to the astral plane, which touches the physical plane and for this reason the forces of darkness can influence the heart more easily than the mind, the soul, or, especially, the spirit. Whatever wrong you do, you cannot drag your spirit into it. It is through your heart that you are most vulnerable. This is why God asks you: 'My child, give me your heart.' But you reply: 'But why, Lord? My heart is for him... or her.' 'Very well, I understand,' says God, 'but give it to me anyway, because all your suffering and unhappiness stem from the fact you do not know how to protect your heart and it can only cause you distress.' So give your heart to God and it will be safe. God at least knows how to look after it. He will not let it come to harm, whereas with the person you love you can never be sure.

So now it is up to you to draw the conclusions that are right for you. But I tell you, so long as you have not dedicated your heart to God, you will continue to be exposed inwardly to great troubles. So many exceptional beings have been led by their hearts into all kinds of chaos and madness. No one is safe from the demons that seek to seize the human heart. This is why we must ask for heavenly protection by giving our heart to God, and then God will send us his servants, angels of light who will make their home in it and work to keep it safe.[4]

It is for ourselves that we should love God, not for him. He does not need us. What could we possibly give him? Our mediocrity? Our wickedness? Our selfishness? Our vanity? What splendid gifts for God! It is we who need him and this need can only be expressed through love. By loving God we love ourselves. Yes, in reality God is us, the higher part of ourselves – which we might call our 'soul mate', if this term were not so often held in derision today. When someone says 'so-and-so has found his soul mate', they often say it mockingly. So let us just say that by loving God, we love the divine part of ourselves, our higher self, and we seek to come closer to him in order to merge with him.[5]

You shall love the Lord your God with all your heart, and with all your soul, and with all your mind, and with all your strength. You now understand the profundity of Jesus' words. To love God is to recover his image within ourselves.

Notes

1 See *Hope for the World: Spiritual Galvanoplasty*, Izvor. 214, Chap. 11: 'Replenish the Earth!'.
2 See *Cosmic Balance – The Secret of Polarity*, Izvor. 237, Chap. 4: 'The Role of The Masculine and The Feminine'.
3 See *The Mysteries of Yesod*, C.W. 7, Chap. 10: 'Look for Purity on a Higher Plane'.
4 See *Love and Sexuality* Part 1, C.W. 14, Chap. 16: The Teaching of Love in the Mysteries'; - *Love and Sexuality* Part 2, C.W. 15, Chap. 3: 'The Sun is the Source of Love', Chap. 14: 'The Task of a Disciple'.
5 See *Love and Sexuality*, C.W. 14, Chap. 19: 'Sister Souls'; - *Cosmic Balance – The Secret of Polarity*, Izvor. 237, Chap. 17: 'The Androgynes of Myth', p. 241-242.

Part IV

The laws
of
destiny

Part I - The laws of destiny

1

The laws of Nature
and
moral laws

I

The law of cause and effect

Religion has repeatedly been accused of inventing moral laws designed to chloroform and enslave people. And it is true that over the centuries, many Churchmen have abused their position and used their power to impose rules and practices that were absurd and even cruel. That I do not deny, but this is no reason to repudiate the reality of the laws governing the psychic and spiritual worlds, because these laws exist and they are similar to those governing the physical world.

Everyone knows physical laws exist; they are a fact of everyday life. If you put your hand into the fire, you will burn yourself. If you do not look where you are going, you will stumble and fall. If you stand in front of a car that is travelling at high speed, you will be knocked down and killed... and I could go on. Our organism, also, is governed by identical laws. If you eat too much or too little, or if you swallow indigestible elements, you undermine your health. If you work too much, you become exhausted, and if you do no work at all, you stagnate, you become stultified. And so on. No one questions the laws of physics or of hygiene. Even if we do not respect them, we at least recognize they exist. But when it comes to moral laws, very few people today are prepared to recognize them. And even if a few still believe in a certain order of things, there are writers, philosophers, artists, and scientists who produce theories, write books, and create works of art aimed at eradicating any remnant of this belief. It is of these moral laws I want to speak, because those who do not recognize them will always lack something fundamental, something essential.[1]

Throughout history, human beings have been given countless dictates, which have varied according to their mentality and their level of civilization and evolution. Actually, there are very few rules that are essential, and let me tell you that, to my mind, the first moral law is to be found in agriculture: you reap what you sow. This is the law of cause and effect. Depending on what you sow (the causes), you will harvest (the effects). All farmers know that if they plant a fig tree they will harvest not grapes but figs, and that they cannot pick cherries from an apple tree. Well, to those who are able to observe and think, this law of agriculture is the most important moral law. On the physical plane it is absolutely true that you reap what you have sown, and it is equally true on the other planes. This means that if you behave selfishly, or with violence or cruelty, it is as though you were sowing seeds and one day you will yourself reap selfishness, violence, and cruelty from others. No use then complaining in indignation: 'How can anyone do this to me?' If you ask such a question you are obviously not even a good gardener.

A gardener does not become angry when something he has not planted does not grow. If he has sown turnips, he will not be upset when they fail to turn out as leeks or strawberries. On the surface, human beings appear to know a great deal about agriculture; they even use phrases like 'he who sows the wind shall reap the whirlwind'. As long as they are dealing with physical processes or events, they may be very clever, but when it comes to matters of the psychic realm, they know nothing at all. And yet everyone can see and experience this irrefutable truth. But instead of accepting it most people lose their way in so-called 'original' considerations and arguments to justify their behaviour. Even if reality proves them wrong, they persist in their error.

The reason why people so often fail to understand this is, of course, that it takes a long time for the effects of these laws to become visible. Neither good nor bad effects appear immediately. It is exactly the same as with the physical organism. If you eat, drink, or smoke to excess you will not necessarily become unwell right away. But it is easy enough to predict that if you do not change your habits fairly rapidly, you will not escape illness. The organism of a person who overdoes things in any sphere is like a wooden structure infested with woodworm: the wood does not crumble from one day to the next, it takes a number of years, and then suddenly the whole structure collapses. Many things work like that in life, but because people do not understand the way the laws work, they base their judgements on the short term, and inevitably draw the wrong conclusions.[2]

When a man behaves like a tyrant or a crook and everything seems to be going well with him – he has plenty to eat and drink, he transacts dealings, or accumulates wealth – people watch him and say to themselves: 'Well, if he is so successful it means there are no laws, there is no justice,' and they try to imitate him. And when someone is honest and does a lot of good all around, he does not seem to be rewarded, and people come to the conclusion that it is no use following his example. Everyone believes that if justice existed, it would be seen to take effect more quickly. In reality, however, you need to observe people and events for a long period of time in order to understand how the laws work. We cannot base our conclusions on one brief instant taken out of context: it is not sufficient. Indeed, if you look at the situation in certain countries, you will find that it has taken centuries to see how they gradually fell into decadence. Those who lived through this decadence were not aware of it. And the same applies to individuals: it is not in the present incarnation that we see the effects of good or bad behaviour, but in the next.

So, you need to try to be more clairvoyant and look beyond the immediate satisfaction of a desire, a need or an instinct. Try to envisage your long-term, permanent, eternal well-being, knowing that justice, seemingly so slow, manifests in reality very rapidly, but does so within you. If you were truly sensitive, you would sense how thoughts, feelings, and acts of goodness instantly switch on a light inside you, and how thoughts, feelings, and acts inspired by the desire to do harm actually darken you, and do so instantly. It takes a long time before the effects show themselves concretely, but within you, the process is instantaneous. If you allow your anger or your hatred to pour out onto others, be aware that before they reach the 'others', these feelings will first pass through you and poison you. Do you want to poison someone? Feel free, but remember that it is you who will be poisoned before they are.

You can only harvest fruits which correspond to the seeds you have planted. Now if you have been plagued with bad weather, if everything has been parched by the sun, or there has been too much rain, or the birds or moles have eaten all your seeds, that is another matter. Such adversities do not change the reality of the law according to which every seed produces its likeness, because the blueprint inside each and every seed cannot be removed. It can temporarily be prevented from producing fruits, but its nature cannot be changed. The blueprint that determines that a seed will produce wheat and not maize cannot be erased. But what I am talking about here is the nature of the seed that you plant, and once the conditions are right, it will germinate and produce fruits according to the blueprint you have recorded, whether good or bad. Yes, because you must realize that everything is recorded.

If, in spite of being always kind and helpful, you are always being sworn at – or worse – that is a minor detail. What is important is to see who reacts in that way, when, and in what circumstances. Perhaps you are too open, too trusting, and then of course, by present-day social standards you will be ranked among the imbeciles who can be abused and should even be resisted. But that is irrelevant, because people and circumstances change, whereas laws are unchanging. And when, once again, values change, when opinions and behaviour change, everything will fall back into place and you will reap what you have sown.

Good always brings good and evil always brings evil. Do good and you will yourself encounter good, even if you do not want to. And if you begin to encounter evil, because there are people who are narrow-minded and ill-intentioned, do not let it concern you too much because this evil is transitory and divine justice will one day restore your rights. Divine justice will take stock of all you have suffered while doing good and your recompense will be all the greater for it. Concern yourself only with continuing to do good, to cultivate good thoughts, good feelings, because, let me say it again, all this good will affect you first, before it affects others, and love, peace, and light will dwell within you. This is what is important. You do not yet realize what good really is; you do not yet know to what extent it is powerful and capable of protecting you. Once you have strengthened good within you, it becomes like a rampart and withstands the evil people can try to do to you, so that you are not affected.

It is high time human beings based their lives on solid, true, irrefutable knowledge which everyone can verify and experience for themselves. Who would want to deny that we reap what we sow? No one! Everyone is convinced of the truth of this law, but only on the physical plane. They do not venture beyond that. You should now venture further, higher, and you will find that the same laws prevail on all planes, for creation is one. The same principles, the same phenomena exist on every level, but in forms that are different and ever subtler. The four elements of earth, water, air, and fire are governed by the same laws, but since they are not of the same nature, there are differences in the way they manifest – more or less slowly, more or less violently – but they are governed by exactly the same principles. So, be aware that the very same principles govern the physical, the psychic, and the spiritual planes. And if we defy these laws established by cosmic Intelligence since the creation of the world, we shall disintegrate.

You will say: 'But how cruel cosmic Intelligence is if it destroys all creatures who oppose it.' No, cosmic Intelligence does not concern itself with any of that. It never wants to destroy anyone, but if, through ignorance or lack of goodwill, human beings do not respect the order of things, the forces they disturb are so powerful that they will be destroyed by them. The poor wretch who wants to march alone against an entire army will soon be wiped out. An insect that keeps beating against a window ends by being battered to death, but is that the fault of the window? Human beings act like insects: they believe they can defy the divine laws and refuse to observe them, and so they are crushed. It is not God who destroys them, it is they who expose themselves to danger.[3]

So, let this be quite clear to you from now on. In whatever sphere it may be, nothing takes place in life that did not first have the conditions for its realization, in other words without there being a cause for that particular effect. When it comes to political, economic, social, or cultural incidents or events, everyone accepts that they have a cause. They can even identify it. But when it comes to the mental, emotional, and spiritual planes, very few people are capable of such discernment. They find themselves in appalling situations and are unable to understand how they got there.[4] And it is impossible to explain it to them, because everything in their head is obscure and illogical. You would need to start from scratch and show them how it all started, where and when they began to err and how they gradually came to find themselves in their present deplorable situation. Above all, they would have to be prepared to listen to what they are told, but they are not. They look for all kinds of unlikely arguments to explain their situation. In fact, the basic argument is usually the same: it is someone else's fault. Yes, it is always because others do not understand them, do not help them, or wish them harm. They, of course, are blameless. They will never admit that at some point there was something in their own head or heart that made them take the wrong turning. They continue obstinately along their chosen path, each time finding new arguments, new reasons to justify themselves, without realizing that the world they are fabricating in their head has nothing to do with reality. And this is how so many end in madness.

In any case, you need to know that the first thing a Master requires of you before recognizing you as his disciple is this awareness of the sequence of cause and effect, because he knows that once you understand this, you will be able to benefit from the knowledge he will give you in all spheres. But if he sees that deep down, you reject this law, then inwardly he will close the door on you, because he will deem you to be a dangerous being.

We reap what we sow. If you study this fundamental law in depth and if you give it broader meaning, it will become a rich and profound system. Most moral and religious teachings are simply different applications of this law. Look at Jesus' precept for instance: *'Do to others as you would have them do to you.'* And what about reincarnation? Reincarnation is also simply one application of this law, in that the way in which you live in this incarnation paves the way for the next. At every moment, through your inner work, you are building your future.

Notes

1 See *Cosmic Moral Law*, C.W. 12, Chap. 7: 'The Laws of Nature and Moral Law'.
2 See *La pédagogie initiatique*, Œuvres Complètes, t. 27, chap. V : «L'apprentissage des lois».
3 See *Angels and other Mysteries of The Tree of Life*, Izvor 236, Chap. 15: 'Binah – The Laws of Destiny.'
4 See *La pédagogie initiatique,* Œuvres Complètes, t. 27, chap. X (2 et 3) : «Les méthodes d'un Maître».

II

The law of recording

You can question the existence of God, you can believe neither in heaven nor in hell, you can ignore sacred scripture, but there is one thing you must never doubt and that is that our thoughts, feelings, and actions are all recorded both within us and outside of us and, therefore, that they leave traces that endure. The knowledge of this law is one of the foundation stones of the moral and spiritual life, for since everything is recorded, we can no longer afford to do whatever we wish. We must watch not only our actions but also our feelings and our thoughts.

Of course, this concept is quite new to many people. Proof that human beings – who are both intelligent and ingenious – have succeeded in developing devices for recording images and sounds can be found in a plethora of photographs, films, tapes and CDs. But the notion that nature should also make recordings seems impossible to many. Well, contrary to what they think, it is precisely because nature makes recordings that human beings can do so too. Everything that exists in the human world is a reflection of phenomena and processes that already exist in the invisible world. Cosmic Intelligence did not wait for photography or the tape recorder to be invented before making recordings. Indeed, it has been making them since the beginning of creation and nature's recordings are far subtler than those human beings are able to produce.

Nature records everything, and true morality is founded precisely on these recordings, on nature's memory. Yes, memory, because nature has a memory that nothing can erase. You think you can do as you wish? Well, it is true, you can, but be aware that everything is recorded and you will never be able to escape from these recordings.

You will say: 'But what does it mean to speak of nature's memory? How does it work?' Well, you must understand that everything that exists in the physical world – mountains, stars, plants, animals, people, and so forth – all have an etheric duplicate. In fact, every one of our manifestations also exists in duplicate. You will understand this better if I draw an analogy with a government department. When a decree or regulation is passed, a copy is made of it – today it would probably be a photocopy. The original disappears, but the copy is kept in the archives for reference. In the same way, whatever human beings do, it is done in duplicate. If they do something good, if they have a good feeling or a good thought, the original of this act, feeling or thought disappears, but it leaves a copy within them, and this copy continues to live and to be active. Similarly, if they do something evil, the evil action leaves them, but it also leaves within them a duplicate of exactly the same nature. People do not know this. They believe that their good or evil actions go no further. Well, unfortunately – or fortunately – a duplicate remains in their subtle bodies.

When they die, they take this duplicate with them – it would be more accurate to say three duplicates, physical (actions), astral (feelings), and mental (thoughts). The originals have long since disappeared; they are irretrievable, it is too late. But they still have within them these faithful and true duplicates. It is with these duplicates – which could be compared to films – that we come before an assembly of highly evolved spirits, and there we have to watch while the film of our entire life is shown. All the copies left within us become visible and audible and we must look at them and listen to them. This showing is not held for the sake of the spirits. They do not need to be informed about people's lives for they know them already. Simply by looking at them they know the degree of evolution they have attained. It is human beings who do not know themselves, poor souls. It is they who are ignorant, and who have to be shown exactly what they are and what their life amounted to.

When human beings arrive in the other world, the celestial entities do not ask them: 'How did you live your life? What did you do? Did you enlighten or help anybody?' No, instead they take from within them a few reels of 'film' and project them onto a screen. And what a show these reels of film make! You will say: 'But that is not possible.' I tell you it is! There are tiny reels, atoms, on which a person's entire life is recorded. Just look at the kind of tape used in cassette recorders or tape recorders; on the face of it, it just looks like an ordinary piece of plastic tape. But put it into the appropriate machine and suddenly you hear ... 'The Barber of Seville'. So, when you arrive in the other world, you will not be questioned. What would be the use? The celestial entities know you would only come up with some excuse to justify your actions. They call you over and say: 'Sit down quietly here.' Then they set up a screen in front of you and you see your entire life unfold before your eyes, in the minutest detail. Now, we are not told how your hair will stand on end. You will ask: 'But do we still have hair once we are up there?' Yes, but hair of another kind. You will have left your physical hair down here, but you have other hair which will stand on end. So, you see, you cannot get away with lies.

All this can be found in all the scriptures of the great religions. Exactly how the deceased reach the world above, how they appear before the celestial judges and so on is irrelevant. I tell you all this in a humorous way, but what is important is to realize that nothing people do during their existence on earth is inconsequential, because everything leaves a trace within. And these traces stay with them in the next world.[1]

Now, whether you believe this or not, you cannot change the facts, and the facts are and will always be these, regardless of what you believe. It is, of course, more sensible to believe and accept them, because once you know the laws, you can understand better how you should change your behaviour.[2]

Proof that everything is recorded can be seen in the way people suddenly remember, many years later, an incident that took place in their earliest childhood. Also, victims of a serious accident in which they were very nearly killed relate how they saw their entire life flash before them in reverse at an incredible rate, like a reel of film unwinding. How is it that nothing is erased? And what happens when someone has committed a crime? Even if they have escaped police investigation, they are constantly pursued by images and words that keep coming back. This is usually called remorse, and whatever they do, they cannot free themselves from it, because the duplicate that has remained inside them gives them no respite.

So you see, there is no need to go and study the scriptures of humankind before believing these laws exist; you can see them at work in yourself. Why do people have these memories, these images from which they are unable to free themselves? Why does their conscience continually reproach them, so that they reach the point where they are unable to eat or sleep until they have confessed and made amends? You will say: 'But history shows that some people never feel remorse for their crimes.' Yes, that is true, monstrous beings who have no idea of what is right and wrong do exist, but I am not talking about them.

In any case it is very difficult to analyze the different guises in which remorse can appear in a human being.

Cosmic Intelligence has had plenty of time to fine-tune everything. If some people choose to believe in coincidence and in chaos, so be it; the Creator has given them the freedom to do so, and one day they will see for themselves. But you at least, who are familiar with this law of recording, must try from now on to watch what you do, because not only do your thoughts, feelings, and actions leave an impression inside you, but once this impression has been made, it is like an imprint, a negative that tends to replicate indefinitely. So try not to make bad negatives, and learn how to make good ones, so that the bad habits you have developed over the years stop repeating themselves. Otherwise, I warn you: the bad negatives will stay with you from one incarnation to the next. As for your good qualities, seek to strengthen them, because what is good can always be made better.

So set to work! But do not waste too much time wrestling with the bad habits you have adopted over the years and which you may never shake off. All deviations stem from the destructive work you have done – consciously or unconsciously – in the past, and at this moment it is better to focus on the positive work you can do for the future. In other words, focus on making new negatives, new imprints, and you will see that once you have embarked upon this work you will be so involved, busy, and inspired by it that you will find in it an endless source of joy, because you will be building the temple of God within you.[3] I know of no work that is superior to that of building within ourselves the temple of God, using the most precious materials, that is, the most noble and unselfish thoughts, feelings, and actions.

Most people are far from having attained this under-standing of the question of recordings. All they are interested in is recording a few items of knowledge in their heads. But, truly, that is not the work I am talking about. The difference between an initiatic school and other schools is that in the latter students acquire knowledge, which may be useful at some point, but which does not transform them. Only the work we do on ourselves can transform us, not what we have read or heard. The knowledge we acquire may induce us to do this work, but it will not transform us if we do not set other forces in motion within us. Whatever we learn, we will remain the same, whereas in an initiatic school we can finally begin true work.

Some will say: 'But I get no pleasure from doing this work.' And that statement shows immediately what category they belong to. All creatures in nature belong to a particular category. Take animals for instance: depending on their shape, their fur, feathers or scales, the food they eat, their habitat, and so on, they are placed in a certain category. Well, nature will put us in a category too one day depending on our predilections. And this categorization is our destiny.

Some people are predestined to be ill, others are predestined to know failure, and others are predestined to be ill-treated, victimized. But it is they who have predestined themselves, who have determined their own fate. You will ask: 'Is it possible to escape that fate?' In this incarnation, no, it is not. It was in our previous incarnation, if we had been intelligent and sensible, that we could have arranged many aspects of this incarnation. The only possibility open to us now is to prepare our next life, provided we work day in day out to make other, better recordings.

I realize that what I am talking about is very difficult to achieve. Where do you find the will-power, the drive within yourself to begin this work and to pursue it? What is important is to be able to make a few new recordings every day, which will be purer and more luminous. And the old recordings? You will gradually begin to cover them with new ones. And this should encourage you. Of course, however well-intentioned you are, you will still continue to make recordings that are not very good, because you will be swept along by those already there, inside you. But at least be alert to what is going on so as to make sure things get no worse. As soon as you become aware you have recorded something unfavourable, react and make reparation in order to prevent the consequences. Whether you have had negative thoughts about someone, said something hurtful, or destroyed something, be aware of what you have done and try to make amends. For the moment at least you may not be able to do much more, but at least do that. Some people do nothing, nothing at all, to make amends for a negative thought or deed. I have seen it many times. Others at least say to themselves: 'I slipped up this time; I was not able to control myself. But in future I shall be more careful.' This can happen to us all, but we should at least be aware of it immediately so that we can make things better – above all, so that we do not do it again.

These truths represent incalculable riches. For my part, I have given up everything in order to know them. I was so convinced of their worth that I was ready to sacrifice everything for them. And what about you? Heaven values human beings according to their attitude toward divine ideas.[4] Do you know the true worth of things? To me, nothing is more important than to know the true worth of everything.

The laws of Nature and moral laws

Notes

1 See *The Fruits of The Tree of Life – The Cabbalistic Tradition*, C.W. 32, Chap. 15: 'Death and the Life Beyond'.
2 See *Cosmic Moral Law*, Volume 12, Chap. 18: 'Morality Comes into its Own in the World Above'.
3 See *Creation: Artistic and Spiritual*, Izvor 223, Chap. 12: 'Building the Temple'.
4 See *A New Dawn: Society and Politics in the Light of Initiatic Science* (Part 2), C.W. 26, Chap. 5 (2): 'The Kingdom of God and His Righteousness'.

III

The law of resonance

All our physical and psychic manifestations are like missiles thrown into the ocean of energies, in that they produce waves, which will inevitably come back to us one day. Our thoughts, feelings, actions, and words, the way we move, even the way we look, all have consequences.[1] Very few people, however, are conscious of the effects they produce. They make threatening gestures, look askance at people, speak unkindly, and entertain negative thoughts and feelings, not knowing that the universe is like an immense wall that sends each of these manifestations back to them like an echo.

Imagine you are standing in the midst of a circle of mountains and you cry out: 'I love you.' The echo replies: 'I love you… love you… love you…' Similarly if you shout: 'I hate you', the echo will reply: 'I hate you… hate you… hate you.' Well, the same applies to everything else in life. Not only does nothing remain without effect, but what is more, as the law of resonance shows, everything we do comes back to us in the end. This is also called the law of repercussion, or the backlash.

However, the effects of our behaviour do not always make themselves felt immediately. Sometimes they reach other people first: family or friends, sometimes even people very far away, whom we do not know, but who receive the waves emitted by our thoughts, feelings, and actions. If you were clairvoyant you would see that the damage caused by chaotic, aggressive manifestations reaches even to the other side of the world. Equally, you would see how something magnificent develops when your attitude and behaviour are harmonious.[2]

Let me draw another analogy, with the experiment of the Dutch physicist Gravesande, in which a series of balls is suspended in a row so that they touch each other slightly. At one end of the row the first ball is lifted up and then released. As it swings back, it obviously hits the second ball. And then we see something astonishing: all the other balls remain motionless, except the last one, which swings out at an angle. This fact is very significant. It is the last ball in the row which is affected by the impact and swings outward whereas the other balls remain motionless, simply acting as transmitters.

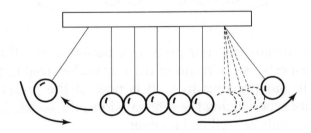

If we think about this law we will see that it finds many applications in our lives. Every country, every society represents a system of interlinked balls, and when one of its members commits a grave fault, the ball that swings outward – in other words the one that pays for that fault – is the last ball in the row. Of course we never know who that last ball represents. Also, we must remember that this law is true for good as well as for evil.

You now understand the way in which all human beings are linked. You think you can act with impunity, but that is not so. For an instant, perhaps, the first ball thinks to itself: 'I have hit my neighbour and nothing has happened.' But this is an illusion. Little does it know that the last ball in the row has been touched. And since that last ball has been touched, it swings out and back again, and the same process occurs in reverse, for once again the vibrations are communicated step by step until the first ball in the row swings out. It receives the backlash.

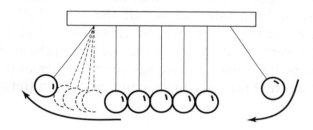

This means that our present situation, with all its good and bad aspects, is the result of the way we behaved in the past or even in our previous lives. It is now, at the present time, that we are experiencing the repercussions, the backlash, which consist of trials as well as blessings.

It is particularly important to know this law when we are the victim of an injustice... and injustices occur only too often. Of course, our first reaction is to seek revenge, or at least to be angry with the perpetrator and wish him some misfortune. Well, reactions of this kind should be avoided, because first of all you do not know the reason for what seems to you to be an injustice. Who knows? you may be experiencing the backlash of something bad you did a long time ago, perhaps even in a previous incarnation. So this injustice merely seems to be an injustice. Instead of letting it eat away at you, tell yourself, therefore, that you are simply paying for previous transgressions. In doing so you will suffer less – for nothing is more painful than to feel oneself the victim of an injustice – and not only will you suffer less, but your efforts to overcome this trial will liberate you. Yes, this is important; you will be liberated. The only way to free yourself from the relentless wheel of fate is by never answering evil with evil.

I am not saying that innocent people are never unjustly persecuted. But if they rebel against this injustice or try to take their revenge, they will create unnecessary torment for themselves. Here on earth, even if we are innocent, it is better to consider ourselves as guilty as everyone else, because in doing so we liberate ourselves. It is not a question of doing nothing. You can – you should even – stand up for yourself and defend your position, but with the only weapons permitted: the weapons of love and light.

You will never be able to prevent malicious people from trying to harm you. But do not concern yourself with them. Instead, try to pray and meditate so as to reach the purer regions of light and love, because only there will you be protected.[3] Not only will the poisoned arrows of your enemies fail to reach you, but they will return to them. This is how initiates, sages, and great masters succeed in defeating their enemies; by leading a pure, noble, and luminous life. It is this life that protects them and rejects all that is negative. They do not worry about it, indeed they often do not even know what is being plotting against them. They focus only on leading a divine life and it is this life that protects them. It acts like a fortress against which the projectiles thrown at them rebound and return to strike those who fired them.

But that cannot happen if you behave exactly as your enemy does, in other words, if you are weak, vicious, and vindictive. Because even if you have been attacked unjustly, if you use the same negative weapons as your enemy in defending yourself, you will be putting yourself on his level and will no longer be protected. If you want to be truly safe, whatever anyone may say or do to you, increase your light, your love, and your generosity. It is instinct, not wisdom, that counsels revenge: someone hits you and, without thinking, you hit back.[4] Some people have reached the point where they are above rancour. However much others malign them, hate them, work against them in every way, it does not bother them. They believe in the power of light and love, and every day, in their spiritual work, they send the purest rays of their spirit and soul to all creatures. And even if there are some that do not receive them, nothing is lost because these rays will come back to them.

You cannot reach this level of consciousness unless you have travelled a long way along the path of inner growth. And most people have not even taken the first steps. Instead, they persist in looking for ways to retaliate. They think that they are justified, that they are in their right. An eye for an eye, a tooth for a tooth, this is how people behave all over the world. If you think that the teachings of Jesus are put into practice, you are very much mistaken. You are, of course, free to do as you wish, to defeat your enemies as you see fit, but sooner or later you will find that in fact you have not succeeded. Even if you kill them, that will not be the end of it. You will keep encountering them, from one incarnation to the next. That is the law. You kill your enemy, but one day it is he who will kill you, and this will continue until one of you is capable of rising higher, of showing more generosity, of forgiving. At that point the cycle ends, the chain has been broken.

It is, of course, far more difficult to work on yourself than to seek revenge, but this work is worth undertaking. If you find that a person who has wronged you truly deserves punishment, turn to the invisible world and say: 'Look, such and such a person has done me wrong, and because of this I am now finding things difficult in such and such an area. I ask you to intervene, so that the wrong I have suffered may be put right.' In this way you are lodging a complaint before heaven, as is done in everyday life before the courts, and heaven will then decide how to act. You, in any case, should do nothing. Never seek revenge of any kind. Use only the weapons of love and light.[5]

Human beings are really quite extraordinary. They want love, they want peace, they want joy, they want wealth, and all they manage to attract is hostility, fighting, sorrow, and ruin. They do not know how to work. If you want something you should not wait until it is given to you; it is you who must begin giving. You want to be loved? Well, all you need to do is to begin loving. When you love you trigger forces of the same nature in the universe and these forces will one day come back to you. Even if you want to escape them you will not be able to... everyone will love you!

Let me give you another image. Imagine a vast park with all kinds of animals, birds, flowers, and fruit trees. But there is one problem with this park: it is surrounded by very high walls, which means you cannot get into it. Now all this wonderful fruit on the trees looks very appealing and you want some of it. What can you do? Suddenly you see some monkeys in the trees. And there is your solution. It just happens that you have some oranges with you, so you go close to the wall and start throwing them at the monkeys. And since monkeys are excellent mimics, they start picking fruit from the trees and throw it at you. All you have to do is pick it up. So, the secret is to throw oranges at the monkeys.

I can hear you thinking: 'What is he talking about? As though we could go to a wall round a park and throw oranges at monkeys.' But this is only an image... 'Oh, all right,' you say, 'if you are talking in images, then we understand.' Well, perhaps you still do not really understand, so let me explain. The universe that God has created is a vast park comprising all the riches human beings could desire. The walls are the obstacles that prevent you from reaching them; the monkeys are the creatures from the invisible world; and the oranges are the light and love you decide to project by means of your thoughts and feelings. And so, what happens? After a while the creatures of the invisible world will copy what you do and send you fruit – that is, blessings – a hundredfold. But you must realize that if you send them bitterness, hatred, anger these too will be sent back to you one day.

Notes

1 See *Life Force*, C.W. 5, Chap. 6: 'Thoughts are Living Entities'.
2 See *On the Art of Teaching from the Initiatic Point of View*, C.W. 29, Chap. 2: 'On Responsibility', Chap. 4 (2): 'On the Living of Knowledge'.
3 See *The True Meaning of Christ's Teaching*, Izvor 215, Chap. 7: 'Father, Forgive Them, For They Know Not What They Do'.
4 Ibid., Chap. 8: 'Unto Him that Smiteth Thee on the One Cheek ...'.
5 See *Love and Sexuality*, C.W. 15, Chap. 27: 'Our Only Weapons: Love and Light'.

IV

The law of affinity

What happens when you throw a ball against a wall? It comes back to you. It obeys the law of resonance, the backlash. As we have seen, this is a law that is applicable on both the spiritual and physical planes. Be it actions, feelings, or thoughts, one day they will have consequences for us in some way. All the more, because to that law we have to add another: the law of affinity. This means that, depending on the nature of your thoughts, feelings, and actions, they will trigger forces and currents of the same nature in the universe, which will make their way toward you in accordance with the law of affinity. It is you who, through your behaviour and your mental, emotional, and spiritual state, determine the nature of the elements and forces that are set in motion far away in the universe and which eventually make their way to you. This means that you can attract all you desire from the great cosmic reservoirs provided that, through your thoughts, feelings, and actions, you project elements of an identical nature to those you wish to receive.

Suppose we lay out on a table a number of tuning forks of various sizes, only two of which have prongs of the same length. If we make these forks vibrate, each will give a different sound. But when we take one of the two identical forks and

235

make it vibrate, the second one, without being touched, will respond to the vibrations of the first by emitting exactly the same sound. You are all familiar with this phenomenon, but what you do not know is that the same thing happens between human beings and everything that exists in the universe. If you endeavour to have only luminous and altruistic thoughts and pure and generous feelings, you will attract from space the entities and elements that have an affinity with your thoughts and feelings.[1] You 'speak' and you are 'heard'. In other words, you generate forces and they respond by making their way to you. You can exchange in this way with all the regions of space and you must know that it is precisely in such exchanges that God offers human beings the greatest opportunities for perfecting themselves. All you have to do is be in tune with those regions from which you wish to receive the benefits.

You ask: 'But how do we achieve this harmony? There are so many details to consider.' Well, you need not worry; it all happens naturally. If you cultivate love, self-denial, leniency, and generosity, the whole of your being will start to bring itself into harmony of its own accord, because you are working with forces that automatically harmonize everything within you. When someone has destroyed his nervous system, did he do so consciously, lucidly, and scientifically? Did he know exactly where and how he was going to disrupt things? No, but by introducing discordant thoughts and feelings into his being, he has ended by creating havoc. He did not need to know the exact location of all his nerve-centres to go out of his mind. Similarly, in order to tune your organism, you must work with pure and luminous thoughts and feelings, which will make all your spiritual centres vibrate in harmony, and then you will also be in harmony with the cosmic organism.

All the initiates who have studied the relationship between human beings and the universe have discovered an absolute correspondence between them. Just as each vibration seeks out a similar vibration with which to merge, all creatures, through their particular vibrations and wavelengths, are in contact with other beings, other entities, and other forces in the universe that have the same wavelengths and the same vibrations. So, through their thoughts, feelings, and actions human beings strike up an affinity with regions and entities that have the same wavelengths and attract them to themselves. But since most human beings do not know these truths, they do whatever seems to suit them at the time and are then surprised to find themselves in situations they never intended.

I have told you so often: we are like fish in the cosmic ocean. Fish live in the rivers, seas, and oceans and attract the elements that correspond to their nature in order to form their bodies – a particular size, a particular head (broad or elongated), a particular tail, a certain type of scales (shiny and colourful or dull and grey). And human beings, who are also immersed in the ocean of life, receive certain physical and psychic characteristics depending on the elements they have attracted to form their different bodies – physical, astral, mental, and so on. The universe is a huge reservoir, which the Creator has filled with all kinds of elements and it is up to us human beings to decide what we want to draw from it. Take a person who is severely disabled in all respects. His condition is the result of previous incarnations, in which, through ignorance or ill-will, he attracted negative entities and currents which now torment him and keep him bound hand and foot. Whereas others, in their previous incarnations, have attracted all the elements that now make them beautiful, intelligent, capable people whom everyone loves and admires. You can see how important it is to know this law of affinity and to set to work immediately to attract particles so luminous that everything will begin to improve within you.

It is a key that I am giving you today: by generating, through your thoughts and feelings, vibrations and emanations of greater intensity, which will travel far into space to seek out from among billions of elements those that correspond to them, you can become master of your own destiny once again.[2] Because once those around you sense that you have become more balanced, stronger, wiser, and more luminous, they will begin to look upon you differently and much will change in your life. As you see, everything in life is connected. But if you continue to ignore or neglect life's fundamental laws, you prevent the forces of nature and the luminous entities of the invisible world from giving you their support, and they will be forced to abandon you to your sad fate.

I do not deny that life is difficult and that every day you – we all – have all kinds of reasons to worry and be distressed. But instead of simply complaining and going round in circles, why not go to those who can help you? You will say: 'Where are they? Where can we find them?' Well, they are there; they are close by all the time, and we can address them and reach them through our thoughts thanks to the law of affinity. As soon as you know this law you are obliged to surpass yourself in order to touch the most sensitive, most subtle chords of your being and make them vibrate, in the knowledge that in space there are forces and entities that will respond.[3] If they do not respond it is because you do not know how to call them. To make them hear your voice you must begin by trying to have a good thought or a good feeling, or do something totally selfless. Then they will sense that you vibrate in perfect concord with them and will be obliged to come closer to give you their love, light, and peace. This law of affinity is one of the greatest laws of magic and it should govern your entire life.

It is your thoughts, feelings, and actions that determine the nature of the elements, forces, and beings that will be awakened somewhere in space and that will, sooner or later, reach you. So, every day, watch and analyze yourself and say: 'This particular thought or feeling has an affinity with elements and regions in space of a specific nature. What will happen to me if I accept it?' If you see that it is good, constructive, then go ahead; otherwise try to rid yourself of it.

Master Peter Deunov said one day: 'A sheep knows it is a sheep and seeks out other sheep. A wolf knows it is a wolf and seeks out other wolves. Human beings know they are human beings and seek out other human beings. Every being chooses its orientation depending on its species. And you, whom do you seek out? If you are light, you will seek out the light.' The greatest laws of creation are hidden in this simple concept that each creature is attracted to that which resembles it. This is how our future is determined; we all determine our own future by the ideal we choose. In the invisible, subtle world above, the process is triggered instantaneously, but it takes time before the effects become apparent on the physical plane. Every day, every hour, every minute, you are determining your future. If you choose the light, the die is cast: you are immediately on the path to eternal glory. And a moment later, if you choose darkness, the same thing happens: you are immediately on the path to hell.

You determine your future at each instant, but it takes centuries for the effects to become apparent on the physical plane. Although in reality nothing down here has changed, something has changed up above, something in the direction you are taking, as when a pointsman operates a lever to make the train change track. This is what human beings do every day. Sometimes a thousand or ten thousand times a day. One minute we are walking toward hell and the next we are on the way to heaven. Down here, on the physical plane, nothing has changed as yet, but every change in direction is recorded. If you want to maintain one direction so that it may continue to shape your life, you must keep a steady course and never stray from it. If you change direction at every moment the passing train will take you to a different region every time.

So, at every moment in their lives human beings determine their fate. This is not yet apparent on the outside, because it takes a long time for forms that have already become crystallized to change. But the laws are relentless and no one can alter them; God himself has breathed them into matter.

Very few people realize where they are going, what direction they are taking. And yet each one of us – whether consciously or not – has already got a ticket for a particular direction. So now, you must consciously get a ticket to the kingdom of God. It should not matter to you how long it will take to reach your destination. You will reach it, that is certain. Whether it takes a long time or a short time depends on the love and intensity with which you wish to arrive at your destination. If you wish it fervently and with unwavering faith, you will soon reach the kingdom of God. 'If you are light, you will seek out the light...'

The law of affinity is at the same time physical, chemical, magical, and spiritual, and can be expressed as follows: by uniting with what is perfect – perfect in intelligence, power, form, colour, and scent, perfect in beauty – human beings benefit from this perfection because they introduce it into themselves. It is an infallible law, and as soon as we know it we can no longer detach ourselves from this idea of perfection. And on this law true religion is based. Why did Jesus ask us to love God? Because by loving him we unite with his perfection and his splendour, and this splendour begins to establish itself within us. As long as we do not respect this law no one in heaven or on earth can help us. Who helped us previously? God himself? No. He does not even know what we are doing. It is this law that springs into action at the merest contact and finds itself obliged to come and give us support and encouragement.

I can speak of all these great laws because I have observed them in nature and verified them in myself. This is why you can now tell me anything you wish and I shall check it against what cosmic Intelligence has written in its great book. If I see it approves, I shall accept it, but if it shows me it contradicts all that is written in this book, I shall reject it.

Notes

1 See *Man, Master of his Destiny*, Izvor 202, Chap. 3: 'Evolution and Creation'.
2 See *Harmony and Health*, Izvor 225, Chap. 1 (2): 'Life Comes First'.
3 See *Creation: Artistic and Spiritual*, Izvor 223, Chap. 11: 'A Living Masterpiece'.

2

Reincarnation

I

The teaching of the Gospels

'Be perfect as your heavenly Father is perfect,' Jesus said, and one wonders how he could have given the crowds of people who followed him such a programme. Human beings have so many weaknesses, so many shortcomings. How could anyone imagine that having heard or read these words, they would be able to attain the perfection of their heavenly Father? Whatever they do, they will not succeed. Or at least not in a single lifetime. Human beings can become perfect, but only at the end of a long process of evolution during several incarnations. Through their efforts, their suffering, their growth in awareness they will one day attain perfection.

You will say: 'But that's impossible. The Gospels do not mention reincarnation anywhere and Jesus did not believe in reincarnation.' Well, think what you like, but if you read the Gospels carefully you will see that there are some passages that can only be understood in the light of reincarnation. If reincarnation is not implied, they remain incomprehensible.

Let us look, for instance, at some of the questions the disciples asked and the answers Jesus gave. One day Jesus asked his disciples: 'Who do people say that the Son of Man is?' What do you think this question could mean? Have you heard many people ask: *'Who do people say I am?'* Do you hear many people wonder what others say about who they are? They know who they are and do not ask questions about what others have to say about it. And look at what the disciples say: *'Some say John the Baptist, but others Elijah, and still others Jeremiah or one of the prophets.'* How can you say that someone is another person, one who died a long time ago, unless you are implying reincarnation?

Another time Jesus and his disciples met a man who was said to be blind from birth. The disciples ask: *'Rabbi, who sinned, this man or his parents, that he was born blind?'* If a disability is a punishment from heaven for a transgression, when could a man who was born blind have committed this transgression? In his mother's womb? What kind of sin could he have committed in his mother's womb? What kind of dishonesty could he have committed? Who could he have killed? Either the disciples' question is very stupid, or it implies a belief in a former life.

You will say: 'But Jesus' disciples were not educated men. They were said to be simple fishermen whom Jesus called as they were bringing in their nets. It would be normal for them to have asked some strange questions.' If their question had been stupid, Jesus would have told them so. The Gospels show that he did not hesitate to reprimand them in some cases. In this instance, however, not only does he not reprimand them, but he replies quite simply, as if it were a perfectly natural question: *'Neither this man nor his parents sinned...'* And this is also an important point. The disciples asked if it was because the parents had sinned that the son was born blind. Why this question? Because they had learned in the law of Moses that disabilities and trials are the consequence of transgressions, but that a person is often able to settle the debt of another. So, when you see people suffering, you cannot tell whether they are paying for their own mistakes or the mistakes of others – those of their parents in particular.

Given that all the trials people have to endure are the consequence of a transgression committed by them or by someone close to them, the disciples asked the question because they knew that a person cannot be born blind for no reason – or simply, as Christians imagine, because God wanted him to be blind. So, Jesus replied: *'Neither this man nor his parents sinned; he was born blind so that God's works might be revealed in him.'* In other words so that when Jesus passed by, he could heal him and the people would believe in him. This means that there are also beings who are willing to bear any kind of illness or disability in order to help humankind. The man who was blind from birth was one of these. He had come to earth with this disability so that those who witnessed when Jesus healed him would stop to think. What is more, St John, who recounts this incident, talks at length about the reactions of the Pharisees and how perplexed they were by this miracle.

Let me give you another example to substantiate my argument. Jesus was told that John the Baptist had just been imprisoned and the passage simply says: *'Now when Jesus heard that John had been arrested, he withdrew to Galilee.'* John the Baptist was later beheaded by order of Herod and some time later the disciples asked Jesus: *'Why, then, do the scribes say that Elijah must come first?'* And Jesus answers: *'Elijah is indeed coming and will restore all things; but I tell you that Elijah has already come, and they did not recognize him, but they did to him whatever they pleased.'* And the passage goes on to say: *'Then the disciples understood that he was speaking to them about John the Baptist.'* So the text clearly says that John the Baptist was the reincarnation of Elijah.

John the Baptist had in fact already been identified with Elijah at the beginning of the Gospel of St Luke, when an angel appeared to Zechariah and announced his wife would bear a son. The angel said: *'You will name him John... With the spirit and power of Elijah he will go before (God).'* Elijah had been a great prophet of Israël, but he was guilty of the death of four hundred and fifty prophets of Baal, having ordered that their throats be cut. He had not been punished for this fault when he was alive, indeed he had had an extraordinary death, since it is said that he had been taken up to heaven in a chariot of fire. But the law is the law, so he had to be punished in a subsequent incarnation. This is why, when he came back in the person of John the Baptist, he in turn had his throat cut.

Jesus stated this law of justice in the garden of Gethsemane when Peter drew his sword, and struck the slave of the high priest, cutting off his ear. Jesus said: *'Put your sword back into its place; for all who take the sword will perish by the sword.'* He knew who John the Baptist was and what fate awaited him. This is why he did nothing to save him, even though he was his cousin (Elizabeth, John's mother, was Mary's cousin). He said these wonderful words about him: *'Truly I tell you, among those born of women no one has arisen greater than John the Baptist,'* but he did not intervene, because justice had to follow its course. We can understand now why Jesus left the country when he was told of John the Baptist's imprisonment. He knew he could not save him.

Reincarnation is based on the law of justice. Every good deed must be rewarded and every fault must be punished, if not in this life then in the next. Jesus knew this law, but brought to it something new. In the Sermon on the Mount, he said repeatedly to the crowd: *'You have heard that it was said... But I say to you...'* Why does Jesus rectify the old Law? He explains this himself when he says, *'Do not think that I have come to abolish the law or the prophets; I have come not to abolish but to fulfil.'*

'To fulfil' means to replace Moses' law of justice with the law of love.[1] An eye for an eye, a tooth for a tooth. This sums up the law of justice, which in reality is simply a form of revenge, and which gives rise to endless consequences. A man commits murder. In his next incarnation the victim comes back to seek revenge and kills his murderer in his turn. But the first man will again seek revenge. And this can go on indefinitely. Jesus came to teach us how to break this cycle: *'You have heard that it was said, "An eye for an eye and a tooth for a tooth." But I say to you, Do not resist an evildoer. But if anyone strikes you on the right cheek, turn the other also; and if anyone wants to sue you and take your coat, give your cloak as well; ...You have heard that it was said, "You shall love your neighbour and hate your enemy." But I say to you, Love your enemies and pray for those who persecute you, so that you may be children of your Father in heaven.'*

By pressing home this concept of reincarnation – which is nothing more than an application of the law of cause and effect (known in India as the law of Karma) – the sages of the past sought to make people aware of the fact that everything they do will one day have repercussions for them. But Jesus went so far in his teaching of love that for anyone who is capable of applying it, knowledge of the laws of reincarnation become less necessary. Thanks to love – and by 'love' Jesus understood the total lack of self-interest that can lead to self-sacrifice[2] – it is possible for human beings to settle their past debts, rise above the consequences of faults committed in previous lives, and liberate themselves. In this way they do not need to return to earth to make amends for their faults, and if they do come back it is because they themselves choose to do so to help their fellow humans.

The philosophy of Christ is that of liberation through sacrifice. We cannot liberate ourselves with hatred, violence, malice, or cruelty. And if Jesus said: *'Love your enemies'*, it is because only love can put an end to old hostilities and thereby break your bonds and enable you to win your freedom.[3] Without love, the law will compel you to return to the same people, in the same conditions, and continue the same hostilities indefinitely.

The key to freedom is love. Only love can break the sequence of cause and effect, which obliges us to reincarnate in order to make amends for our faults. Intellect and will-power are vital to a person's evolution, but they cannot make them free, because they do not contain this element of generosity, selflessness, and sacrifice which compels them to surpass themselves. This element dwells in the heart... it is love. So Christianity does not have to insist on reincarnation, because it teaches sacrifice and only through sacrifice are we able to progress more rapidly and more efficiently along the path of evolution.

Now let this be quite clear; it is not because I talk to you about sacrifice that you should go and throw yourself into extraordinary ventures, which will lead to ruin, destroy your health or put your life at risk. You will not settle your karmic debts by behaving senselessly. If you truly seek to follow the teaching of sacrifice you can start with very simple things, which – as you will find out once you try – are not as easy as they seem. For instance, try to learn to give without expecting recompense or thanks, like the sun, which never stops giving without expecting anything in return. Human beings always expect something in return for what they give – praise or thanks at the very least – and everyone finds this quite normal.[4] But these are the rules of the earth, not of the sun. If you help someone, render him a service, stand up for him in front of others, train yourself not to expect any benefit from these actions, because this is how you will grow and become more noble.

You will say: 'But does that mean that the good we do will never be recognized?' No, it will be recognized, but you must not wait for that. In the short term you must find your reward within yourself. There is one law we should never doubt: we reap what we sow. If we do good, therefore, sooner or later we shall reap the benefits. But do not wait for them. Whatever good you can do, be it in deeds, words, feelings, or thoughts, do it, and then let time do its work. Even if you do not wish it, one day all this good will pursue you to reward you. There is nothing you can do about that... no use trying to hide.

To love human beings without ever expecting anything in return, to help and enlighten them – this is what we must learn to do naturally, just as the sun shines, as springs flow, as birds sing, as trees bear fruit.[5] It does not matter whether or not you are seen to be doing good, whether or not you are appreciated, this is work you must do. This is the true sacrifice taught by Jesus.

Notes

1 See *A New Dawn: Society and Politics in the Light of Initiatic Science* (Part 2), C.W. 26, Chap. 5: 'The Kingdom of God and His Righteousness'.
2 See *Life Force*, C.W. 5, Chap. 9: 'Sacrifice'.
3 See *The Seeds of Happiness*, Izvor 231, Chap. 18: 'Our Enemies are Good for Us'; - *A New Dawn: Society and Politics in the Light of Initiatic Science* (Part 2), C.W. 26, Chap. 2: 'The True Religion of Christ'.
4 See *The Seeds of Happiness*, Izvor 231, Chap. 16: 'Give Without Expecting Anything in Return'.
5 Ibid., Chap. 17: 'Love Without Asking to be Loved in Return'.

II

Making sense of fate

There is not much in religion – or even in life – that makes sense if you do not believe in reincarnation. If you ask a priest or a minister to explain why some people are blessed with all kinds of physical, intellectual, and moral qualities and succeed in everything they undertake, while others are born into conditions where they are condemned to be ill, impoverished, stupid, and delinquent, and where they experience only failure, they will tell you it is God's will. They may expound some complicated theories about predestination and grace, but that will not make things clearer for you; the inference will be that it is the will of God.

Now, before we analyze this response, let me tell you a little anecdote. One day Mullah Nashrudin[1] walked into an inn where a few villagers were gathered. He was carrying a bag full of walnuts. One of the villagers asked him: 'What have you got in the bag, Nastradine Hodja?' And he replied: 'Walnuts, and I'd like to give you all some.' 'How generous you are today, Nastradine Hodja!' They were all rather surprised because Nastradine Hodja was not in the habit of giving things away. 'Yes,' he insisted; 'I want to give you all some walnuts, but you will have to choose: I can distribute them either as God would do it or as people would do it. Which do you prefer?' And since everyone knows people are miserly, whereas God is rich and very generous, they asked for the walnuts to be distributed in God's way. 'Very well,' said Nastradine Hodja, and he began handing out the contents of his bag. To the first, he gave three walnuts; to the second he gave just one; he passed the third person without giving him anything; to the fourth he gave a handful; to the fifth two handfuls; to the sixth nothing, and to the last he gave all that was left in the bag. Then everyone exclaimed: 'But Nastradine Hodja, what has come over you? You said you would hand out the walnuts in God's way.' Nastradine Hodja replied: 'What are you complaining about? Have none of you ever noticed how God gives some people a little, others a lot, and yet others nothing at all? Well, that's what I did.'

So you see, something that human beings see as an injustice must be deemed just when it comes from God. How can we accept that? We have to admit, after all, that God is God. It is his will, it is magnificent and we have to accept it. But then how can he be angry when those he has deprived of every good quality commit a fault? Since he has denied them his blessing, why does he punish them? He who is all-powerful, could he not give them some goodness, honesty, intelligence, and wisdom? Not only is it his fault if they commit crimes – since he has given them nothing good – he then punishes them for their crimes. That is where it all starts to go wrong. God can do as he wishes, of course, no one can blame him for that, but then why is he not more consistent, more logical? He should at least show sinners some leniency. But no, instead he sends them to hell. And of course, once in hell, they are there for eternity – or so they say... Here again I feel something is not right. I ask myself: how long have they been sinning? A few decades. Well, then they should remain in hell for a few decades. No longer, and certainly not for eternity.

We really do need to use our reason... But no, we are not allowed to reason. Although the Church speaks of a God of love, a God of mercy and of grace, it has made him into a veritable monster of injustice and cruelty. And this we must accept without argument, because it is a crime to reason. But is it not a crime to present this image of God and cause human beings to live in incoherence and despair?

All kinds of doctrines have emerged during the course of the centuries and all they have done is add to the confusion around the issue of justice and grace. I do not wish to go into details here, but I would like to say this: at first glance it is difficult to reconcile the two notions of justice and of grace and to understand how they manifest. The truth is that no one deserves salvation, not even the best of us. If justice were always to be done, it would reduce us to dust. Only the grace of God saves us. But do not be misled into thinking that grace is an arbitrary manifestation of the Deity, who does only what suits him.

An example may help you understand better. Suppose a man has undertaken to build a house. After a while he finds he is short of funds and cannot finish the work. So he goes to a bank and asks for a loan. The bank – not being stupid – makes enquiries about his financial situation, because it wants to know whether he will be able to pay back the loan. If the information the bank receives is good, it will give him the money he needs. Well, to a certain extent you could say that grace acts in the same way. If grace visits a particular person, it is because it has made enquiries and found that this person has already done good work in previous incarnations. At the moment he is in difficulty, but because of what he has already achieved, he deserves to be helped, to have his task made easier. Grace is neither blind nor fickle, as we are tempted to believe, and if we want to receive it one day we have to work long and hard to earn it.[2]

As long as we refuse to accept reincarnation we shall never understand the laws of destiny. With reincarnation on the other hand, everything becomes clear; we begin to understand that God is truly the greatest master, the most noble, the most just, and if we are so impoverished and limited, it is our own fault, because we have been unable to make good use of all he bestowed on us at the outset. We have wanted to make costly experiences, and since God is generous and understanding, he has allowed us to do as we wished, saying: 'Of course they will suffer, they will fall down, but no matter. I shall continue to give them my riches and my love. They have numerous incarnations before them and one day they will find their way back to me.' So, God has left us free to do as we wish and now all the misfortunes we encounter are our own doing.

Why has the Church laid the entire responsibility of our fate at God's door? It has done away with the belief in reincarnation thinking all it had to do was brandish the threat of hell to induce human beings to improve more quickly. But not only have people not improved, but they have become ignorant. This is why we need to get back to the belief in reincarnation, otherwise God seems a monster and human existence becomes senseless. Many Christians would be willing to accept the notion of reincarnation, but they are waiting for the Church to make it official. When will this be? God knows! I have often talked about this with members of the clergy and have found that many believe in reincarnation, but they are afraid to say so because they want to avoid problems with their superiors.

As long as we do not acknowledge reincarnation we cannot really understand our present situation or the events that shape our lives, and we cannot know how to work for a future life. If we do not know the truth, how can we lay out a path for ourselves, how can we find our way? As long as the clergy does not enlighten the faithful about the law of cause and effect, which continues to act from one life to the next, all their sermons and moralizing will serve very little. How many people still believe they will burn in hell for eternity for their wrongdoing? Fewer and fewer. And since they now know that the Church tried to exploit their credulity and frighten them with all this, it has ended by becoming a joke.

Of course, there are many people who do not believe in reincarnation but who naturally possess great moral qualities. This simply means they have worked in previous incarnations to acquire them. But there is no absolute certainty that this will last. In certain circumstances instincts such as fear, desire, the desire for revenge, and so on, may gain the upper hand and then they will not show such goodness and honesty. In this case, it would mean that their morality was not founded on a solid base, in other words, on a knowledge of the laws.

Now once again, let us be quite clear on this. To accept the notion of reincarnation is truly useful only insofar as it teaches us that our fate is governed by laws of mathematical precision. Just as the way we are living now is the result of the way we lived in the past, so our future depends on the direction we give our life now. This is why I tell you that it serves very little purpose to go and see a clairvoyant to find out about your previous lives. Some people have repeated to me what a clairvoyant had told them, and I was amazed. I learned that one kind, gentle, humble man who would not have hurt a fly, had been Napoleon in his former life. What a rapid transformation! And another, who was intellectually very limited, had been Shakespeare. Well, I have no objection, but it seems somewhat unlikely. And then there have been people who have come to me claiming to be reincarnations of saints, geniuses, kings, queens, pharaohs, or initiates.

I am not saying you should never believe any of this. But you cannot really know what you are dealing with if you are unable to verify these things – and would that really be useful? What use are revelations about your past lives? You gain nothing from them. Especially if the person you consult overwhelms you with phantasmagoria – as some do, in the desire to have you eating out of their hand – and this can only lead to confusion and distract you from your true work. The tendency we see more and more, now that the concept of reincarnation is beginning to gain ground within Christianity, is not at all good. Belief in reincarnation should not serve to tell yourself or others cock-and-bull stories, but only to make you aware that laws do exist.[3]

As soon as you acknowledge the law of reincarnation you begin to understand that every event in your life has its reason, because everything has a cause, distant or less distant. This understanding will of course affect your feelings and emotions, because once you understand that everything has a meaning, you will no longer rebel against heaven – the worst possible reaction – and you will no longer try to resolve your problems by dishonest or violent means. Once you realize that all your misfortunes are the result of past transgressions, you will begin to accept them, stop blaming others for them, and no longer seek to avenge yourself. Belief in reincarnation, therefore, will urge you to strengthen your will; you will try to avoid doing anything reprehensible – for which you know you would have to suffer – and put all your efforts into building a luminous future.

If people have such difficulty in finding a meaning in life, be it theirs or that of others, it is because they think of their present life as detached, cut off from the past and the future. So, of course, many things remain beyond their comprehension.

When, for instance, you read about the lives of certain prophets, saints, or initiates, you could say: 'These were magnificent people and still they suffered, they were martyred. How can this be? They surely did not deserve such treatment.' Well, they did, but the causes of their trials must be sought in an earlier life. Even those who have succeeded in re-establishing divine order within themselves in one incarnation have not necessarily paid off all their past debts. They now have to pay them – and pay them to the last penny.

As for you, who follow a spiritual teaching, you too may be subjected to trials. You have chosen the path of goodness and light, you have decided to live in accordance with the divine laws, but that does not mean your life will be transformed and you will be sheltered from everything. You need to have settled all your past debts before reaching the point where you suffer no more misfortune. If you are still burdened by debts, you will have to pay them, whatever your current life may be. There is no escaping that. You will be free only when you have honestly acquitted these debts. So this is clear: you are following a divine teaching, you live in the light, you do only good from this point onwards, that is understood, but remember that all this will produce results only in the future, not right now. At present, knowing these laws allows you to understand the reason for your current circumstances and gives you the means to improve them in the future.[4] When you are up against problems, therefore, do not rebel, and do not let them destroy you either. Accept them and say: 'Lord God, now I understand; if I have trials to overcome it means I am liberating myself, and that is very good. I will stop rebelling and asking you to spare me.'

You will say: 'But Jesus was crucified; did he also have karmic debts to pay?' No, his case is totally different and here, in fact, we touch upon the fundamental question of sacrifice. There are human beings who, in order to help their fellow-beings, accept to sacrifice their life and bear great suffering although they have no more debts to pay off. But these are rare exceptions. If you want to evolve, do not start imagining you are one of these exceptions, but pursue your work in the knowledge that you will be free only when you have made reparation for all your faults.

Many people imagine that freedom is all about doing what they please. If their desires do not lead them to break the divine rules, then yes, they will become free. If not, they will become increasingly enslaved. Since we are all children of God we have a certain degree of freedom and we can use it to do what is good as well as what is wrong. But only those who endeavour to do the will of God will one day know true freedom.[5] Freedom is in the spirit. As soon as human beings begin to use their consciousness and their intelligence to work to control their instinctive tendencies, to purify them and add a spiritual element to them, they will gain their freedom. To win freedom is a long-term undertaking, but every day you can get closer to your goal.

Imagine you are taking a trip on a cruise-liner. You have no choice but to follow the itinerary and visit the scheduled ports of call. But on the ship itself you are free: you can come and go as you please, go up on deck, admire the view, go down to your cabin and read, play chess, watch a film, or chat whilst you relax in a deckchair. You can also squabble with your travelling companions, try to seduce them, rob them of their possessions, and so on. But the details are not important. I am using this image of a cruise-ship merely to illustrate that on board this ship on which you have decided to travel, you enjoy a certain degree of freedom. Well, fate could be compared to a cruise-ship on which you are travelling. There are some things in life that are pre-determined, such as the country and the family into which you are born, your physical body, your temperament, and so on. But you also have a mind, a heart, and a will and they allow you to utilize the conditions you have been given in your own particular way. So, if you wish to have better conditions in a future incarnation, try to start work on yourself here and now so as to deserve those conditions.

In the meantime, be aware that you also have the ability to overcome the obstacles you must face. Here, in this incarnation, your freedom begins with your decision to accept the trials God sends you. He has sent you these trials because you deserve them and their purpose is to make you reflect so that you understand a number of truths you had not yet understood. If you do this, heaven, which is watching you, will tone down the trials you face, not outwardly – because these trials have to be overcome, these events lived through – but inwardly, in other words you will not experience them in the same way.

Let us say for instance that it is written in your destiny that you will have an accident. The accident happens and you are immobile for some time. It is then up to you to decide how to use this time. You can spend it reading, thinking, listening to music; you can start learning a new language or you can spend your days watching rubbish on television, complaining, and rebelling against your fate. You are not free to choose events, but you are free to live these events intelligently or stupidly. Once you have understood this, you will have progressed a long way on the path of evolution.

The events in our lives are predetermined. What is not predetermined is our response, the way we choose to live these events. Our freedom lies in the inner attitude we choose to adopt toward them. Those who never cease to complain or rebel against fate not only do nothing to change events, but they also deepen their misfortune. Whereas if you try to overcome your discouragement in the face of a major loss, not only will your sorrow be eased, but by adopting this approach you will be working for your next incarnation, you will be accumulating the purest and strongest materials with which to build your future existence.

Never forget that it is not events that count for most in your life but your attitude toward them. And this rule applies not only to unhappy events, but to happy ones as well.[6] If you do not know how to welcome good fortune, if you show yourself to be careless, selfish, ungrateful, if you do not know how to make your good fortune aid your evolution and that of others, what should have been gold will be reduced to ashes, and these ashes will not make good building material for your future incarnation. So you see, do not let yourself become concerned with happy or unhappy events, with successes or failures; your concern should be with yourself and the way in which you live these events, successes and failures.

Notes

1 Mullah Nashrudin is a popular figure in the Islamic tradition.
2 See *Le grain de sénevé*, Œuvres Complètes, t. 4, chap. III : «Que celui qui est sur le toit...» p. 46-51.
3 See *The Mysteries of Fire and Water*, Izvor 232, Chap. 11: 'The Cycle of Water: Reincarnation'.
4 See *Freedom, the Spirit Triumphant,* Izvor 211, Chap. 3: 'Fate and Freedom'.
5 Ibid., Chap. 5: 'Sharing in the Freedom of God'; Chap. 6: 'True Freedom: a Consecration of Self'.
6 See *Youth: Creators of the Future*, Izvor 233, Chap. 8: 'Learning to Handle Success and Failure'.

III

We create our own future

Some people consult clairvoyants to find out what their future holds. Well, let me tell you there is no need to do this, because it is very easy to know what your future has in store.[1] You may of course not be able to guess what your occupation, your encounters, your financial gains or losses, your illnesses, accidents, and successes will be, but all that matters very little. What is very easy to foresee is the essential, and that is whether you will make progress on the path of evolution, whether you will be free, whether you will live in peace and light. If you love everything that is great, noble, just, and beautiful, and if you work with all your heart, all your mind, and all your will to achieve it, then your future is already mapped out, and one day you will live in conditions that correspond to your aspirations. This – and only this – is what is important to know about your future. All the rest – possessions, glory, relationships, even health – is all secondary. And it is secondary because it is transient; it can be given to you and then taken away again. When you leave this earth, all that will truly remain with you is what corresponds to the aspirations of your soul and spirit.

Our present is the result of our past. This is why we have almost no power over it. It is the effect, the logical consequence of that past. The thoughts, feelings, and desires we had in previous incarnations have triggered in the universe forces and powers of the same nature and they in turn have determined our qualities, our weaknesses, and the events in our present life. This is why it is virtually impossible to change during this incarnation that which has been determined by our past. The only thing that remains in our power, is to prepare the future. Most people have still not understood this. They have endless discussions about whether man is free or not, some claiming that he is and others that he is not. In fact, they are asking the wrong question. Freedom is not a condition given or withheld forevermore. As far as the present is concerned, our freedom is very limited, because the present is the consequence of a past which we cannot change. The past has to be lived out and endured, accepted. For the future, on the other hand we are free, we can create the future we want.

This is the most important truth to know in order to understand the direction our work should take. Otherwise what happens? Not realizing you can improve your situation for the future, you submit to the present, letting yourself slide into increasingly deplorable behaviour, with the result that in your next incarnation you will be even more limited and enslaved.

You can begin to prepare your future today. You can choose the best orientation through your aspirations, thoughts, prayers, and imagination, in order one day to manifest as beings of peace, goodness, and light.[2] But make sure that once you have chosen your orientation, you do not stray from it. Learn to channel your energies and direct them towards this luminous world of harmony and love. Even if some clouds appear from time to time they will not last. Insofar as you maintain the right orientation inwardly, the day will come when you stray no more. This is what is important, and I only concern myself with what is important. For the rest you can go and see all the clairvoyants you like, but remember they will never touch upon the essential.

Whatever happens, continue to build your future. Do not allow yourselves to become discouraged. Your suffering and trials will soon seem like waves of a storm above which you are gliding. If you begin to feel crushed by the trials you face, it is because you have not been able to maintain a clear view of your luminous future. Your outlook has become blocked, but it is blocked because you yourself have blocked it, and it is now up to you to open the window to see the sun.

Many will say, of course, that they are working for the future, for their future and that of their children. And I know; they put money in the bank, they buy shares, they take out life insurance, and so on, and this is how they think they are working for the future. But what do they call the future? The future is not merely the thirty, forty, or fifty years they may have left on this earth, nor even the lifetimes of their children and grand-children. The future, the real future, is their future incarnations, and we must all prepare our future incarnations by practising qualities and virtues.

Far too many of you continue to be obsessed by material acquisitions for yourselves and for your children. Of course you need to provide for yourselves and your families; you must have the necessities of life. But why waste your time and energies chasing after all the other things you do not really need? Life is so short. For how many years will you be able to enjoy these acquisitions? Not only can you not take them with you to the next world, but you will not even remember you owned a mansion, or held the post of managing director, or minister, or president. Everything is erased so quickly.

This future that human beings claim to be working for is so near it will soon be the present, and a present that will soon be erased in turn. So they are working in a void... for nothing. Indeed, all the events they are due to experience in this life really belong to the present. The future is something else, and you do not yet truly know what it is. The future I speak of is eternity, infinity, and this is what we have the power to create. We do not have the power to erase the past or to change the present, but we do have the power to create our future. God has given us this power. Through thought, desire, and will we can do everything. So long as we are not aware of this power we do very little to improve our situation. Sometimes, in fact, we only manage to make it worse.

I know that, hearing me speak like this, some of you will think: 'But what planet does he think he is living on? Life is so complicated, so difficult with all its worries, trials, illnesses, and so on. And he talks of a future of perfection and splendour. He is living with his head in the clouds. Does he really believe he can convince us with such an unrealistic philosophy?' Well, let me tell you, I know as well and even better than you what you call the realities of life – deprivation, adversity, hostility, infamy – but I have never allowed myself to dwell on this reality, because I know that it is a minor and insignificant aspect, a shadow of true reality.

Try to set aside a few minutes each day to thinking about creating your future, knowing you have the same power over this future as God himself. There is little you can do to influence the present, but when it comes to the future you are all-powerful, because you are all sons and daughters of God. All the great masters, all the great initiates teach us that a human being is a spirit, a flame that has sprung, like the earth itself, from the Eternal God. We have a long way to go, and even if we become numbed and cold, and sink into darkness along the way, we are predestined to return to the regions we came from.

So never forget that your future is to become like God himself. If you forget this wisdom, this light, do not be surprised to find yourself beset with disappointment, bitterness, and despair. And then, of course, you will begin to give doctors and psychiatrists some work to do. So many people find themselves at the edge of the abyss. They are said to be suffering from depression, from nervous debility, neurosis – the list of medical conditions is endless. But in reality they all suffer from the same malady. They have forgotten the true nature of humankind, our divine essence and our ultimate predestination: our return to the Eternal Father. So link yourself to the sun as you think about your luminous future.[3]

People often wonder what life on earth will be like in ten, fifteen, or a hundred years time. Of course this is important, but what is most important is to know that one day you will shine like the sun, that your presence will fill the atmosphere, that the scent of your soul will fill the air, and that symphonies will be heard wherever you go, because all your cells will sing. Imagine this magnificent future for at least a few minutes every day and suddenly you will find courage and the ability to smile will come back to you.

Some of you will think: 'But he is making fun of us! We are so feeble and handicapped. What kind of glorious future can we dream of?' Let me tell you straight away that this kind of statement shows you are not reasoning correctly. It is not those who are happy and fulfilled who need to wish and imagine, but those who are unhappy, and they are capable of doing so a hundred times more powerfully than the others. So, if you feel disadvantaged, now is the time to create through thought a future of riches and splendour.

Think for a moment: what happens when you know you are about to inherit a great sum of money or are about to take a fantastic trip? The anticipation of what you will do with the money or what you will see and do on your trip gives you immense joy. So can you not do the same with something far more important than money and trips, in other words with your divine future? It will still be imagination, of course, but this imagining does not remain ineffectual, because the thoughts and feelings that bring to life this divine future within you actually influence and transform your destiny.

Now, listen carefully to what I am saying: you must use all the years you have left on this earth to prepare your future incarnation by asking for the best. In this way you will be launching plans that will crystallize in the future. The present crystallization will resist and refuse to change, but that is normal, for it cannot be replaced until it completely worn out. But when you return to earth, all the good you have created will materialize in a new structure, an⸱ ʰis structure will also be strong and able to withstand the forces of destruction. I repeat: the work we do today cannot bring great changes for this incarnation, only for the next. So do not be discouraged if you do not see the results of your efforts yet. Wait. Be patient. In a future incarnation, once the present form has disappeared, you will see the new form, the one you have worked on, and you will be amazed by its splendour.

You are heirs to heaven and earth. Your heritage is there, but as you are still too young you cannot take possession of it. Why despair and become discouraged because you have to wait a little longer? 'Yes,' I hear you say, 'but in the meantime my life is miserable, I work my fingers to the bone, no one has any respect for me, they even insult me.' Yes, but that is necessary. For educational reasons, the King your Father has sent you to work out a short apprenticeship. Yes, because education exists also in the kingdom of God. In fact, this is true education. God says: 'When this child's reign begins, he will have far-reaching powers over millions of creatures, but what will happen if he has not first developed goodness, patience, generosity, and courage? He will be malicious, lazy, capricious, and cowardly.

He will behave like a despot, imagining that everyone is there merely to serve him. So I shall let him have his kingdom only when he has proved that he will not abuse his power and wealth. Not before.'

Hope for everything then, but in the meantime, make sure you work.[4] Hope shapes and realizes the future on the subtle planes because it is a magical force. Let me assure you, I know your situation, and if I give you these methods, it is not because I want to make fun of you, but because I want to be of use to you; I want to give you something worthwhile. Do with it as you see fit. I simply tell you what is best for you and it is then up to you to choose.

It is written in the Book of Genesis that humankind was created in the image of God, but when we talk of the sublime future that awaits them very few people take this seriously. Yet, if we really believe that humankind was created in the image of God we must be logical and accept all the implications. And one of these implications is precisely this, that human beings are destined for a divine, sublime future. We have no right to deny half of this truth, for what other future could there be for the image of God?

Notes

1 See *Looking into the Invisible – Intuition, Clairvoyance, Dreams*, Izvor 228, Chap. 5: 'Should We Consult Clairvoyants?'.
2 See *Creation: Artistic and Spiritual*, Izvor 223, Chap. 3: 'The Work of the Imagination'; - *The Powers of Thought*, Izvor 224, Chap. 2: 'Thinking the Future'; Chap. 5: 'How Thought Materializes on the Physical Plane'; Chap. 11: 'Creative Prayer'.
3 See *La pédagogie initiatique*, Œuvres Complètes, t. 28, chap. X : «Le modèle solaire».
4 See *'In Spirit and in Truth'*, Izvor 235, Chap. 17: 'The Kingdom of God is Within'.

Part V

Answers
to the question
of evil

Part I - Answers to the question of evil

1

God transcends
good and evil

Among all the questions human beings reflect upon, there is one that haunts and torments them, and to which they have great difficulty finding a satisfactory answer. It is the question of evil: what is evil and why does it exist? The truth is that this question will remain insoluble as long as they persist in thinking of evil as independent of and cut off from good.

A passage of the *Zohar* describes God as a very beautiful, very noble head with a beard and long white hair. This white head is reflected in an expanse of water, and the reflection emerges as a black head with an ugly scowl. What does this image teach us? That what we call evil – or the devil – is merely the reflection of God in matter, the shadow God casts in matter. When certain religions present the devil as the adversary of God, an adversary against which he must continually do battle, they are mistaken. God does not combat the devil; that would mean that he combats himself.

How can religions, which claim to be monotheistic, hold theories and exhibit attitudes that contradict the very basis on which they are founded? They say that God has an enemy, the devil, who is as powerful as he, as if God were not the one and only Lord. If there is an entity capable of opposing God, who created it? Another, more powerful God? What kind of religions

The symbol of Solomon
(From Eliphas Levi: *Dogma and Ritual of High Magic)*

can these be whose God has an enemy he is unable to bring down? A God who needs human beings, weak and feeble as they are, to come to his assistance... is this what we think of the greatness and omnipotence of God? We are degrading God if we deem him incapable of defeating an adversary. Have you considered that? The result of this misconception is, of course, that many people attribute to the devil powers that surpass those of God. If someone exhibits exceptional gifts or performs miracles, they believe it is the devil who makes that possible, not God. All God does, as far as they can see, is to keep human beings in a state of weakness and mediocrity. It comes as no surprise, therefore, that some men and women have ended by signing pacts with Satan. It is only logical. Why serve an incapable, powerless God, when knowledge, gifts, and powers

273

come from his adversary, the devil? This is what happens when the keys to true knowledge are lost.

Even today there are fanatics who, obsessed by the idea of the devil, imagine they see this adversary of God continuously trying to edge his way into human beings' lives in one shape or another. So, convinced that God has given them the mission to act as his soldiers, they undertake to fight all these 'enemies', these hellhounds, these sons of the devil, and try tirelessly to destroy them and call down eternal damnation upon them. But this is criminal behaviour! Such ignoramuses should learn there is no such thing as eternal damnation... not at least as they understand it.

In fact, what is damnation? People say it is 'to lose one's soul'. When a human being delights in evil, when he persists in working consciously against God's plans, against the light, he burdens himself so much and becomes so dark that in the end his human soul separates from his divine soul. The divine soul, in the form of a spark, leaves him and returns to the ocean of primeval light, and once the human soul is deprived of this spark, it disintegrates and disappears. This is true death. Otherwise, whatever the errors and transgressions committed, the human soul (what we call 'soul' is in fact made up of several souls)[1] is always able to purify itself thanks to the divine soul, to which it is connected and which always seeks to carry it along toward the light.

As for those who persecute others under the pretext of taking God's side, in fact they make themselves auxiliaries to the devil and constantly reinforce him. Why go to war against the devil? As I have said before, the devil is the servant of God. He has a role to play. God uses him to spur human beings on, to urge them forward. God does not need human beings to help him fight the devil. God manages quite well by himself, because in fact he uses him.

You know the Book of Job in the Old Testament; it begins with a conversation between God and Satan: *'One day the heavenly beings came to present themselves before the Lord, and Satan also came among them.'* Just imagine: Satan attended this gathering in person; he stood among the sons of God. He could have been behind them or next to them, but no, he stands among them, as if he occupied the same rank as the spirits of light. What is more, God speaks to him alone – and what a conversation they have! *'The Lord said to Satan, "Where have you come from?" Satan answered the Lord, "From going to and fro on the earth, and from walking up and down on it." The Lord said to Satan, "Have you considered my servant Job? There is no one like him on the earth, a blameless and upright man who fears God and turns away from evil." Then Satan answered the Lord, "Does Job fear God for nothing? Have you not put a fence around him and his house and all that he has, on every side? You have blessed the work of his hands, and his possessions have increased in the land. But stretch out your hand now, and touch all that he has, and he will curse you to your face." The Lord said to Satan, "Very well, all that he has is in your power; only do not stretch out your hand against him!"'*.

And you all know how the rest of the story went. All kinds of misfortunes befell Job. He lost all he had, including his children, his herds, and his houses. But he did not rebel. Some time later the heavenly beings gathered again, and the Lord said to Satan: *'... He still persists in his integrity.'* Then Satan answered the Lord: *'Skin for skin! All that people have they will give to save their lives. But stretch out your hand now and touch his bone and his flesh, and he will curse you to your face.'* And the Lord said to Satan: *'Very well, he is in your power; only spare his life.'* And so Job was subjected to great suffering, abandoned by everyone, sitting among the ashes, his body covered in sores. But he did not revolt, he kept his integrity. In the end God was so touched by his faithfulness, he restored everything to him: his sons and daughters, his houses, his cattle, his wealth, his health, indeed he blessed him with more than he had in the beginning. And all his friends who had mocked and criticized him came to pay their respects.

It is interesting to note that God, while sanctioning Satan's torment of Job, imposed certain conditions. The first time Satan was not allowed to touch Job's person, so he took away his herds, his servants, and his children. The second time, Satan received permission to cover Job's body in sores, but he had to spare his life. And each time Satan obeyed and did not torment Job more than had been agreed with God, which proves that what we call devils or evil spirits do not oppose God but respect his will. All those entities that descend among human beings to put them to the test, to lead them into temptation and make them suffer are merely employees, assistants, who are there to teach them a lesson, to make them evolve.

This account at the beginning of the Book of Job obliges us to think. Goethe used the idea in *Faust*, which starts with a conversation between God and Mephistopheles about Faust.

We shall never understand the issue of evil clearly as long as we do not accept that the devil is in fact a servant of God. Imagine this: a little girl is keeping watch over some cows near her village in the country. She sits and knits or reads while her big dog lies faithfully by her side, ready to do what she asks of him. The cows are peacefully grazing and all is well. Until, that is, one of the cows ambles into the neighbour's field. That is bad news; there are bound to be problems. So the little girl sends her dog off, saying: 'Go on, bite her!' Being an obedient creature, the dog gets up and rushes, barking, toward the cow to nip her leg. Of course the cow, who is afraid of the dog, immediately comes back to her master's field, and the dog, delighted with its achievement, lies down again beside the little girl. A while later another cow wanders off, and once again the girl sends her dog, because of course the cows are not allowed to break the rules and leave their own field, even if the grass in the neighbour's field looks more appetizing. If they stray, the dog is sent after them.

And the same goes for this gentleman the devil. When human beings begin to break the rules, they meet the same fate as the cows that stray into the neighbour's field. In other words the devil goes after them, because he is under orders to chase them and bring them back into the God's pastures. Once back on the right path, they are no longer pursued; the dog is still there but it is not biting them any longer. We have to understand that the devils and all the spirits of hell are God's servants who have been charged with 'watching over' human beings. Did you think it was the angels who put us to the test and pursued us? No, they have other matters to keep them busy.

Like Job, all sages, saints, and prophets have been tormented by evil spirits, sent to tempt them, to put them to the test, and make them stronger as a result of these trials. These spirits are servants. They go where they are sent. They obey orders, nothing more. They do not do as they please, because they are not allowed to. So why should God decide to annihilate them? They are in his service. Do you massacre your servants?

The first monotheistic religion was the Jewish religion. Moses wanted to form a people that knew this truth of one God. Even the initiations of some polytheistic religions taught the existence of only one God. The other gods were simply personifications of the forces of nature. If God is not unique, everything becomes senseless and falls apart. Nothing can be explained if we do not accept this oneness.

Nowhere is the number Two separated from the number One.[2] Every object, every being has two extremities, two poles, but the object or being is still one. The number One is the first and only number. It is because you have not yet understood this that you believe One and Two exist separately, in other words that God and the devil exist as two opposing entities of equal strength. No, this is false. The devil does not exist separately in opposition to God. The devil is an aspect of God's oneness. He is far off somewhere deep in the Whole, but he is part of it, he remains bound to it. It is impossible to separate from God, from the number One.[3]

All those who have not been content to abide by the number One, which represents God himself, have found the devil who came to torment them. In certain eras of Christianity there were so many paintings and sculptures depicting the devil and the sufferings of the damned in hell that people forgot about God. Of course, what did the poor 'Good God' represent compared with the devil who was so powerful and drew so many creatures into the flames of hell? What an aberration, what a fall! The greatest mistake human beings can make is to abandon the number One. Because if you think of the number One, everything that is negative and hostile disappears, including the devil: only God remains.

You will say: 'But if God is omnipotent, why does he not, despite our supplications, draw us out of our misfortune and suffering?' Because supplications are not enough. Human beings must first get all those wrong ideas out of their heads because they form a screen between them and God which prevents him from helping them. As long as they continue to maintain these ideas, God will seem remote, inaccessible, and deaf. The devil on the other hand, seems very near. Ask people and you will see that they think this: 'This God we have been praying to for so long, where is he? He hears nothing. Is he asleep? The devil on the other hand, is wide awake, he is there straight away.' This is true, but the reason is that human beings have themselves put this distance, created this chasm between them and God. In reality no other being is as close to us and loves us as much as God does, and no other being wants to help us as much as he does. But we must rid ourselves of all that prevents this love from reaching us.

The sun causes the planets to move and produces upheavals in the universe simply by changing the currents it emits, but it is powerless in front of a window where the curtains are drawn. If you have closed your curtains you can plead as much as you like: 'Come on in, my dear sun, come in, shine your light on me, you are so beautiful.' The sun will say: 'I can't. You must open the curtains first.' And you expect God to open the curtains for you? Well, let me tell you – at the risk of being thought sacrilegeous: 'God can do everything, but he is powerless in front of your closed curtains. It is up to you to open them.'

God has no adversaries. It is impossible for him to have any. Everything bows before him, everything obeys him, for he is the Creator. The devil does not exist as a separate entity who opposes God as his equal. People who claim the devil has appeared to them have imagined it. Just as there are spirits of light, there are spirits of darkness, and it is this collectivity of dark spirits that is referred to as the devil. The white head and its dark reflection in fact represent two worlds, both inhabited. But the devil is not a single entity separate from and opposed to God. He is a collective force, fed and strengthened by the negative thoughts, feelings, and actions of human beings. One could go so far as to say that the devil is a fabrication of human beings who have not understood the question of good and evil.

The devil can also be said to be a part of human beings themselves, more specifically their lower self. How did this come about? Well, over the course of their incarnations people have never ceased feeding this part of them through their weaknesses and vices, and in doing so they obstruct the path to heaven. However, human beings also possess a luminous entity, their higher self, which they have nourished through their thoughts, feelings, and actions inspired by goodness, love, and sacrifice.[4] If human beings made the effort to bring order into their inner life, what they call the devil would disappear. All that would remain would be the two antagonistic forces with which they must learn to work, just as God works with both the powers of darkness and the forces of light. God transcends good and evil. Is this new to you? Yes, good and evil are subject to a higher authority. They are two currents attached to the Throne of God.

In the Sephirothic Tree the Throne of God is symbolized by the sephirah Kether. The force that reigns in the sephirah Kether governs the universe with the help of two opposing currents – emissive and receptive, positive and negative – which we call good and evil. So good and evil are like its two hands. And sometimes – why not? – one hand strikes the other. The origin of what unites these opposing forces is on high, and this is why the question of good and evil can never be resolved on the physical plane.

Let me give you another image. When people in the old days wanted to draw water from a well, a large horizontal wheel was often used to which oxen, horses or even men were harnessed. To an onlooker it would appear that some were going one way and the others the other way, and one might conclude that they were walking in two opposite directions. If, however, you could observe the scene from above, you could clearly see that in fact they were all walking in the same direction and were all engaged in the same work.

This example helps us understand that good and evil, which appear to work against each other, are in reality two forces harnessed to the same task. But because we do not see them from above, that is, from the spiritual point of view, we think they are two opposing forces. If you look at facts and events from below, in other words from the level at which they occur, you come to the wrong conclusion. If, however, you try to elevate yourself and look at them from the viewpoint of wisdom, of the spirit, you will see a circle, a wheel, and will understand that good and evil are two forces harnessed together to make the wheel of life turn.

If these two, seemingly opposing currents, are in reality working toward the same goal, it is because they are connected at the centre. And in the universe this centre is God, the third entity which is above good and evil.[5] Our task, therefore, is to rise to this third entity, which uses the two others to achieve a goal that neither knows. Good does not know everything, neither, of course, does evil. The one who knows everything is he who transcends good and evil: God. It is to him we must turn saying: 'Lord, you who have created so many things, so vast and so deep, look at me now. I am lost among them all. My intelligence is too limited for me to see clearly. Send me your angels to tell me how to understand and to act.' When we unite with the Creator of the universe, with the eternal Principle, our consciousness migrates and moves from the region of darkness where suffering, anguish, and terror dwell, and goes to unite with the Centre, the creative Principle, Creator of all things. And since he is their Creator, he knows the role of all elements, all forces, all creatures, and he enlightens us. We are incapable of knowing, but he who transcends good and evil, can know everything, so it is to him we must turn for help.

When you have recourse to God, you are uniting with a third entity. Why does religion never mention this third entity? Religion always presents good as equivalent to God. No, good, like evil, is the servant of God. Because we think we know something about good, we claim to know God. But God is more than good. I tell you, God is above and beyond good and evil. Just as mental energy and sexual energy are the polarization of one and the same force, good and evil are also the polarization of one and the same force. You will ask: 'What are you saying? How can mental energy and sexual energy be one and the same force? Is the force that drives a brute to take advantage of a woman and abuse her the same as that which inspires the highest feats of the mind?' Yes.[6] And if you tell me that this upsets you, let me tell you that God did not arrange things to suit us. He made things as they are to make us work.

I realize how difficult it is for you to understand and accept this, because it turns everything you know about good and evil upside down. It seems these notions are incrusted in your very flesh and they are impossible to uproot. But as long as you do not change your ideas, you will continue to feel powerless in the face of evil. Good alone is not enough. Since it has so far failed to resolve the problem of evil, since it is continually battling against evil without ever triumphing over it, it means that it is not enough. But neither has evil succeeded in defeating good. It burns it, persecutes it and massacres it, but good is constantly reborn, constrantly grows and spreads everywhere, because it too is tenacious. Tenacious, yes, but not omnipotent!

So we must stop identifying good with God. Since good is unable to overcome evil, it means that it is not God himself, only half of him, and evil is the other half. Good and evil are brother and sister, if you like, but they are not the father. And it is to the father we must turn, because it is he who commands the son and the daughter, or if you prefer, the two brothers. To turn to the Father is to become a servant of God and not just a servant of good. We must therefore go higher in order to serve God, who governs good and evil. This is where the true sanctuary lies.

Of course, up above there is no evil, and insofar as good can mean perfection, one could say that to be the servant of good is to be the servant of God. But good as we understand it intellectually, in other words as the opposite of evil, is still not God. Good is only half of the equation. And if we venture no further to discover the higher principle that governs good and evil, we shall never understand their interaction, their games, and their battles. Good and evil are actors hired to perform in the play of life. Because if evil did not exist, good would probably do nothing; it would go to sleep. Evil is a spur to good.[7]

Evil can be compared to certain characters in a play. Whether it be a tragedy, a comedy, or a drama, it is they who make things happen. While everyone else is busy going about their business, someone suddenly appears on the scene whose ambitions, love, pride, greed, jealousy or stupidity disrupt a family or a place of work, and everyone has to suffer the consequences of their behaviour, to fight and defend themselves, and find ways to overcome the crisis. At the end of the play some have been killed, fallen ill or become insane, whereas others have acquired great wisdom because they have been able to utilize these difficult conditions. There would never have been a play if the disturbing element had not intervened and allowed the plot to develop. And maybe, if evil did not exist, life would not move on either.

Look at how things work in general: human beings wish for good, and when this long-awaited good finally comes, they very soon begin to feel bored and sometimes even lose their taste for life. Yes, because they were too comfortable. Evil had forgotten them, and to be completely forgotten by evil is not so wonderful either, because life loses some of its flavour. We have to admit that it is evil that gives spice to life. People aspire to good – or so they claim – but it seems they need evil to spur them on.

I can give you further examples to help you understand how these forces we call good and evil work. Take the circulation of the blood for instance. If we had only arterial circulation, we would be poisoned because wastes would not be eliminated. It is the role of the venous circulation to eliminate waste. The venous circulation is the other half of the whole, in other words it carries the blood to the lungs, where it is purified, and once it is pure it enters the heart from where it is sent out through the arteries. It is from the heart, therefore, that pure blood, i.e. good, flows. But this 'good' begins to pick up impurities again right away, and so it goes on. We see the same phenomenon with road traffic. One stream of cars travels on the left-hand side of the road and another on the right. If they were only allowed to travel in one direction, how could they return home?

So, evil does not lie in the fact that opposing forces exist, for they both have their part to play in life's work. Evil arises only if, instead of doing the work designated by cosmic Intelligence, the two forces collide or intermingle. If arterial and venous circulation become mixed up, you have cyanosis. If traffic travelling in one direction collides with the oncoming traffic you have an accident. Or take the example of fire and water: what extraordinary things can be achieved by putting water over a flame – with something to separate them of course, otherwise the heat will evaporate the water and the water will extinguish the flames. This is what happens in all spheres of life to those who are ignorant.

All these examples should help you understand that good and evil are two antagonistic but complementary forces harnessed to the same work.[8] Moreover – do not be shocked by this – good is not capable of doing all the work if evil does not give a helping hand. You will say: 'A helping hand? But evil is an opposing force.' Exactly! It has to be an opposing force. When you want to cork or uncork a bottle you use both hands. One pushes in one direction and the other in the opposite direction. It is thanks to these opposite movements that you draw the cork or put it back in. And who controls these forces? You. It is you who think and decide, and the forces obey. It is you who represent the third entity here that transcends and governs the other two.

You see how such a simple example from daily life can help you understand. Get into the habit of observing nature and all the little things that happen every day. They will teach you about good and evil infinitely better than the works of philosophers and theologians. Everything I tell you is simply a conclusion drawn from observations you too can make every day simply by reflecting on the slightest events in nature or in everyday life and thus learn to interpret its language.[9] This is where we find answers to the most important philosophical problems, and they are presented even more clearly and simply than in books of philosophy, which are so complicated and abstract.

Notes

1 See *Langage symbolique, langage de la nature,* Œuvres Complètes, t. 8, chap. I : «L'âme»; chap. II : «L'être humain et ses différentes âmes».

2 See *Cosmic Balance – The Secret of Polarity*, Izvor 237, Chap. 1: 'Cosmic Balance and the Number Two'.

3 See *Truth: Fruit of Wisdom and Love*, Izvor 234, Chap. 17: 'Truth Transcends Good and Evil'.

4 See *'Know Thyself' – JnanaYoga*, C.W. 17, Chap. 8: 'The Higher Self'.

5 See *Langage symbolique, langage de la nature,* Œuvres Complètes, t. 8, chap. III : «Le cercle (le centre et la périphérie)».

6 See *Angels and other Mysteries of The Tree of Life*, Izvor 236, Chap. 17: 'Yesod, Tiphareth, Kether, the Sublimation of Sexual Energy'.

7 See *Cosmic Balance – The Secret of Polarity*, Izvor 237, Chap. 7: 'Alternation and Antagonism – The Law of Opposites'.

8 Ibid., Chap. 8: '"To Work the Miracles of One Thing" – The Figure of Eight and the Cross'.

9 See *The Living Book of Nature*, Izvor 216.

2

The only way to triumph
over evil is to learn to use it

No one can deny that most people seek the good, but since they are rarely in agreement as to what is good, all these contradictory goods finish by producing evil. That is the sad truth: each one is so busy working for the triumph of his or her 'good' – which is not the good of others – that the result is evil. This is what we need to reflect on. The greatest human tragedies do not stem from something that is evil in itself, which appears from who knows where, but from the faulty understanding of human beings who have decided to call the things that suit them 'good' and those they object to 'evil'. And because what suits some disturbs others, and *vice versa*, the problems persist.

You will never get everybody to agree on what good and evil really are. This is why we should not be too concerned with the resolution of the question, and certainly not think of going to war against evil in the hope of annihilating it so that good may prevail. If we try to annihilate evil, we will also annihilate good. This is what Jesus was saying in the Parable of the Wheat and the Weeds,[1] in which the master tells the slaves who ask whether they should gather up the weeds growing in his wheat field: *No; for in gathering the weeds you would uproot the wheat along with them.* We should not fight against evil to free ourselves from it, for that is impossible. We should instead find the methods and the attitude that will enable us to make use of it.

No theory, however subtle, will ever resolve the problem of evil. We can resolve it only by action, by learning to transform it. Otherwise our ignorance and weakness simply reinforce it. As I have said before, God is not the good. Or rather, he represents the good for one who has succeeded in transforming evil. Let us get back to the example of the circulation of the blood. Our blood is the intermediary between the air and the cells of our tissues. When the blood has become contaminated, does nature solve the problem by emptying it out of the body and replacing it with new blood? No, it is purified by the oxygen our lungs receive from the air they inhale. So one could say that nature has found a way of transforming evil into good. And we must learn to do the same.

We experience evil as hostile forces, but in reality these forces have no hostility toward us. Their hostility is all in our imagination because they bother us. Indeed, how could we not see elements that paralyse or poison us as hostile? Everything that does not vibrate in harmony with us, that bars our way or darkens and troubles our consciousness, appears to us as an enemy. That is natural. But does it always have to be so? No, if we succeed in transforming these elements, they will become forces that are beneficial to us. Shall I give you some examples?

Fire, lightning, water, and wind were initially all enemies of human beings. People struggled against them and exhausted themselves in the process. The day human beings began to domesticate them, however, they understood that if they had been enemies before, it was because they had not known how to control them in order to use them. Why not accept that we can do the same with other forces in life? In reality evil represents extremely powerful forces, with which we do not have a good relationship because we do not know how to channel them. And of course, everything we are unable to control can only be harmful to us. Electricity is a prime example of what human beings can do to channel an energy, which in its raw state would instantly destroy them. Just look at all the transformers, networks of cables, wires, circuit breakers, etc. We have now succeeded in controlling electricity so well that even a child can start up the most complicated appliances simply by pressing a button.

There you are: it is quite simple, quite clear. If we examine the forces we usually think of as evil, we become aware that in fact they are not, because in nature evil does not exist.

Just look at the earth; the earth is more intelligent than human beings, because all the waste and pollution we throw at her is received as a very precious material and transformed into plants, flowers, and fruits. And just think about coal for a moment: how did it become coal? And oil? And what about precious stones?[2] So, since the earth and certain initiates possess this wisdom, since God possesses this wisdom – for he does not want to destroy evil – why should we not try to acquire it as well? For thousands of years human beings have prayed: 'Lord God, annihilate evil.' But God scratches his head and smiles and says: 'These poor creatures; as soon as they understand that evil is necessary they will stop begging me.' But until then the prayers continue. Of course we have to pray, but this is what you should be asking: 'Lord God, teach me how you have created the world, how you envisage things. Give me this understanding, this wisdom, this intelligence, so that, like you, I may be above evil, so that it may not touch me, and I may be able to use it to realize great things.'

So many examples show us that what is evil for some is not necessarily evil for others. Some animals have an extraordinary resistance to fire, others to cold, others to poison, and yet others to a lack of food. There are even some that do not die when they are cut in two. The concepts human beings have formed about evil are of their own making. They are not universally valid. And this is what I want to get you to understand: these are our ideas, our concepts, but other creatures think differently on the subject of evil, because they have evolved to the point where they are able to use it.

I could give you many more examples. It is all right to pour water into your stomach, for instance, but pour it into your lungs and you will be in trouble. To let air into your lungs is good, but air in your stomach is not so good. The conclusion we can draw from this is that what is good in one situation becomes bad in another. Even light can be good or bad depending on who is exposed to it; people with sensitive eyes find bright light painful. This also shows that human beings cannot know what evil is as long as they judge it according to their weaknesses and imperfections. Once they begin to come closer to perfection, they will change their point of view. This is why the opinion of ordinary people concerning evil differs so widely from that of initiates and sages. Behind the terrifying aspect that inspires fear in the weak, initiates are able to see a beneficial force, even a friend, in evil.

The best way to become weak is to look upon evil as an enemy. When you encounter a drawback, learn to consider it as a footing, a solid base on which to ground your work. When you have been climbing in the mountains, did you not notice that it was the sharp edges and the rocks that made it possible to climb up? If you want your life to be smooth, without any sharp edges, how will you ever reach the top? And on the way down, what a tumble you would take if there were no bumps and rocks to hold on to. It is thanks to them that you are still alive. So do not ask for your life to be smooth, without suffering, without drawbacks, sorrow, or enemies, because if that were so you would have nothing to hold on to to help your ascent. If all your wishes were granted – an easy life, filled with pleasure and money – inwardly there would soon be nothing left of you. Fortunately, heaven does not listen to prayers like that. Everyone asks to live in comfort and opulence without realizing that they are asking for their own misfortune.

I know it is difficult to accept what I am saying. Every day I introduce you to one aspect of the philosophy of the initiates and you are often saddened, even in revolt, because these ideas do not fit in with yours. But if you cling to your ideas you will never be free of the difficulties with which you are constantly wrestling. Accept this philosophy of the initiates, therefore; otherwise, every time you should be singing a hymn of thanksgiving and praise to the Almighty, you will manage to feel miserable.

Since evil represents forces and materials you have not yet learned to master, you should tell yourselves that it is still possible to reach a higher level where you will succeed. Something which is still beyond us may represent an evil. So it is up to us to rise above evil in order to change it into good. Take very small children for instance: if you give them the same food and drink as adults they may die, but once they are a little older and have become stronger it can no longer harm them. These are facts of everyday which we can all see, but we fail to draw conclusions from them. And the conclusion to be drawn here is that you must become stronger and understand things in greater depth.[3] If you do this, evil will no longer cast a shadow over you or poison you as it has done in the past, but will make you stronger, more luminous, and more alive.

The evil we are not able to utilize remains evil. As soon as we are able to use it, it becomes good. This truth gives you immense possibilities. Nothing will be able to stop you. Since, as you have seen, humanity has succeeded in utilizing the forces of nature – the wind, waterfalls, tides, etc. – on the physical plane, it must also be possible on the psychic plane. It is simply a question of attitude. The most important thing to remember is that you must not let yourself be floored by these forces, nor must you try to confront them directly, because there too you would be defeated.

What do we do to protect ourselves from storms, tornadoes, snow or hail? Do we go outside and shout at them to calm down? Maybe this is so in fairy tales, where magicians order the forces of nature to do this or that, but not in everyday life. In everyday life we work on our house to make sure it is sound, we check the insulation, we install an efficient heating system. Yes, people know what to do on the material plane, but when it comes to their inner life they act like ignoramuses. They want to eliminate evil but they do not know how.

There have been occultists who wanted to attack evil directly; they declared war on it and have died as a result. They did not know the truths I reveal to you now. They ventured into the battle on their own against formidable forces, and inevitably they were crushed. I am not saying that an initiate should not and cannot fight evil, but he must first prepare himself, purify himself in order to allow God to become strong within him and to manifest his omnipotence through him. Several passages in the Gospels show Jesus doing battle with evil by driving out demons, but he did so in the name of his heavenly Father, with whom he identified. Besides, he did not annihilate them, he simply drove them away.

Only God himself can annihilate evil. Human beings have neither the stature, the capacity, the strength, nor the methods to do so. Read the Apocalypse which says that the Archangel Michael will seize the dragon, the symbol of evil, and lock it up for a thousand years. This should make us think; since the Archangel Michael himself, who possesses all powers, does not annihilate evil but only binds it, how could human beings, poor creatures that they are, possibly succeed?[4] All those who have wanted to attack and annihilate evil should of course be praised for their drive, their courage, and their spirit of self-sacrifice, but it has to be said that they missed the point. Because whatever we do, there will always be this double reality: good and evil, light and darkness, life and death, and in no instance does one triumph over the other, neither good over evil, nor evil over good.

You will say, of course, that when you see how things work in the world, it seems easier to do wrong than to do good. Yes, this is true, but it is not because good is weak and evil powerful. No. The reason is that here on earth the conditions humankind has gradually created are far more conducive and favourable to evil. You want to do wrong? Well, there is a whole crowd of people ready to help you. But try to do good and things are different. No one follows suit. It is as if good were paralysed, chloroformed, powerless. In the lower realms this is always so, and human beings live too much in the lower regions. But as soon as we manage to escape these regions the opposite happens. Evil is suffocated, shackled, and bound. When we live in the higher regions it is impossible to do wrong. And if we want to do good, it is plain sailing.

Let me give you an example. Suppose it is winter, everything is damp, covered in snow. It is impossible to get even a few twigs to catch fire. But in the summer, when it is hot, one tiny piece of glass that focuses the rays of the sun is enough to set the whole forest ablaze. It is as if the entire forest had agreed to catch fire, because the conditions were favourable. If you try to fire a canon when the powder is damp it will not work, and so on... You can understand now that if evil is far more powerful than good here on earth, it is because human beings give it the best conditions. One day everything will change. Evil will not be able to manifest because it will no longer find favourable conditions. In the meantime, however, evil is well and truly there, and the only real weapon we have against it is to try to use it for good.

Now, since we can never conquer evil, we must henceforth replace the words 'fight, kill, uproot, and eradicate' – which express an erroneous conception – with other words such as 'harness, assimilate, channel, orientate, sublimate, and utilize' – which express a far more advanced, more spiritual perception. When we do this the black of coal becomes a luminous red. Once we accept this new philosophy, whether we are faced with an enemy, an illness, or any kind of temptation or weakness, we will always have the best conditions in which to work, become stronger, and find a final solution to our problems.

So, this is my advice to you. When you are tempted to look upon an incident, a situation, or an inner state as an evil, ask yourself: 'Is it really evil? Is it not in fact a hidden good?' As long as you do not ask yourself this, you will fight or rebel and will not benefit from this evil, which was in fact a good that you were unable to recognize.[5] Rarely are human beings able to see what is good and what is bad for them. Success has so often led people to disaster. Conversely, obstacles and failure have often become the true cause of future triumphs for those who were able to utilize them.[6] But you need to have experienced a great deal, studied much, and overcome many trials before you can see how true this is.

I often feel when I speak to you that something within you is resisting. You say to yourselves: 'But what is he talking about? Telling us to use evil, to harness and orientate it... Can't he see what awful conditions we live in?' Yes, I do see. Indeed I see the same thing everywhere. But I also see other things. I see positive things, favourable conditions that are there but which you do not see, because you are so obsessed by your difficulties that you see nothing else. What I see above all are the positive, favourable conditions you carry within, the incredible treasures and riches in your intellect, your heart, and your will, while you yourselves only see your external circumstances – the wife or husband who might leave you, the children who do nothing but get into mischief, the neighbour who wishes you ill, your professional worries, and so on. But there are so many other things to see: all those riches you carry within and which can help you triumph over circumstances. This is the most worthy and the most glorious work you can do.[7]

Do not worry if this work does not immediately produce tangible results. You are too eager for material, visible, tangible achievements; this is why you suffer so many disappointments, but none of this is long-lasting. Decide therefore to work with the one who is the most inaccessible, God himself. Then you will truly achieve results, inwardly, in your consciousness, and these results will be instantaneous. For what is most distant is in fact closest, and what you imagine to be nearest is in reality the furthest away. You cannot experience something simply because you wish to experience it; you cannot obtain something simply by wishing to obtain it. Only when you work on the realities furthest away will you experience them within you instantly.

If you are looking for instant success, aim at what is the furthest away. From now on, tell yourselves: 'I now understand where the truth lies, where power lies, and where true life lies: in this unique centre that is above good and evil.' So think about this centre, merge with it continually, believe only in it, seek nothing else, work with it alone... for in this way you will begin to transform evil into good.

The only way to triumph over evil is to learn to use it

Notes

1 See *The Tree of the Knowledge of Good and Evil*, Izvor 210, Chap. 4: 'Until the Harvest'.
2 See *A New earth – Methods, Exercises, Formulas and Prayers*, C.W. 13, Chap. 6: 'Methods of Purification', p. 94.
3 See *The Tree of the Knowledge of Good and Evil*, Izvor 210, Chap. 10: 'The Science of the Initiates, or the Inner Lamps'.
4 See *Life Force*, C.W. 5, Chap. 4: 'Pitting Oneself against the Dragon'; – *The Book of Revelations: a Commentary*, Izvor 230, Chap. 11: 'The Archangel Mikhaël Casts Out the Dragon', Chap. 15: 'The Dragon is Bound for a Thousand Years'.
5 See *Spiritual Alchemy*, C.W. 2, Chap. 9: 'Spiritual Alchemy'; – *Harmony and Health*, Izvor 225, Chap. 1: 'Life Comes First'; - *The Seeds of Happiness*, Izvor 231, Chap. 12: 'The Spirit is above the Laws of Fate'.
6 See *Youth: Creators of the Future*, Izvor 233, Chap. 8: 'Learning to Handle Success and Failure', Chap. 14: 'The Will Must be Sustained by Love', Chap. 15: 'Never Admit Defeat', Chap. 16: 'Never Give Way to Despair'.
7 See *On the Art of Teaching – from the Initiatic Point of View*, C.W. 29, Chap. 1: 'On the Spiritual Work', Chap. 3: 'On Building the New Life'.

3

'Evil can be
compared to tenants'

In one of his lectures Master Deunov once said: 'Evil can be compared to tenants who come into your house and stay there for years without paying rent.' This statement may surprise many people, because the notion that human beings are inhabited by other entities is not so wide-spread. Although in the Gospels, Jesus expressed the same idea: *Those who love me will keep my word, and my Father will love them, and we will come to them and make our home with them*. Which means that human beings are constructed in such a way as to be able to harbour other entities. Unfortunately, what is true for God, for Christ, for the holy Spirit, and the spirits of light is equally true for evil spirits, to which the Gospels also refer very clearly. On several occasions they mention that Jesus delivered people who were possessed, one of these being Mary Magdalene, from whom he banished seven demons. When Jesus asked the evil spirit that possessed the Gerasene man: *What is your name?* the spirit answered: *Legion*, because an evil spirit is never alone. He has a crowd of helpers to wreak havoc on the poor unfortunates in whom they make their home. The literature of every country tells of people possessed by evil spirits, and every religion has rites of exorcism with the appropriate prayers and formulas with which to drive them out.

A human being is not a single entity. Every individual harbours a large number of other inhabitants.[1] Evil spirits – referred to as 'undesirables' in esoteric literature – are creatures of a lower order who set up house in human beings and inspire them to do all kinds of senseless or criminal acts. The people in question do not know what is happening to them. They do not even realize that it was they who attracted these creatures in the first place through their thoughts, feelings, and way of life, but once these entities have entered them, they settle down and expect to receive 'room and board' free of charge. They eat and drink and soil and wreck everything.

Of course, if you tell someone with mental problems that these problems come from the fact that he has invited evil spirits to come and set up house within him, he will not only not believe you, but he will be furious. As for the doctors, psychiatrists, and psychoanalysts who treat such people, they would call *you* insane. But it is the truth nevertheless, the sad truth. All unreasonable deeds, all criminal acts are dictated by undesirables, and it is up to human beings themselves not to attract them. I do not wish to describe these spirits here – their shape, their emanations, and so on – because by speaking about them one connects with them and attracts them. I will simply tell you that each time our thoughts, feelings, and actions are not totally beyond reproach, we pave the way for these undesirables.[2] You must not be misled into thinking that the advent of these entities always manifests in a spectacular way, with screams, wild gestures, rolling around on the floor, or the shouting of profanities. No, such cases are exceptional. These undesirables have other ways of manifesting their presence.

When you study zoology you find that the different animal species – insects, beasts of prey, mammals, reptiles, or birds – all need a certain type of food. Some eat seeds, others grass, or meat, or worms, and some, like jackals, hyenas, and vultures, feed on carcasses. So, before you can feed an animal, you need to know what food is suitable for it. Or take another example: if you leave food lying about on the table, very soon flies and ants will appear. Where do they suddenly come from? How did they find their way? They have antennae to guide them from afar. Remove the food, and the flies and ants will disappear. Now if we carry the analogy through we can conclude that if you harbour certain thoughts, desires or feelings that are neither luminous nor pure, the entities that enjoy these impurities will very quickly appear – for they too have antennae with which to detect the food they like – and they will make their home within you. Try, therefore, to have better thoughts, better feelings, better desires. Then those undesirables will leave you because there will be no more food for them, and you will at least be able to breathe freely. You see, it is quite clear. But very few people know how to read the book of living nature that lies open before them. You will say that these are such small details. True, but their significance for our mental, spiritual, and emotional life is immense.

Every thought, every feeling emits electro-magnetic currents which can nourish either good or evil. This means that depending on the quality of our thoughts and feelings we either attract magots, elementals, and demons and drive away luminous spirits who cannot bear their nauseating emanations, or we attract highly evolved spirits, whose presence repels the harmful creatures engulfed in the centre of the earth. 'Engulfed in the centre of the earth?' you will say, 'How can this be?' Yes, just go back to the Gospels and you will see that when demons were driven from the body of a demoniac they begged Jesus not to send them back into the abyss.

Unfortunately this field is not well known, and it is because of this ignorance that many physical and psychic problems are impossible to cure. So long as science does not recognize that these invisible entities exist, so long as it continues to reduce everything that takes place in a human being to a physico-chemical process, its results will remain limited. I do not deny the reality of these physico-chemical processes, but they are themselves the result of psychic phenomena produced by living creatures. Yes, they are merely results of something else. If scientists expect to find these entities under their microscopes or on their scalpels they will have to wait a long time. The fact that you cannot see an object or being is no proof that it does not exist. Can you see microbes and viruses? So, just as you open the door to microbes when you allow impurities into your physical body, you open the door to demons if you allow impurities to enter your astral and mental bodies. When Jesus had healed someone or driven out his demons, he said: *Go your way, and from now on do not sin again.* In other words: do not let impurities enter you again.

Maybe one day technology will find a way to build devices that allow us to see the entities of the invisible world. It has already made such advances in the study of the subtle planes of matter. In the meantime, psychologists should take seriously the assertions of true clairvoyants, who say that they can see entities entering and taking possession of human beings, or leaving them. Most people cannot see this, but some who are capable of analyzing themselves can occasionally sense that a beneficial or an evil entity has entered and produced changes in them. When you are suddenly troubled, plagued by bad impulses, it means you have been visited by undesirables. Why? Because you have prepared food for them. Conversely, when you suddenly feel inspired or have an upsurge of generosity and goodness, it is because luminous entities have visited you, because you set out food for them.

Our physical body could be likened to a house with a number of floors, all of which are occupied. The cellar, the ground floor, the first floor, the second, the third, and so on all have their occupants. And even up in the penthouse there are tenants with instruments with which they observe heaven and pass on its messages. A human being's level of evolution is judged by the number and especially the quality of the occupants he or she has attracted and by the harmony that reigns among them.

There are times when you feel there are two different beings inside of you. When one of them manifests, you are good and reasonable, and when the other enters you, you become a dreadful person. Well, many other entities can manifest in us, but let us just focus on two for the moment. Neither physiology nor psychology can explain the existence of these contradictory manifestations in human beings. Biologists study the cells, but they know nothing about the entities that inhabit these cells, because they only study their 'houses'. They are content to describe the shapes (hexagonal, round, etc.) and the structure (membrane, cytoplasm, nucleus) without any idea of the souls that inhabit them or of the life that flows within these souls. And yet this is where the explanation of everything that takes place within a human being is to be found. We are made up of a multitude of inhabitants, but to simplify things let us divide them into two categories: good and evil, luminous and dark.

The example of a house brings to light some very interesting things. A house is often occupied by tenants, and these tenants can be of two different types. One group is not very scrupulous, they damage the floors, dirty the walls, saying: 'Who cares about the landlord'. The others, on the contrary, embellish the house. They redecorate, they replace the curtains, they do up the outside of the house, they put flowers on the balconies. Similarly, two types of tenants inhabit human beings. Some come in and destroy a person completely; they wreck the stomach, wound the heart, soften the brain, and so on. Whereas others move in and set about embellishing, cleaning, purifying, and consolidating everything. You have become familiar with both types through certain sensations you have had, through the suffering or joys you have felt. But you do not know what they look like, and you do not always know exactly when they enter or leave you. Is there no concierge in your house? Well, that is a great mistake, because a concierge (this is symbolic) would immediately alert you to all the comings and goings. When a bad tenant moves in he gradually destroys your equilibrium and your peace. All those desires and passions that torment you... they are your bad tenants, and by the time you realize they are there, it is often too late, and it is very difficult to get rid of them.

So it is human beings themselves who attract the undesirables that set up house within them, and they do so by breaking certain laws. Once these undesirables are there, they cling. Well, you should never have let them in in the first place. Initiates sometimes use magic and pentacles against evil spirits. If you have ever read *Faust* (of course, Faust was not a high initiate, but he had some knowledge of the occult) you will know that above his door he had placed a pentagram to stop evil spirits from entering and good spirits from leaving.[3] There are pentacles we can use to protect ourselves once they have been prepared by magic formulas and rites, and many occultists use the pentagram. In everyday life we see signs saying 'No Entry', 'Private Property', or 'No Dumping'. Well the same prohibitions exist in the spiritual realm, but on that level they are conveyed by symbols and talismans, which the spirits understand and respect. It is important to know, however, that a talisman can be effective only if we work physically and psychically in harmony with what it represents, with the powers and virtues it contains.[4] Those who are weak and depraved will not be able to ward off the undesirables, regardless of what talismans they possess.

It is important to be clear about this question of undesirables. Whether we like it or not, all kinds of phenomena and manifestations prove that they exist. What are vices for instance? Everyone recognizes they exist, but how do we explain them? Here is a man who is good, intelligent, well educated, and who has all kinds of qualities, but he also has a vice he is unable to overcome: he is an alcoholic, or a drug addict, or he ruins himself by gambling. Try as he may, there always comes a time when he succumbs. Time and time again you see exceptionally talented artists, men of science, or philosophers fall prey to destructive passions. How do you explain this? You could say it is due to some trauma or a bad habit adopted under the influence of family or society, but in reality this explains nothing.

Conventional science is still unable to explain these phenomena. Only initiatic science can do so, and it will tell you that the vice this person is unable to overcome is caused by the undesirables he invited into himself and which he is now obliged to feed. Without realizing it, by his own deplorable behaviour he has reinforced them so much that he is now dominated by them. They have settled within him so as to exploit him and reduce him to slavery.

I once had a visit from a writer. In response to a question, I explained that in the invisible world there are spirits who live at the expense of human beings. He was indignant and said: 'But that is impossible. It's unjust.' – 'Of course it is unjust,' I told him, 'but look at what happens with animals. Some live in freedom, but so many others work for their masters, for human beings who exploit them or slaughter them even, for food or to sell their meat or their skins. Is that just? No. And you must realize that human beings are not alone in committing such injustices.' I am not saying it is wrong to domesticate animals. That is quite a separate issue. At the moment we are talking about human beings and I am simply explaining that they too can be exploited by dark spirits on the astral and mental planes. These spirits milk them and take their fat, their flesh, their bones. They even sell them, because they too have shops. Yes, it is a sad fact. Very few men and women are truly free. Most of them are exploited.

Take for instance the question of sexuality. Those who give free rein to purely sensual, egotistical love, reach a point where they are obliged to recognize that their organs function independently of their will, and they are unable to stop them or held them in check. They can do nothing more than witness what is happening. So there must be other forces at work – elementals, maggots, undesirables, underground spirits – which seize upon them and take everything they have. They see that a feast is being laid on and they come running. In days gone by (even today in some eastern countries), when a wedding or the birth of a child was celebrated, a banquet was given and everyone, even beggars from the street, came to eat and drink. Everyone was invited. Well, when a man and a woman allow themselves to be swept away by their sensuality, they too are holding a feast. They produce quantities of food to please the lower spirits, and these spirits come because that is the custom. Who is regaling themselves? Who takes everything that is there? Not the man and woman, that is certain. They pay the bill and others feed themselves at their expense. These entities force their way in like burglars, but burglars of the worst kind, for it is not objects they steal, but all that human beings have in their hearts and heads: they steal their inspirations, their ideas, their enthusiasm, and their plans. And at the end of it all those two poor creatures no longer have the same enthusiasm, the same desire to evolve. They now have other, totally prosaic desires. Even their love withers. Yes, it is very important to study and observe everything that happens in our lives, and through the law of analogy, to learn to interpret it.

Do things have to be this way? No, of course they do not... and that is a whole science in itself. If a man and woman know how to prepare themselves consciously so as to purify and spiritualize everything, so as to consecrate everything within them, the emanations of their love can be food for the angels. Then they will no longer be impoverished; quite the contrary, they will be richer, more beautiful, and in better health. Why does ignorance have to govern everything? Human beings seek only pleasure without realizing that in doing so they are inviting all kinds of lower entities to feed themselves at their expense. If people were more enlightened, if they sought the light, the light would also tell them to give a banquet, but instead of attracting all the undesirables from the astral plane, they would attract angels and divinities who would come and rejoice with them. And when these celestial entities depart, they leave presents behind them, and the human beings receive a hundred times more than they gave. They suffer no loss. Instead, they receive revelations and magnificent impulses; they become younger, they resurrect. You see, you need to know who should be on your guest list and who should not.

Once the undesirables have gained access it is difficult to control them or drive them away, because that requires extraordinary knowledge and will-power. This is why it is so important not to attract them in the first place. What methods can we use to avoid attracting undesirables? The first is purity; purity on all planes.[5] Then light and heat. Purity starves them to death, because there is no food for undesirables in purity.

Light makes them flee and heat burns them. Of course all this is symbolic. Light is wisdom, the proper understanding of things, which enables you to detect danger from afar. Heat is love for a divine ideal. And purity is our every effort to lead an exemplary life in all spheres so as to prevent these creatures from making their home within us. If they try to worm their way in, they will immediately be ousted, because purity, wisdom, and love repel them.

So you see, in our teaching we have all we need to understand the laws of life. It clearly shows that everything depends on us. Even if we have committed errors in the past which have allowed undesirables to enter us, remedies do exist. We must turn them into reasonable beings, convince them that instead of wrecking our house it would be better if they embellished it by contributing in some way. If they are musicians they should bring us music, if they are painters they should paint some pictures, if they are scholars they should reveal the secrets of nature to us. Some of these creatures really are very learned and very capable, but instead of helping us they take away our strength. Whereas the luminous spirits who come and make their home within us give us everything they possess. Incidentally, some of these good spirits who come and help us are relations. They are parents and grandparents who want to support their children or grandchildren. These are family spirits. Some of them are altruistic and highly evolved, while others are less so. When for instance a grandfather has smoked a pipe all his life, he wants to go on smoking through his grandson, and so the grandson smokes. He is unable to give it up because the grandfather is very obstinate and clings to his pipe. Of course this is only an image, but it sums up all the deplorable tendencies inherited from the family.

A man may say: 'Well, I don't have anything to do with these undesirables.' What he does not realize, unfortunately, is that the undesirables already have a good grip on him... and they are not letting go. This is why, at some point, you will have to take this issue seriously and learn how to behave towards all these evil entities, how to educate and enlighten them. As I have said, it is difficult to drive them out. For that, you need to be very strong and very powerful, otherwise it is you who will be brought down. You must help them and even pray for them, show them a great deal of goodwill and love, otherwise they become irritated and bring you down. Yes, instead of trying to throw them out, it is better to talk to them and try to get along with them. Some clairvoyants have seen this: when someone who was being tormented by an evil spirit went to see them, the clairvoyant spoke to the spirit, prayed for it or read the Gospels to it. Then the clairvoyant could see that the spirit listened and sometimes even left its victim, who had seen none of this. The only thing he was aware of was that something had changed, but the clairvoyant could see the spirit leaving.

I too have had many experiences in this respect. So for me there is no doubt; I firmly believe in these things. You would do well to believe in them also, otherwise you will never improve your situation. These creatures really do exist. Some are relatively understanding, evolved, and enlightened, but others are of a totally inferior order and are good for nothing. Even if you explain things to them they still do not understand. Such creatures have to be handled very differently. But whatever you do, never try to fight, because as I have said, it is dangerous; you would be overcome. You must invite other very luminous and powerful spirits to come and dwell within you and to fight in your place, because they are capable of doing so. They have all the means, all the weapons they need. As for you, do not fight.

I repeat: instead of trying to find out how to drive out undesirables, you would do better to try not to attract them in the first place, and for this you must give them no food. This is why it is vital for human beings to think about how they spend their energies. These energies have been given to them in order to live, and most people do not realize how precious they are and how highly God values them. They waste them without ever thinking about where they came from or all the trouble nature went to to produce them and give them to them. The way people pursue amusement, their outbursts of anger, their excesses of sensuality, their selfish and criminal deeds all prove that human beings are incapable of appreciating the riches received from the Creator, for they use them to feed the spirits of hell. Heaven will hold them responsible. They are very knowledgeable about things scientific, but they have never heard that they are responsible for the use they make of their energies. This is not something that is taught at a university.

So, you must always be aware of how you use your energies. Ask yourself what orientation, what goal you have given them. This is something I tell myself everyday, just as I am telling you now. Whatever situation I am faced with, I always ask myself: 'How will this further my progress?' And when the conclusion is that it will not bring me anything positive, that it will mostly be a waste of time and energy, I move on, because I know that I would only be feeding undesirables.

In everything I tell you there are points on which you will be able to dwell only when circumstances allow and others upon which it is important to reflect every day.[6] Take note of what I have just said about the way we use our energies, because it is something you should think about every day. I will not always be there to remind you. Many other things I have spoken about can be left aside, but not this. Be aware every day in all circumstances how you are using your energies. Make yourself aware. It is not so difficult. You can do it anywhere you like.

In the street, in the underground, at the dentist, in the kitchen while you are cooking, you can look within yourself and ask: 'If I embark on this or that activity, will my time and energies be well spent?' This is the only way to sustain life within you.

Jesus said: *Let the dead bury their own dead; but as for you, go and proclaim the kingdom of God.* These words are symbolic, and they should be understood in the broadest sense. It goes without saying that one dead person will never bury another. But someone who has strayed from divine life can already be considered to be dead and to be burying the dead. In other words, he is giving himself to activities that gnaw at and exhaust him. And as he associates with others in these activities, they are all burying each other. As for you, if you wish to live, you must follow the one who will give you divine life.

Notes

1 See *«Au commencent était le Verbe»*, Œuvres Complètes, t. 9, chap. XII : «Il y a plusieurs demeures dans la maison de mon Père».
2 See *The Mysteries of Yesod*, C.W. 7, Chap 4: 'Purity and the Spiritual Life'; Chap 5: 'Purity in the Three Worlds'.
3 See *The Symbolic Language of Geometrical Figures*, Izvor 218, Chap. 4 (II): 'The Pentagram'.
4 See *The Book of Divine Magic*, Izvor 226, Chap. 5: 'Talismans'.
5 See *The Mysteries of Yesod*, C.W. 7, Chap. 15: 'Fasting'; Chap. 16: 'Washing'; Chap. 17: 'True Baptism'; Chap. 18: 'Work with the Angels of the Four Elements...'.
6 See *Golden Rules for Everyday Life*, Izvor 227.

Part VI

Spiritual
alchemy

Part I - Spiritual alchemy

1

How to extract
the quintessence

Human beings are so accustomed to living on a superficial level that it is difficult to make them understand the importance of mental work. And yet mental work offers them possibilities that no other activity can ever give. This is why it is vital to make the distinction between work in a general sense and the work of thought.

Let me illustrate this. You need tons of iron or copper ore to produce only a small quantity of metal – the rest is the matrix, which is discarded. You also need wagon-loads of rose petals to extract just a few litres of essential oil, but one litre of rose oil is worth a fortune. And you can imagine how much a few grams of radium or uranium are worth! So you see, you need an enormous amount of material to extract only a very small amount of what is very precious: the quintessence. Now what I want you to understand is this: all the work that most human beings do – even intellectual work – amounts to moving tons of raw ore, the crudest of materials, whereas mental work, which is true work, allows you to extract the quintessence.[1] As long as you have not learned to work with thought so as to control yourself and direct your energies toward the higher regions, it is as though you were amassing wagon-loads of ore, and you run the risk of being buried under it.

Even if you possess all the wealth in the world, you will continue to feel poor, empty, worried, and dissatisfied as long as you have not extracted the quintessence. For it is not quantity that can satisfy you, but quality, the quintessence, this imponderable something that gives meaning to life.[2] Yes, understand this well; your possessions, your activities are of no real benefit to you in themselves. They can only be of benefit to you if you are able to extract the quintessence, that is, if you are able to give them meaning, because it is the meaning that nourishes and enriches. Quantity is the physical world, stones, earth, and so on. Quality is the spiritual world, the divine world, meaning. No amount of success or material possessions can give life meaning, because in fact 'meaning' is not a tangible substance, it is not material and you can only find it very high up, on the subtle planes. On the lower planes you find only forms, nothing more. Of course you can give forms a content, which is created through emotion, the feeling you get when you really love an object, a person, or an activity. But emotion is transient, and at some point in time you will feel the void again and will suffer. So you must strive toward something more than the content, and that is the 'meaning'. Once we find the meaning we find fulfilment.

Unfortunately, we have to admit that in nearly all their activities human beings are merely breaking stones and accumulating ore. They never manage to extract the quintessence, because you need a different kind of activity to extract the quintessence, and this activity is on the higher mental plane. Only through initiatic teachings can human beings find the quintessence. Indeed, an initiatic school could be likened to a distillery or a refinery. And what do they distil or refine there? The total life-experience of human beings, all they have accumulated in thoughts, emotions, feelings, all the experiences they have had, all their mistakes even, and all their suffering.

In an initiatic school the disciples learn to extract the quintessence from life. They study the laws and how they function, they understand why they are stagnating and not progressing in one area, whereas in another they are making progress, enjoying success, and becoming spiritually richer. This is how they learn from experience and acquire true wisdom.

The quintessence is the most essential, the most perfect part of something. It is like a perfume whose fragrance is released into the atmosphere without itself ever losing any of its substance. Once you have succeeded in finding the quintessence of your life, of your being, you have found what is most precious. An example will help you to understand this better. Let us say you had an excellent meal yesterday, but this meal was only sufficient for yesterday; today you need to eat again. The memory of yesterday's meal does not satisfy your hunger today. But if, when reading a book, looking at a painting, or listening to some music, you suddenly find you have touched upon a truth that transforms your view of things, this revelation will continue to last tomorrow and the next day. Through this book, this painting, or this music your spirit has risen very high and has found a meaning. It is as though an eternal element had penetrated you, never to leave you again. Once you have found this meaning, it will be yours for ever.

If people never make up their minds to do this work of the mind – which alone can bring order and direction to life – they will gradually sink to the lower regions of consciousness. And it is there that they will find hell, because we all carry hell within us. Human beings contain both heaven and hell, and it depends on each one to go toward one or the other. So do not allow yourselves to be influenced by all those ignorant people who seek to distance you from spiritual life by persuading you that you will be happier without it.[3] That is not possible. You will not find the full meaning of life either in your family or

318

in your profession, in art, in travel, or in anything else. These may help you come closer to this meaning, but they do not contain it. And the proof of this lies in the fact that no family, no career, no amount of travelling, and no art has ever stopped a man or woman from committing suicide. Of course you also have to continue to work in the world, practise your profession, earn money, look after your family, but do not ignore the only means that will lead you toward a richer, more meaningful life. Everywhere around me I see people working against their better interests because they have eliminated everything essential, everything that could give them knowledge and control: the work with thought.

This mental work needs to be started at a very early age, for it takes time, patience, and perseverance. It is easy to mine the depths of the earth and bring to the surface thousands of tons of rock and soil. What is difficult is to extract the precious ore contained in all that rock. Mental work is also difficult; it is an undertaking that takes time. Many people become discouraged and abandon their meditation because it does not produce quick results. Why are they in such a hurry? To extract what is most precious takes time, a great deal of time. What quintessence can be extracted in just a few minutes? So, once you have embarked on this mental work, you must not abandon it, because only then will you achieve real results.

Just look at all the poor countries, which are mostly desert, where fantastic underground riches have been discovered: oil, natural gas, gold, diamonds, etc. Well in the same way, if someone – however underprivileged or unfortunate – understands these truths and sets in motion the process of searching, sorting, and distilling, he will draw a quintessence, a wisdom, from his mistakes, failures, and misfortunes. He will discover the laws and understand the designs of Providence and will find the path for the future.

Believe me, it is worth embarking upon this work. Once you begin to be able to extract the quintessence from your life, you will become precious, extremely precious, just like the poorest country that one day discovers a diamond mine. Even the most destitute and most despised of beings can become rich this way, rich with wisdom, with virtue, acquired by distilling their life-experience. Everyone is able to undertake this work with the mind, because thought, true thought, is different from the intellectual faculties needed to study. We should not confuse the two. True thought can be found in very simple and unassuming human beings, in country folk, craftsmen, even in illiterate men and women belonging to what are referred to as primitive tribes or cultures.

You must understand that thought is the instrument heaven has given us with which to extract the quintessence from our lives. It is of course up to us to know where and how to concentrate our thoughts. Everyone thinks, but the question is, how do they think? If you start to poke about in a pile of manure it will release a foul smell. This is often how people think; they poke about in the filth that is in them... and what a stench! Even when they are not really concentrating they are still thinking – more or less – but they are thinking in the wrong way. I am not saying people should make an effort to think. No. They are doing that already, for thought precedes and governs everything. Even those who are lazy think, but their thoughts drift like leaves in the wind. And others think about how to steal, cheat, murder, and so on.

When I speak of thought I am speaking of an instrument we must use to come closer to an inner world of light, certainty, and peace. If thought does not bring us closer to the world of light it will bring us closer to the world of darkness, for it is linked to both.[4] So you must try to tear your thought away from the lower powers to which it is subjugated and give it a celestial direction. Otherwise you need not be surprised if you feel you are living in hell. Even if you are well dressed, covered in medals, a welcome guest at sumptuous receptions where prominent persons come to congratulate you, in reality you will be in hell. Whereas, if you have learned to do real work with your thoughts, even if you are alone and abandoned by all, you will live in joy, because heaven and earth are within you. They belong to you.

So continue to earn money, acquire knowledge and whatever else you like, but try also to set aside some time in which to seek the quintessence. Because even though you possess the entire world, if you do not possess the quintessence, you will always be wondering what you can do with all that you have. You will feel crushed, disorientated, in a void. Never forget that whatever your circumstances, this quintessence, which gives meaning to life, can only be obtained through the work of thought. At times when you have suffered misfortune or incurred a major loss and are in despair, remember that you still possess your power of thought. Concentrate your thoughts, direct them to the divine world so that you are in touch with the higher entities and you will gradually feel that, as if by a process of alchemy, a glimmer of light, a new strength and peace emerge from this misfortune or loss. This is what it means to extract the quintessence that gives meaning to your life.

The meaning of life is the reward you receive for a patient and constant inner work on yourself through thought. Once human beings have reached a certain stage of consciousness, heaven gives them an atom, like a droplet of light, a quintessence that impregnates all the matter of their being. From that point on their lives take on a new dimension and intensity. They experience events with a new clarity, as if they had been granted the understanding of the reason for all things. Even death no longer frightens them because this atom, this electron reveals the immensity of an eternal world where there are no more dangers or darkness and where they sense they are already walking in the boundless space of light.

Notes

1 See *Harmony*, C.W. 6, Chap. 10: 'The Hara Centre', p. 209-210; - *Youth: Creators of the Future*, Izvor 233, Chap. 6: 'Knowledge Cannot Give Meaning to Life'.
2 See *The Seeds of Happiness*, Izvor 231, Chap. 6: 'The Meaning of Life'.
3 See *La pédagogie initiatique*, Œuvres Complètes, t. 28, chap. I : «Pourquoi choisir la vie spirituelle».
4 See *'Know Thyself'* Jnana Yoga, C.W. 18, Chap. 3 (I and IV): 'The Power of Thought'.

2

The image of the tree – grafting

Human beings have often been compared to a tree, and this comparison has such a wealth of meaning that we are still far from having discovered all its aspects.

If you look at the composition of a human being you see that the upper part is destined for activities of a noble, subtle nature – seeing, hearing, speaking, and thinking – whereas the lower part digests, eliminates, and excretes, functions which are considered far more trivial. But both the noble and the trivial activities occur in the same individual, and if he tries to reject the latter because they are neither spiritual nor aesthetic, he will die. We cannot separate our lower from our upper part. We do in fact carry both around with us everywhere. We do not leave one half behind somewhere and take only the other half, which we happen to find more presentable. So why separate them in our minds?

You will say: 'But we haven't separated them.' Oh yes you have! Look at how people behave in general. They either give free rein to their instinctive tendencies without allowing their higher faculties any say in controlling or directing them, or they attack and attempt to annihilate these instinctive tendencies as if they were enemies of their evolution.[1] Well, in both cases

324

they are making a mistake, because they are separating the upper from the lower. Cosmic Intelligence intended that our higher faculties should draw their energies from our lower functions, because these are like indispensable roots, which the human tree needs in order to extract from its soil the substances which it will then transform in order to flower and bear fruit. Look at how a tree transforms the raw sap it absorbs through its roots into sugar-sap. This transformation takes place in the leaves thanks to the light of the sun. In the same way, thanks to spiritual sunlight, we too can transform the raw sap within us – our instinctive tendencies – into sugar-sap, which will feed the flowers and fruits of our soul and spirit.

Nature has given us so many signs for our enlightenment. You are familiar with the process of grafting in which the gardener inserts into the stem of a vigorous wild pear tree a scion of a high quality pear tree, which will gain from the vigour of the wild tree and produce succulent pears. Well the same process can occur in our psychic lives. When you read the biographies of some of the most remarkable people, you are sometimes surprised to see how many of them had abnormal or even criminal and monstrous tendencies. It is difficult to understand how this is possible when we do not know the composition of human beings. In reality it is very simple: because of their lower tendencies, which they constantly had to confront, these people succeeded – consciously or unconsciously – in performing grafts on themselves. The more terrible and fervent their passions (their roots), the more succulent the fruit they bore and the more remarkable their achievements.

Saint Paul said: *A thorn was given to me in the flesh... Three times I appealed to the Lord about this, that it would leave me, but he said to me, 'My grace is sufficient for you, for power is made perfect in weakness.'* So we should not fight all those weaknesses that affect us on an emotional, spiritual, and mental plane and try to rid ourselves of them because they are a source of great riches within us. These weaknesses, these 'thorns in the flesh', oblige us to work in depth, to come closer to God. Heaven leaves us with our weaknesses in order to spur us on in our spiritual work, because what seems like a weakness is in fact a strength. If we have light within us, if we have love and the will to do so, we can use all the instinctive tendencies that torment us. They are a mine of materials from which we can constantly draw elements to transform. This is how we can become great alchemists.

So be happy! You are all very rich, since you all have weaknesses. But you need to know the rules of spiritual alchemy to be able to make them useful for your work.[2] Let us look once more at the diagram of concentric circles, because it is a key that opens the secret doors of nature and of our soul.

Symbolically, a human being represents a tree with roots, a trunk, branches, leaves, flowers, and fruit. But although all have roots, a trunk, and branches, how many are visited by the spring? Most human beings are trees without fruit, flowers, or even leaves... they are winter trees, sad and black, without leafy finery. Every human being has the potential to grow flowers, but it requires much work, great knowledge, and a great deal of time for these flowers to blossom, to give off their scent, and to produce fruit. You can see from the diagram how the roots are linked to the fruit; they are the point of departure, and the fruit is the point of arrival. As soon as the fruit is ripe the roots stop work. Then the fruit, with its seeds or stones, is the point of departure for future roots, from which a new sapling will begin to grow. There is also a relation between the trunk and the flowers, and between the branches and the leaves. The same applies to human beings, in that our physical body is linked to our spirit, our heart to our soul, and our intellect to our higher mental body.

Higher nature

Atmic body	*Truth*	Fruit
Buddhic body	*Love*	Flowers
Causal body	*Wisdom*	Leaves
Mental body		Branches
Astral body		Trunk
Physical body		Roots

Lower nature

    The leaves, flowers, and fruit are wisdom, love, and truth. The leaves represent wisdom, the flowers love, and the fruit truth. With the help of great wisdom the leaves transform the raw sap into sugar-sap, just as alchemists transform metals into gold with the help of the philosopher's stone. Flowers are linked to love: their colours, their scent, the pure substance of their petals attract all creatures. They contain the nectar insects come and gather. Fruit represents truth, which is the result of the union of wisdom and love.

    Study yourselves and you will see that that which is stable, strong, and steadfast within you are the roots, the trunk, and the branches, in other words that which corresponds to your purely personal tendencies, instincts, and passions. From time to time some leaves appear in your mind in the form of luminous thoughts, some flowers appear in your soul in the form of warm and caring feelings, and fruit appears in the form of impersonal, unselfish deeds. Unfortunately, this fair season does not last long. Inspiration, the subtler states of our superconsciousness, are fleeting, and you find yourself as you were before – selfish, jealous, prideful, sensual, vain, bad tempered, lazy, and defamatory. And then you ask yourself: 'But what is happening to me? A moment ago I was in the best of moods, and now...' And you feel discouraged, as if heaven had abandoned you. Well no, heaven has not abandoned you, but it does want you to work, so it gives you the conditions and the means to do so.

Now let us go back to the example of grafting. Human beings have become expert in the technique of grafting, but when it comes to the psychic or spiritual sphere, they have neither the same competence nor the same skill. This is why we see so many people of great worth – scientists, writers, artists, philosophers, politicians – ending miserably, all victims of passions or vices they were not able to overcome. If they had been familiar with the laws of grafting they would have been able to graft qualities and virtues onto those weaknesses. You will say: 'But how do we set about doing this?' Well, you need to link those crude forces to a high ideal, to a celestial entity.[3] No one is perfect when they arrive on earth. Even the greatest initiates have been obliged to make grafts by linking themselves to the most sublime beings and ideas. By taking an upward direction, their energies thus made the flowers of their soul and spirit blossom and the fruit ripen.

And let me tell you something: there exists a large distribution centre for such grafts, and that is the sun. This is where you need to go for grafts. When you watch the sun rising in the mornings, say to him: 'Oh my dear sun, I would like to understand so many things, but I feel so limited. This is why I turn to you, you who are light, warmth, and life. Give me a few grafts of your wisdom, your love, and your strength.' He will give them to you... and free of charge, I can assure you. Everything is in the sun and you can ask it for all the grafts you wish: purity, beauty, goodness, intelligence, patience, and so on. But do not ask for them all at once. Ask for them one after the other, otherwise while you are busy with one, the others will dry up and die.

Some of you are wondering whether I am joking. No, I am speaking seriously. I have spent years establishing the truth of what I am telling you. I have not yet told you everything about this question, but what I do not tell you, the sun will reveal to you. It is the sun that taught me everything I know.

A master, an initiate, and a great saint can all give you some grafts; it is possible, because symbolically, through their wisdom and love, they are representatives of the sun. But none of them can compare with the sun. If you knew how to look at it, fully aware that it is the best representation of the Deity, you would sense that its rays have the power to replace all that is used, impure, or dark within you, and your thoughts, your emotions, and your actions, everything would become different. Unfortunately most human beings who experience marvellous sensations when they eat, drink, smoke, play or kiss, feel nothing when they are in front of the sun. And this is because their vibratory level is too low. All that is lower impresses them and has an effect on them, whereas the rays of the sun leave them cold.

A disciple who is advancing on the path of evolution becomes more sensitive to the rays of the sun, and they produce truly celestial revelations, delights, and sensations in him. And this is another totally new notion. Psychology has not yet discovered that it is we who determine that the rays of the sun produce momentous phenomena in our souls and our hearts that are capable of regenerating and resuscitating us. But of course this is not done overnight. This requires preparation, otherwise we will always remain outside the reach of the sun.

But the most powerful, the most sublime grafting of all is, of course, to unite with God by saying: 'Lord God, I feel that if I am left to transform myself on my own, I shall never succeed. So, use me, work through me. I am in your service, I will carry out your wishes. Come and manifest through me.' It may not be God himself who comes to you, but he will send one of his angels or archangels, as he did to the patriarchs, the prophets, the apostles, and all the saints. And then your tree – that is, you yourself, who had as yet produced only inedible fruit – will begin to bear delicious, fragrant fruit. What has happened? You have dedicated the crude forces surging within you to the service of heaven, and heaven has accepted them and will transform them. All instinctive, negative tendencies can be transformed in this way, and note that I use the word 'transformed', not annihilated, because that is impossible. In fact, if we were able to annihilate them, the outcome might be even worse. It has often happened that people from whom certain vices had been uprooted have fallen prey to even greater vices.

Look at how religion has envisaged sexual energy in the past. So many unfortunate men and women tried to escape their torment by taking refuge in a monastery. They wore hair shirts, flagellated themselves, deprived themselves of food and sleep... with the result that they were even more tormented and obsessed. Because this is not the way to master your sexual energy. You master your sexual energy by loving, not by running away or fighting it. Onto the tree of sexuality you must graft the branch of the most noble, most elevated, and purest love.[4] Then the sap that travels up from the roots will circulate through the branches and up to the brain, where it will produce light and inspiration.

And how should you deal with your anger? You may already have destroyed many a friendship and compromised your future because of your anger. Well, you can even transform these wild forces that explode like thunder by deciding not to waste your energies any longer on such explosions, but to use them to strengthen yourself inwardly so that you may bear difficulties more easily, to defend just and noble causes. In this way, instead of trying to destroy what seems bad you will build what seems good and great.[5]

And what about vanity? What is vanity? The desire to be noticed, valued, appreciated, in   ˆand, invited, even photographed. Of course this tenden   is normal, there is nothing really reprehensible about it. Everyone has a need to be appreciated and acknowledged. It could even be said that Cosmic Intelligence has put this tendency into human beings in order to force them to evolve. It often happens that people, in their desire to win the approval or admiration of others, manage to surpass themselves. People who were frightened, but who did not want to destroy the faith their family or country placed in them, have become true heroes.

The same is true for an artist. An artist never ceases to perfect his art so that his public should never tire of him and his work. This is only natural. But too much time and money, too much energy is wasted in winning recognition from others. People wear themselves out, because all their other energies, their intellectual and moral energies are all diverted, absorbed, and used up by vanity. Not to mention the hostility this attitude provokes, because those who want to be noticed make an exhibition of themselves and make a great deal of noise. They try to make themselves known, which of course offends others who happen to have ambitions of their own. They too seek success and glory, and so conflicts abound. But is this reasonable? Is it really worth going to such lengths to find glory before fellow human beings? And how long will this glory last?

This is why those who are enlightened should graft the desire for divine glory onto this instinctive tendency to vanity. We must seek to please heaven, not human beings, because God alone knows what tortuous paths we would have to travel in order to satisfy them. Those who are enlightened put themselves at the service of heaven in order to deserve to be welcomed among the chosen. From that moment on, they are not concerned about whether other human beings acknowledge and value them or not. They continue to work because they know they are working for eternity, and one day they will achieve true glory, everlasting glory. Human beings have been created to share in divine glory, and this idea is also expressed in the Gospels in the parable of the feast where the guests must appear in ceremonial dress. Only those who have donned fine jewellery and festive clothes are made welcome at this feast, because these symbolize the divine glory to which they have managed to elevate themselves.

All these examples should make it clear that only the work you do on yourself really counts, whatever your weaknesses or shortcomings may be.

Indeed, qualities and virtues do not have any absolute value. So many people possess great virtues. But what do they do with them? Nothing. Whereas others have all kinds of faults, but they want to improve, and by working on themselves every day they become able to accomplish great things. If they did not have those faults they might never do anything. I assure you, one often sees people who achieve great things because they work on their faults, and others who, satisfied with their qualities, achieve nothing much. Well, be aware that heaven is concerned not so much with your qualities, as with what you do with those qualities.

The only important thing is the work we do on ourselves in order to put both our faults and our qualities at the service of a high ideal. So many people moan about sinful human nature which bears within it the seeds of evil. But it is no good bemoaning it; the only thing that is needed is to work. Each one of our defects – be it vanity, arrogance, anger, jealousy, sensuality – must be put to work. This is true alchemical work.

Notes

1 See *Love and Sexuality*, C.W. 15, Chap. 8: 'Materialism, Idealism and Sexuality – 'On Earth as in Heaven'.'
2 See *Spiritual Alchemy*, C.W. 2, Chap. 9: 'Spiritual Alchemy'.
3 See *True Alchemy or the Quest for Perfection*, Izvor 221, Chap. 12: 'The Sublimation of Sexual Energy'.
4 See *Spiritual Alchemy*, C.W. 2, Chap. 1: 'Gentleness and Humility'.
5 See *True Alchemy or the Quest for Perfection*, Izvor 221, Chap. 10: 'Vainglory and Divine Glory'.

3

The fire of sacrifice

Since human beings carry within them all the realms of nature, it should come as no surprise that there are also animals in them. Yes, our instincts and passions represent a whole collection of animals. Many of our inner states can be compared to tigers, wild boars, crocodiles, snakes, scorpions or octopuses, whereas others resemble birds full of kindness and gentleness. If you think that prehistoric animals like mammoths, dinosaurs or pterodactyls have disappeared, think again. They are all still within us, in a different form, in our lower astral and mental bodies. You must understand that it is not the physical shape or size of these animals that matter, but their nature, the quintessence of their manifestations. I shall say no more for the time being because there is no need to go into detail. What is important is to know that we are inhabited by different animal species and to learn the best way to handle them. As human beings we have a very important role to play in creation. Our task is to tame, harmonize, and reconcile everything within us so that the wild animals that dwell within us become domesticated and agree to work for us.[1]

Human beings have worked wonders in animal domestication, and this has brought them great benefits. But what they have not yet understood is that there are animals within them which also need to be educated. They let them struggle freely among themselves and do a great deal of damage... in other words, the human beings behave exactly like them, tearing each other apart and devouring each other. Of course, with human beings there are the clothes, the houses, the décor, a few books, and a few works of art to distinguish them and hint at a certain degree of culture, but their inner life leaves a lot to be desired. It is a collection of wild beasts – the same instincts, the same appetites, the same blind impulses. Do not think that we have rid ourselves of our animals. We think that because we cannot see them they do not exist. But they exist... In our thoughts and feelings, they exist. Brutality, voracity, cruelty, guile – these are all animals. Our task now is to tame and quieten them, and get them to serve our divine self. Those who succeed in domesticating the wild beasts within them can rely on the work these creatures do, and thanks to them they will live in plenitude.

Look at what happens in parts of the countryside or in countries that are still wild. If children, poultry, or cattle are not watched and protected, wild animals may attack and eat them. In the same way, if a human being fails to protect himself, every now and then wild animals will come and devour his children. What children are these? The good thoughts, good feelings, and good inspirations he has brought into the world.[2] If they are not protected, they will be eaten by the hostile forces that are only waiting for the right moment to wreak havoc. And then this person wonders why he is poor, wretched, and weak. So many have come to me complaining: 'I had great plans and now they have all evaporated. I have lost my inspiration, my enthusiasm...' I could reply: 'That was your doing. You have not been vigilant; you went to sleep and wild animals came and ransacked everything.' But I do not say this, because I know they would not believe me. But then how do you explain the fact that all that positive energy has disappeared? This question of the animals in human beings is very important. To be able to control them you need to be strong, and this strength can only be gained through purity, light, and love.

It is said in India that certain ascetics and yogis who have withdrawn into the forests are not bothered by wild animals, which just seem to walk around them without doing them any harm. And in the days when the Christians were being persecuted, there were instances when the wild animals in the arenas spared certain victims. Yes, animals can be sensitive to the purity, light, love, and inner strength emanating from a human being. But the animals I have in mind are the ones within. You do not need to be warned about the other kind – it is not every day that you will find yourself walking in a forest where wild animals roam, and you will not be delivered up to lions in an arena – but you will come face to face with your inner animals every day. And in order to tame them you must increase the light, the purity, and the love within you, in other words move closer and closer to the Godhead. Then these animals will begin to sense you are becoming their true master, and they will be obliged to obey. Otherwise they will continue to devour you.

Animal sacrifice held a very important place in ancient religions, and this is still the case in some present-day religions. The animals had their throats cut and were burnt. Why? It is said in the Old Testament that the smoke from the sacrifices rose up to God's nostrils like a pleasant smell. Can you imagine how God's nostrils delighted in the smell of roasting animal fat! But this is just an image. Burnt sacrifice was offered to God as an act of worship and thanksgiving and in reparation for faults committed, or as an offering so that prayers might be answered. Certainly the fact of renouncing wealth as valuable as cattle represented a major sacrifice for people in those days. But these immolations of animals also had their origins in magic, in that before being burnt the victims had their throats cut, and the energies contained in their blood were diffused into the atmosphere and fed the entities of the astral plane, whose help was needed for the realization of the people's prayers.

When Jesus came to earth, he brought a new kind of teaching. He said: *you shall love the Lord your God with all your heart, and with all your soul, and with all your mind, and with all your strength.* This is considerably more of a sacrifice than all those holocausts. Why immolate innocent animals? In what way do our faults, our suffering, or our wishes concern them? The animals we must sacrifice are within us – our weaknesses, our desires, our bad habits – and only the fire of divine love, by inflaming our heart, our mind, our soul, and our spirit, is capable of burning them. Yes, the only fire that should burn our inner animals is our love for the Creator. Then the 'blood' of the inner animals we sacrifice also releases energies that feed our prayers and divine aspirations and prepare the conditions for their realization. These days Christians no longer immolate bulls, oxen, sheep or birds, but this does not mean they have learned to offer their inner animals in sacrifice. They leave them to run free, and since they have no divine fire within them to consume their animals, it is they who are devoured.

In nature, all creatures serve as food for others; this is the law. And on the psychological level, people are well aware of this law. One often hears people say: 'It's either him or me. If I don't eat him, he'll eat me.' But it is not enough simply to know this law. We must apply it to our spiritual lives. And the struggle of good and evil is also simply a question of eating.[3] Good consumes evil and evil consumes good. If you are weak, evil will consume you, but if you are armed and you know how to defend yourself, it is you who will seize evil and consume it, in other words you will use its energy for your own benefit. Initiatic psychology is based on the understanding of this truth. Remember that it is said in the *Talmud* that at the end of time, the righteous will eat the flesh of the Leviathan, the aquatic monster which represents the devil. The Leviathan will be cut up, salted, and prepared by God (maybe he is already keeping it in a freezer somewhere) and given to the righteous to eat. Just imagine the amazing feast that awaits us! If we took this literally I think anyone with the slightest sense of aesthetics would be quite disgusted. So we have to interpret it, and here is the interpretation: since the Leviathan, which is a monstrous animal, is to become a delicious meal for the righteous, it means that, if we know how to immolate the animals within us, they will become a source of wealth and blessings.

Meditate on this universal law which governs the relationship between creatures. Each one endeavours to absorb another in order to feed itself. Plants live on the ground and feed on minerals; animals eat plants; and human beings eat animals, or at least – and this is preferable – their products. And who eats human beings? Human beings feed the creatures of the invisible world, and the type of food they are able to prepare will determine who comes to feed on them. If the matter within them is putrescent, they will be devoured by undesirables, which are attracted by these impurities. But if, through the purity and light of their thoughts and feelings, they are capable, like bees, of preparing honey, they will attract celestial entities. And to be consumed by celestial entities is great happiness, indescribable joy and bliss for human beings, because not only do they remain intact, but they become richer by having been consumed in this way. This is why all religions say that man should offer himself to God as a sacrifice. It is an image to show that the spiritual ideal of man is to be absorbed by God, or more accurately by the inner representative of God, our higher self.

Perhaps you think God does not eat or drink? Well let me tell you, I have discovered exactly the opposite. I have seen him enjoying great feasts. He has created us in his own image, so it follows that since we eat, he must eat too. Otherwise, whom do we resemble in the act of eating? God nourishes himself, and he does so by eating the best food with which the creatures nearest to him provide him: those entities that are pure light and pure love. And it lies also within our power to offer him such food.

Those who are not willing to sacrifice their inner animals end by identifying with them. A truly spiritual person is one who has understood there is nothing more desirable than to be eaten, absorbed by God, and this is why he offers himself to him in sacrifice. But how many people really understand what sacrifice is? The word inspires fear in human beings because they wrongly associate it with suffering and death. When Jesus said: *those who want to save their life will lose it, and those who lose their life for my sake will save it,* he was of course not thinking of physical death, but about dying on the lower plane of vices and passions in order to begin to live on the divine plane.[4] By sacrificing the animals within us and offering them to the celestial entities, we do not in fact die, but resurrect. Because by being eaten – symbolically speaking – our matter is transformed, deified.

Nutrition, which is a form of combustion, is based on the principle of transformation of matter. All creatures nourish themselves, be they plants, animals, or human beings, and in doing so they transform the matter they absorb by impregnating it with elements it did not previously possess. It is the task of every realm in nature to absorb matter from lower realms in order to make it evolve. Cosmic Intelligence could no doubt have found other ways, but this is the one it has chosen. It decided that, in order to live, every creature would absorb matter from the realm below it so that it might rise to a higher realm. And the same is true in the realm of the spirit. Human beings offer themselves as food to God in order to transform their psychic matter and make it divine.

We can therefore say that sacrifice is the transformation of one substance into another, one energy into another. We find one of the best examples of this in wood and coal. You take some coal or some dead branches and you set fire to this black, dirty, ugly material. In doing this you are accomplishing a kind of sacrifice, and the material you are burning becomes heat, light, and beauty. If you do not want to make sacrifices, of course, you are quite free not to do so, but you will remain in the cold, in the dark, and surrounded by ugliness. Look around you: earth, water, and air are there before you and all around you. You can see and feel them. But for there to be fire, we must first light it.[5] Of course fire exists in nature under different forms, but when we need fire, we must first capture it, and once captured, we must maintain it, feed it. Be it wood, coal, candle wax or lamp oil, the flame needs feeding. So, combustion is a sacrifice, and if we do not sacrifice anything, there will be neither heat nor light.

As long as human beings live an ordinary, selfish life they will remain inert and black, like dead branches. Only when they succeed in attracting the fire of the spirit within them, as did Jesus' disciples on the day of Pentecost, will they give out light and heat. And this fire needs to be tended by being fed. You will say: 'But after a while there is nothing left of the tree as it burns, and the fire goes out.' Yes, that is true of trees, but human beings can burn indefinitely. Once lit, it is possible for them to go on burning for ever. Human beings have accumulated so many things inside them over the years, and it is all combustible. All their selfish and passionate tendencies, all the manifestations of their lower nature – arrogance, vanity, jealousy, anger, sensuality, and so on – are like dead wood. If they could throw all of these into the fire, not only would they be rid of them, but their heart would be warmed and their intellect enlightened. But instead of burning them, they carefully squirrel them away, and they themselves slowly waste away beside a pile of dead wood. They wait to find themselves in the cold and the dark, to be faced with major difficulties, before they begin to think about having a fire. And then, as in periods of terrible cold when people have to burn their furniture to keep warm, they begin to burn the old rubbish that has accumulated within them over the centuries. But they have to experience great calamity first. Until then they are terrified of getting rid of it, and see this sacrifice as an impoverishment, a loss. Which shows they have understood nothing. Of course there is something that disappears, but only when this something has disappeared can something better take its place. Only then can light and warmth take its place. If you have understood this, do not wait to find yourself in this situation. Go and find all that is mouldy, rotting, or moth-eaten, and burn it in the fire of the spirit.

To light a fire... Yes, nothing we do in life is meaningless, even our simplest acts can have deep significance. Every time I light a fire I am struck by the immensity of this phenomenon of sacrifice. Lighting a fire reminds us that in order to have light, inner light, the light of the spirit, there has to be sacrifice, something inside of us has to be burnt.

If we want to keep the divine fire alive within us, we must feed it every day with pieces of our lower nature, our personality, because our personality is the 'wild beasts' within us, the dead wood. Our personality is specially predestined to feed our spirit. Until now you were not quite sure what purpose your personality served, and since it plays you some pretty bad tricks, you wondered how to rid yourself of it. You must not rid yourself of your personality, because without it, as I have said, you will not be able to survive on earth. Whereas with it, you have a great deal of combustible material with which to feed your spirit. The only way to achieve results on the spiritual plane is by sacrificing something of your personality every day.

Several forms of combustion already take place naturally in human beings. Nutrition is one form of combustion, breathing is another, and it is thanks to these forms of combustion that life is possible.[6] But this is still only a vegetative or animal life, and I am talking about the spiritual life. Things are different there, because it is no longer the physical body, but the astral and mental bodies that are involved. And although these are not visible, they have enough combustible materials to last for centuries.

So, try to rid yourself of this idea that sacrifice represents suffering and deprivation, otherwise you will never want to sacrifice to transform any of your dark, shabby, impure elements into light and heat, into love and wisdom. The initiates understand this. That is why they offer themselves as a sacrifice to the divine fire every day so that they may be consumed.

Many complicated books have been written about the experiences of mystics. In reality it is all very simple. The experience of mystics is the experience of fire, of the sacred fire that human beings feed every day by throwing bits of their lower nature into it, just as we throw dead wood onto a fire in the fireplace. If you watch a fire burn, you will see that these pieces of wood, which up until then were separate and dispersed, are united by the fire into one and the same light, one and the same heat, and they are obliged to think and feel like fire. So, bring on your dead branches, your black and twisted branches, and throw them into the blaze of the divine fire, because it is in this blaze that you will find the secret of true life.[7]

Notes

1 See *The Key to the Problems of Existence*, C.W. 11, Chap. 19: 'Your Inner Animals'.
2 See *Hope for the World: Spiritual Galvanoplasty*, Izvor 214, Chap. 11: 'Replenish the Earth!'.
3 See *The Key to the Problems of Existence*, C.W. 11, Chap. 8: 'The Image of the Tree – The Individuality Must Consume The Personality'.
4 See *Spiritual Alchemy*, C.W. 2, Chap. 2: 'Except Ye Die Ye Shall Not Live'.
5 See *The Mysteries of Fire and Water*, Izvor 232, Chap. 14: 'How to Light and Tend Fire'.
6 Ibid., Chap. 2: 'The Secret of Combustion'.
7 Ibid., Chap. 17: 'Trees of Light'.

4

From movement to light: replacing pleasure with work

When you see how much energy human beings put into activities that give them pleasure, it is obvious that if happiness were synonymous with pleasure, they would all be living in perfect bliss. But often the opposite is true, and there where they find pleasure, also lurk misfortune and unhappiness. Human beings prefer to choose what is easy, pleasant, and nice without seeing how detrimental this can be to their evolution. They do not have the wisdom to opt consciously for certain difficulties and to realize that snares, disillusionment, and bitterness often lie behind what appears to be pleasant.

Pleasure is a momentary agreeable feeling, which misleads us into thinking that if we can sustain it for as long as possible we will be happy. Well, this is not so. Why? Because most of the activities that give us these pleasant feelings so quickly and easily are not on a very high plane. They only touch the physical body, the heart, and the intellect, and such satisfactions are limited and ephemeral.

Those who expect to find happiness in pleasure are like alcoholics. They pour themselves a drink, and yes, they feel good. They forget all their worries, and from this they conclude that drink is good for them. Yes, if you look no farther than the next few minutes or few hours it may seem magnificent.

But what happens a few years later? The loss of their faculties, the inability to lead a normal family and social life, accidents, degradation, perhaps crime. Well, in many circumstances people behave like alcoholics. They think that everything that appears pleasant at the moment will remain so for eternity. Unfortunately this is never the case.

So be careful of the direction you choose, because once the first moment of pleasure is past, you risk having to pay very dearly for your lack of insight. There are certain pleasures that feed the soul and the spirit, this is true, but they are not usually the ones human beings choose. You only have to look at the things which give most people pleasure.

By seeking pleasure, people think mainly of themselves, because their pleasure is only for themselves. They do not seek the pleasure of others, only their own. In this way they become limited and debased, because in order to obtain and keep this pleasure, they often have to use reprehensible methods, and if at some point they find themselves deprived of this pleasure, they become aggressive, unjust, cruel, and vindictive, in other words they manifest all the tendencies of their lower nature.

Of course I am not saying we should deny ourselves all pleasure and gratification; that would be silly. In any case it is human nature that drives people to seek pleasure, and without it life would lose its appeal and would become dull and dreary. Pleasure enlivens and puts colour into our existence. You will say: 'So we are justified in what we are doing.' Yes, but it depends on how and where you look for your pleasure. It is amazing how many different activities people enjoy, from the most innocent, such as fishing or collecting stamps, to the most dangerous, like cheating, destroying, committing theft and aggression of every kind, even risking one's life. Human nature is incredibly resourceful. But if the pursuit of pleasure is not directed and controlled by reason and wisdom, it is not acceptable.[1] It may be acceptable in its initial impetus, because it is a natural instinct, but not necessarily in its accomplishment, and it should not be given the freedom of realization without prior consideration and reflection. Be it greediness, sensuality, aggressiveness, the need to dominate, all these instincts are forces that are not wrong in themselves, but they become criminal if they are not controlled and directed by another factor, i.e. reason.

We all have instincts and appetites, that is normal, but that does not mean we have to do only what pleases us, without thinking. If heaven has given us a brain it is so that we may use it to orientate ourselves correctly. You could compare a human being to a ship sailing on the ocean of life. On board the ship are sailors, whose job it is to stoke the boilers that keep the ship moving, and up above is the captain, with his compass, in charge of steering the ship. The sailors are our instincts, our appetites. They are blind, but they keep us moving forward. And the captain is our intelligence, the wisdom that gives us direction and sees to it that the ship does not run aground or collide with another ship. Unfortunately, human 'ships' often founder because the captain has let the sailors do as they please.[2]

The greatest disillusions await those who are guided and ruled by pleasure alone, because they do not see the consequences of the choices they make. We need to be guided by reason. Only reason sees the consequences of the direction we intend to take, and it warns us: 'Careful, here you will come unstuck. But there you will be all right, go ahead.' Unfortunately, most people are convinced they will not know fulfilment if they cannot do as they please, and for this they are prepared to break all the rules, all 'taboos' as they say. They want to be free. But what sort of freedom is this? The freedom to indulge in all kinds of excesses and follies, even to destroy themselves. Because once we free ourselves from light, from wisdom, from good sense in order to taste a few moments of pleasure, we are bound to suffer. It is inevitable. And we will even suffer physically. We will become ill, because illness is simply the manifestation on the physical plane of the disarray we have allowed to set in on the psychic plane.

To want to overthrow the prejudices and rules of a narrow moral code in order finally to be oneself is not necessarily a bad thing, on the contrary. Provided, of course, you realize that above the laws of human morality are the eternal laws established by Cosmic Intelligence, and whether we like it or not, if we transgress those laws we will pay dearly through sorrow, suffering, and illness. I told you this long ago: it is easy to see that new diseases will emerge because of the way human beings live their freedom, and in some cases these diseases will be incurable.

Pleasure is never a trustworthy guide, because what is pleasant at first often ends in a much less pleasant way. It is pleasant to have a really good meal in the best restaurant, but when the time comes to pay the bill, that is not so pleasant. Why imagine we can eat our fill without paying? In the psychic life, as in our physical life, everything has to be paid for. In one way or another, everything has to be paid for. Here too there are markets and shops where everything is displayed for you to help yourself, but once you have helped yourself, you must pay. And it is here, when faced with this idea of paying, that we must pause and say to ourselves: 'Is it really worth it? It will be too costly. This pleasure is transient, there will soon be no trace left of it, and it will take me years to pay off my debt.' Do not think I wish to deprive you of joy and happiness. No, all I ask is that you replace all these joys that are so costly, with joys which, on the contrary, will enrich you, joys of the spiritual life.

You will say: 'All right, we understand, but then what must we look for in the place of pleasure?'
– 'Work.'
– 'Work?'

Yes. You will protest that you already work every day and that you do not feel like depriving yourself of what brings you a little joy and satisfaction. If you really think that, it means you have not understood what true work is. True work does not cancel out pleasure. On the contrary, it gives a far more subtle, far more complete pleasure, one that will not leave you with any regrets.

To replace pleasure with work is to replace an ordinary, selfish, harmful activity with a more noble and generous activity, which broadens your consciousness and triggers new possibilities within you. It is not a question of depriving yourselves of pleasure, but simply of not giving the priority to pleasure as the goal of your existence, because pleasure weakens and impoverishes you. Imagine someone using their furniture – tables, chairs, beds, wardrobes, doors, windows, and so on – to heat their house because they are cold. After a while nothing will remain. Well, the same is true for those who allow themselves to be guided by pleasure. All the emotions and sensations they experience are gradually burning all their reserves. And all that lies in store for them is the impoverishment and darkening of their consciousness.

Pleasure, which is of course at first so pleasant, slowly gnaws away at you only to destroy you in the end. Work, on the other hand, is hard at first but in time it brings you strength, richness, and happiness. Instead of lingering on first impressions, which are often false, you must think carefully and foresee the effect your decision will have in the long run. Yes indeed, people look for one thing and find another, because they rely on appearances. But ugliness is lurking behind beauty, misery lurks behind wealth, and weakness behind strength. The wise are those who succeed in seeing through the veil of appearances to discover reality. And once they have discovered this reality it is up to them to decide, with full knowledge of the facts, whether or not to satisfy their desires.

When human beings seek pleasure they do not realize that in reality they are seeking God. All creatures in the entire universe are driven by the need to seek the Creator, and only him, because he lies at the origin of everything. God himself is behind all pleasure, all joy. Even the glutton who thinks only of eating is seeking God through food, because God is in this joy of eating, and nothing and no one can give joy apart from God. Even the most debauched seek God, but instead of going directly to him, they seek him along tortuous and muddy paths, which although they do not know it, lead them not toward heaven but toward the sewer.

God has infused a particle of his quintessence into every being and every thing. This is why we can find him everywhere. But if we scatter ourselves here, there, and everywhere, it will take us billions of years to find him. To find God straight away we must look for him through light and purity. As long as human beings do not have the true knowledge – which often, poor creatures that they are, they reject – they will continue simply to manage as best they can. In other words, they will want to unite with God, but instead they will encounter devils.

Those who let themselves be guided by pleasure are forced to cross the boggy regions of the astral plane, which are full of 'creepy crawlies' of all kinds that pester, sting, and bite them. Whereas those who have understood the necessity of replacing pleasure with work will discover the regions of light. Let me give you an example which goes back to the prehistory of humankind.

Matches and lighters are recent inventions, and our distant ancestors had several ways of making a fire. One of these, which can still be used today, involved rubbing two sticks of wood together, because they had observed the law of physics by which friction produces heat, and after a while the heat transforms into light as a flame appears. You all know this phenomenon. But have you ever thought of carrying it through and realizing that since this is a physical, mechanical phenomenon it must have an equivalent in the psychic sphere? No, people always notice facts, but then they leave them aside, empty of meaning, without trying to understand and interpret them.

So here is the interpretation. You take two sticks of wood and rub them together. The rubbing is a movement; this movement produces heat; and heat transforms into light. Movement, heat, and light correspond symbolically to the three basic principles that make up the human psyche. Movement corresponds to the will; heat corresponds to feeling; and light corresponds to thought. So, just as you can produce light on the physical plane, you can also generate it on the psychic plane.

If we examine this process in relation to love, we will make some very interesting discoveries. What do human beings do in physical love? Symbolically we could say that, like the two sticks of wood, they rub against each other to produce heat, in other words a pleasurable sensation. All right, but why do they stop there? Why do they not go on to the light? Why do they not become more enlightened, more lucid? Why does their love not give them a better understanding of things? Why does it not reveal all the splendours of the universe to them?

Movement and heat – at the moment this is all that people understand by love. No more. They stop midway, they do not go as far as light. But in order to produce light it is not enough merely to seek pleasure, because pleasure absorbs all the energies and prevents light from appearing. Therefore it is quite simple, quite clear: do not stop midway but go on to the light.[3] Of course there are many attractive, seductive things to see and taste along the way. Yes, but if we allow ourselves to be held up by them we will not reach the goal that must be the end result of all activity, the light.

The majority of human beings stop midway because they find things there appealing, sparkling. But this is also where you encounter the sirens, and if you allow yourselves to be seduced by their singing you will be destroyed. Remember the story of Ulysses in the *Odyssey*. Ulysses was wise and knew that in the course of his travels he would encounter the sirens who would try to lure him with their singing in order to devour him. He therefore took precautionary measures by plugging his companions' ears with wax so that they could not hear these voices, which they would have been unable to resist. He himself did not plug his ears because he wanted to hear the sirens, but he told his companions to tie him to the mast, and that if he ordered them to untie him they should tighten the ropes even more. As the ship approached the island of the sirens and Ulysses heard their voices he lost his head. He wanted to go to them and shouted: 'Untie me! Release me!' He even threatened to kill his companions if they did not obey him. But they kept to their instructions and tightened the ropes. Well, the sirens represent the midway point in the course, and you must not stop midway. Of course this is where charms and seductions will tempt you, but if you do not stop, you will not succumb.*

You are also familiar with the episode of the flower maidens in Wagner's opera *Parsifal*. One day Parsifal reaches

---

* A remarkable coincidence is that the episode with the sirens is in Book XII of the *Odyssey*. That is exactly halfway through the account (the *Iliad* and the *Odyssey* are both made up of 24 books) relating the return of Ulysses to his homeland, Ithaca. Editor's note.

a meadow where some pretty young women, the flower maidens, try to seduce him. But behind these women, these flowers, serpents are hidden. These stories – and there are many similar ones in the literature of the world – contain great esoteric truths. Ulysses and Parsifal symbolize the disciple who encounters temptation on the path of initiation, but he must not linger there, because if he does he will lose his life. He must go on to the summit, because once he has arrived there he will receive everything. Everything is given to him: rest, food, love, and knowledge.

This adventure can be portrayed slightly differently again. You have a mission to accomplish, and in order to do so you need to go through the forest. But as you walk through, you discover some tiny wild strawberries growing by the side of the road. So you start to pick them, wandering here and there, without realizing you are wasting a great deal of time. Of course, the strawberries are so beautiful and succulent. But then night falls, and it is too dark to find your way. You are lost. You begin to notice all the cries of animals, the creaking of the branches, and you are frightened. Yes, this is what happens to disciples who stop along the way because of the beautiful strawberries; they lose their way in the forests of life. You say you never go and pick strawberries... That is quite possible, but those strawberries can also be women, men, pubs, casinos, night-clubs, and so on. The strawberries are symbolic. Tiny strawberries can also be very big strawberries.

Well, the strawberries, the sirens, the flower maidens... these are pleasure, and if you succumb you are lost. And so, contrary to what many people believe, gaining pleasure is not the solution to the problems of sexuality, for pleasure represents only the midway point, and if human beings stop there, they will increasingly have extremely costly experiences. They will feel tied down, bound; they will lose their freedom, their

356

inspiration, their subtlety, their lightness, their grace. When a butterfly's wings receive too much humidity it can no longer fly. Well, that is what pleasure is: too much humidity. When I see people whose wings can no longer carry them – figuratively speaking – I do not need to ask them where they have been. I know they have exposed their wings to humidity. It is quite obvious to me that it is this humidity that prevents them from flying. It will take a long time for the light to dry off all this humidity. So, believe me, do not allow yourselves to be deluded by pleasure. It will only stop you midway and devour you. Go on until you reach the light.

Would you like to know when I discovered that the French were the most intelligent people on earth? It was the day I first heard the song *Plaisir d'amour* in Paris – *the pleasures of love last only a moment, the sorrows of love last all your life.* I had never heard that in Bulgaria! This is why I hold the French in such high esteem... But you know, I do not understand why, having found this great truth, they continue to behave as if they had not found anything at all.

In reality, when you have found love, true love, nothing and no one can make you lose it. You possess it for ever.[4] Yes, but only if you replace pleasure with work. You will say: 'But how? It seems quite impossible.' Well, it is possible. Work begins when a person decides to cease wasting his energies on seeking pleasure, but to use them to set in motion other, higher centres in his brain. Instead of allowing whirlwinds and volcanic eruptions to rage within him, he is attentive, he keeps his lucidity and his control in order to channel these currents and direct them. And this is how he awakens new faculties in his brain which will make him a genius, an initiate, a divinity. This is how you transform heat into light, by replacing pleasure with work. And it is then that true pleasure really starts to take hold, not one that degrades you, but one that elevates and ennobles you.

357

Of course many will claim that lucidity kills pleasure. No, thought has also been given to human beings to enable them to live true love better. Without it the animal, primitive part of their being would increase its hold on them. It is thought and understanding through thought, that must control, direct, and sublimate your energies. If, while manifesting your love, your thought remains lucid, if it is vigilant, if it controls, and directs these forces, you will not, of course, feel pleasure as many people understand it, that is, the gross, crude, and uncontrollable animal pleasure which is devoid of nobility and spirituality. But thanks to your thought you will be able to work spiritually and instead of changing into lead, your pleasure will change into pure gold, into rapture, into ecstasy.

Look, for instance, at how attentive you need to be in the simple act of making coffee. Not only do you have to get the right amount of water, coffee, and sugar, but the temperature needs to be right too. And you need to keep a watchful eye on the saucepan or it will all boil over. So you see, even for something as simple as making coffee or heating milk you need to be vigilant. And yet, when it comes to something as charged with consequence as the sexual act, it is quite extraordinary to see how people imagine they can abandon themselves completely to forces they know nothing about and do whatever they like without thinking.

Men and women today believe they have won a great victory by obtaining sexual liberation. Yes, it is true, it is a great victory against the hypocrisy and narrow-mindedness that reigned for generations. But has the problem of sexuality been resolved thereby? After repression comes the release. By rushing to experiment with something as fundamental and complex as sexuality, they expose themselves to every kind of physical and psychic abnormality. To resolve the problem it is not sufficient merely to promote the use of condoms and contraceptives or to allow abortion... and to prohibit them is not the solution either.

'So what should be done?' you ask. The question has to be explained and clarified. It should be explained to human beings what exactly sexual force is and in what way it is related to love. I have spoken to you about this hundreds of times.[5] Sexual energy is an age-old power which it is impossible to fight, but this is no reason to allow yourself to be totally swept away by it. There are ways to channel and orientate it so that it contributes to an individual's psychic, moral, and spiritual development. But few men and women are capable of understanding why it should be controlled. They all imagine that sexual relations will make them blossom and enrich them. They do not truly understand the issue.

Every physiological manifestation involves combustion. Simply by talking or thinking we burn materials, and this combustion produces waste. And this is even more so for emotions. Have you not suddenly felt exhausted after a moment of great sorrow or even of great joy. We need to rest or even sleep to give our organism the chance to recoup. Yes, with every manifestation, every sensation, and every emotion some materials are spent. So how can anyone imagine that nothing is spent, nothing is lost in sexual effervescence? It is here in fact that the cost is the greatest, because not only does it involve a loss of physical energy, but also the loss of the most subtle, the most precious psychic energies. And once these energies have been spent, wasted, we are deprived of everything that could give us inspiration and impetus toward the world of beauty and light.[6]

Of course, those who want nothing more than to live an ordinary, prosaic life can allow themselves to be carried away. They do not have to be especially vigilant or make efforts to control themselves. Such control would in fact harm their physical and psychic health. They would become a terrible burden for their family and others around them because they would feel frustrated and would become embittered, hardened, and intolerant. If vigilance and control are to have a purpose, there must be a very high ideal, a desire to make something great, beautiful, and noble of one's life. If you do not have the need to add an element of spirituality and light to your life, then your efforts are pointless.

I understand it is difficult to hear me talk about control when so many advocate sexual freedom and back up their attitude by seemingly valid arguments. Of course you do not want to be deprived of pleasure, but there is pleasure and pleasure, and you might at least try to see what advantages there are for you in renouncing some of these pleasures. It is not a question of depriving yourself of everything and finding yourself in a void. No, when I speak of renouncing pleasures, I only mean that you should replace certain gross, physical pleasures with other subtler and more spiritual ones. When a doctor finds that a patient is destroying his health by eating the wrong kinds of food, by consuming too much fat, sugar or alcohol, he does not advise them to stop eating or drinking altogether. He knows that in any case the patient would not follow this advice – or worse still, if he did follow it he would die! So he simply tells him to replace the wrong foods with others, which are lighter and healthier. And this is also my advice to you, but in a different sphere. I am not suggesting you starve yourselves to death, simply that you eat differently.

But understand me well, to renounce certain sensual pleasures is meaningful only if they are replaced with spiritual acquisitions and joys. The Church and moralists in general have done their work very badly in that they have imposed rules of abstinence without really explaining the reasons, and this gave people the impression that they were expected to live in privation, in a desert. But the time has now come to explain; people are not so stupid or narrow-minded that they cannot understand. And even if they do not understand immediately, it is no use prescribing a code of conduct without explaining its purpose. The renunciation of certain habits is meaningful only if they can be replaced with other, better ones. Otherwise the old habits will continue to torment the poor unfortunate creature who tried to give them up, and they will get the better of him in the end because he has not generated within himself other needs capable of resisting them. As long as people do not understand this, they will continue to have very painful experiences, and then of course they will soon abandon their efforts.

Initiatic science does not say that renunciation necessarily means privation. In the spiritual life, renunciation does not necessarily go hand in hand with loss.To renounce is to replace, in other words, to transpose pleasure to a higher plane. The activity is the same, but with elements that are purer and subtler, and above all the aim is more disinterested. When you decide to reduce the physical manifestations of love, it must be in order to live its spiritual manifestations more fully, otherwise it would be stupid and senseless. And we have seen this: those who sought to renounce physical love without seeking to replace it with love on the spiritual plane exposed themselves to great danger, because this is no longer sublimation but repression.

At the mere mention of sexual self-restraint people become terrified. They think: 'But if I renounce, I'll die.' And it is true, they will die. If they have not understood that the purpose of renouncing is to live a purer life, with joys that are more intense, then they will die. Nature has arranged things very well: we eat, we drink, and we breathe, and none of this has to be abolished. We only have to refine these needs, to transpose them to a higher plane.

So, renunciation – or sacrifice, as some say – is only a figure of speech. Renunciation does not mean deprivation, only transposition, in other words the repetition on a higher plane of what you did on the lower plane. Instead of drinking water from a swamp polluted by all kinds of micro-organisms, move higher and drink from a crystal-clear spring. Not to drink at all would result in death. If you are told not to drink, it does not mean you should not drink at all, only that you should not drink from a sewer. You must drink, but it must be celestial water, ambrosia, the drink of the gods, the drink of immortality.[7]

So stop thinking that renunciation leads to death. On the contrary, renunciation gives life. By accepting certain privations we transform one energy into another, and we become richer. And this is true life, the transformation of one energy into another, into one that is purer and subtler. The whole of nature continually gives us examples of this process, but as long as we fail to transpose these examples onto the spiritual plane, we stagnate, and it is this stagnation that leads to death.

Of course these are very subtle truths which you may not yet be able to understand very well. But you will, with time. By meditating on these truths and by making inner adjustments, you will succeed in seeing them more clearly. I am not saying this is easy, but this way of seeing things deserves your attention and efforts. Instead of worrying over the prospect of a life of privation, try to understand that pleasure is the consequence of an action that is more or less in harmony with other energies, other substances, other presences. So, if an action is in perfect harmony with the divine world, the pleasure derived from it is widened and multiplied to infinity. You do of course at the moment enjoy certain pleasures, but these are very crude and inferior, and you have to pay so dearly for them that they are not worth it. We must all enjoy pleasure, yes, but it must be a pleasure that is so wide and subtle that it can reveal to us the entire universe, that it makes us luminous, beautiful, expressive, powerful, and useful to the whole world. Pleasure like this, I agree, is worthwhile, and Nature will not deprive you of it.

For thousands of years human beings have been repeating the same practices, the same patterns of behaviour to such an extent that they are not able to conceive that Cosmic Intelligence has planned possibilities, opportunities along the path of their evolution that are more beautiful and more spiritual. This evolution consists of sublimating sexual energy, to direct it upwards in order to feed the brain and render it capable of the most extraordinary creations. As long as human beings do not know how to use this energy for spiritual work they will waste it and continue to impoverish themselves. Everyone knows that sexual energy naturally follows a certain course, but that they can direct it in a different direction, and that in fact Cosmic Intelligence has set up within them a whole system of channels and devices to direct this energy to the brain, this they do not know. These channels and devices are there, they have been waiting there for thousands of years. All we need to do is to devote ourselves to releasing them to make them work and direct the energies correctly. Otherwise we are like appliances through which we have forgotten to run power. How can these possibly work?

So many people speak of sexual energy as a terrible pressure that has to be released. Yes, but through this 'release' they lose a very precious quintessence, which could have been used for their spiritual enrichment. Imagine you are a building, one hundred and fifty stories high. If you had no pressure, how would you make the water rise up to the top floor to allow the residents to drink, to wash, and to water their plants? You need pressure for energy to rise. Without pressure it can never reach the top, and instead of the cells being aroused for great works, they are numbed, chloroformed, capable only of making the organs of the physical plane function. As long as human beings do not learn to bring themselves under control in the sexual sphere they will nullify all their possibilities of becoming divinities. Our salvation lies in our efforts to surpass ourselves and make the energies converge upwards.[8]

How can I make men and women understand that, according to God's plans, sexual energy can be used for sublime creations? They look for pleasure at any cost. In this way they not only impoverish themselves, but they sense inwardly that they have nothing to be proud of, because they have let themselves be swept along by their instincts. This feeling is an indication that they are straying onto the wrong path. Why do they not take this into consideration? If they agreed to make some effort, not only would they see they are acquiring riches, but they would also experience even greater pleasures and joys. We can all live a life of beauty and good sense provided we choose the best attitudes and methods with which to ennoble and enrich ourselves inwardly.

But it is not given to everyone to be able to control their sexual energy. And this is why, before launching yourself into such an adventure, you must think carefully and especially know yourself well. If you are aware that you still need physical pleasure too much, it is best if you do not abruptly abstain, because that will only make things worse. If, however, you deeply feel the need to live something more subtle, more spiritual, to understand the splendour of the divine world, and to help fellow human beings with your love, you may choose this path. Heaven does not demand from everyone that they be able to sublimate their sexual energy, but it does ask each and everyone of us to make at least some effort toward achieving this and not to stop midway. At whatever level we find ourselves, we must never abandon the desire to rise up through the clouds to contemplate the Sun and the light.

What I say about love and sexuality is also valid in all other spheres of psychic life. Seek to give all your actions a luminous goal. Whatever you do, let light be your goal. Do nothing merely for your pleasure and you will discover that everything works together. In other words, as soon as the light and heat are there – that is, understanding and love – pleasure will necessarily follow. Believe me, it is to your advantage to make work your goal in life, to ensure that every moment of the day is a new opportunity to progress along the path of control, harmony, and light. And you will see, it is in this work that you will one day taste the nectar and ambrosia, the food of the gods.

Notes

1 See *Cosmic Moral Law*, C.W. 12, Chap. 2: 'The Importance of Choice – Work not Pleasure'.
2 See *The Egregor of the Dove or the Reign of Peace*, Izvor 208, Chap. 3: 'Aristocracy and Democracy'.
3 See *Love and Sexuality*, C.W. 15, Chap. 4: 'The Goal of Love is Light'.
4 See *La pédagogie initiatique*, Œuvres Complètes, t. 28, chap. I : «Pourquoi choisir la vie spirituelle».
5 See *Sexual Force or the Winged Dragon*, Izvor 205, Chap. 2: 'Love and Sexuality'.
6 See «*Au commencement était le Verbe*», Œuvres Complètes, t. 9, chap. X: «Le péché contre le Saint-Esprit est le péché contre l'amour».

7 See *The Mysteries of Fire and Water*, Izvor 232, Chap. 7: 'Water is Born of Mountains'.
8 See *Sexual Force or the Winged Dragon*, Izvor 205, Chap. 8: 'Spiritual Love is a Higher Way of Feeding Yourself'; Chap. 10: 'Open Your Love to a Higher Path'.

5

Learn to eat
and so learn to love

'You Are Gods'

Over the ages our conceptions of love and sexuality have, of course, evolved. Primitive people behaved with extreme brutality and crudeness in this respect. They were ravenous beasts, volcanoes in eruption, raging oceans. Only gradually, as human consciousness was awakened – and, with it, a spiritual life began to emerge – did new elements come into play, elements such as respect for others, tenderness, and gentleness. And yet, in the majority of cases even today, love is still a primitive manifestation. The passionate, instinctive love that human beings have been practising for thousands of years is so deeply ingrained that they do not really know how to refine and ennoble it. It is true to say that nothing is more difficult, but it is also true that nothing is easier when you know a few rules.

Love is divine life which descends from heaven and reaches into the densest regions of matter to irrigate them and bring them to life. This life gushes, pure and crystal-clear, from the summit of the mountain, but as it flows down like a river it gathers impurities from the regions it is obliged to pass through. It is the same energy that comes from the sun, the same light, the same heat, the same life that manifests itself everywhere in the universe. But human beings, ignorant as they are, continually disfigure it by considering it to be no more than a means of propagating the species or an instinct the satisfaction of which gives them pleasure. They do not realize that this is a divine energy, the most powerful and the most fundamental, and that it is their task to restore it to its initial purity, to the purity it had in the beginning, on high.[1]

By alert thought, focussed attention, and intelligent self-control we can all work on ourselves so that this energy becomes as limpid once again as the light of the sun. Of course there are a certain number of rules you must know, but you must not wait until you are holding someone in your arms during love-making to apply these rules. Since the rules are the same in all spheres, you can practise during your various day-to-day activities, even before loving someone and manifesting this love.

Every day you prepare food and you eat, do you not? But you do not swallow everything that comes to hand. You sort things out first, because there is always something dirty or indigestible that needs to be washed off or discarded. Human beings, who are more evolved than animals, go through this sorting process when it comes to food, but when it comes to feelings and thoughts they swallow everything. And it is worse still when it comes to love and sexuality. They do not know that this food – love – that they are about to eat and to give to their beloved to eat needs to be cleansed. If it is not, germs of disease and death, which their consciousness was incapable of discerning, will creep into their mutual exchange. Yes, death finds its way into a love that lacks consciousness, control, or light. And yet this is the love that is sung, praised, and glorified everywhere. So few people know any other kind.

You may be a little surprised that I compare love with nutrition, but the laws are the same. Why do men and women

369

seek each other out? Hunger and thirst urge them on. They are hungry, they are thirsty, and they want to eat and drink. Love is just like nourishment; the same needs and the same processes are involved. As I have so often said: when you eat you must forget everything else and allow yourself to think only of linking this process of nutrition with the whole universe, so that all these energies may serve not only to feed your physical body, but may also be directed upwards to feed your subtle bodies. People who have not understood the process of nutrition will not understand that of love either, because they obey the same laws of spiritual alchemy. By eating automatically or simply for pleasure without doing any spiritual work, you are not preparing yourself to do any spiritual work during the exchanges of love either, and you will remain crude, limited, and dissatisfied. If, for years, I have so often stressed this seemingly insignificant question of the way you eat, it is because I have a very specific goal in mind.[2] By starting with nutrition, by learning to eat according to new rules, you will become capable of finding nourishment also in the fragrances, the emanations, the rivers that flow from the divine Source. Everything begins with a proper understanding of nutrition, from now on, therefore, endeavour to take it seriously.

Before you sit down to a meal you wash your hands, and – although such practices are gradually disappearing these days – you say a prayer to invite the Deity to partake of your meal. You can gain a great deal from the practice of washing your hands and inviting God to your table. Before approaching your beloved, before taking him or her into your arms, you will know how to invite the angels to partake of this feast.

And since nutrition is a sacred act, it is preferable to get into the habit of eating in silence. Do not think that the practice of silence during meals is appropriate only in a convent.[3] In silence you prepare the right conditions to receive materials which will contribute to the construction of your physical and psychic organs.

When you take the first mouthful, chew consciously, for as long as possible, until it disappears in your mouth without your even having to swallow it. The state of mind in which we take the first mouthful is very important. It must be taken in the best possible frame of mind because it is this first mouthful that actuates all the inner cogwheels. Never forget that the essential moment in any act is its beginning. The beginning gives the signal for forces to be released, and these forces do not stop half-way, they continue to the end. If we begin in a harmonious state, then all the rest will evolve harmoniously.

Eating slowly and chewing well aids digestion, of course, but you also need to be aware that the mouth, which is first to receive the food, is like a laboratory. It plays the role of a real stomach on a subtler plane by absorbing the finest – and therefore the most active – particles. It is the cruder materials that are passed on to the stomach. And then of course, since human beings possess not only a physical body but other bodies which are the seats of their psychic and spiritual functions (the etheric, astral, mental, causal, buddhic, and atmic bodies) the question arises of how they can nourish these. I have said you need to chew your food well, but mastication is primarily for the physical body. To nourish the etheric body[4] you need to add breathing. Just as air revives a flame – all you need to do to rekindle a fire is to blow on it – deep breathing during a meal aids combustion. Digestion is a form of combustion, as are breathing and thought. The only difference is that the degree of heat and the purity of the matter varies with each process. It is good, therefore, to stop and breathe deeply from time to time as you eat, so that the combustion allows the etheric body to withdraw subtler particles from the food. And since our etheric body is the vehicle of vitality, memory, and sensitivity, it is to our advantage to allow it to develop properly.

As for the astral body, it feeds on feelings and emotions, elements that are even more immaterial than etheric particles. If you are sensitive you will feel that food is nothing other than a love letter written by the Creator. How could you ignore this letter? How could you not reply to it with love? Just look at how men and women respond when they receive a letter from the person they love. They read it fervently, over and over, they are happy, they keep the letter safe. But the letter from the Creator is thrown into the waste paper basket, it is not worth reading... Well, I believe that food is the most eloquent of love letters, the most powerful, since it brings us life and strength. And to learn to read this letter is true communion.[5]

Take a fruit; what does the Creator tell us through a fruit? He says: 'I want you to become delicious like this fruit. At the moment you are hard, sour, and tough. You are not yet ready to be eaten, so you must educate yourself. Look at this fruit; if it is ripe it is because it has been exposed to the sun for a long time. Like this fruit, expose yourself to the sun, to the spiritual sun, who will see to it that all that is bitter, sour, and indigestible in you is transformed. It will also give you beautiful colours.' This is what God tells us through the food we eat. So, by dwelling on your food with love for a few moments, you are preparing your astral body to extract very precious particles from it, particles that will change the quality of your feelings. And then you will feel the urge to behave with generosity and kindness. You will feel at peace and in harmony with nature and with human beings.

To nourish your mental body you must learn to concentrate on your food by reflecting on the fact that it is made up of energy particles not just from the earth, but from the entire universe. The truth is that food materializes on earth in exactly the same way that children materialize in their mother's womb. In the beginning plants and fruits are spirits in space, but just as we are unable to work on the physical plane if we do not have a physical body, these spirits must conform to the laws of matter in order to act effectively here on earth and sustain life. They do this by incarnating. If, therefore, you are more attentive, if you understand the richness and value of the food you eat, you will be able to receive and decipher the messages it conveys. It will tell you how the particles of which it is made up have crossed the universe, what beings have worked to make it grow, what entities have devoted themselves day and night to infusing it with such and such a property so that it may be useful to the children of God. It has even recorded the imprints left behind by all those who have worked in the fields or walked near it. Indeed, the knowledge we gain by eating is a living knowledge, because it impregnates all the substance of our being. Do not be misled into thinking that it is sufficient to read, study, and think to develop your intellectual capacities. No, study and thought are vital activities, but they are not sufficient to feed our mental body.

Lastly, beyond their etheric, astral, and mental bodies human beings possess other, even subtler bodies. These are the causal, buddhic, and atmic bodies, the seats of the higher mental body, the soul, and the spirit, and these too need nourishment. You nourish them by allowing a feeling of gratitude toward the Creator to penetrate you. This sense of gratitude will open the doors of heaven through which you will receive the greatest blessings, for gratitude is capable of transforming crude matter into particles of light which will be distributed in every part of you, in your brain, your solar plexus, and all your organs. You will begin to realize you have other needs and other joys of a higher nature, and greater possibilities for action will be open to you. You will say: 'But how? Does gratitude have such powers?'

Yes, because gratitude is the consciousness of what we owe to the Creator. And it is this consciousness, when it is focussed on the food we eat, that is capable of opening up that food in order to release the energy it contains. In reality this process is identical to that we see in a nuclear power plant. If we really knew how to eat, a very few mouthfuls would be enough. We would draw enough energy from them to move the entire universe.

Like all living creatures, human beings eat to stay alive. But is there not another reason? Everything we do has more than one reason, one aim. Let us take an example very close to home. What do worms do? They swallow the earth and then expel it. By passing the earth through them in this way, they work on it in order to aerate it, thus making it richer and more fertile. Well, human beings do the same with the food they eat. With their psychic and spiritual faculties they belong to a level of evolution far superior to that of the matter they absorb, and so, by passing through them in the process of nutrition, matter is enriched and refined.

As human beings, we must understand that we have been assigned the noble mission of transforming and sublimating the matter of creation. We have been given the power to improve and embellish all that we eat, all that we touch. This is the task we have been set: to make matter pass through us in order to put a divine mark on it. Nutrition is a process of the highest alchemy. If we do not understand this, we are missing something vital. Our task is to put the stamp of the spirit on matter, to spiritualize everything, deify everything, and if we succeed in this, we are acknowledged, appreciated, and chosen by the luminous spirits, who will always be with us because we are fulfilling our task as children of God.

And let me tell you something that will surprise you: as long as human beings are incapable of giving the act of nutrition a greater, deeper dimension, they have no right to call themselves civilized. To me that is the test. Once human beings have learned to eat with enlightened consciousness, in the grateful awareness that the entire universe has worked to produce the fruit, vegetables, and grain through which they receive life, then yes, they may speak of culture and civilization.[6]

Nutrition, as I understand it, reveals all the secrets of the universe to me. To me it represents a limitless world. From now on, try to take the time to eat according to the rules of divine science, for in this way you will also learn to transform your sexual energies into energies of light. We need to eat to maintain our health, but without neglecting the mental work through which we transform energy by directing it heavenward.

Food is matter that needs to be transformed. So, when you take your food, dedicate it to heaven saying: 'Lord God, come and eat with me, come and nourish yourself at the same time.' And you can also invite the angels and archangels to share your meal. Once you have learned to do this, you will have a firm foundation from which to progress to other regions, in particular to the regions of love.[7]

You will say that I am asking the impossible of you. No, this is where you are mistaken. I am not asking anything of you. I am merely explaining the question, because I know that once you know the truth of something, once you know the ideal solution, even if you are still not able to achieve any great results, you will be making progress. Once we know a truth it begins working within us. If we do not know it, of course, we can never attain it, but if we know it, if we understand it, we have already gone part of the way, because we are linked to this ideal, this poetic image of perfection.

Notes

1 See *Hope for the World: Spiritual Galvanoplasty*, Izvor 214, Chap. 7: 'Love's Goal is Light'.

2 See *Hrani yoga, le sens alchimique et magique de la nutrition,* Œuvres Complètes, t. 16, p. 9-44.

3 See *The Path of Silence*, Izvor 229, Chap. 5: 'Silence, A Reservoir of Energies'.

4 See *«Au commencement était le Verbe»*, Œuvres Complètes, t. 9, chap. XIII : «Le corps de la résurrection», p. 225-228.

5 See *Hrani yoga*, Œuvres Complètes, t. 16, chap. XVIII : «La communion», p. 189-194.

6 See *The Yoga of Nutrition*, Izvor 204, Chap. 11: 'The Laws of Symbiosis'.

7 See *«Au commencement était le Verbe»*, Œuvres Complètes, t. 9, chap. X: «Le péché contre le Saint-Esprit est le péché contre l'amour», p. 152-169.

Part VII

The organs
of spiritual
knowledge

Part I - The organs of spiritual knowledge

1

The aura

Everything that has existence – human beings, animals, plants, and even stones – emits particles, produces emanations, and it is this fluidic atmosphere that surrounds objects and beings which we call the aura. The aura, therefore, is a kind of halo which is invisible except to clairvoyants. Indeed, many people do not even realize it exists, although subconsciously they sometimes sense its presence.

In human beings the aura can be compared to the skin, which has three basic functions: it protects the physical body, gives it sensitivity, and provides a medium of exchange with the outside world.[1] The aura fulfils the same functions and can therefore be said to be the skin of the soul. It envelops and protects the soul, gives it sensitivity, and as a medium for cosmic currents, it makes an exchange possible with all other creatures, even the stars.

All the cosmic, planetary, and zodiacal influences that are poured out into space ultimately reach us, and it is the quality of our aura – its sensitivity, purity, and colour – that determine whether or not we receive certain currents and energies. Negative currents cannot reach those who possess a powerful and luminous aura, because before reaching them they come up against their aura, and it is the aura that rejects them. The aura functions like customs officers at the border: it lets nothing through without checking. Most of the time, it acts without our consciousness, but it can also warn us. So we can distinguish different functions of the aura, but in reality they are all interlinked – the functions of sensitivity, protection, and exchange are all in action at the same time.

Now what are the factors at play in the formation of the aura? Exactly the same as those needed in the formation of the skin. There are skins that are coarse, rough, and dry and others that are supple, fine, and soft. Anyone, or almost anyone, is capable of judging the quality of someone's skin at a glance. And what does the quality depend on? On the entire organism, on whether it functions properly at the physiological level as well as the psychic level.

Human beings form their own skin, and in the same way they form their own aura, which is the emanation of their different bodies, from the physical to the most subtle, each one of them contributing its own particular qualities. The etheric body forms an aura that penetrates that of the physical body, and the aura of the physical and etheric bodies combined reveals a person's health. The astral and mental bodies, through their activity or inertia, their qualities or defects, add other emanations, other colours to this initial aura, and thus reveal the nature of a person's feelings and thoughts. And if the causal, buddhic, and atmic bodies are awakened, they add even more luminous colours and more powerful vibrations. It is the emanations of these three higher bodies that form the body of glory to which Saint Paul refers in his Epistles. The body of glory, like the aura, is an emanation that flows from human beings, but whereas the aura reflects a person's defects as well as his qualities, the body of glory is the expression of the most intense spiritual life.

That which we call the aura, therefore, is a very complex reality: it is the fusion of all the emanations from the whole being. This is why, when an initiate wants to know a person, he does not so much observe his outer appearance – his physiognomy, gestures, or language – but he tries to sense his aura. The initiate observes the fluidic atmosphere which surrounds a human being and which can be neither disguised nor camouflaged. Some people are true camouflage artists. They have perfect control of their gestures, their voice, the way they look, and the way they speak. But what they do not know is that they have no power over the subtle manifestations of their inner life. Their thoughts and feelings create forms and colours which they can neither change nor hide. This is why everything is apparent to a true initiate. He immediately senses whether a person lives in harmony or in disarray, whether he emanates something constructive, beneficial, vivifying, and luminous, an atmosphere in which others can become stronger and purer or, on the contrary, one in which they become bogged down. A person's aura also says something about his health, for it reflects the condition of the liver, the lungs, the brain, and so on. And just as there are no two people with the same fingerprint, there are no two people with the same aura, because the aura represents an individual's most personal characteristics.

As I have said before, everything that exists possesses an aura. Minerals, metals, and crystals project certain forces which form a kind of small coloured magnetic field around them. In plants the etheric body adds its vitality, its need to grow, thus making their aura more intense, more alive than that of minerals. In animals the aura is even richer, for animals already have an astral body, the body of desires and emotions. Generally speaking they have not yet begun to develop their mental body – except for some, such as dogs, horses, elephants, monkeys, and dolphins, in which biologists discern the beginnings of mental faculties. Although these faculties are still rudimentary, through contact with human beings, the mental body of animals begins to develop, because human beings contribute a great deal to their evolution by looking after them, loving them, and caring for them. As for human beings, they are currently developing their mental body in a phenomenal way, and even though they do not always do so in the best way, those who know how to direct and control their thought strengthen their aura enormously.

But if we want to know what the aura can truly be, we must turn to initiates and great masters. Through their elevated thoughts and their love for the Creator they develop their causal, buddhic, and atmic bodies, whose emanations form an aura of extraordinary splendour with colours in perpetual motion, like fireworks. Their aura is also very vast. It is said that the aura of Buddha stretched several leagues. Yes, great masters are capable of extending their aura so far that they can take an entire region under their protection, and at the same time their aura penetrates the aura of all those who live there, thus impregnating them with their luminous and beneficial influences. Great masters have no other desire, no other goal but to widen their aura so as to reach and take under their wing the greatest possible number of creatures. It is through their aura that they purify the atmosphere around them, that they embellish, illuminate, and vivify creatures. It is through their aura that they work on the vegetation, that they change atmospheric currents. And it is also through their aura that they achieve a knowledge of things that far surpasses intellectual knowledge. Thanks to their powerful and luminous aura they soar upwards to the sublime regions where they learn how God created the world and discover what he has written in the stars, the mountains, the lakes, the birds, the animals, and the plants.

An initiate who has spent thousands of years working on developing love, wisdom, purity, and disinterestedness within himself possesses an immense aura in which creatures come to bathe, in which they sense that they are nourished, pacified, strengthened, and led in a divine direction. This is why disciples can receive great blessings from the aura of their master, but only if their consciousness is awakened, because if it is not, whatever their master does, they will remain closed to his influence.[2]

Disciples should not be content, however, simply to benefit from their master's aura. They too must work on their own aura, and in order to do this they must improve the way they live, endeavour to behave justly and with nobility, and have disinterested thoughts and feelings. Those who believe that the way they act and think and feel is not important, because morality and religion have now become outdated and must be discarded, darken their aura, and it begins to produce only dirty, lifeless colours, chaotic and inharmonious vibrations. They should not be surprised, then, if they so often meet with failure: it is because their aura is rejecting everything that would be beneficial to them and attracts everything that is detrimental.[3] People who seek strength, light, and love must learn to work on their aura.

The aura is like a magical instrument in the hand of an initiate. Since it is part of him, everywhere he goes he has a beneficial effect on the realms of minerals, plants, animals, and human beings. But that is not all. With his aura he even helps the disincarnated, of which there are billions and billions in space. Yes, even there, in the other world, his aura succeeds in reaching them. I know this because I have studied the question. A master improves the destiny of an infinite number of creatures in the astral and mental worlds. On earth he may devote his efforts to just a handful of people, but on another level he is in constant contact with a multitude of beings who come and seek warmth and light from his aura and take a little of his vitality in order to evolve.

Yes, the true work of an initiate is not even here, among human beings. His work is far more intense on the other side, even if we see nothing of this. The great masters who, with all their heart, all their soul, and all their spirit, have realized the ideal of serving God have awakened their causal and buddhic bodies so that their vibrations reach the creatures that live on other planets. And in the same way, the great masters who live in other worlds reach earthly creatures, thus producing an exchange not only in the solar system but in the entire cosmos. God has set no limits or boundaries in the universe, and if love is said to be omnipotent, it is because it can travel through space to reach the stars and touch the most distant entities.

Why have saints always been portrayed with a halo around their head? The halo symbolizes the aura. There is a science of colours according to which every virtue is expressed by a particular colour, and the colours produced by these virtues make up the aura. A saint is a being of great purity who seeks to come closer to God, to be one with him in order to know him and become like him, and in this desire for knowledge he attains such penetration, such wisdom, that a golden colour springs from deep within his soul and envelops him. There are many shades of yellow, from the very pale, very delicate, to the intense yellow of gold, and every shade has a meaning. There is a great deal to be said on this subject, for it touches on the alchemical problem of how to transform all matter into fluidic gold.

Every characteristic of someone's aura – its purity, luminosity, beauty, power, and scope – is determined by the virtues the person has cultivated. If a person is pure, his aura becomes limpid and transparent; if he is wise, it becomes increasingly luminous; if he lives a very spiritual life, it vibrates intensely; if he has great will-power, it becomes very powerful; if he is inhabited by great love, it grows wider, it amplifies and becomes immense. And its beauty, that is, the beauty of its colours, depends on the harmony that reigns among all the qualities and virtues. The aura has many more nuances, but I have given you the most important.

So, people who always have good thoughts, who have faith, hope, goodness, and purity receive all the riches of nature, and nothing bad can penetrate them. They are protected, as though by a shield. And indeed, the shield carried by the knight in fairy tales symbolizes his aura, and his sword symbolizes his thought, which he projects outward. The aura, this enclosure that surrounds us, is an expression of the feminine principle, and the thought we project is the expression of the masculine principle, the active and dynamic principle. The sword, like the lance and the arrow, has always represented the active masculine principle. In astrology, Sagittarius shooting his arrows is the symbol of the initiate who projects his thoughts.[4] He shoots his arrow to protect the city of the initiates.

Look at how, on the physical plane, human beings have been able to perfect the tools and appliances they use to work or defend themselves. Vacuum cleaners have replaced brooms; tractors have replaced carts; tanks, guns, and missiles have replaced arrows, lances, and bayonets. But on the spiritual plane human beings remain poor and destitute, even though it is a sphere in which methods and tools abound. Everything we have been able to find on the physical plane has its equivalent on the spiritual plane.

On the physical plane our skin and clothes protect our body, and on the spiritual plane it is our aura that fulfils this function.[5] No protection is more effective than a pure and luminous aura. Of course, all the magic formulas, figures, and objects mentioned in esoteric tradition have a purpose, they all have a deep meaning, but no formula, no talisman is as powerful as the aura. Before addressing the spirits – the infernal spirits in particular – in order to neutralize them or drive them away, a magus traces a circle inside of which he writes the names of God or draws symbols; this circle represents the aura.[6] You cannot confront the dark spirits with impunity if you are not surrounded by a strong protective circle, a powerful aura. It can also be said that, in general, you will not achieve any spiritual results if you have not drawn around yourself this circle of the aura, formed by all the virtues and divine forces.

Many people dabble in magical practices without knowing the origin of the symbols they use or the meaning of what they do. They are content simply to follow the rites indicated in the books without knowing that it is within themselves that they must draw a circle with the names of God, in other words, acquire the virtues that form an aura of purity, sanctity, light, and love. Being ignorant of these things, they are still vulnerable, whatever they do. The circle exists only on the outside; on the inside they are not prepared and, therefore, not protected. When it is said that a magus holds a magic wand or a sword in his hand, stands within a circle, and reads formulas from a book, that is correct, but each of these elements corresponds to an inner acquisition.[7] The initiate reads from a book, and this book represents the knowledge of all the forces and all the spirits of nature. The magic wand or sword represents the will with which he must write, that is, act. And the circle is the aura he has formed through his practice of the virtues.

As our aura develops we become better able to commune with all the regions of space. Look at the planets of the solar system; they are millions of kilometres apart, but in reality they touch each other. Yes, they touch, they are merged and form one whole. They only appear to be separate. Let me give you an example that will help you understand. Take the planet Earth. A certain area of it is taken up by the continents, and water takes up an even greater area. But the gaseous atmosphere that envelops the planet flows out into space, and its volume is several times that of the earth. And we can take this even further, beyond the atmosphere, because Earth has an etheric, an astral, and a mental body, each of which is increasingly subtle and immense. Yes, planet Earth is an animate, intelligent creature that also has a soul and a spirit. And as the same is true for all the other planets, we must assume that all the celestial bodies touch each other, because their auras interpenetrate. Their physical bodies are a long way from each other, but their auras, their emanations merge. This is how the planetary influences mentioned in astrology can be explained. Thanks to their auras, the planets interpenetrate, acting on one another and on the creatures that inhabit them. How? This is another point that needs some explanation.

One of the functions of our aura is to enable exchanges between the outer stars and the stars within us. For, yes, there are also stars within us. Since man was created in the image of the cosmos, all the planets also exist within him, and, as in the universe, they rotate around his inner sun. A dark, colourless aura cannot attract beneficial planetary currents; it attracts bad ones. It is said that some planets are 'benefic' and others are 'malefic'. But if this is so, why does the same planet act favourably on some people and unfavourably on others? It is simply that those who receive the bad influences have not prepared themselves to capture the good ones. In fact, all planets are benefic, but the way they act on a human being depends on his aura. If his aura contains elements that do not allow the beneficial influences of a planet to reach him, the currents emitted by this planets become distorted, break up, and produce

388

harmful effects. Whereas if a person's aura is pure and powerful, all influences, even bad ones, are beneficial.

Mars, Saturn, Uranus, and Pluto are considered to be malefic planets. In reality they are mainly so for those who are not receptive to their beneficial influences. For instance, the good qualities of Mars are will-power, daring, the desire to overcome difficulties, to reach the goal one has set oneself. Its negative traits are, of course, violence, cruelty, and the need to destroy. The good or the bad aspects of planets manifest themselves in a human being depending on whether that person's aura is pure or cluttered with elements, which, by affinity, attract negative influences.

This law is valid for all the other planets. It is the quality of our aura that attracts the virtues of Saturn (patience, stability, the desire to know) or its faults (sadness, stubbornness, bitterness); the virtues of Jupiter (greatness of soul, generosity, kindness, mercy) or its faults (ambition, vanity, the desire to dominate and crush others); the good qualities of Venus (beauty, charm, thoughtfulness) or the bad (sensuality, thoughtlessness, infidelity). So, the issue for disciples is to learn to work on their aura in order to receive only the favourable influences of the planets. Contrary to the opinion of the majority of astrologers, the good or bad influences of the planets on human beings are not determined solely by the sign and the house in which they are situated or by how they are aspected. These influences will manifest differently depending on a person's degree of evolution. This is why it is said that the stars dispose but do not determine.

Light attracts light, and darkness attracts darkness. If your aura is dark and chaotic, all the harmonious, pure, and luminous forces will stay outside, and only that which is colourless, ugly, and harmful will penetrate you because your aura will let through only that which resembles it. Now that you see how important this question of the aura is, you must bear it in mind so as to develop a good protective screen around you and a good instrument with which to perceive the invisible world and the hidden side of things. It is also thanks to your aura that you can be in contact with celestial entities, which, seeing light and colours from afar, will answer your calls. Suppose you are sailing on the ocean at night: if your boat is not lit up, no one will see it. But if you send out signals, if you project light into the darkness, you will be seen immediately, and communication will take place.

Our existence on earth is like sailing on an ocean at night. We are plunged in darkness, and if we do not send out luminous signals from within us, the invisible beings, the angels, and the archangels will not see us. So we must project light, and it is the aura that projects light. Someone who possesses a very luminous aura will be detected by heavenly workers, and if he calls on them, they will be able to find their way to him, thanks to this light. The world is sometimes referred to as a 'vale of tears and darkness'. But it is not surprising that human beings go unnoticed when they suffer and moan: they emit no light! They must send out signals of light, and it is through their aura that they can do this.

It is thanks to the aura that we can attract the attention of celestial beings. And it is also thanks to the aura that we can have access to the regions where these beings live. As you know, you need a pass to be allowed access to certain places. Once you have that, the doors are open. This is true on the physical plane, and it is equally true on the spiritual plane. In order to gain access to certain regions of the invisible world you need a pass, and this pass is your aura, the colours it contains. To be admitted to a specific region, your aura must contain the colours of that region. If, for instance, you possess the colour gold, you will be welcomed in the libraries of nature and all its secrets will be revealed to you. Blue will take you to the regions of music or religion; red to those of life and love, and so on. It is your aura, therefore, that opens the doors to the invisible. The colours contained in our aura are our pass to the regions to which they correspond, and the spirits that inhabit these regions welcome us and come to our aid.

The aura is an organized, hierarchical world. Like the Tree of Life it is divided into regions, which are inhabited by the archangels, the angels, and the spirits of nature, but also by infernal entities. It all depends on the life an individual leads. A person who has received the grace of being inhabited by luminous spirits displays wonderful qualities. Whereas one who has attracted malefic entities is said to have a mental illness or to be possessed or under a spell. So, we have to work on ourselves for years to make our aura into an antenna that is capable of attracting all that is truly beautiful and beneficial in the universe. If I ask you: 'Do you really value your health, your beauty, your peace, and your happiness? Do you really want to be loved?' you will answer: 'Yes, of course, that's what we want.' Then why do you do nothing to achieve this? All these blessings will not fall into your lap by chance. To work on your aura is the best way to attract them. Through love you vivify your aura, through wisdom you make it powerful, and by a pure way of life you make it limpid and bright. The virtues you succeed in developing determine the qualities with which you endow your aura.

Everything is determined in the universe, and every virtue attracts a specific blessing. It would take too long to talk about all the nuances, but you can think about them yourself. If you are observant, you may have seen this in the simple situations of everyday life. You hear someone talking, expressing himself with strength and conviction, and this strength of conviction influences others. But if you analyse his words, you may find that he has said many foolish things. There are intelligent people, on the other hand, who talk intelligently but who lack the ability to persuade, and no one listens to them. Strength of persuasion is one thing, and intelligence is another. In the same way, different virtues give the aura its different qualities. You must meditate on this and you will come to understand that by working every day to enrich your aura with new qualities you will attain your highest aspirations.

So how does one work on one's aura? You can do this in two ways. The first is through conscious effort, in other words, by concentrating on the purest and most luminous colours. You contemplate them, you nourish yourself with them. But in order to gain a correct idea of the seven colours you need a prism. The colours you see in nature, on flowers and birds, are never exactly those of the light of the sun, whereas with a prism you will see what red, orange, yellow, green, blue, indigo, and violet really are. And once you have visualized these colours well, you can begin to practise imagining that they flow from you and surround you, and that your thoughts and feelings, as they pass through this luminous and colourful sphere, are charged with this light and these colours, in order to transport them into space.

The second way is to work on the virtues of purity, patience, leniency, generosity, kindness, hope, faith, humility, justice, and altruism. You work on these virtues, and it is the virtues themselves that form your aura. This method is, of course, the most reliable. For if you concentrate on your aura every day, but at the same time you are living a totally mundane life and violating the divine laws, you will be building up on the one hand, but tearing down on the other. Ideally, therefore, the two methods should be used concurrently, in other words, by leading an pure and honest life, full of love, while, at the same time consciously working on your aura through your imagination.

As long as you do nothing to change your mediocre life, all your exercises of concentration on your aura will be useless. It is exactly the same when it comes to your health: if you are content to take medicines without changing your life style, those medicines will be merely palliative. How difficult it is to make human beings understand that the only truly effective method is to change their way of life!

A pure aura will first bring improvements within you, but it will also transform the atmosphere around you, and this is why other people will begin to love you. Without knowing why, they will feel good when they are with you. In reality, what they are feeling is a presence, the presence of luminous beings that your aura has attracted. Unfortunately, most human beings are so unaware that they never know why or how they attract what is good or what is bad.

I have worked with the colours of the prism all my life, and to me it is one of the most pleasant and poetic exercises that exist, so I invite you to do the same. Take a prism, direct it toward the light of the sun, and see how it diffracts the light into seven colours as it passes through it.[8] When you have gazed on the true colours for a while, close your eyes and imagine you are surrounded by violet, then by blue, then green, and so on. Or you can begin with red to finish with violet, visualizing each colour in turn for a few minutes. When you repeat this exercise every day you will feel so good it will astound you. And when someone in your family or one of your friends is unwell, unhappy, or discouraged, if you really want to help them, do the same for them. Send them the most beautiful colours of the prism. Yes, so many good things can be achieved with the aura and colours.

You can do all these exercises on colour in the morning as the sun rises. Look at the sun, see the aura that surrounds it. See how the colours flow from it and spread out into space, and say: 'I too want to surround my being with lights: blue, violet, gold...', then immerse yourself in this splendour. Contemplate these colours, imagine they travel far, very far, that all creatures are bathing in this marvellous atmosphere, that they are all swimming in this light, that they are impregnated with this light, and your aura will become a blessing for them. You can do this. There are no limits. It is human beings who set limits for themselves. You must have an ravenous ambition for what is good. Set yourself a very high goal and tell yourself: 'I shall reach that goal.' Even if you do not reach it, this distant, inaccessible ideal will continue to pull you upwards.

Disciples who have understood the teachings of their master reach the point one day of being able, like him, to send their love to the entire creation, to the entire universe, and this love reaches beyond the stars. Yes, for some this is a reality. They send their love to the stars, and the love of the stars returns and breaks over them like a wave, and they swim in love, they live in universal love.

The aura

Notes

1 See *'In Spirit and in Truth'*, Izvor 235, Chap. 9: 'The Skin'.
2 See *The Path of Silence*, Izvor 229, Chap. 10: 'Speech and the Logos'; - *What is a Spiritual Master?*, Izvor 207, Chap. 8: 'The Disciple and His Master'; Chap. 10: 'The Magical Presence of a Master'.
3 See *Love and Sexuality*, C.W. 14, Chap. 10: 'A Spiritual Filter'.
4 See *The Zodiac, Key to Man and to the Universe*, Izvor 220, Chap. 8: 'The Fire and Water Triangles'.
5 See *'In Spirit and in Truth'*, Izvor 235, Chap. 8: 'Garment of Light'.
6 See *The Book of divine Magic*, Izvor 226, Chap. 2: 'The Magic Circle of the Aura'.
7 Ibid., Chap. 3: 'The Magic Wand'; Chap. 4: 'The Magic Word'.
8 See *The Splendour of Tiphareth*, C.W. 10, Chap. 11: 'The Spirits of the Seven Lights'.

2

The solar plexus

I

The solar plexus and the brain

In studying the human nervous system, biologists have established that the sympathetic nerve-system is made up of a chain of centres running from the brain down to the base of the spinal cord, and of a peripheral series of nerves and ganglia linked by networks of nerves called plexuses. The solar plexus, located at the level of the stomach, is one of these. The ganglia of the sympathetic system are divided as follows:

– Three pairs of intracranial ganglia lying along the trigeminal nerve;
– Three pairs of cervical ganglia linked to the heart;
– Twelve pairs of dorsal ganglia linked to the lungs and the solar plexus;
– Four pairs of lumbar ganglia linked to the solar plexus and via the solar plexus to the stomach, intestines, liver, pancreas, and kidneys;
– Four pairs of sacral ganglia linked to the rectum, the genitalia, and the bladder.

The solar plexus

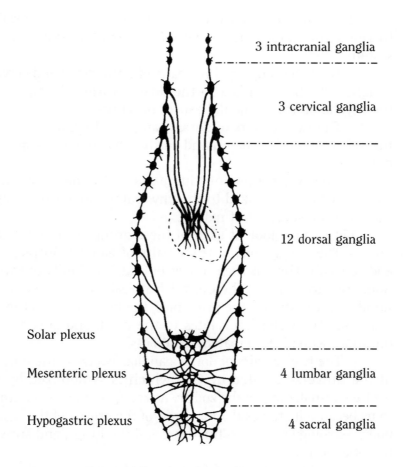

3 intracranial ganglia

3 cervical ganglia

12 dorsal ganglia

Solar plexus

Mesenteric plexus

Hypogastric plexus

4 lumbar ganglia

4 sacral ganglia

Network of ganglia of the sympathetic system

That makes twenty-six pairs. And this number is not due to chance. The Cabbalah teaches that twenty-six is the sum of the four letters of the name of God, the Tetragrammaton Iod, Hé, Vav, Hé: יהוה for י Yod = 10, ה (Hé) = 5, ו (Vav) = 6, ה (Hé) = 5.

The name of God, therefore, is constructed according to the same laws as those which govern the sympathetic system.

– The two groups of three pairs of intracranial and cervical ganglia, which are linked to the divine world, correspond to the psychological or mental aspect of nature.

– The twelve pairs of dorsal ganglia, which are linked to the spiritual world, correspond to the physiological aspect of nature.

– The two groups of four pairs of lumbar and sacral ganglia, which are linked to the physical world, correspond to the anatomical aspect of nature.

Let us now look at each of these groups in more detail:

– The two groups of three pairs of ganglia (intracranial and cervical): Three is the number of God, the Trinity of Father, Son, and Holy Spirit. The Cabbalah reveals the secrets of this number, for it studies the principles, the factors that act in the universe. The Cabbalah relates to the head, and answers the question 'who': Who created? Who acts?

– The twelve pairs of dorsal ganglia: Twelve is the number of the universe created by God which is symbolized by the twelve constellations of the zodiac. Astrology reveals this number to us because it studies the functions of the organs of the cosmic body. Astrology relates to the heart and the lungs, and answers the question 'when?'.

– The two groups of four pairs of ganglia (lumbar and sacral): Four is the number of alchemy because it represents the four states of matter: earth, water, air, and fire. Alchemy answers the question 'what?'.

These twenty-six pairs of ganglia of the sympathetic system are thus divided into five groups, and these five groups are linked to the five virtues of Christ: purity, justice, love, wisdom, and truth.[1]

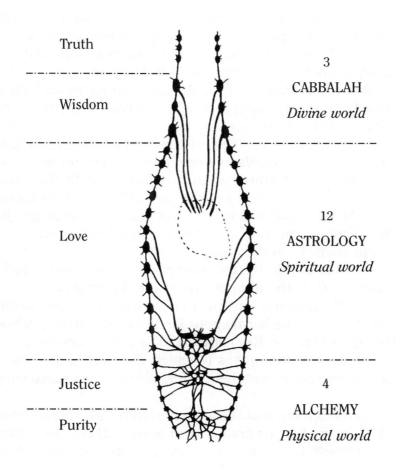

Truth

Wisdom

3

CABBALAH

Divine world

Love

12

ASTROLOGY

Spiritual world

Justice

4

ALCHEMY

Physical world

Purity

Network of ganglia,
corresponding to the virtues and numbers

– Purity is linked to the four pairs of sacral ganglia that make up the base of the chain of ganglia, because purity is the basis, the foundation.

– Justice corresponds to the four pairs of lumbar ganglia situated in the region of the kidneys, which are linked to Libra ♎, the symbol of balance and equilibrium. It relates to the organs of nutrition: the stomach, liver, intestines, and so on. When a person fails to nourish himself correctly, the balance is upset and the suffering that follows reveals that justice had to intervene to restore order.

– Love is linked to the twelve pairs of dorsal ganglia. Love is a force which expands us (we see this expansion in the act of breathing) and unites us with all beings, with the entire universe symbolized by the twelve constellations of the zodiac.

– Wisdom is linked to the three pairs of cervical ganglia, which, through the cardiac nerves, are linked to the heart. True wisdom stems from the heart.

– Truth is linked to the three pairs of intracranial ganglia, because truth is the summit, the goal to be reached.

Truth, wisdom, love, justice, and purity bring us into contact with all the harmonious forces of the universe, whose blessings we receive. Each virtue enhances the performance of the ganglia and the organs to which the ganglia are linked, just as every fault against these virtues disrupts their functioning.

A relationship exists between the sympathetic nerve-system and the brain. But the brain cannot act directly on the organs. It acts through the medium of a conductor, the orthosympathetic system, of which the solar plexus is the most important centre.[2] This is why an initiate works to bring this connection between the solar plexus and the brain to the level of consciousness, because once this connection is established, he is able to reach and strengthen the organs of his physical body.

There is a link between psychic states and physical states. Through the agency of the solar plexus a feeling of sadness, for instance, acts on the sympathetic nerve paths, which act as vasoconstrictors and begin to contract the arterial system. Thus the contraction generated by a feeling of sadness hampers the flow of blood and consequently also digestion, respiration, and so on. To stimulate the nerves that dilate, on the other hand, we must call on joy and love. Every day, on awakening, we should say: 'Lord God, our Creator, I thank you that I am alive and well, that I can breathe, walk, sing, look, and listen, because these are invaluable treasures.' If human beings grow old so quickly it is because they do not know how to call on joy and love every morning.

The things that most disturb the solar plexus are the chaotic manifestations of the astral body, such as fear, anger, jealousy, and impassioned love. And since the solar plexus is where our strength is stored, the result of this disharmony is total demagnetization. When you have had a fright or a shock, your strength immediately drains from you, your legs are no longer able to support you, your hands shake, your head becomes empty. This means that your solar plexus has used up all its strength. But if the solar plexus can be emptied, it can also be filled, and this is what disciples must learn: how to replenish the solar plexus. Let me give you a few methods.

Every tree is a reservoir of energies emitted by the sun and the earth. So choose a large tree, stand with your back against it and put your left hand on your back with the palm of your hand touching the trunk of the tree and with the palm of your right hand on your solar plexus. Concentrate on the tree and ask it to give you strength. You will receive this strength with the left hand and you pour it into your solar plexus with your right hand. It is a kind of transfusion of energy.

You can also strengthen your solar plexus by watching and listening to a flowing spring, waterfall or fountain. These are seemingly insignificant actions, but they produce great results. People often watch water flowing, but they do so without being aware of the work they could do with it for their spiritual advancement.[3] Besides, have they ever really thought about the use we could make of all the elements nature gives them?

If you are at home, you can stretch out on the bed, place both hands on your solar plexus and imagine you are drawing energies from the entire cosmos. You can also plunge your hands – or better still, your feet – in water.[4] Whenever you feel demagnetized, troubled or tense, put some hot water in a bowl and bathe your feet in the water, focussing totally on what you are doing, and then wash your feet with great care. If you have difficulty meditating, take a foot bath and you will have a sense of harmony in your solar plexus, and this harmony will be reflected in the way your brain functions.

How to have a direct influence on the solar plexus is a science that will be studied in the future. For the moment, however, it has its own way of life, and human beings can do very little about it until, some time in the future, they learn to influence it directly. But how can we influence the solar plexus indirectly? By endeavouring to lead a pure, sensible, balanced life.[5]

So many people look exhausted, depressed, and stressed. They are in this state because they do not know how to work with their solar plexus. If a person's face is dreary and lacklustre, it means that their solar plexus is not functioning properly. But you, at least, should try to use the methods I give you to make your solar plexus more active and more vigilant. Then gradually you will begin to sense an improvement not only in your physical equilibrium, but you will also get better results in your spiritual work.

You will say: 'But spiritual work is done with the brain.' Yes, but only part of it. The main work is done by the heart. Why do we talk about the intelligence of the heart? Even the Gospels refer to the heart as an organ of understanding. But which heart are we talking about? Not the physical heart, of course. The true heart, the initiatic heart, is the solar plexus. The solar plexus grasps the great truths of spiritual life. The brain is merely able to do a little talking, studying, and writing – and a great deal of boasting – often without a clear idea what it is talking about. Just look at how things happen in the world: people explain, talk, and write, but in reality they do not really understand much, because it is impossible to understand properly with the brain. You have to feel, you have to experience things to understand them, and this understanding comes about through the solar plexus.

So, what does the relationship between the brain and the solar plexus consist in? We have seen how the solar plexus controls the majority of the functions of the physical body, but we must also realize that it is the solar plexus that created the brain and continues to feed it. Yes, the brain is a creation of the solar plexus, and this is why the solar plexus feeds it and sends it 'subsidies', but once it stops 'subsidizing' it, the individual loses his power of action: he becomes somnolent, has headaches, and is incapable of reflection.

The brain is not cut off from the solar plexus, but if it does not always enjoy its support it is because it is not yet able to communicate with it. The solar plexus, however, is itself a brain, but in reverse: the grey matter in the brain is on the outside and the white matter on the inside, but in the solar plexus it is the other way round. The grey matter, made up of nerve cells, enables thought; whereas the white matter, made up of nerve fibres, enables feelings. Thanks to its white matter on the outside, therefore, the solar plexus can feel everything that goes on inside the organism, in all the cells. And this is why it can constantly ensure that equilibrium is restored. The brain, on the other hand, feels nothing until things go very wrong, and then it does not know how to remedy the situation. When your heart beats too fast or too slowly, or when you have stomach ache, the brain can do nothing about it. In fact it is not up to the brain. But if you give your solar plexus the right conditions to function normally, it will restore the equilibrium.

As the human brain has developed, human beings have acquired a self-awareness which has enabled them to become individuals. The solar plexus on the other hand brings us into contact with the ocean of universal life. It is in communication with the entire cosmos, and this is not the case for the brain.[6] In reality this communication could be established, but the brain is not yet sufficiently developed, given that it was formed far more recently than the solar plexus. The brain is not yet fully organized, but it will become so in the future, because its task is to record all knowledge and to conceive notions that are still unimagined. Until such time, it is the solar plexus that is in charge. Together with the Hara centre – situated slightly lower down, with which it is in close communication – it is the solar plexus that controls everything.

Contemporary humanity is destroying itself because it attaches too much importance to the activities of the brain – studying, working with figures, worrying, criticizing, and so on. And since the brain is not well prepared to withstand great stress, many nervous illnesses today are the result of the brain being overburdened. In order to restore equilibrium, human beings must learn to redistribute the work between the two centres of the solar plexus and the brain.

The brain is only an instrument, and this instrument is not independent. But for an instrument to be in good working order it must be cared for. Take any machine, even an ordinary flashlight: if you reduce the current, its output will not be the same. Well, the brain is like a flashlight, but in most people it is not a very good one. It is a candle that produces hardly any light. So it must be plugged in to the inexhaustible source, the solar plexus, which will give it all powers. Why did the ancients called this plexus 'solar'? Because it is linked to the sun, the heart of our universe.

The relationship between the solar plexus and the brain is that of two complementary poles. It is exactly the relationship of man and woman, in that cosmic intelligence has given both men and women certain powers, but these powers are so different from each other that they can manifest fully only when they are united and work together in harmony toward the same goal.[7] What men can give, women cannot, and vice versa, but when they combine their powers, they become creators. It is therefore important to understand how these two organs, the solar plexus and the brain, are polarized into masculine and feminine, how they act upon each other, and what power they have over matter.

The brain expresses itself; it speaks, gives orders, organizes, and even makes a commotion, shouting, and gesticulating. But who enables it to do this? The solar plexus. It is the solar plexus that sends energies to the brain, but we do not see it. It is there, hidden and silent; it does not reveal itself, and no one even suspects its existence. The brain is active, dynamic, but it tires easily if the solar plexus does not send it subsidies. This is why, when you want to meditate or do some intense intellectual work, you should not focus your mind abruptly on the subject of meditation or on the task before you, otherwise it will seize up and you will achieve nothing. Begin by concentrating on your solar plexus and when you feel you have reached a state of peace, of dilatation, then set to work. Your brain will then be nourished and supported by the energies it receives from the solar plexus. And if, while you are working, you sense that your brain is beginning to seize up, massage your solar plexus in an anti-clockwise direction and a few minutes later you will feel that you are in the clear once again and you can get back to work.

You must learn to share activity between the brain and the solar plexus, just as in a true marriage, in which the man and the woman live in harmony and share the work. Your brain will then be able to reveal all the riches of the solar plexus. All the knowledge of the universe, from the most distant past, is contained in the solar plexus, and it is up to the brain to bring it out and give it expression. The brain is nothing more than an instrument whose task is to draw out into the light of day the riches embedded in the depths of our being.

The white matter in the brain, which is on the inside, communicates with the white matter of the solar plexus, which is on the outside, and the brain's grey matter, which is on the outside, communicates with the grey matter of the solar plexus, which is on the inside. And the cross-over occurs in the neck. This is why, when you feel that the communication between the two is failing, you can also gently massage your neck in the area of the cervical vertebrae. The neck is the vital pathway for our inner currents to flow through. If you squeeze a person's neck too tightly you can kill him.

Once you have learned to concentrate on your solar plexus, you will have all its energies at your disposal and will be able to send them to your brain. How clear and simple it is! The two principles can be seen at work everywhere. Would you like me to give you another example? A tree has roots, a trunk, and branches. The roots release and transmit the energies needed for leaves, flowers, and fruits to appear. You cannot see the roots, but remove them and everything you can see will disappear. The visible is always the result of something invisible that is hidden deep down. In us the solar plexus represents the roots, and our trunk and limbs represent the trunk and branches of the tree. A human being is like a tree. We have roots, a trunk, branches, and in the brain are leaves, flowers, and fruits. The solar plexus is the roots of the brain and it is this that is the most important. It is always the roots that are the most important, because if something is amiss with the roots, everything else collapses. You see, this is an irrefutable argument.

When you want to meditate you choose a spiritual subject on which to focus. Then you can follow your train of thought, see how it develops, almost make out its content and its colours, and all this is the work of the brain. But if, during the course of your meditation, you succeed in rising to a higher level, you will sense that your brain stops working and your solar plexus becomes active. You no longer understand things intellectually, analytically, but you understand them in a global way, you vibrate in harmony with them, a feeling of fulfilment pervades you, and your meditation becomes contemplation. You are no longer thinking; you are contemplating something magnificent... and you are intensely alive. You sense that you understand things much better than with your brain, but you do not know *how* you understand them. It is simply a fact. Yes, because with your heart, your solar plexus, you have succeeded in touching the heart of the universe.[8]

You can study things, assess them and understand them, but that does not yet mean you have touched the heart of the universe. These are merely preliminary conditions. You can touch the heart of the universe only with your own heart. When your heart, your solar plexus, begins to feel, to love, to live with great intensity, then you will touch and stir the universal heart, the heart of God, and from this heart energies, forces, and currents will come to you that will vivify and enlighten you. Yes, once you succeed in projecting from your heart an immense energy of love, then, in accordance with the laws of affinity and of resonance, the other heart will respond. To touch the heart of the universe is to know, to feel, to penetrate the plans and schemes of the Deity, of the universal Soul. But you will achieve this neither through science, nor through book-learning, nor through speeches, however eloquent.

If you want to touch the heart of the universe you must vibrate on the same wavelength, in other words, you must emanate the same selfless love. When what you wish and ask for concerns not only your own self-interest, but the good of humankind and the entire universe, then your desire vibrates on the same wavelength as the heart of the universe. And as the heart of the universe is the source of life, the source of happiness, beauty, poetry, and music, the source of all that is splendid and divine, then you will receive this life, this happiness, this splendour... you will taste fulfilment.

You have to touch a person's heart if you want something from him. If you do not succeed in touching his heart, he may not even hear you. There are days when you plead with heaven, hoping to move it to pity or to impress it, but that is pointless. The only reply you will get is: 'We don't understand what you are saying', and the door will shut in your face. And then there are other days when you say nothing, you simply gaze, and heaven says: 'Come, enter. Here, take this.' Why is this so? Well, you have to find the secret.

I have already spoken to you about crystal receivers. Some time ago, when radios were not as sophisticated or as popular as they are today, many people made their own crystal sets. To receive radio broadcasts, you had to move a small needle on the crystal until you made contact. When the needle touched certain points you could hear talking or music, whereas on other points you heard nothing. I thought a lot about this phenomenon. You move the needle from right to left along the crystal and you hear nothing. This despite the fact that you are touching it. Yes, but you are not touching its heart, for this crystal too has a heart. And as soon as you touch its heart, you hear music. The universe also has a heart, but we do not know its laws, and this is why we are not able to establish contact in order to tune in to its waves and receive revelations.[9]

To be able to touch the heart of the universe you must intensify your love. This work takes place in the solar plexus. You project and direct a force, an energy, but you do it without the intervention of the brain. You are fully conscious, you direct these energies and sense that you are reaching another level of understanding and knowledge. How can we explain this? It is simply that there is another form of thought, another form of understanding which you have to try and discover. I could talk to you about this at greater length, but what use would that be? You would not understand, because in order to understand, you must have had this experience. Work, therefore, work to change your life, to live a harmonious life. Then and only then will you be able to trigger the forces contained in the solar plexus, because the law of the solar plexus is harmony. It is by introducing harmony within you that you enter into communication with cosmic life.

A child in its mother's womb is joined to its mother by the umbilical cord, which is located in the area of the solar plexus. It is through the umbilical cord that she nourishes her child. At birth this link is cut, which is why birth can be seen as simply the passage from a state of dependency to a state of independence, of freedom. But in reality, human beings are not yet fully independent. Their solar plexus is joined to Mother Nature by another umbilical cord, an etheric cord, and Mother Nature carries us in her womb, sustains us and nourishes us, and we must work to strengthen and enrich this link.

'You Are Gods'

Notes

1 See *The Symbolic Language of Geometrical Figures*, Izvor 218, Chap. 4: 'The Pentagram'.
2 See *Spiritual Alchemy*, C.W. 2, Chap. 6: 'The Miracle of the Loaves and Fishes'.
3 See *The Mysteries of Fire and Water*, Izvor 232, Chap. 3: 'Water, the Matrix of Life'.
4 See *Spiritual Alchemy*, C.W. 2, Chap. 7: 'The Feet and the Solar Plexus'.
5 See *L'homme dans l'organisme cosmique,* Fascicule n° 4.
6 See *The Splendour of Tiphareth*, C.W. 10, Chap. 17 (I, II): 'Day and Night – Consciousness and the Subconscious'.
7 See *Cosmic Balance – The Secret of Polarity*, Izvor 237, Chap. 4 (IV): 'The Role of The Masculine and The Feminine – Man and Woman'.
8 See *Harmony*, C.W. 6, Chap. 8: 'The Human Intellect and Cosmic Intelligence', Chap. 11: 'The Initiatic Heart'.
9 See *Love and Sexuality*, C.W. 15, Chap. 1: 'A Question of Attitude'.

II

Oil in the lamp

Then the kingdom of heaven will be like this. Ten bridesmaids took their lamps and went to meet the bridegroom. Five of them were foolish, and five were wise. When the foolish took their lamps, they took no oil with them; but the wise took flasks of oil with their lamps. As the bridegroom was delayed, all of them became drowsy and slept.

But at midnight there was a shout, 'Look! Here is the bridegroom! Come out to meet him.' Then all those bridesmaids got up and trimmed their lamps. The foolish said to the wise, 'Give us some of your oil, for our lamps are going out.' But the wise replied, 'No! there will not be enough for you and for us; you had better go to the dealers and buy some for yourselves.' And while they went to buy it, the bridegroom came, and those who were ready went with him into the wedding banquet; and the door was shut. Later the other bridesmaids came also, saying, 'Lord, lord, open to us.' But he replied, 'Truly I tell you, I do not know you.' Keep awake therefore, for you know neither the day nor the hour.

Mt 25: 1 – 13

Reading this parable you have no doubt been struck by some of the odd details. All those who have been invited to the feast must bring a lighted lamp. One assumes, therefore, that the room is dark and everyone must bring something to light it. Have you ever heard of such a thing? And how is it that the so-called wise bridesmaids refuse to give up some of their oil? How stingy of them! And what kind of bridegroom is this who does not hesitate to close the door in the face of the five bridesmaids who go out to meet him? Is their sin so great that they deserve such punishment? What an unpleasant and uncivilized person the bridegroom must be. He wakes up everyone in the middle of the night and then leaves five poor girls standing outside simply because they arrive late, having first had to go and buy some oil. Is it really worth waiting for such a disagreeable man who makes such a fuss over a little oil?

Unusual details like these are found in all the parables, but it is in just such details that the initiates find evidence of the deep wisdom of the Gospels. In view of the contradictions and absurdities in this parable one is forced to conclude that the lamp, the oil, the bridegroom, and even the bridesmaids are symbols which need to be interpreted.

Let us begin with the bridesmaids. Five wise and five foolish bridesmaids. Why did Jesus choose the number five in this parable? Why not four or six? Because five is the number of the five fundamental virtues, kindness, justice, love, wisdom, and truth. Thus the five wise bridesmaids represent these virtues, whereas the five foolish bridesmaids represent the corresponding faults.[1]

Let us now look at the lamp these bridesmaids had to bring to light up the room in which the feast was held. We no longer use oil lamps today, but as symbols, the oil and the lamp play a very important role in our lives. Let us suppose, for instance, that you are anaemic: your vitality is diminished, you are somnolent and worn out. In other words the lamp of your body is running short of oil and is beginning to go out. A lamp with a flickering flame is sometimes taken to the hospital, where more oil is poured into it and the flame burns more brightly. In this case the 'oil' is the blood received by transfusion. In reality, this 'oil' is everywhere in nature. Plants draw it from the soil, from the air, from the sun's rays, and thanks to it they manufacture the sap, symbol of this living sap that flows also within us. Where? In our solar plexus.

The solar plexus is the reservoir of our vital forces, the storage battery of all energies. And if we know how to replenish this store on a daily basis, we will have a source from which to draw the strength we need at any moment. In other words, our lamp will give us the means to wait for the one who is to come, for the one the bridesmaids were waiting for, the bridegroom, and who may come to us every day in the form of light, wisdom, inspiration, and love.

The oil symbolizes our life force, the sap that nourishes our cells. You have all had many experiences in which you have noticed, for instance, that if you have been able to act with wisdom, kindness, generosity, and self-control for a whole week, you are able to handle problems more easily in the days that follow. It is as if a prop, a new strength had developed within you, in the cells of your nervous system, which enables you to sustain great efforts and withstand great stress. Those who lead a sensible, luminous life, full of love, feel a force growing within them that can be likened to the oil of a lamp. And then, even if they are tired and exhausted, they feel this inner force working to refresh them.

You see now how the parable of the ten bridesmaids has a very profound meaning. To initiates this meaning is perfectly clear. And if Jesus spoke of bridesmaids or 'virgins', some wise and some foolish, it is precisely because the solar plexus is linked to the astrological sign of Virgo. The solar plexus is the 'heart' Jesus was referring to when he said: *'Out of the believer's heart shall flow rivers of living water'*.

The five wise and the five foolish bridesmaids represent two types of human being (both women and men, of course): those who know how to prepare the oil for their lamp and those who do not know how. If you expend all your energies in fits of anger, in intrigues and sensual pleasures, then when the bridegroom arrives – in other words, when an opportunity to receive heavenly blessings arises – you will be weak and exhausted, and you will suffer because you will realize what you are missing. Even if you are present, you will feel inwardly excluded, because you have not learned to prepare this oil, the preparation of which requires a great deal of time, and no one else can give it to you or prepare it for you. Nature provides us with a little of this oil in the food we eat and the air we breathe, but it is primarily up to us to learn to prepare it inwardly through our feelings and thoughts.

The five foolish bridesmaids who did not prepare the oil for their lamp were not able to enter and join the bridegroom. This is what the sentence: *'Truly I tell you, I do not know you'* suggests, in other words, 'You have never prepared any oil. You come here for the first time today. You have made no efforts, no spiritual progress in your life. I have never seen you before. I do not know who you are. Go away!' The bridegroom is not bad, but he does not allow himself to be disturbed by the 'foolish'. We all know how harsh nature can be. When we have used up all the most precious forces she has given us, she is in no hurry to give them back. If we have been ill, convalescence is often long, and recovery is sometimes impossible. But can we say that nature is cruel when it is we who have been foolish?

416

The sentence: *'Keep awake therefore, for you know neither the day nor the hour'*[2] is also important. 'Keep awake' does not mean 'do not sleep', because all the bridesmaids had fallen asleep, the wise as well as the foolish, and the parable does not say that this was a mistake. Keep awake means be awake spiritually, because you do not know at what time the beloved will come. And this beloved, this mystical bridegroom, is the Holy Spirit.[3] If, through prayer and meditation and the purity of your life, you are able to prepare the spiritual oil in your heart and soul, you will one day be visited by the Spirit. Whether you are a man or a woman is unimportant. The wise bridesmaid of which Jesus spoke symbolizes the human soul, preparing to receive the Holy Spirit. It is for the Holy Spirit that she must have oil, because the Holy Spirit is a flame. A flame has to be nourished, and oil is its nourishment.

The Holy Spirit is none other than the bridegroom of light, and he will come only if you have sufficient oil to feed his flame.[4] You now understand why it is said that on the day of Pentecost the disciples received the Holy Spirit in the form of flames, tongues of fire that burned above their heads. It is because they had filled their lamps with oil, this spiritual quintessence which alone can attract the bridegroom, the divine Spirit.

Notes

1 See *New Light on the Gospels*, Izvor 217, Chap. 9: '. The Parable of the Five Wise and the Five Foolish Virgins'.
2 See *The True Meaning of Christ's Teaching*, Izvor 215, Chap. 9: 'Watch and Pray'.
3 See *The Mysteries of Fire and Water*, Izvor 232, Chap. 18: 'The Coming of the Holy Spirit'.
4 Ibid., Chap. 9: 'Feeding the Flame'.

3

The Hara centre

People travelling to India are sometimes surprised to see that although many sadhus and yogis eat almost nothing, they have a well developed belly. Also, most the statues of Buddha and other sages show them with a prominent stomach. Why? Because to Orientals a well developed belly is a sign of power, of strength, of spiritual reserves which have been built up, particularly through breathing exercises, which strengthen that part of the body. And look at the Japanese: many of them have a belly that is very large in proportion to the rest of the body, and they are strong, well-balanced, and have considerable intellectual ability. This is because they work at developing what they call the Hara centre. This centre is situated four centimetres below the navel. Hara in Japanese means 'belly', hence the expression 'to commit hara-kiri', meaning to commit suicide by disembowelling oneself. To the Japanese sages the Hara centre is the source of life, of equilibrium, and they teach methods to develop it. People who have worked on their Hara centre are remarkable for their extraordinary energy and equilibrium.

A great many disorders currently suffered by Westerners are caused, as I have already told you, by their having disrupted the equilibrium. The majority of their activities revolve around the brain, as if it were the centre, whereas in reality it is only the periphery. This is why, when they experience a shock, they are unable to recover their balance, because the inner centres that would remedy the situation no longer function. If they knew how to work with their Hara centre, how to develop it, they would never feel exhausted, however much nervous energy they expended.

Of course there is a problem in this regard for Westerners, in that they generally consider the centres located in the lower part of the physical body to be unworthy of contributing to the development of their psychic and spiritual lives. Even I, for years, when I spoke to you about the centre, when I told you that you should find your centre, I was almost always referring to the divine centre within you, to your spirit, your higher self. I did not broach the subject of this centre below the navel, because it has taken years and years to prepare you to penetrate and explore it in order to know the true origin of your being. For your origin is here. It is no good looking for it on the outside, because it is not on the surface. You need to delve, delve deep down to this region of the Hara centre, which corresponds to the psychic region that Westerners call the subconscious.[1]

The Hara centre is mentioned in many esoteric books, but in very different ways. And even the writings of some Christian authors show they know this centre. In his book *The Twelve Keys,* the alchemist Basil Valentine invites the disciple to descend to the centre of the earth to find the philosopher's stone. He says: '*Visita Interiora Terrae; Rectificando Invenies Occultum Lapidem, Veram Medicinam*' – 'Visit the bowels of the earth. By rectifying you will find the hidden stone, the true medicine'. If you take the first letter of each word you get the word VITRIOLUM. *Visita Interiora Terrae...* The earth into which we must descend is, of course, not our planet but our own earth, our physical body. The 'bowels' are the Hara centre, and when you understand what this centre represents, you will be able to decipher the symbolism of the crib in which Jesus was born.*

The three most important deities of the Hindu Pantheon are Brahma (the creator), Vishnu (the preserver), and Shiva (the destroyer), and Hindu scriptures say that Brahma resides in the belly, Vishnu in the region of the heart and lungs, and Shiva in the brain. Why is it Brahma, the creator, that resides in the abdomen? If the abdomen were really such an unworthy region, and the brain, on the contrary, so noble, surely Brahma should have be situated in the brain? But this is not the case: it is Shiva – identified as the destroyer – that resides in the brain. Why? Because the brain – that is, the lower mental faculty, which analyses, separates, dissects, and breaks things down – cannot give us an accurate understanding of reality. In fact it represents a threat to our equilibrium.

Since the abdomen is the part of the body where beings are formed, it is extremely important and there is nothing shameful about it. Why would life begin in a shameful place? If Cosmic Intelligence has chosen this region, it is because it considers it sacred, so why should human beings scorn it? Of course it is not especially beautiful, at least not according to human notions of beauty. But why is it that life stems from there? Not only is it in this region that a pregnant woman carries her child, but the child, through the umbilical cord, draws all strength and nourishment from it. The Russians call the entire region of the solar plexus and the Hara centre '*jivot*', and '*jivot*' in Bulgarian means 'life'. Yes, because this is where life first appears before spreading into the other organs. So the brain, too, is dependent on this centre from which it receives

* See Part IX: 'The Feast of Christmas'.

422

life. Like the solar plexus, the Hara centre represents our roots. And if we go down into the roots to see what nature has put there, we discover a world with an extraordinary wealth of materials and energies.*

The source of life is located in the abdomen, and this is where the Father, Brahma, the creator lives. But before we can feel and communicate with him, we need to work for many years and to learn not to rely so much on Shiva, the brain.

For years I have been teaching you only about the world of above, that is, the world of consciousness, of light. This time of preparation was necessary before you could delve into the depths of your being without danger. To know yourself truly, you need to know the two regions and learn to work with them, with that which is up above and that which is below. Why is Jesus said to have descended into hell?[2] Above are the centres of the brain and below is this centre that Japanese sages call Hara. The Hara centre represents the subconscious, the hidden depths of a human being, and of course, these regions are very dangerous. This is why it is important to explore the terrain starting from the top, and once you are strong, once you have the weapons and tools you need, you can descend into the depths.[3]

The greatest material riches are found under the ground – gold, precious stones, precious metals, coal, oil, and so on – and a multitude of entities and spirits work on them. Well, in the psychic as well as in the physical world, materials and wealth are below, not above. But hell and monsters also exist below, and this is why we must learn to protect ourselves before

* The Greek god of hell, Hades, 'the invisible', was also known as Pluto, 'the giver of riches', and was sometimes depicted with a horn of plenty. (Editor's note)

going below, otherwise we shall be swallowed up. It is for this reason that initiates, who are true pedagogues, first teach their disciples the realities of the higher world, because to face darkness you need light.

Human beings are no more capable of direct contact with their Hara centre than with the solar plexus, because they have no way of reaching their subconscious. They can only reach it in a roundabout way, by the way they live. However, I can give you a method: begin your meditation, and after a few minutes place both hands on your abdomen while concentrating on the Hara region. But you must do this exercise only in a spirit of purity, for your own spiritual evolution and the good of humankind, otherwise other centres nearby will be awakened and you will be dragged down into the dark regions of your being. This is why you must prepare yourself before working with the Hara centre. Once you are prepared you can delve into these depths without danger. Because these are the true depths, the deep chasms of human beings.

You need to be pure, strong, and well protected in order to explore the world below, and this is not the case with so many today who, like psychoanalysts, embark on the exploration of the subconscious. They do not realize what forces they are facing, and the results, both for themselves and for their patients, are often negative. Nevertheless, psychoanalysis, even if it is practised clumsily, is a sign that the time has come for human beings to explore the dark and unknown regions of their being. At the moment they are just scratching the surface. Of course it is true that psychoanalysts have discovered part of the subconscious, but they are still a long way from knowing all the regions and entities that live and work there. The day they are capable of exploring the Hara centre, which is embedded deep in the subconscious, and of understanding how it is linked to superconsciousness, then yes, they will have made great progress.

In the meantime, initiates know more than psychoanalysts. When they speak of 'joining the tail and the head of the serpent' they are using this image to say that the Hara centre, the centre below, must unite with the higher centre, the chakra Sahasrara, located at the top of the head. But as long as we have not first worked in a more accessible sphere it is dangerous to want to venture into these regions. The spiritual life has its own programme. We must begin by purifying and strengthening ourselves, and when finally we begin to see our way clearly and we feel strong, then we can afford to descend into the depths of the chasm. These experiences await all of you, but you must prepare yourselves.

So these were just a few words about the Hara centre. You think that it is not much, but in reality it is already a great deal.

Notes

1 See *Man's Psychic Life: Elements and Structures*, Izvor 222, Chap. 12: 'The Subconscious'.
2 See *Truth: Fruit of Wisdom and Love*, Izvor 234, Chap. 17: 'Truth Transcends Good and Evil', p. 190-193.
3 See *Love and Sexuality*, C.W. 14, Chap. 2: 'Taking the Bull by the Horns – The Caduceus of Hermes'.

4

The Kundalini force
and
the chakras

St John's *Revelations* concludes with the vision of a heavenly city, the new Jerusalem, with its foundations adorned with precious stones, its walls of jasper, and its doors, each one a single pearl. Through this city flows a river: *'Then the angel showed me the river of the water of life, bright as crystal, flowing from the throne of God and of the Lamb through the middle of the street of the city. On either side of the river is the tree of life with its twelve kinds of fruit, producing its fruit each month; and the leaves of the tree are for the healing of the nations.'* How can a tree have its roots on either side of a river?

If we are to interpret this vision of the new Jerusalem we must first understand that, in reality, the city represents a human being.[1] The river of the water of life descending from the throne of God is the current of energies that flows from the brain down through the spinal column. The Tree of Life in the centre of the city is the solar plexus, and the roots of the Tree are the twelve pairs of dorsal ganglia and nerves located on either side of the spinal column, which, in turn, are twelve branches producing twelve lots of fruit. These fruits are related to the twelve signs of the zodiac, of which man is the synthesis.[2] We must eat these fruits, for they represent the qualities and virtues of the constellations of the zodiac. In order, these are: Aries, activity; Taurus, sensitivity and kindness; Gemini, a taste for study; Cancer, perception of the invisible world; Leo, nobleness and courage; Virgo, purity; Libra, sense of cosmic equilibrium; Scorpio, understanding of life and death; Sagittarius, the link with heaven; Capricorn, control of self and of others; Aquarius, brotherliness and universality; and Pisces, sacrifice. These are the qualities of the fruits of the Tree of Life.

Thus the roots embedded in the banks on either side of the river of life referred to by St John represent all the nerves and ganglia situated on either side of the spinal column. The spinal column links heaven to earth – our heaven, that is, the brain, to our earth, the belly. Beneath the earth burns a fire that causes violent eruptions from time to time. But this fire also burns within us, at the base of the spinal column. This underground fire, which is the fire of the belly and the genitalia,[3] corresponds to what the yogis of India call the Kundalini force. And although at the moment, the spinal column has a purely anatomical and physiological function in most people, there are initiates who, by awakening the Kundalini force, have succeeded in bringing their spinal column to life in view of an immense work of spirituality and magic.

The Kundalini force lies dormant at the base of the spinal cord. This is the 'strength of all strengths' referred to by Hermes Trismegistus in the Emerald Tablet. Once awakened it can move either upwards or downwards. If it moves up, the person in question enjoys the greatest spiritual development. If it moves down it produces the worst kind of physical and psychic disturbance. Those who awaken the Kundalini force without first becoming pure and fully in control of themselves, fall prey to unrestrained sexual passions and a demonic lust for power that puts them in opposition to the entire world. This is why disciples are advised not to attempt to awaken Kundalini before having worked on purity and humility. For this force, this 'strength of all strengths' can destroy as well as create.[4] Tantric science teaches that Kundalini sleeps seven slumbers and that it must therefore be awakened seven times, because it is buried under seven layers of increasingly subtle matter.

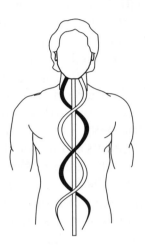

It is relatively easy to awaken Kundalini from its first sleep. But the question is not so much of how to awaken it, but of how and in which direction to guide it. The direction Kundalini takes is determined not by a person's will, but by his qualities and virtues. When the Kundalini serpent awakens, it goes at once to where it will find nourishment. If this nourishment is in a person's inferior self, then regardless of any efforts he may make, that is where Kundalini will go, and for the individual this means hell, true hell. In order for the serpent to move upward it must be attracted by the higher side. The Kundalini force rises up through the Sushumna canal, in the spinal cord. On either side of the Sushumna canal the two currents Ida (polarized negatively and linked to the Moon) and

Pingala (polarized positively and linked to the Sun) rise in an intertwining spiral. The traditions of ancient Greece and Judaism also present this process with the symbolic images of the Caduceus of Hermes and the Sephirotic Tree. And even contemporary science has found technical applications of it with the laser.[5]

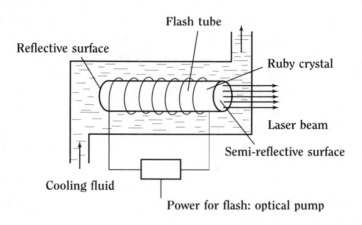

The Ida current ends at the left nostril and Pingala at the right. This is why breathing exercises are considered to be the most effective way of awakening the Kundalini serpent. When you close your right nostril and breathe in through your left nostril you produce a current that flows through the Ida canal. This current passes through the Muladhara chakra, the centre where the serpent sleeps, thus producing a slight vibration that begins to shake it from its torpor. When you block your left nostril and breathe in through your right nostril, the current passes through the Pingala canal, and again gives the serpent a few impulses. Thus, as you do your breathing exercises every morning[6], you are gently awakening the Kundalini force. But you must be careful not to prolong these exercises too much.

When I was in India I heard talk of all the different methods used by the yogis to awaken Kundalini. Some of them are incredible, going to the point of introducing a silver wire into a place that I shall not name. There are some who are ready to go to ludicrous lengths to possess the powers that can come from awakening this force. But true Hindu initiates teach that before the serpent Kundalini is awakened, a yogi must free the Sushumna canal by leading a pure life and by appropriate exercises. This work of purification is necessary, because when Kundalini awakens, it sets in motion the whole of a person's psychic life. It is a fire that burns everything in its path. This is why the way must be clear so that it may move through quickly and reach the crown chakra, Sahasrara. If it finds obstacles and impurities in its way, it cuts a path through them by producing fires and earthquakes.

Jesus says in the Gospels: *'Enter through the narrow gate...'*,[7] and *'..., it is easier for a camel to go through the eye of a needle than for someone who is rich to enter the kingdom of God.'* Both these phrases refer to the awakening of the Kundalini force. The central canal is extremely narrow, and the force that brings illumination can move through it only if the person has removed all obstacles from its path, and it is this force that sets the chakras in motion.

What are the chakras? After centuries of observation and dissection with increasingly sophisticated tools, anatomists have gained a very detailed knowledge of the human body and its physical structure. But they are still a long way from having found that which initiates have discovered of the subtle anatomy of human beings, by means of clairvoyance and spiritual experiences. One of the most impressive discoveries is that made by the initiates of India about the system of the seven chakras. For thousands of years they have been teaching that beyond their physical body, in their etheric and astral bodies, human beings possess subtle centres lying along the axis of the spinal column. They called these centres 'chakras', (which in Sanskrit means 'wheels') or lotuses.

In ascending order they are:

– at the base of the spinal column: Muladhara, the four-petalled lotus;

– immediately above the sexual organs: Svadhishthana, the six-petalled lotus;

– in the region of the navel and solar plexus: Manipura, the ten-petalled lotus;

– in the region of the heart: Anahata, the twelve-petalled lotus;

– at the front of the throat: Vishuddha, the sixteen-petalled lotus;

– between the eyebrows: Ajna, which has two large petals, each divided into forty-eight smaller petals, giving ninety-six in all;

– on the top of the head: Sahasrara,[8] the thousand-petalled lotus. In fact Sahasrara has 960 outer petals and a central corolla of twelve petals, which gives 972 petals in all. The twelve petals of the corolla are golden yellow and the outer ring of 960 petals is violet, and the two rings spin in opposite directions.

There is no visible sign of these spiritual centres in the physical body, but the organs close to which they are located are directly influenced by them. Since the chakras are activated by the awakening of Kundalini force, these subtle centres are inactive in the majority of people. Once the Kundalini force begins to stir to activity, the yogi's work consists of making it rise up through the other chakras, where it actuates and releases the powers they contain. Tantric tradition describes Kundalini

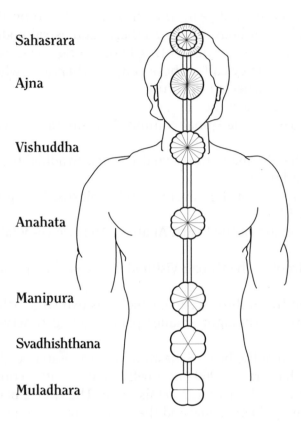

Sahasrara

Ajna

Vishuddha

Anahata

Manipura

Svadhishthana

Muladhara

as a serpent coiled three times on itself inside a triangular form at the heart of the Muladhara chakra. When it is awakened in favourable conditions, it is like a flame that spirals upwards along the spinal column, working on each chakra with its tongue in order to weld and combine the different elements that will enable it to spin. A chakra is an extremely fragile system of very fine wheels which only the serpent Kundalini can adjust and set in motion. It is when a chakra begins to spin, that the powers and faculties associated with it can begin to manifest.

The chakras differ from each other in colour, in the number of their petals – in other words, in the rate and intensity of their vibrations – in the divinities that inhabit them, and above all, in the virtues and powers their awakening bestows on a human being. Muladhara bestows life force; Svadhishthana creative power; Manipura collective consciousness; Anahata universal love; Vishuddha wisdom; Ajna clairvoyance, and Sahasrara omnipotence and freedom. A feminine deity, or Shakti, inhabits each chakra. Their names are, in ascending order: Dakini Shakti, Rakini Shakti, Lakini Shakti, Kakini Shakti, Shakini Shakti, and Hakini Shakti. When Kundalini has completed its journey and arrived in the chakra Sahasrara, it reaches Shiva, the masculine principle. The masculine and feminine principles, the head and the tail of the serpent, come together in a blinding light, and from that moment on the yogi, having reached the summit, is free from all constraints. But so few have reached that point.

The Book of Genesis says that Adam and Eve lived in the garden of Eden, in which, among all kinds of other trees, grew the Tree of Life and the Tree of the Knowledge of Good and Evil. God forbade Adam and Eve to eat the fruit of the Tree of the Knowledge of Good and Evil, but the serpent managed to persuade Eve to eat the forbidden fruit, and Eve persuaded Adam to do the same.

In the light of Tantric science, we see that the Tree of the Knowledge of Good and Evil corresponds exactly to the series of chakras lying along the spinal column, and the serpent coiled at the foot of the tree is Kundalini. The serpent spoke to Eve saying: 'If you eat the fruit of this tree, in other words, if you awaken your chakras, you will become like God, you will be omniscient, clairvoyant, and omnipotent.' So, of course, Eve was tempted, and so was Adam. But it was all premature; they were not ready to withstand the forces involved. They should have continued to eat the fruit of the Tree of Life, in other words, to draw their energies from the solar plexus, for thanks to those energies they knew neither tiredness, nor suffering, nor death. Yes, the Tree of Life is the solar plexus, whereas the other tree, the Tree of the Knowledge of Good and Evil, is the spinal column. Adam and Eve were in too much of a hurry to eat of its fruit. They should have waited until God allowed them to do so, when the time was right.

And the situation of human beings is exactly the same today. Those who know how to nourish themselves with the solar plexus, which is linked to the sun, can again enjoy the fruits of the Tree of Life. They draw strength from the Prana, the Elixir of Everlasting Life. Whereas those who want to eat the fruits of the other tree before they are sufficiently strong and pure, put themselves in the gravest danger. They endeavour to awaken Kundalini, they speak with the serpent, and the serpent leads them toward death, spiritual death.

The best advice for Westerners is not to attempt to awaken the Kundalini force, but to live a pure life, in accordance with the divine laws. Kundalini will then awaken when the time is right. Nothing should be rushed. Any other approach may cause a great deal of damage, for this force is like a fire capable of destroying even certain organs of the body. When you allow things to follow a smooth, natural course, you will awaken harmoniously to the consciousness of the divine world.

I sense a great desire in you to strive to reach this awakening of your consciousness. But don't be in a hurry; it will come in due course. All the exercises and practices of our teaching are so many different forms of yoga which will, one day, enable you to awaken the Kundalini force. Many people think they need to go to India to find true spirituality. A trip to India is wonderful, but you should also realize that the teaching of the Universal White Brotherhood, which examines and studies in depth the true teachings of Christ, offers a yoga suited to our times and adapted to Westerners.

Notes

1 See *The Book of Revelations: a Commentary*, Izvor 230, Chap. 17: 'The Heavenly City'.
2 See *The Zodiac, Key to Man and to the Universe*, Izvor 220, Chap. 10: 'The Twelve Tribes of Israel and the Twelve Labours of Hercules in Relation to the Zodiac'.
3 See *Angels and Other Mysteries of The Tree of Life*, Izvor 236, Chap. 12: 'Malkuth, Yesod, Hod, Tiphareth, Archangels and Seasons', p. 139.
4 See *Sexual Force or the Winged Dragon*, Izvor 205, Chap. 5: 'The Dangers of Tantric Yoga'.
5 See *Light is a Living Spirit*, Izvor 212, Chap. 9: 'The Spiritual Laser'.
6 See *The Fruits of the Tree of Life – The Cabbalistic Tradition*, C.W. 32, Chap. 16: 'Human and Cosmic Respiration'.
7 See *New Light on the Gospels*, Izvor 217, Chap. 5: 'The strait gate'.
8 See *Man's Subtle Bodies and Centres*, Izvor 219, Chap. 6: 'The Chakras'.

Part VIII

Living
in eternal life

1

'And this is eternal life,
that they may know you,
the only true God'

After Jesus had spoken these words, he looked up to heaven and said, 'Father, the hour has come; glorify your Son so that the Son may glorify you, since you have given him authority over all people, to give eternal life to all whom you have given him. And this is eternal life, that they may know you, the only true God, and Jesus Christ whom you have sent.'
Jn, 17: 1-3

Those who have meditated on these verses in St John's Gospel have wondered about the link Jesus sees between the knowledge of God and the possession of eternal life. How can knowledge give eternal life?

For many, to know God consists of reading theological treatises which discuss his attributes, his power, how he created the world, and so on, but it is not that. In any case, the question of knowledge itself is not very clear. Philosophy and psychology touch upon it, as does biology, which studies the different centres of the brain and the nervous system, their structure, and the connections that exist between them. But despite the discoveries made in these fields, the act of knowing remains a mystery.

'And this is eternal life, that they may know you...'

Life as a whole is simply a succession of acquisitions of knowledge. We read books and newspapers, we listen to the news, to lectures and conversations in order to 'know' about any number of things, but this knowledge can sometimes be like a poison to us. Or perhaps we try to 'get to know' people, to make the acquaintance of those who are rich, learned, influential, or seductive... but what will result from these acquaintances? Usually the desire to know is motivated by self-interest, in that we think to gain by it, and then the result turns out to be just the opposite. A fly looks at a spider's web with curiosity; it has no idea that at the centre of this network of threads sits a very wily creature that has spun this web for its own purposes. If the fly ventures in, it will indeed make the acquaintance of the spider, but it will lose everything else. Life is full of spider's webs and snares waiting for us. It is not good to want to touch, feel, taste, look at, and listen to anything and everything on the pretext that we want to learn what it is, for in this way we may be putting our health, our equilibrium, and even our life at risk.

The only knowledge really worth acquiring is the knowledge to which Jesus refers when he says: *And this is eternal life, that they may know you, the only true God, and Jesus Christ whom you have sent.'* But it is not enough to read, study, analyze, or think in order to know, because true knowledge is not acquired solely with the intellect. Intellectual knowledge remains external, superficial. We only truly know things and beings if we merge with them. Moses, who was a great initiate, gave the word 'know' its true meaning when he wrote, *The man knew his wife, and Abraham knew Sarah.* And from this 'knowing' each time a son was born. This proves that true knowledge is a union, a fruitful fusion with a being or an object. You meet someone, you exchange a few words with him, and then you say you know him. No, you do not know him.

443

You have made his acquaintance, but you do not know him. Once you become one with him, then you will know him, not before. And this is even more true when it comes to God. As long as we have not merged with him we do not know him. Only fusion, union, ecstasy allows human beings to know God.

For there to be knowledge, there must be two elements, one active, positive, and the other passive, negative, or if you prefer one masculine and the other feminine. And these two elements must unite so that one penetrates the other.[1] In order to know something, it must, as it were, penetrate us. If we want to know its flavour, we must put it into our mouths. If we want to know its scent, our nose must absorb the aromatic particles that emanate from it, and so on. And if we want to know the cosmic Spirit, we must also allow him to penetrate us.

'And this is eternal life, that they may know you, the only true God.' In the Cabbalistic tradition the essence of God is contained in the Tetragrammaton, the four letters of his name: Yod Heh Vav Heh י ה ו ה .[2] These four letters correspond to the four principles that operate within man, that is, the spirit, the soul, the intellect, and the heart.

– Yod י is the creative masculine principle, the primordial force that is at the origin of all activity, the spirit, the father.

– Heh ה represents the feminine principle, the soul, the mother who attracts, absorbs, and preserves the creative principle and allows it to work within her.

– Vav ו represents the son born of the union of the father and the mother. He is the firstborn of this union, and he also manifests as an active principle, but on a lower level. Vav ו , the son, is the intellect, which follows in the footsteps of the father, the spirit. In fact, you can see that the letter ו is like an elongated Yod י .

– The second Heh ה represents the heart, the daughter, who is the repetition on a lower plane of the mother, the soul.

Thus the four letters of the Name of God represent the spirit (the father), the soul (the mother), the intellect (the son), and the heart (the daughter).*

And because human beings are created in the image of God we find these four principles in their faces. The eyes represent Yod, the spirit; the ears Heh, the soul; the nose represents Vav, the intellect, and the mouth the second Heh, the heart.

In summary, therefore, there are four forces:

י Yod, the spirit, corresponds to the eyes;

ה Heh, the soul, corresponds to the ears;

ו Vav, the intellect, corresponds to the nose;

ה Heh, the heart, corresponds to the mouth.

These four forces, therefore, are linked to the four senses: sight, hearing, smell, and taste. And the fifth sense? The fifth sense is touch, and the organ of touch is the hand with which we work. Thus, to the four letters of the Name of God is added a fifth letter, the Shin ש . This letter is seen in the middle of the name of Jesus, Joshua יהשוה , which symbolizes the incarnation of God in matter. Through the person of Jesus, the

---

* The Cabbalah therefore sees the Name of God as a diagrammatic representation of the family unit. And the interpretation given to the Vav and the second Heh (the accordance of the son and the father, and of the daughter and the mother), is echoed in almost the same terms in C. G. Jung's studies into the 'intensity of kinship'. *In Modern Man in Search of a Soul*, Jung reports on his research using tests based on the association method to determine the degree of resemblance between the members of one family. He writes: 'The difference between fathers and sons equals 3.1... The closeness between a father and his son is a primordial fact: the son having been considered since the beginning of time as a rebirth of the father... The difference between mothers and daughters equals 3.0, which is the smallest difference found; daughters are a repetition of their mother.' (Editor's note)

Christ, the four aspects of God represented by the spirit, the soul, the intellect, and the heart of God are incarnate in man. As an expression of the cosmic principle named Christ, Jesus is the Word made flesh. It is he who made it possible for the four spiritual principles to manifest. This is why he is also represented in the form of a hand, the five fingers of which correspond with the five virtues – love, wisdom, truth, justice, and goodness – arranged on the pentagram, which is the Christmas star and the symbol of perfect man.[3]

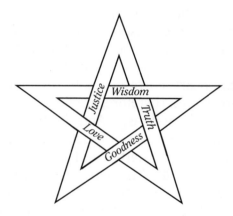

Jesus is the son of God who descended to earth to teach us how to manifest. In order to become perfect beings we must not remain on the spiritual plane of the spirit and the soul, nor on the psychic plane of the intellect and the heart, but learn to manifest their powers and qualities through our physical body, of which the hand, with its five fingers, is a symbol. Jesus said: *'My father is still working, and I also am working.'* In other words: my father works in the heads, hearts, souls, and spirits of human beings, and I too work among human beings, here, in matter, with my hands.

446

The Creator has given human beings all the elements they need to live eternal life, but the thinkers and theologians who have not understood this have made eternal life into something completely abstract. This must be quite clear to you, therefore: the more importance you attach to your five senses, the more you are careful to use them as instruments of your heart, your intellect, your soul, and your spirit, the closer you will be to knowing the supreme realities, which no book, no philosopher, no scholar will reveal to you. Revelation comes from within, and it cannot deceive you; it is the result of the enlightened use of your five senses.

Eternal life consists in forming a bond, in opening our spirit, our soul, our intellect, and our heart to all the virtues of the Name of God and of his Son. Once we have achieved this, we will be nourished by the inexhaustible Source, just as an electric bulb is fed by a generator. By opening our heart to purity, our intellect to light, our soul to spiritual love, and our spirit to divine omnipotence, we will be able to manifest on earth in accordance with the example given by Jesus.

This is eternal life, that they may know you, the only true God... To know God is to vibrate in unison with him through our heart, our intellect, our soul, and our spirit. And through this knowledge we attain eternal life, the highest state of consciousness.

In order to obtain eternal life we must be fused into one with God, so that his life, true life, begins to flow within us, and this fusion can come about only through love. This is why Jesus also said: *'You shall love the Lord your God with all your heart, and with all your soul, and with all your mind, and with all your strength.'* As soon as we fuse into one with him, we begin to communicate with the Whole, and eternal life floods into us and bathes us in light. You will say: 'But eternity is never-ending time.' Yes, but eternity is one thing and eternal life is another. You can live eternal life without living eternally. Eternal life does not mean time drawn out to infinity. Eternal life can be lived in a single second, because it is a state of consciousness.

Let me explain with an image. Take a stick. A stick is a straight line with a beginning and an end. It represents a piece of something that is limitless, and however you go about it, you will never be able to measure what is limitless with this 'limited' fragment. But suppose that the stick is flexible. Then you can bend it until the two ends meet and it forms a circle which has no beginning and no end. This circle represents the 'limitless', eternity. And so, each moment of our lives that is united with the divine Source enters the circle and becomes eternal life. The nature of that moment changes, its quality changes, because it is no longer a detached fragment of a whole. We could say that every point on a straight line is a point in time, and every point on a circle is a point in eternity. On the line of time, each second we manage to unite to the divine Source enters the circle of eternity.

This same truth was expressed by Jesus when he said: *'I am the vine, you are the branches. Those who abide in me and I in them bear much fruit, because apart from me you can do nothing. Whoever does not abide in me is thrown away like a branch and withers.'* This means, 'if you want to obtain life, light, wisdom, and love, unite with me. I am the vine, and the vine is alive because it is planted in the ground, it has its roots deeply embedded in the earth, and it gives life.' The vine and the branches symbolize human souls which are united with God, for the soul draws its strength from God himself. Just as the branch that is detached from the vine withers and dies, the soul that is detached from God also withers and dies. Everything that becomes detached from the tree – the leaves, the flowers, the fruit falling from the branch – is cut off from the source of life and dies. Therefore, if we detach ourselves from the Whole, from the cosmic Tree, we too will die. Only the soul that remains linked to the Tree grows and flourishes.

As long as the fruit remains on the tree it is alive because it draws life from the tree. But as soon as it is detached, it loses its freshness and very quickly becomes inedible. The substance, the matter subsists, but this cannot last long since the fruit is condemned to live on its own resources. When water gushes from the spring it is fresh and life-giving because it is animated by the life of the spring, but once taken from there, it loses this freshness. And the rays emitted by the sun are alive and powerful, but once they come into contact with dust and all the other impurities on earth, they become weak and impoverished and are obliged to return to the sun to be revitalized.

But let us go back to the image of the fruit. Before eating a piece of fruit you often remove the skin or the shell as well as the core or seeds. The peelings still contain a few particles of life, but you discard them and they then become food to insects and other animals. Those who do not remain linked to the Tree of Life, in other words, who abandon a higher state of consciousness, also eat nothing but peelings. Their existence cannot be plentiful, full, and divine, because they are in contact only with elements that are losing their purity and freshness. So you must do your best to unite with immensity, with that which has no beginning and no end, then your consciousness will become vaster and more luminous, and new life, the life of eternity will flow within you.

In order to be nourished and to develop, each branch must remain connected to the vine, and then it will produce flowers and fruit. It is by linking yourself to the divine Principle, to Christ – so that you live the life of Christ – that you will be able to transform your personal, limited, and purely human consciousness into a consciousness that has no limits, a consciousness that is universal, a consciousness that has become a consciousness of eternity. You must try, more and more, therefore to free yourself from all the prosaic preoccupations that restrict you and weigh you down. Forget about your imperfections and shortcomings, and concern yourself with the divine Principle within you. In this way you will live eternal life.

Do you understand now? We do not need to live for billions of years in order to live in eternity. In fact, even if we did live for billions of years, it would still not be eternity. Eternal life is not a question of duration, it is a state of consciousness. We are creatures who are limited by time, we have a beginning and an end, but in this limited existence we can find eternity through the intensity of our spiritual life. Only the spirit is of the same order as eternity.

The vine, the tree, the spring, the sun are all symbolic representations of the Godhead. So when I tell you to connect with the vine, or the tree, or the spring, or the sun, these are simply different ways of telling you the same truth: it is in the link with the Godhead that you will find eternal life. Eternal life is a quality of life, an intensity of life, and if you succeed in leading this intense life, even if it is only for a fraction of a second, you enter eternity.

This is the key to these two passages in the Gospels: *'I am the vine, you are the branches'*, and *'This is eternal life, that they may know you, the only true God, and Jesus Christ whom you have sent'*. These are simply two different expressions of the same truth, which is that human beings must find their way back to union with the divine Source and never be separated from it again, for separation represents spiritual and physical death. The whole of nature can be a means to help us unite with the divine Source, but the most powerful and most effective means is the sun. The sun is the symbol of the living river that emerges and flows down to give water and life to the whole universe, the symbol of God himself, and the sun can best help us to find our way back to the Creator, to vibrate on the same wavelength, to become the branch connected to the vine. The sun is the vine, and if we unite with it we shall become the branches and will have eternal life.

An application of this truth can be seen in the area of human love. When men and women who are in love detach themselves from the divine Source in order to live exclusively in their love for one another, forgetting that they belong to the immense whole, they see this love gradually losing its glow and crumbling away. If they were to link with immensity, with the divine Source, their love would remain luminous and beautiful, because it would escape the limits of time. This is true for love and for all other areas of life. Those who detach themselves from the Source die.

In reality, nothing and no one can ever break away from universal life; neither the smallest particle of dust nor the smallest atom can escape it. The rupture occurs only on the level of consciousness, and of course it leads to other ruptures on other planes. But even in the midst of extreme chaos, human beings are always linked with the universe, with the lower regions of the universe. The only thing they can do, therefore, is move from one region to another, from one apartment, or floor, to another, just as you can move your living quarters from an upper to a lower floor... even down to the basement. But you cannot detach yourself completely from the cosmos; no one has ever managed to escape the influence of cosmic forces and energies. This must be quite clear to you; no one can detach themselves from the universal forces. The only thing you can do is change conditions or regions – move to more or to less favourable conditions – but any changes you make will occur only in your consciousness.

This is why I urge you to return to the Source. Thanks to the sun – or, if you cannot see the sun – then thanks to the divine principle within you, remember every day, whatever you are doing – working, resting, walking, or eating – to restore your link with the Source. In this way you will gradually enter universal life – or, to put it in human terms – fraternal life. Indeed, what do you do in a spiritual brotherhood? Those who have understood know they are there to learn to free themselves from their purely personal life in order to enter the life of the collectivity, the life of immensity.[4] In reality everyone already lives in this immensity, but they are not aware of it. They must now become aware in order to establish this link and attune themselves to universal life.

Eternal life is nothing more than a higher level of life, a higher intensity of life.[5] It is the intensity of our life that gives it its eternal dimension. We will not live eternally on earth because we have had a beginning and we will have an end, but we can make sure that each moment of our existence is not merely a fragment of time but is animated by such intense vibrations that it embraces the whole universe. It is this living, vibrant moment that becomes eternity.

No doubt most people find it impossible to grasp fully the nature of time and space, but everyone is able to understand what intense life is. You all know from experience that some days the pace of life slows down, just as with plants, which have only a vegetative life. You go about your business as usual, but inwardly you feel flat. And then there are other times when you feel you are dilating, vibrating in unison with the whole universe. You will ask: 'How can we make our life more intense?' Through purity, through love, and through sacrifice.

Of course, the world in which we live has its demands, and we cannot abandon our day-to-day commitments to go and set up house in eternity. We can, however, for a few minutes each day, endeavour to bring ourselves into harmony with the divine life, which has no beginning and no end. Little by little this will become a habit; you will begin to get a taste for it and realize, all of a sudden, that it is not so difficult after all. And this is the greatest joy a human being can experience, to be always connected, always in harmony, always in unison with the divine hierarchies. Do this exercise, and you will find that all the particles of your being that are still uncontrolled, that do not yet sing in harmony, will begin to be tamed thanks to this practice, to the taste you have acquired for bringing yourself into harmony with the divine world.

It is up to you, now, to get into the habit of doing this exercise. And never say: 'I don't have the time. There are more important things that need doing, more pressing matters to see to.' Reasoning like this will leave you bogged down in heartache and torment because you will have cut the link with the Source of eternal life. And once you sever this link, you become subject to time. To be subject to time means to be exposed to all possible tribulations and to suffer. This is what Jesus meant when he said: *'Whoever does not abide in me is thrown away like a branch and withers; such branches are gathered, thrown into the fire, and burned.'* The fire in which the branches burn is of course symbolic. It is the fire of suffering that tortures human beings as long as they imagine they can lead their own life while severing their inner link with God.

Why come to a spiritual teaching if it is not to learn the essential? It is pointless; you will be wasting your time. And the essential is to bring yourselves into harmony with the infinity, the eternity of God in order to taste the sublime quintessence that will turn you into branches laden with fruit.

Earlier on I used the image of a stick and showed you how the straight line, which represents a fragment of time, can become the symbol of eternity if the two ends are joined together. In ancient books initiates depicted the serpent in three different ways: slithering along the ground, rising up in a spiral, and finally, forming a circle as it swallows its own tail. These three representations correspond to the three stages of human development: on the physical plane (the serpent slithering along the ground), on the psychic plane (the serpent spiralling upwards along the spinal column), and on the spiritual plane (the serpent swallowing its own tail). When human beings succeed in joining the two ends, the head and the tail of the serpent, to form a circle, they enter the harmonious and creative movements of eternity. And then all emanations, all energies are harmoniously organized and distributed, so that all conflict and disharmony between them disappear. All the points on the periphery, which are all at the same distance from the centre, produce sublime interactions. The initiate who succeeds in forming this circle within himself becomes powerful and luminous like the sun and lives in eternity.

Spiritually, a human being must become a circle. Before a child is born, it is curled up in its mother's womb. You will say that this is an economical solution devised by nature so that the baby takes up less room. Possibly... And then, after birth the child stands up. But spiritually he must be a circle again, in other words, he must move out of his personal, limited consciousness in order to live a cosmic life, a universal life, the life of eternity.

The serpent that swallows its own tail symbolizes sublimated sexual energy. To begin with, as I have just explained, the serpent glides along the ground, and if it bites you, you will be poisoned, and that will be the end of you. So it needs to be transformed, that is, to rise up. And the serpent rising along the spinal cord is the movement of the Kundalini force spiralling upwards to reach the chakra of the head, Sahasrara. Once it has reached the summit, it becomes a circle because, symbolically, the head and the tail are joined. An initiate's work, therefore, consists of mastering his sexual energy so as to direct it to the brain. In this moment he enters the perfect movement of eternity. All his energies are transformed into light, into love, and all of humankind benefits from it.[6]

When human beings are content with sensual love – the straight line – they live in time, that is, in an unstable situation: they swing between being happy and being unhappy, between hope and disappointment. One day they love, and the next they love no longer. But when they enter the circle, when they embrace true love, they escape these fluctuations and taste eternal life. This is a very profound question, which you will understand later on. Sexual energy must not be ill treated. You must not kill the serpent, but its venom should be made curative so that it heals all illnesses. This idea is expressed by the Caduceus of Hermes, which was the symbol of Aesculapias, the healing god, and which is still used by doctors and chemists.[7] The Caduceus represents the serpent that has transformed its venom in order to cure the ills of humankind. Like the serpent swallowing its tail, the Caduceus is the symbol of sublimated sexual energy that becomes therapeutic. It is the universal panacea sought by sages. Yes, the universal panacea referred to in alchemical treatises is the cosmic force of sublimated love.

In the field of metals, time is represented by lead and eternity by gold, because gold does not tarnish. Gold is influenced by the sun and lead by Saturn. Saturn is also a personification of time: it is the Greek god Cronos who devours his children. In order to escape being devoured, we must enter eternity. Thus the passage from time to eternity is also an application of the alchemical process of transmuting lead into gold. To transmute lead into gold is to transform life in time into eternal life, to transform the old Adam into Christ. Now, you can see the correspondences that exist between all these symbols.

You are familiar with many symbols, but for the moment you see them as unrelated objects, and this is why you do not understand them. In order to understand them you must bring them to life, in other words discover in your day-to-day lives the links that exist between them.[8] For your evolution, the time has come when all these symbols must be animated, brought to life. Those of you who are attracted to this subject and who have the mental capacity to do so will find in these symbols a wealth of material for your work, your fulfilment, and your joy.

Notes

1 See *Cosmic Balance – The Secret of Polarity*, Izvor 237, Chap. 3 (I): 'One and Zero'.

2 See *The Fruits of the Tree of Life – The Cabbalistic Tradition*, C.W. 32, Chap. 4: 'The Tetragrammaton and the Seventy-Two Planetary Spirits'.

3 See *The Symbolic Language of Geometrical Figures,* Izvor 218, Chap. 4 (I): 'The Pentagram'.

4 See *Love and Sexuality*, C.W. 15, Chap. 29: 'Towards a Broader Concept of the Family'; – *A New Dawn: Society and Politics in the Light of Initiatic Science*, C.W. 25, Chap. 2: 'The Dawn of Universal Brotherhood'.

5 See *Light is a Living Spirit*, Izvor 212, Chap. 8: 'Living with the Intensity of Light'.

6 See *Angels and other Mysteries of The Tree of Life*, Izvor 236, Chap. 17: 'Yesod, Tiphareth, Kether, the Sublimation of Sexual Energy'.

7 See *Cosmic Balance – The Secret of Polarity*, Izvor 237, Chap. 9: 'The Caduceus of Hermes – The Astral Serpent'.

8 See *The Symbolic Language of Geometrical Figures*, Izvor 218, Chap. 1: 'Geometrical Symbolism'.

2

'Know Thyself'

'Know thyself.' Many, many interpretations have been proposed for this formula, which was inscribed over the entrance to the temple of Delphi. To some it means that human beings must know their own limitations and have the wisdom not to pit themselves against the gods. To others it means that we must know our own character, with all its strengths and weaknesses. A knowledge of our own strengths and weaknesses is, of course, necessary, but it is not sufficient. This is not what the knowledge of self truly entails. Do you really think that if this formula had no broader and deeper meaning than that, the Greeks would have inscribed it over the entrance of one of their most sacred sanctuaries?

Most people know only some of their aspirations, some of their tendencies, good or bad, and then they say that they know themselves. No, they are mistaken. They know neither who they are nor what they need in order to fulfil their true nature. And the fact that, more often than not, they confuse their 'self' with their physical body proves that they do not know who this 'self' is. You only have to look at what human beings are interested in, what they devote most of their time and energies to: food, clothes, comfort, cars, and pleasures of all kinds. This proves they do not know themselves.

For disciples of initiatic science, to know yourself means to extricate your consciousness from the narrow circle of your lower nature in order to merge with the limitless consciousness of the cosmic Being who dwells and works within, until at last you can say: 'I am He'. In other words: only He exists, and I exist only insofar as I succeed in identifying with Him, in merging with Him.

As I have already explained, true initiatic knowledge is a fusion, a merging through an act of love. By saying: 'know thyself', the initiates were saying that a human must merge with that other part of himself, that higher self that dwells above in the region of the spirit. In this way he enters a space where there are no longer any boundaries, where there is no longer a division between the higher and the lower, and all the strengths and riches of the true self are imparted to the small self. The small and the great self form one within him, and he has achieved the symbol of the circle, the serpent biting its own tail. The tail (his lower nature) and the head (his higher nature) are joined together. And this is the aim of initiation: to learn to join the head and the tail of the serpent.

As long as human beings have not found themselves, all their energies are scattered and lost. But as soon as the two poles are united, tremendous powers accumulate in the circle, in the centre; they are collected, condensed, and preserved so that they may be put to work. Yes, the head and the tail... True knowledge is the result of the union of the head and the tail.

In the belief that they will come to know themselves through others, human beings are constantly seeking each other out. Men seek out women, and women seek out men with whom to unite. Of course, in this way they will learn something about themselves, but very little, because they cannot find themselves by looking outside. They only disperse and waste their energies in this way. Through their exchanges with others they may learn certain things and experience certain joys, but these joys are short-lived. They soon move away from each other and separate... in fact, they move so far away that they end by opposing each other. They want to be as one, but it cannot be done! They will always be two separate, different people who will have many experiences together, some interesting, of course, but also some disappointing and painful – examples of this are plentiful in life. Human beings will succeed in truly finding themselves only when they stop looking for themselves on the outside, through another person, and start looking within and seeking to realize the symbol of the serpent that bites its tail. Their strength will then be concentrated, light will dawn, and they will live eternal life.

To know yourself is to bring the two ends of the serpent together within you, because these two ends are polarized. If you are a man you represent the spirit, and the other end of yourself is the feminine principle, matter. Conversely, if you are a woman you represent matter, and the other end is the masculine principle, the spirit. This is why, when the two principles are joined together you find fulfilment. If you look outside yourself you cannot be sure to meet the entity that will truly complete you. If you are a man, the other pole seems to be a woman, and if you are a woman, it is a man. But this complementarity is not perfect, and this is why so many encounters end in conflict. Perfect encounters do occur occasionally, but they are extremely rare. Whereas the other part of you that is within you is perfectly complementary, and the only true fusion is the fusion you achieve with it. Only within yourself can you realize the ideal union of the masculine and the feminine, the spirit and matter, in other words of that which is above and that which is below.

In the Emerald Tablet, Hermes Trismegistus says: 'That which is below is like that which is above, and that which is above is like that which is below, to accomplish the miracles of one thing.' Above is the spiritual plane. Below is the physical plane. All that exists on the physical plane corresponds to an element, an entity on the spiritual plane. This is why we must learn to restore the contact between the two planes, the higher and the lower. This is true marriage: the joining of the head and the tail of the serpent, of heaven and earth. Yes, because true marriage is not only the coming together of a man and a woman, of the masculine and the feminine, but also that of the higher and the lower, the higher self and the lower self.

It is in their consciousness that human beings are separated from themselves, and it is in their consciousness that they must become one by seeking to come closer to this higher part that they do not yet know, so as to unite with it. This is the meaning of the precept: 'Know thyself'. But what exactly is this 'self'? What is 'yourself'? Your arms, your legs, your brain, your lungs? No. Is it your feelings, your thoughts, your desires? No again. Your true self is a fragment of God, a spark, an immortal spirit, something infinite, very far away, very high. It is there, in this immortal, omniscient, omnipotent entity, your higher self, that you must find and know yourself. Then your consciousness will merge into the Eternal Godhead, it will draw on the strength, the light, and the love of the Almighty, and you will enter into immensity, into divine splendour, into eternity.

Thus there are two poles: the self that is here, the consciousness you have of yourself, of your lower self, and the sublime self of which you are not yet conscious. And as you seek to know yourself above in your sublime self, that self seeks to descend, to manifest in you, to know itself through the dense matter in which you are incarnated. It knows itself as it is above, but it also wants to know itself below, through matter. So, thanks to your efforts to elevate yourself, you allow your higher self to descend in order to take possession of your matter. This double process is symbolized by the seal of Solomon. Within you, spirit and matter come together at last. You make it possible for your matter to be elaborated, illuminated by the spirit, while, at the same time, you give your spirit matter in which to create.[1] This is difficult work, of course, but it is the only work worth doing because it is the work of God. Indeed, to work on your own matter is to do the work of God. God works on his own matter, and this is why he dwells in fulfilment, why he is omniscient and omnipotent.

Human beings are creatures whose reality is far greater than what we can see of them. What is walking around here on earth is their tail.... And where is their head? So long as these two poles are still separated, human beings will be content to slither along the ground. The tail must join up with the head so as to know it. That is, the lower self must join up with the higher self, which is above, in heaven. Once this contact is restored there is a constant and harmonious flow of energies. When at last the two poles join up, when that which is below unites with that which is above, then human beings know themselves and experience fulfilment.

The greatest achievement possible for a human being is the union of his lower self with his higher self, the union, in other words, of the riches of matter with the power of the spirit, which alone knows how to use these riches. This is the secret of marriage. If you are content to seek the other pole outside of yourself, you will be wasting your energies. True marriage must be with yourself; it is within yourself that you must achieve the union of the masculine and the feminine, the higher and the lower.[2]

But an entire existence will not be enough to reach the higher consciousness that enables you to sense that you have touched your divine self. From time to time you will have a glimmer, a flicker of light, but very soon you will again feel separate, lacklustre, poor, and weak. This is quite normal, but you must not simply wait passively for the state of grace to visit you again. You must consciously endeavour to move closer to your higher self, and you will succeed all the more readily if you learn to look for it in the sun. In fact, without realizing it you are already in the sun. You cannot feel it, but there is a small part of you, a very subtle element of your being that lives in the sun.

Science has not yet managed to study human beings fully; it does not know the immensity, richness, vastness, and depth a human being represents. What science sees of them – their physical body – is not really them. Human beings possess other bodies made of ever subtler matter, and this is why, taking into account their higher self, we can say that they already live in the sun. If they are not yet aware of this, it is because they work exclusively with their brains, and the brain can grasp only the physical world.

This part of ourselves, this entity that lives in the sun, is our higher self. Yes, our higher self does not live in our physical body; if it did it would achieve astounding things. From time to time it makes contact with our brain, but since the brain is not yet ready to handle such vibrations, to bring itself into unison with the higher self, this self goes away again. The work we do every morning with the sun, through meditation and prayer, is aimed at restoring this link, at building a bridge between our lower self and our higher self in the sun, so that it may make its home permanently within us.

Therefore, when you go and watch the sun rising in the morning, tell yourself that you are already in the sun and from there you can look at this person sitting down there – this person that is you. In thought you disassociate and go out of your body, then you look down and smile at yourself and say: 'Just look at that odd little creature down there! And to think that it's me! I really must help him. I'll help him by sending down all the beauty, the love, and the light I discover up here.' Through this simple exercise of the imagination you can begin each day to rebuild the bridge. No one knows how long it will take to join the higher and the lower, because this bridge is not built with metal, concrete, or steel. It is built of a different material, a far subtler material from the mental plane. You are all invited to do this work, but are there many candidates to go so far?[3]

Once you have reached the sun, you can imagine that you visit the Archangel Michael who rules it. You talk with him, he takes you in his arms to reveal his secrets to you and give you his light, and then you send rays of this light down to this being below, this being which you think of as you, but which is not really you. In this way you will begin to feel an immense expansion of your consciousness; a heavenly peace will flood into you, and then will come revelations and still more revelations... And in this way you will taste eternal life.

Notes

1 See *Cosmic Balance – The Secret of Polarity*, Izvor 237, Chap. 14: 'The Work of the Spirit on Matter'.
2 Ibid., Chap. 15: 'Union of the Ego with the Physical Body'.
3 See *The Splendour of Tiphareth*, C. W. 10, Chap. 9: 'A Master Must be Like the Sun and Remain at the Centre – Some Prayers to Say at Sunrise'.

Notes

1. See Octavio Paz, *Sor Juana: or, The Traps of Faith*, trans. Margaret Sayers Peden (Cambridge, Mass.: Harvard University Press, 1988).

3

Merging
with the cosmic Soul
and Spirit

When mystics say they are seeking God, the God they are referring to is not an entity outside themselves but the complementary part of their own being which they are seeking in order to achieve perfect unity. Until they find it, they feel that they are divided, mutilated beings. They seek to commune with God through their higher self, since this higher self is the purest reflection of the Deity. This is a spontaneous, intuitive process, but it is one which can be analysed, for it rests on basic psychic realities.

It is said that God created man in his image. But who is God? Many philosophers, theologians, and mystics have sought to answer this question, but none has truly succeeded, because God cannot be explained with words. And only when we finally merge with him shall we know who he is.

I have already shown you how this entity we call God is at the same time masculine and feminine. When we talk of the cosmic Spirit and the universal Soul, we are referring to God as one single polarized entity. In the same way, every human being is both man and woman. Of course, on the physical plane human beings are one or the other, but on the spiritual plane they are both male and female, or rather masculine and feminine, for their soul is feminine and their spirit is masculine.

On the spiritual plane, therefore, a human being – like God – is androgynous.

Let us consider for a moment this concept of the androgyne. In the dialogue known as *The Banquet*, Plato relates the myth of the primitive androgynes, creatures who were said to have lived on earth long ages ago, and who were both male and female. They were spherical in shape and had two faces, four arms, four legs, and two genital organs: the male and the female. These beings were exceptionally strong, and realizing their strength, they decided to attack the gods and seize power from them. This worried the gods greatly, and they tried to find a way to weaken them. It was Zeus who found the answer: all they had to do was cut them in half. And this they did. And that is why man and woman, the two separate halves of a single being, have wandered the world ever since, looking for each other in order to unite and regain their original wholeness.

This idea of the primitive androgyne, the perfect being who possessed a nature that was both feminine and masculine, can be found in some form or other in most great religious and philosophical traditions. We even find traces of it in the Book of *Genesis*, since some Cabbalists have interpreted the episode when God takes a rib from Adam and makes it into Eve as a reference to the division of the sexes. Alchemists see this polarity of the masculine and the feminine in the mineral world, and they express it with the symbol of the *Rebis*, the 'Two-thing'. The Rebis is an egg-shaped figure (the egg is a symbol of totality) enclosing a body with two heads: a man's head with the sun (the masculine principle) above it and a woman's head with the moon (the feminine principle) above it. All these traditions hold this idea that creation is the result of the polarization of a whole. Every creature, being only the half of a whole, feels perpetually incomplete and can live at peace only when it finds its complementary half.

469

Thus the whole human adventure is nothing more than the quest for a lost half. Everywhere around us we see men and women looking for each other. They do not even know why they search for each other, but they do so instinctively. An inner voice tells them that they will regain their primordial unity once they are together. Now and again, for a few minutes, a few seconds, they have a taste of indescribable happiness, a mysterious expansion of their being, but this does not last. It is inevitably followed by disappointment and sorrow. But because they never give up hope, they continue to search by changing the subject – or the object – of their search.

Why is this so? Why do human beings fail to achieve their deepest aspirations? Why? Because it is not on the physical plane that the union of the masculine and the feminine must first come about. The physical plane should be only the outcome of work previously done on the psychic and spiritual planes. Otherwise the best you can hope for are ephemeral pleasure and enjoyment. If some – and such people are very rare – have succeeded in achieving this unity on a long term basis on the physical plane, it is because they had previously done a great deal of inner work. Every human being must first seek to unite the two principles within themselves. This is the philosophy of androgyny, and it is the most exalted of all philosophies.

This is why the most significant point in Plato's myth is that, in order to weaken the creatures who threatened the power of the gods, Zeus decided to cut them in half. The implication is obvious: the power of a human being lies in the possession of the two principles. It is because they possess both the masculine and the feminine principle that human beings are like the gods.

In truth, despite their mutilated state, human beings still possess the two principles physically. Yes, they are present in the mouth.[1] The tongue is a masculine principle and the lips are a feminine principle, and together they have a child: the word, speech. This is why the true power of a human being lies in speech. Just look at how, by nothing more than words, human beings can achieve as much as with any material means. They can build up and break down, they can gather together and scatter, they can restore peace or start a war, they can heal or cause illness. When the primitive androgynes were split in two, one could say that, symbolically, woman kept the lips, the feminine principle, and man the tongue, the masculine principle. And this is why, in order to regain their original strength, they now seek each other out in order to unite. That is the remote origin of the impulse that makes men and women continue to seek each other out.

Even if this seeking often takes the form of pleasure or recreation, its deeper purpose is to find the unity of the divine Word, the oneness of the creative principle which is both male and female. In the upper part of their bodies both men and women possess the two principles: the tongue and lips are together in the mouth. So although a man or woman alone cannot create a child, through speech both are creators apart from each other, thanks to the two principles contained in the mouth.[2]

The Gospels are an illustration of this truth. It is thanks to this omnipotence of the Word that Jesus performed miracles. He told the paralytic: *'Stand up and take your mat and walk.'* When he raised Lazarus from the dead, he stood before the tomb and cried with a loud voice: *'Lazarus, come out!'* When he brought the daughter of Jairus back to life, he took her by the hand and said: *'Little girl, get up!'* When he healed a man with an unclean spirit, he ordered the spirit: *'Be silent, and come out of him!'* When he cured a leper, he said: *'I do choose. Be made clean!'* When he calmed the storm, he said to the sea: *'Peace! Be still!'*[3]

I have often explained to you that we can learn a great deal from the way our body is built. As far as the two principles are concerned, our body shows us that it is only below on the physical plane that they are separate. Physically, a human being has to be either a man or a woman (hermaphrodites are extremely rare). But up above, on the divine plane, the two principles are united, as they are united in the mouth. And this is why human beings are creators on the higher planes, where they are free and live in fulfilment.[4] The problems arise from the fact that as they descend into matter, men and women become so obsessed with their outward appearance that they forget that on high, on the divine plane, they are the two in one. Yes, through their soul and their spirit, every being is a reflection of the divine androgyne, the cosmic Soul and Spirit, the heavenly Father and Mother, the two entities which, in reality, form but one and which we call God.

Initiates, who understand the immense wisdom that Cosmic Intelligence has put in the mouth, know that up above, on the spiritual plane, they possess the two principles. And this is why they endeavour every day, in their meditations, to penetrate the infinite light that we call the universal Soul, in order to fertilize her by projecting into her their thought and their will. And once they have achieved this, they abandon themselves to the universal Spirit, so that he may possess them and project into their souls living seeds, which will germinate and become inspirations and joys.

But once again, when I say 'above' you must understand that this 'above' is not at a great distance, light-years away in space. The 'above' is also within us, the higher part of us, our soul and our spirit. There is of course no possible comparison between the soul and spirit of a human being and the cosmic Soul and Spirit, but in their essence they are identical. And this is why our soul and our spirit need to merge with these divine entities, with the eternal masculine and the eternal feminine. As our soul rises it unites with the cosmic Spirit, and our spirit unites with the universal Soul. There is, thus, an exchange between our two spiritual entities and the two divine entities, as the masculine part of our being unites with the feminine part of God and the feminine part of us unites with the masculine part of God. But a great deal of work needs to be done before this union can be achieved.

The initiates and great mystics are beings who have not only understood this reality, but who have given up everything to realize it in their lives, and their joy knows no bounds. What did you think? That they were poor wretches, who for some reason – probably because they were slightly cracked – abandoned all terrestrial pleasures to live in solitude, in deprivation, in the desert? Not at all! They are beings who have gone in search of the greatest riches, the greatest fulfilment. All religions teach that we should pray and adore God, but why? These precepts are based on a reality, on laws regarding relations that exist between man and God, between the soul and spirit of man and the cosmic Soul and Spirit. I cannot reveal everything to you, because these are the greatest mysteries of initiatic science, but I can at least put you on the right track.

The soul and the spirit are not notions invented by woolly-minded thinkers. They are realities that correspond to cosmic realities. Whatever you call them, human beings possess a fragment of these two creative principles. Our bodies are created in the image of the universe,[5] and our souls and spirits – which we cannot see – are reflections of the two great masculine and feminine principles, the universal Soul and the cosmic Spirit. You will say: 'But then why are we so limited on the physical plane?' Because in your previous incarnations you did not pay enough attention to your soul and your spirit. It was to the intellect and the heart that you gave priority, and although the intellect and the heart represent the lower aspect of the soul and the spirit, as they were not enlightened by the soul and spirit, they have led you in the direction of self-interest and selfish desires. But the intellect and heart in turn fashion the physical body, for the physical plane is always fashioned by the forces of the planes directly above it, in other words the forces of the astral plane (the heart) and of the mental plane (the intellect).[6] The first task of every spiritual person, therefore, is to purify, enlighten, and ennoble their heart and their intellect through the powers of the soul and the spirit.

Everything that exists on the physical plane has first been created above on the divine plane by the cosmic Spirit and the universal Soul. Their union and their interaction fill space with constellations, nebulae, galaxies and all the creatures that inhabit these galaxies. We too are their creations and, like them, we have the power to create. Yes, we too can create as God creates. We shall be able to create once we have become conscious, once we have freed ourselves from our limitations, once the masculine and feminine principles within us have come into full possession of their resources. And to achieve this we must unite with God. Prayer, meditation, and contemplation are the only means we have at our disposal in order to understand all the divine mysteries and become creators.[7] In our desire to elevate ourselves in order to penetrate the universal Soul, our spirit fertilizes this light that is the substance of creation. And in return our soul receives the seeds of the cosmic Spirit and produces divine children: illuminations, joys, acts of goodness and nobility.

When we pray, when we meditate, our soul is attracted by the universal Spirit and our spirit is attracted by the universal Soul. And when they meet we experience perfect fulfilment. It is this encounter that gives meaning to our prayer and our meditation. Otherwise, why pray? Prayer is not a question of making demands on God: 'Lord, I need this, I want that'. Prayer gives us the opportunity to find the true dimensions of our being. The purpose of prayer is, in fact, this encounter between something within us and something of the same nature in the universe. It involves a cross-over, the meeting of two polarized entities. And this cross-over is the greatest secret of religion: the human soul seeks the divine Spirit and the human spirit seeks the universal Soul. Our soul is fertilized by the cosmic Spirit and our spirit fertilizes the universal Soul. God is androgynous, and in their soul and spirit, human beings are also androgynous.

If men and women were sufficiently evolved to achieve this encounter of their souls and spirits in their love, this love would be an inexhaustible source of riches and joys to them. Unfortunately, the encounter is often only between their bodies, and this can only result in misunderstanding and disappointment. This is why, until you reach the level of evolution which will enable you to give each other this fulfilment, try at least to seek it up above by forming a bond with the cosmic Soul and Spirit.

Those who succeed in reaching the regions of divine light and love receive currents of very pure and very powerful particles that penetrate to the depths of their being and nourish all the cells of their body. But to receive this light requires a great deal of preparation, because it is a current of untold power, and if the way is not clear, if it encounters impurities, it burns everything in its path.[8] It is a terrible fire that can produce the worst kinds of disorder in the psychic and even the physical organism: unbridled sensuality, mental confusion, and physio-logical disorders of the heart and the brain.

Initiatic science is not concerned only with intellectual knowledge; it deals with issues that affect the whole human being and all its inner workings, and this is why we must be extremely careful. To work with the soul and the spirit is to work with the two creative principles and, therefore, to touch the most powerful entities and currents of the universe. Inasmuch as they create life, men's and women's genital organs are, on the physical plane, the equivalent of the soul and the spirit, and anyone who plays the sorcerer's apprentice with the powers of the soul and the spirit triggers formidable forces even within his own body, forces that he will very soon be unable to control.

Yes, you must realize that these exercises demand a great deal of preparation. It is not enough simply to want to meet the cosmic Spirit and the universal Soul. In order to achieve this, you have to start by working to purify yourself.[9] As I have said hundreds of times already – and I say it again, because I see that it is still far from being understood – it is dangerous to try to enter the spiritual world if you have not first purified yourself. Let this be quite clear: the desire to touch the universal Soul and the cosmic Spirit must be inspired by the highest ideal, by the sole need to perfect yourself and to serve the will of God. This is true initiation.

If initiates and certain mystics are capable of a life of chastity, it is because their exchanges on the subtle planes are so rich that they do not need to descend into matter. They drink and are nourished from springs and in regions that are unknown to the majority of human beings, regions in which all exchanges occur in the utmost light and purity. And they are visited by angels and archangels, the sun and the stars look down upon them, and human beings, sensing the presence of something exceptional in them, give them love and trust. In this way they are fulfilled, totally fulfilled. What more could they need?

True initiation is an inner process at the end of which a human being is able to merge with the complementary part of his being. This is why initiates never feel deprived, never alone. It is not carnal relationships that make men and women feel less alone. As so many could tell you, even though they have had multiple encounters and experiences, they still suffer from inner solitude and aridity. Yes, because our encounters must first take place within, on the psychic and spiritual planes. We will only find below what we have first realized above. We will only find on the outside what we have already realized within.

So never forget that true union can take place only inwardly, with the divine principle that is within you. When you succeed in igniting the spark, you will suddenly feel your whole being vibrating in unison with immensity, melting into the universe, and your entire existence will be transformed. The important thing is to experience this union at least once. It is like a drop of light that will continue to live within you. You have found yourself, and you must continue to sustain this union until you reach the perfection of knowledge and power. This is when the real work starts.[10] You have reached the other bank, you are on the road to perfection, but there is still a long way to go. You have captured a drop of light, and thanks to this drop you are already able to drink and rejoice. But you do not have the ocean yet. So you must continue until you are one with the ocean of divine light. Then you will truly have found yourself.

In his wisdom, his immensity, his generosity, God has given men and women the means to experience love on the higher planes of the soul and spirit. Instead of being unhappy because you have had so many disappointing experiences and have still not found the ideal companion with whom to go through life, remember that God has prepared you to know the fullness of love in the fusion of your soul and your spirit with the universal Soul and the cosmic Spirit. Just as the water from the skies feeds the tree down to its roots, this energy that comes from above will flood into you and impregnate you by depositing particles of light in all the organs and limbs of your body, right down to the soles of your feet.

Notes

1 See *Langage symbolique, langage de la nature*, Œuvres Complètes, t. 8, chap. X : «Comment les deux principes sont contenus dans la bouche».

2 See *The Fruits of The Tree of Life – The Cabbalistic Tradition*, C.W. 32, Chap. 11: 'The Living Logos'.

3 See *New Light on the Gospels*, Izvor 217, Chap. 7: 'The Calming of the Storm'.

4 See *Angels and other Mysteries of The Tree of Life*, Izvor 236, Chap. 16: 'Chokmah, the Creative Word'.

5 Ibid., Chap. 11: 'The Body of Adam Kadmon'

6 See *Harmony*, C.W. 6, Chap. 6: 'How Thought is Materialized on the Physical Plane'.

7 See *'Know Thyself' – Jnana Yoga*, C.W. 18, Chap. 6: 'Concentration, Meditation, Contemplation, and Identification'; Chap. 7: 'Prayer'.

8 See *Angels and other Mysteries of The Tree of Life*, Izvor 236, Chap. 14: 'Yesod, Foundation of the Spiritual Life'.

9 See *A New Earth – Methods, Exercises, Formulas and Prayers*, C.W. 13, Chap. 6: 'Methods of Purification'.

10 See Cf. *Vie et travail à l'Ecole divine*, Œuvres Complètes, t. 31, chap. III: «Le véritable sens du mot travail», p. 104-109.

Part IX

The paths
of
divinization

Part I - The paths of divinization

1

The feast of Christmas

It is not by pure coincidence or because they were instituted by some religious leader that there are four cardinal feasts – Christmas, Easter, the feast of St John, and the feast of the Archangel Michael. They exist because they correspond to cosmic phenomena.[1] During the course of the year the sun passes through four cardinal points: March 21st is the spring equinox; June 21st is the summer solstice; September 21st is the autumn equinox; and December 21st is the winter solstice. During these four periods, great influxes and currents of energy are produced which influence the earth and all its inhabitants. If, therefore, we are attentive and receptive to these influxes and if we prepare ourselves to receive them, great transformations can occur within us.

According to Christian tradition, Jesus was born on December 25th at midnight. On December 25th, the sun has just entered the constellation of Capricorn. Symbolically, Capricorn is linked to mountains and grottoes, and it is in the depths of a grotto that the child Jesus can be born. During the rest of the year nature and human beings have been very active, but as winter approaches, work slows down, the days get shorter and the nights longer, and the time is ripe for meditation and contemplation, a timely occasion for human beings to enter the depths of their being and make ready for the birth of Christ within them.

When the sun leaves Capricorn, it enters Aquarius, and Aquarius is water, the lustral water of baptism, pure life gushing forth, creating new currents. On leaving Aquarius the sun enters Pisces, the sign in which is the miraculous catch of fishes of which Jesus spoke when he said to his disciples he would make them fishers of men.

But let us return to the birth of Jesus. Every year on December 25th at midnight, the constellation of Virgo rises over the horizon, and this is why it is said, from the astrological point of view, that Jesus was born of a virgin. On the opposite horizon is Pisces, and in mid-heaven the magnificent constellation of Orion can be seen, with the alignment of the three stars, which, according to popular tradition, represent the Three Kings.

Let us leave aside the question of whether Jesus was really born on December 25th at midnight. What is important is that on this date in nature the Christ-principle is born, the light and warmth that will transform everything. And the event is also celebrated in heaven. The angels sing and all the saints, the great masters and the initiates come together to glorify God and celebrate the birth of Christ, the cosmic principle, who is truly born in the universe.

And what are human beings doing on earth at that time? They are in bars and night-clubs, eating and drinking and making merry. And the most extraordinary thing is that even the most intelligent think that it is normal to celebrate Christmas in this way. Instead of being aware of the importance of an event that occurs only once a year, while the whole of nature is busy preparing for new life, human beings have their minds on other things. And this is why they gain nothing from it; on the contrary, they lose the grace and love of God. What can heaven give a being who remains insensible to these divine currents? Disciples, on the other hand, prepare themselves, because they know that on the night of Christmas, Christ is born into the world in the form of light, warmth, and life, and they create the right conditions for this divine child to be born also within them.

Jesus was born two thousand years ago in Palestine, but this is the historical aspect of Christmas, and as you know, the historical aspect is of secondary importance to an initiate. The birth of Christ is, above all, a cosmic event. It is the first manifestation of life in nature, the beginning of all outpourings. But it is also a mystical event; in other words, Christ must be born in every human being as the principle of light and divine love. This is the true birth of Christ. As long as human beings do not possess light and love, the divine child will not be born within them. They may celebrate and wait for his coming as much as they like, but nothing will happen.[2]

Jesus was born two thousand years ago, and in memory of this event people go to church and sing that he came to save them from sin. And of course, since they are already saved, they feel free to go on sinning, eating, and drinking to their heart's content for the rest of eternity. This is how Christians understand the birth of Jesus. Very few are prepared to study, to make an effort to prepare this birth within them. If the birth of Jesus on earth two thousand years ago was enough, why is the Kingdom of God still not established on earth? Not only was it not enough, but the truth is that God has sent several of his sons to earth. How can we possibly think that the coming of Christ into the world is something that happened only once two thousand years ago? In the first place, that would be incompatible with the immensity of God's love. We say that God is love; is it then possible that, only once in all the millions of years human beings have been living on earth, God sent his Son to preach for no more than three years in one tiny country? Where was that love before the birth of Jesus? What was it doing? And after Jesus would God have deserted the world for ever more? Really... that is quite ridiculous.

The truth is that Christ has appeared on earth in different forms many times – and on other planets too, throughout the universe –and he will come again in the future. If you cannot accept this, you are neither religious, nor Christian, nor anything at all. You believe in unlikely things, but you refuse to believe what is sensible. You keep saying: 'God is love, God is love', but what use is that if you do everything in your power to prove the contrary? You are told that this love manifested itself on earth just once... and you were not even there.

We cannot deny the historical significance of the birth of Jesus, but it is the cosmic and mystical aspects that are essential, because the birth of Christ – of which the birth of Jesus is only one aspect – is an event that occurs in the universe every year, and because Christ can be born within us also at any time. For some he has already been born, for others his birth will come soon, and for still others it will come some time in the future. Everything depends on the conditions prepared by the individual. And this is why it is very important to prepare for this feast of Christmas well in advance so that you may fully understand its significance.

Of all the Gospels, it is in that of St Luke that we find the birth of Jesus described in greatest detail. Let me read you a passage from it:

In those days a decree went out from Emperor Augustus that all the world should be registered. This was the first registration and was taken while Quirinius was governor of Syria. All went to their own towns to be registered. Joseph also went from the town of Nazareth in Galilee to Judea, to the city of David called Bethlehem, because he was descended from the house and family of David. He went to be registered with Mary, to whom he was engaged and who was expecting a child.

While they were there, the time came for her to deliver her child. And she gave birth to her firstborn son and wrapped him in bands of cloth, and laid him in a manger, because there was no place for them in the inn.

In that region there were shepherds living in the fields, keeping watch over their flock by night. Then an angel of the Lord stood before them, and the glory of the Lord shone around them, and they were terrified. But the angel said to them, 'Do not be afraid; for see – I am bringing you good news of great joy for all the people: to you is born this day in the city of David a Saviour, who is the Messiah, the Lord.

This will be a sign for you: you will find a child wrapped in bands of cloth and lying in a manger.' And suddenly there was with the angel a multitude of the heavenly host, praising God and saying,

'Glory to God in the highest heaven,
and on earth peace among those whom he favours!'

When the angels had left them and gone into heaven, the shepherds said to one another, 'Let us go now to Bethlehem and see this thing that has taken place, which the Lord has made known to us.' So they went with haste and found Mary and Joseph, and the child lying in the manger. When they saw this, they made known what had been told them about this child; and all who heard it were amazed at what the shepherds told them. But Mary treasured all these words and pondered them in her heart. The shepherds returned, glorifying and praising God for all they had heard and seen, as it had been told them.

After eight days had passed, it was time to circumcise the child; and he was called Jesus, the name given by the angel before he was conceived in the womb.

When the time came for their purification according to the law of Moses, they brought him up to Jerusalem to present him to the Lord (as it is written in the law of the Lord, 'Every firstborn male shall be designated as holy to the Lord'), and they offered a sacrifice according to what is stated in the law of the Lord, 'a pair of turtledoves or two young pigeons.' Now there was a man in Jerusalem whose name was Simeon; this man was righteous and devout, looking forward to the consolation of Israel, and the Holy Spirit rested on him. It had been revealed to him by the Holy Spirit that he would not see death before he had seen the Lord's Messiah. Guided by the Spirit, Simeon came into the temple; and when the parents brought in the child Jesus, to do for him what was customary under the law, Simeon took him in his arms and praised God, saying,

> *'Master, now you are dismissing your servant in peace, according to your word;*
> *for my eyes have seen your salvation,*
> *which you have prepared in the presence of all peoples,*
> *a light for revelation to the Gentiles and for glory to your people Israel.'*

No doubt you have read or heard this account many times. Many of the details in it are symbolical, and two passages are particularly mysterious. Why does it say, *'Mary treasured all these words and pondered them in her heart?'* The implication is that there was something she could not say. If it had been what she had heard from the shepherds, she could have spoken of it, since the shepherds were telling everyone. So it must have been something else that she was keeping in her soul, something sacred. Then there is the question of who Simeon was. The Gospel says that the Holy Spirit rested on him, which means that he was very pure. I do not want to talk about Simeon, for that would upset Christian consciences, but who was he? And what was his connection to Jesus?

As for Mary and Joseph, the fact that they had been chosen to be Jesus' parents means that they had prepared themselves already. They must have done great spiritual work in their previous lives to be worthy of receiving Jesus into their family. For in this respect, too, there is justice and certain rules and laws. It is God who made these rules and he is not going to break them himself. When God chooses creatures it is because they fulfil certain conditions. Of course *'God is able from these stones to raise up children to Abraham'*, but by first making them develop through the vegetable state and animal state before they reach the human state. Just as with a child, the seed must also go through all kinds of forms and states before taking on the appearance of a human being.

In the same way Jesus had to go through certain stages before becoming the Christ. This again is something Christians are unable to accept. They believe that Jesus, son of God, was God himself and that he was born perfect. But then why did he have to wait until he was thirty to receive the Holy Spirit and perform miracles? Even if God in person has to incarnate on earth, he is willing to abide by the laws he himself established. The Lord respects himself, you see. This is how the initiates see things. Everything is logical, everything is ordered, everything makes sense. Now, was it the Holy Spirit who engendered Jesus? Yes, it was. On the divine plane it was the Holy Spirit. On the physical plane, however, there also had to be someone, so that on this plane too there would be a reflection of the Holy Spirit. There had to be a conductor of the Holy Spirit on the physical plane so that the correspondences between the three worlds would be perfect, so that everything would be holy, luminous, and pure on all three planes: the physical, the spiritual, and the divine.

Was Jesus 'conceived of the Holy Spirit'? Certainly! Inasmuch as his conception was not sullied in any way by lust, passion or sensuality, we could say that he was conceived of the Holy Spirit. This is how Mary's virginity[3] must be understood, for virginity is a spiritual rather than a physical quality. Many women are virgins physically, but inwardly...? But I shall say no more about this. I have already said a good deal about it when speaking about Simeon.

The birth of Jesus has to be understood in the three worlds. That is, as a historical phenomenon, a psychic and mystical phenomenon, and a cosmic phenomenon. And today it is the mystical aspect that most concerns me. In his account of the birth of Jesus, St Luke has retained only the images of those events that occur for every human being. It is these symbolic images that we shall examine now.

For a child to be born there has to be a father and a mother. Joseph, the father, represents the intellect, and on a higher level, our spirit. Mary, the mother, is our heart, and on a higher level, our soul. When the heart and the soul are pure the child is born, but he is not born of the intellect and the spirit, he is born of the Holy Spirit, the pure flame that impregnates the human soul and heart. The intellect and the spirit represent the masculine principle within us, which provides the right conditions for the Holy Spirit to take possession of the feminine principle, the heart and the soul, so that the divine child can be born.

When Mary and Joseph sought refuge in the inn, there was no room for them, and this means that human beings who are busy eating, drinking, and enjoying themselves never have room for one who has received the divine child. The child has already been conceived in him as a Light – perhaps an ideal or idea he has been cherishing and nourishing. But where can he now go with this child? No one is prepared to open their door to him. In other words, no one understands him. But then he finds a stable. The stable with the manger is a symbol, a symbol first of all of poverty and difficult external conditions. Indeed, for one in whom the Spirit dwells it will always be this way: those around him will not appreciate or welcome him. But thanks to the light that radiates from him and shines above the manger, others will see him from afar and come to visit him.

This light, represented by the five-pointed star, is an absolute reality. It shines over the heads of all initiates in whom the feminine principle – their soul and heart – has given birth to the Child Jesus conceived of the Holy Spirit. And then the intellect – Joseph – instead of being jealous and repudiating Mary, must humbly accept the situation. Instead of behaving like a brute and shouting: 'That child you have brought into the world is not mine! Get out!' he should say: 'It is God who has touched Mary's heart and soul. I was unable to do it.' Thus the intellect must not be angry, but must understand and say, 'This is something totally beyond me.' And it must keep Mary as his spouse. To repudiate Mary is to repudiate half of one's own being and become like those who, ruled exclusively by their intellect, have banished their receptive dimension, all gentleness, humility, and intuition.[4] Many people have repudiated Mary because she delighted in receiving the Holy Spirit.

You must understand that Mary and Joseph are symbols of our inner life. Those who have repudiated Mary have become dried up. All they have left is their intellect, which does nothing but destroy and criticize and is never content. Joseph, however, respected Mary. He stood by her and said to himself: 'She is expecting a child. I may not be the father, but I shall protect her, because she needs my support.'

And what about the star? The star is a phenomenon which is always present in the life of a true mystic, a true initiate: a star in the form of a luminous pentagram shines above him.[5]

And since 'as above, so below', this pentagram exists on two levels. In the first place, man himself is a living pentagram, and secondly, when he has developed to the full the five virtues: goodness, justice, love, wisdom, and truth, another pentagram represents him on the subtle plane above, in the form of light.

The star that shone over the stable means that a light radiates from every initiate in whom dwells the living Christ. This light can be seen by others from afar, and they sense that something very special is manifesting itself through that being, and that 'something' is Christ. Then all those who represent authority, the rich and the powerful, come to pay him homage. Even high-ranking religious leaders who imagine that they have already reached the summit also sense that they still lack something, that they have not yet reached this level of spirituality, and they too come to learn, they come to bow down and bring gifts.

This explains the presence of the Three Kings by the manger in which Jesus lay: *Wise men from the East came to Jerusalem, asking, 'Where is the child who has been born king of the Jews? For we observed his star at its rising, and have come to pay him homage.'* These Magi were the High Priests of the religions of their respective countries, and they came because they sensed the presence of this light. Also, being astrologers and having seen certain exceptional configurations in the sky, they had concluded that an extraordinary event was about to take place on earth. The birth of Jesus, therefore, also corresponds to a phenomenon that took place in the heavens two thousands years ago.

The Three Kings – Melchior, Balthazar, and Gaspar – brought gold, frankincense, and myrrh, and each of these gifts was symbolic. The gold brought by Melchior meant that Jesus was king; gold is the colour of wisdom which shines over the heads of initiates like a crown of light. The incense brought by Balthazar meant that Jesus was a priest; incense represents the realm of religion, and therefore of the heart and love. And myrrh, brought by Gaspar, is a symbol of immortality; it was used to embalm the bodies of the dead and preserve them from destruction. These three gifts, therefore, correspond to the three realms of thought, emotion, and the physical body. And each of them also corresponds to a sephirah: myrrh corresponds to Binah, eternity; gold corresponds to Tiphareth, light; and frankincense corresponds to Chesed, love for all humankind.[6]

Let us now take a closer look at the stable, where an ox and an ass are said to have sheltered. There is no mention of any other animal in this stable, only an ox and an ass. Why? For centuries this story has been repeated without being understood, because the key to universal symbolism has been lost. The stable represents the physical body. And the ox? You know that in ancient civilizations the bull – and here of course we must draw a parallel between the ox and the bull – was seen as the generative principle. In Ancient Egypt, for instance, Apis the bull was the symbol of fertility and fecundity. The bull is ruled by Venus and represents sexual energy. The ass, on the other hand, is ruled by Saturn and represents the personality, our lower nature – also referred to as the Old Adam – who is obstinate and headstrong but a good servant. And these two animals were there to serve Jesus. But how could they serve him? Well, let me reveal to you something absolutely essential.

When human beings first begin to work to achieve self-perfection, they come into conflict with the forces of their personality and of their sexuality. An initiate is someone who has succeeded in mastering these two forces and making them serve him. Yes, you see, he puts them to work; he does not annihilate them; he must not annihilate them. The fact that those two animals were there is proof that they were useful. How? What did they do? They warmed the Infant Jesus with their breath. So, when an initiate has transmuted his inner ox and ass and made them his servants, they warm and vivify the new-born child within him with their breath. And then, not only do they no longer torment him, but they become beneficial forces. Breath is a sign of life, and the breath of the ox and the ass is a reminder of the breath by which God gave the first man a soul. The ass and the ox served the Child Jesus, and this means that all those who bear Christ within them will be served by the forces of their personality and their sexuality, because these forces can be extraordinarily useful if we know how to harness them and put them to work.

Then an angel appeared to the shepherds who owned the stable and who were keeping watch over their flocks in the fields. When the angel told them of the birth of Jesus, they were filled with wonder. They picked up some lambs and took them to the child as an offering. This means that those who have shares in our physical body – in other words, our family spirits, whether reincarnated or not – and who possess wealth (the wealth that is symbolized here by the sheep, the lambs, and the dogs) are told about what is happening. They are told because they have all played their part in building the stable – the physical body – and they gather round, exclaiming: 'Oh wonders! Who would ever have believed that such a great honour would befall our stable?'

All your family spirits, therefore, whether up above or here on earth, receive the news that a splendid event has taken place in your heart and soul, and they come to bow down and bring you gifts. Yes, the entire world is eager to serve this child. But you first have to bring him into the world. No one will come and serve you if you have not brought the child into the world, neither will angels come to you and sing to the glory of God, for angels come to sing only to celebrate the birth of the divine principle.

But let us get back to the symbolism of the manger. Why was Jesus, the son of God, born in a manger, on a bed of straw, rather than in a fine crib in a room of a large and magnificent house? This is another detail that is symbolic.

You will understand in what part of the body the manger is to be found if you remember my talks about the Hara Centre in which I explained the role this centre can play in the spiritual life of those who know how to work with it. Although the name Hara, meaning 'belly' in Japanese, suggests that this centre, situated a few centimetres below the navel, is mainly known in Japan, it has in fact always been known to initiates. It is this very centre Jesus referred to when he said: *'Out of the believer's heart shall flow rivers of living water.'* This 'heart' is the Hara centre and the manger in which Christ is to be born is there, between the ox and the ass, between the liver and the spleen.

I can see you are astonished by what I am saying, because you thought Jesus would be born in your head. Have you ever seen a baby born from its mother's brain? No. Well take some time to think about it. People tend to think of the belly and the entrails as something rather disgusting, but the fact is that God has chosen that area for the perpetuation of the human race. And it is here too, in the Hara centre, that the disciple must give birth within him to this new consciousness: the Infant Christ.

Nothing is more important than to work to bring the divine child to birth within us. Once we have achieved this, heaven and earth will break into song. At the four corners of the world, beings will understand that a new light has been born, and they will come to visit you and bring you gifts. Of course there will also be Herod (there have always been Herods) who will be furious and want to kill Jesus. He will tell the Three Kings: *'Go and search diligently for the child; and when you have found him, bring me word so that I may also go and pay him homage.'* Fortunately there will also be an angel who will come to warn us, as Joseph was warned: *'Get up, take the child and his mother, and flee to Egypt, and remain there until I tell you; for Herod is about to search for the child, to destroy him.'* So an angel of the Lord went to the Three Kings and told them not to return to Herod, so they went back to their own country by another way. This means that people who come to Jesus, to the Christ-principle, will never be able to return from whence they came and will have to go a different way.

And do you know why there is the tradition of a midnight supper on Christmas Eve? This too is symbolic. When the child is born, his coming must be celebrated with singing and a feast – without overdoing things, of course – because the child needs food. The first food a child receives after birth is its mother's milk. While it was still in her womb she fed it with her blood, but once it is born she feeds it with her milk. There are two colours here, red and white, and colours are also symbolic.[7]

They are already present at conception, when the red is supplied by the woman and the white by the man, and they are present again when the woman nourishes her child with her blood for nine months and later with her milk. And these same colours are found in our blood, with the red and white corpuscles.

Red and white represent the two principles on which life is based. Red, blood, is the life force, love, and it is thanks to this blood, to our love, that the Infant Christ can become flesh and blood within us. After birth the child is nourished with milk, in other words with purity, with light. And just as a mother never ceases to care for her child after it is born, so we too must continue to care for the Christ Child once he is born, but in a different way. This is why we watch the sunrise in the morning, so that we may nourish ourselves with its light.

Now, let us consider the words the angels said to the shepherds: *'Glory to God in the highest heaven, and on earth peace among those whom he favours!'* Do you understand these words? Why do they speak of peace among men and glory on high? Because when the divine child is born, he glorifies God, and peace descends on the soul of the man or woman in whom he is born. This child, the fruit of the love between the father and the mother, brings peace because he brings fulfilment. This is the meaning of the formula given by Master Peter Deunov: *Bojiata lubov nossi peulnia jivot*, in other words: 'divine love brings the fullness of life.'[8] The divine love that brings the fullness of life is the love brought by the Infant Christ. Love is nothing more than the herald of the child who is to come. This formula has very profound significance, and the Master did not give it to us so that we should simply repeat it mechanically, but in order that we might work with it so that our soul may be touched by God's love and conceive the child, the Christ. And when this happens, what marvellous changes take place!

In every area everything is transformed for the better, everything becomes luminous. It is well worth working for a whole year, several years, a whole lifetime, to bring about the birth of Christ within us.

By interpreting a few passages from this chapter by St Luke, I have sought to show you certain aspects of your inner life, so that you may come to realize that the birth of Jesus is a mystical event that can occur in each and every human being. So hold on to this image of the manger, with Joseph and Mary, and the Child Jesus lying between the ox and the ass, and the bright star shining above the stable. You will understand the meaning better now.

And do not forget that the feast of Christmas lasts for several days after December 25th. Up above, in heaven, a celebration is going on and you must take part in it, if only in thought. In the same way that the birth of a child offers the hope of life, so the birth of Christ each year in the universe expresses the hope that God has not abandoned human beings. In spite of the fact that they continually transgress his laws, he continues to extend their credit by sending them a Saviour, because he does not want a single soul to be lost. Even people who have committed the gravest errors must pick themselves up and move on. Of course they will suffer, that goes without saying. They will have to pay for their mistakes, they will have to make amends, but God gives them every opportunity to move on, to progress. The one thing you must not do is become discouraged and stop making an effort to evolve.

Now I would just like to add this: you may doubt that Christ ever existed historically. Some people doubt this and have demonstrated that he did not exist on the basis of evidence just as scientific as that produced by those who say he did exist. So where does the truth lie? Well, I would say very simply that the historical aspect is not really so important. Suppose that someone manages to produce irrefutable proof that Jesus never actually existed, that the whole story is a myth: one thing remains certain, and that is that the Gospels were inspired by an exceptionally great spirit. The mere fact that someone was capable of writing such things, of such depth, of such luminosity, is enough to take your breath away. Any other question becomes superfluous.

Notes

1 See *The Fruits of The Tree of Life – The Cabbalistic Tradition*, Complete Works, Volume 32, Chap. 17: 'The Cardinal Feasts'; - *Angels and other Mysteries of The Tree of Life*, Coll. Izvor No. 236, Chap. 12: 'Malkuth, Yesod, Hod, Tiphareth, Archangels and Seasons'.
2 See *Les splendeurs de Tiphéreth*, Œuvres Complètes, t. 10, chap. XVI : «Le Christ et la religion solaire».
3 See *«Au commencement était le Verbe»*, Œuvres Complètes, t. 9, chap. X: «Le péché contre le Saint-Esprit est le péché contre l'amour», p. 169-173.
4 See *'Know Thyself' – Jnana Yoga*, Complete Works, Volume 18, Chap. 4: 'Knowledge: Heart and Mind'.
5 See *The Symbolic Language of Geometrical Figures*, Coll. Izvor No. 218, Chap. 4: 'The Pentagram'.
6 See *The Fruits of The Tree of Life – The Cabbalistic Tradition*, Complete Works, Volume 32, Chap. 2, The Number Ten and the Ten Sephiroth, pp. 37-38.
7 See *The Book of Nature*, Coll. Izvor No. 216, Chap. 9: 'Red and White'.
8 See *Hrani yoga - Le sens alchimique et magique de la nutrition*, Œuvres Complètes, t. 16, chap. II (4) : «Formule à réciter avant et après les repas».

2

The second birth

As we have seen, everything recounted in the Gospels about the birth of Jesus may not be true from a historical point of view, but it is absolutely true from a symbolic point of view, and that is what is really important, for this birth can take place in every human being. This is what we call the second birth, and Jesus himself referred to it in one of the most mysterious passages in the Gospels in which a Pharisee named Nicodemus went to visit Jesus by night.

He said to him, 'Rabbi, we know that you are a teacher who has come from God; for no one can do these signs that you do apart from the presence of God.' Jesus answered him, 'Very truly, I tell you, no one can see the kingdom of God without being born from above.' Nicodemus said to him, 'How can anyone be born after having grown old? Can one enter a second time into the mother's womb and be born?' Jesus answered, 'Very truly, I tell you, no one can enter the kingdom of God without being born of water and Spirit. What is born of the flesh is flesh, and what is born of the Spirit is spirit. Do not be astonished that I said to you, You must be born from above. The wind blows where it chooses, and you hear the sound of it, but you do not know where it comes from or where it goes. So it is with everyone who is born of the Spirit.'

Let us have a closer look at Jesus' reply: *'no one can enter the kingdom of God without being born of water and Spirit.'*[1] What does it mean to be *'born of water and Spirit'*?

In order to be brought into the world a human being requires a physical mother and father, and in order to enter the kingdom of God a human being requires a spiritual mother and father. To enter the kingdom of God, therefore, is to be born anew, born from above, and according to Jesus, this birth can only occur thanks to our mother, water, and our father, the spirit, that is, fire, because symbolically the spirit is represented by fire. Just as the birth of a child is the result of work done by the father on the mother, entry into the kingdom of God is the result of the work of fire on water.

In the language of symbols, fire therefore represents the spirit, and water represents primordial matter. Water and fire are the expression of the two great masculine and feminine principles which manifest from the highest to the lowest level of creation.[2] When fire and water work together they produce energy, and this energy is a power that can be put to work. In inventing the steam engine, human beings made an amazing, vitally important discovery, but it has been put to use only on the physical plane to drive machinery, which does not amount to much. The masculine and feminine principles of fire and water are represented within us by the intellect and the heart, or on a higher level by the spirit and the soul. To enter the kingdom of God we need these two principles; the one or the other alone is not enough. We need the two combined for this work.

If we manage to elucidate Jesus' words: 'to be born of water and Spirit', we see that they confirm the interpretation I have given you of the feast of Christmas. What I said about the mystical dimension of the birth of Jesus is exactly what Jesus himself said about the second birth. The few words with which he answered Nicodemus showed that Jesus too possessed this knowledge of fire and water, which is the science of the two great cosmic principles, the masculine and the feminine.

Everyone knows what the first birth is. It is the coming into the world of a child conceived by a physical father and mother. And when a child comes into the world, it possesses all the organs it needs for its terrestrial life. To survive on Earth we need to breathe, eat, grasp objects, walk, talk, and so on, and nature has therefore given us lungs, a mouth, a stomach, arms, legs, vocal chords, etc. The first birth, therefore, could be said to be our entry into the physical world, which is the world we must study and in which we must work in order to develop. But this is not enough, for there is another world that is pure light, pure love, pure beauty, and we must penetrate this world too one day in order to explore it, hear its music, smell its scent, contemplate its flowers, its trees, its lakes, its mountains... You will say: 'Does that world also contain all these things?' Yes, since the world below, which is ours, is in the image of the world above, all the beauty of the visible world also exists in the invisible world.

Just as with physical birth, conception is also necessary for the second birth, and this conception takes place in the spiritual world as the spirit unites with pure matter to conceive a divine child. And of course, when a child is born in the spiritual world, it too can breathe, walk, talk, and work. This is the second birth: to be able to enter and live in a universe of another dimension.[3] You will say: 'But is it I who am born a second time or someone else who is born within me?' Well, in reality, whether it is you or another makes no difference. But let us say that it is you who are born, for it is you who feel that you have acquired another consciousness, other thoughts, and other feelings; it is you who enter a world which has existed from all eternity but which you were not able to enter before, because you had not yet been born a second time.

When the soul and spirit unite, they bring into the world a seed which develops into a new consciousness, and it is this consciousness that opens the doors of the kingdom of God. This new consciousness manifests itself as an inner light that drives out darkness, as a heat so intense that even if the entire world abandoned you, you would never feel alone, as a plentiful life that springs from you wherever your feet take you, as an influx of forces that you dedicate to the building of your inner being. It manifests also as joy, an extraordinary joy at feeling yourself to be in unison with all the evolved souls that dwell in the universe, a joy at being part of this immensity, and, what is more, the certainty that no one can rob you of this joy. In India this state is referred to as buddhic consciousness. Christians call it the birth of Christ.

You can now understand better why we say that a true initiate is androgynous, that is, a being in whom the masculine and feminine principles exist in perfect harmony. To bring the divine Child to birth within him, an initiate must be both father and mother, man and woman. As the father he sets off the process of conception, and as the mother he sets off the formative process. He forms and nourishes the child. An initiate is a being of fulfilment; he lacks nothing because he possesses both principles.

The birth of the divine principle is such an exceptional inner event that if you are given the grace to experience it one day, it will be impossible to mistake it. It is as though heaven lay open before you and you sense the presence of a being who supports you, who enlightens, protects, and delights you. Even in your darkest moments, at times when you feel utterly discouraged, you sense that this being is there, helping you. You sense a presence, a contact that is never broken. It is as though beside you, within you, there is a flame that never goes out. When you most need it, it gives you all its light and warmth, but at all times it is there, like a pilot light.

The second birth is birth into the divine world, and this time it is the person himself who decides to be born and who achieves it through his own efforts. No one asked for your opinion when it came to being born on the physical plane. Others called you into being and fashioned you. Nothing depended on you – although, in reality, it did depend on you to some extent, for, to put it simply, your destiny is decided by the Twenty-four Elders on the basis of the way you lived in previous lives.[4] When it comes to the second birth, however, it is you who are in charge, you who decide to be born into the world of light. Consciously, patiently and with intelligence, you build another consciousness, so that you may be born into the kingdom of God.

No one can enter the kingdom of God without being born of water and Spirit. This means that we cannot be born again if we do not possess the two principles of the father and the mother. The mother is water, the love of your heart sublimated by the soul. The father is fire, the wisdom of your intellect sublimated by the spirit. If you do not possess these two principles – love which is the feminine principle and wisdom which is the masculine principle – you cannot be reborn. A child always presupposes a father and a mother. Well, without love and wisdom there are no parents, and a child will never be born. You have already been born once, that goes without saying, but you have not yet been born of love and wisdom. To be born a second time you need a father and a mother who are more advanced, more evolved than a physical father and mother. You need love and wisdom, and then the child who is born will be truth, the kingdom of God of which Jesus spoke.

You will say: 'What do you mean by truth being the kingdom of God? This is not how philosophers and theologians define truth.' Yes, I know, truth has been given all kinds of definitions, which have only served to confuse the issue. It is impossible to say what truth is, because it does not exist as such. Only wisdom and love exist. This is why so many people who claim to possess truth are, in fact, mistaken. That is obvious when one sees that they do not act with wisdom and love. It is a person's behaviour which reveals whether he lives in truth or not, not the theories and extravagant notions he presents to others.

Those who act with love and wisdom live in truth, and even if they say nothing, everyone will come to sense this in the end. And if you feel that it is difficult to know truth, I would like to say to you that it is not. If you really want to find truth, all you have to do is to go forward in love and wisdom.[5] Yes, be quite clear on this, you will never find truth in isolation, because it cannot be conceived without the input of love – heart and soul – and of wisdom – intellect and spirit. Your love and your wisdom will lead you to truth, to the kingdom of God.

If there are so many different and contradictory 'truths' being bandied about in the world today, it is because they reflect the distortions of the human heart and mind. When someone says: 'As I see it, the truth is…', he is talking about his own truth, and that truth expresses his own heart and mind, which may be inadequate and distorted, or, on rare occasions, very elevated. If truth were independent of the heart and mind, everyone should have discovered the same truth. But this is not the case, as you well know. Everyone discovers different truths. Everyone, that is, except those who possess true love and true wisdom; they all discover the same truth and this is why they all, basically, speak the same language.

It all depends, therefore, on the harmonious development of the heart and the mind, and on a higher plane still, of the soul and the spirit. If we are not vigilant, we will drift further and further away from truth. People may write books to put their point of view across to the general public, and of course they will be sincere, but what they write will not be the truth. For sincerity is one thing and truth is another. You can be sincere and still be mired in the worst possible error. You must try to justify yourself on the grounds that you are sincere.

If truth remains so obscure it is because people think of it as something abstract. But truth is the world in which we live. We are tied to it, we are one with it. We cannot detach ourselves from it. We live in truth, we eat it, we breathe it, and we should therefore stop thinking that it will come to us from without. Those who expect to meet something outside of themselves of which they will be able to say, 'This is the truth' are very much mistaken. We can only move closer to truth by studying love and wisdom and by endeavouring to manifest love and wisdom.

Every time you introduce elements of love and wisdom into your thoughts and feelings you take one step closer to truth, you touch a certain aspect, reach a certain level of truth. And these aspects and levels are infinite in number. It is necessary to have found truth but at the same time to continue to seek it, in other words you must cling, once and for all, to these two irrefutable principles of love and wisdom, while at the same time continuing to look for the most appropriate ways of putting them into practice. In this way you will one day feel that you are being born a second time.

Notes

1 See *The Mysteries of Fire and Water*, Izvor 232, Chap. 1: 'The Two Principles of Creation, Water and Fire'; Chap. 8: 'Physical and Spiritual Water'; Chap. 14: 'How to Light and Tend Fire'.
2 See *Cosmic Balance – The Secret of Polarity*, Izvor 237, Chap. 16: 'The Sacrament of the Eucharist'.
3 See *Christmas and Easter in the Initiatic Tradition*, Izvor 209, Chap. 3: 'Birth on the Different Planes of Being'.
4 See *Youth: Creators of the Future*, Izvor 233, Chap. 11: 'Did you Choose Your Own Family?'; *Angels and other Mysteries of The Tree of Life*, Izvor 236, Chap. 15 (I): Binah: The Laws of Destiny'.
5 See *The Second Birth – Love, Wisdom, Truth*, C.W. 1, Chap. 1: 'The Second Birth'; Chap. 3: 'Truth is Hidden in the Eyes'; Chap. 4: 'Wisdom is Hidden in the Ears'; Chap. 5: 'Love is Hidden in the Mouth'; Chap. 6: 'Love, Wisdom, and Truth'; - *Truth: Fruit of Wisdom and Love*, Izvor 234, Chap. 2: 'Truth, the Child of Wisdom and Love'; Chap. 3: 'Wisdom and Love; Light and Warmth'.

3

The resurrection
and
the last Judgement

If you consider only what Christians have been taught for centuries, the question of the resurrection of the dead and the last Judgement is extremely vague and obscure. In order to make these subjects clearer to you, let me begin by reading you a passage from the Gospel of St Mark.

Some Sadducees, who say there is no resurrection, came to him and asked him a question, saying, 'Teacher, Moses wrote for us that if a man's brother dies, leaving a wife but no child, the man shall marry the widow and raise up children for his brother. There were seven brothers; the first married and, when he died, left no children; and the second married her and died, leaving no children; and the third likewise; none of the seven left children. Last of all the woman herself died. In the resurrection whose wife will she be? For the seven had married her.'

Jesus said to them, 'Is not this the reason you are wrong, that you know neither the scriptures nor the power of God? For when they rise from the dead, they neither marry nor are given in marriage, but are like angels in heaven. And as for the dead being raised, have you not read in the book of Moses, in the story about the bush, how God said to him, "I am the God of Abraham, the God of Isaac, and the God of Jacob"?

510

He is God not of the dead, but of the living; you are quite wrong.'

Mk 12: 18–27

There are some important points here which I would like to consider, in particular Jesus' reply to the Sadducees: *'Is not this the reason you are wrong, that you know neither the scriptures nor the power of God?'* This sentence needs closer scrutiny because it may be the key to understanding all the rest. Yes, the power of God... what role does the power of God play in the resurrection of the dead? And Jesus continues: *'For when they rise from the dead, they neither marry nor are given in marriage, but are like angels in heaven.'* And what are angels in heaven like? In the first place, of course, they do not have a physical body, but they are also asexual in the sense that although they do not have sexual organs as we know them, they have other organs which are far superior, and by means of which they too make exchanges.[1] Exchanges exist not only in the world of human beings but throughout the universe. No creature is excluded. All creatures make exchanges of love, the only difference being the expression and the quality of these exchanges. If you knew how much angels loved each other! Perhaps you will say: 'We thought that they were so pure they didn't need love.' But God is love, and God lives in all creatures, so how could they not know love? The question is to understand the nature and the manifestations of this love.

Concerning the resurrection of the dead, Jesus said: *'He is God not of the dead, but of the living...'* This is another point that is not understood. So, these are a few important points that we need to study so that we may begin to understand the extraordinarily important question of resurrection.

For two thousand years now Christians have talked about resurrection and read passages from the Gospels that tell of

Jesus' resurrection. A small group of women came into the garden and found an angel by the tomb, but Jesus was no longer there. He later appeared to Mary Magdalene and subsequently to his disciples, and so the story goes on. But let us leave these passages aside today and concentrate on the meaning of Jesus' words in the excerpt I just read to you.

You all know how the majority of Christians understand resurrection: a person dies and is buried, and then he waits in his grave until it is time to rise again in his physical body in order to be judged. Since the beginning of human history, therefore, for millions of years, all those who have died have been waiting for judgement day. And that day has not yet come, and it will not come until the end of time. Well, for my part, I do not believe in this kind of resurrection. Why? Because the people concerned are no longer the same beings.

When a person is buried, more or less the same thing happens to them as happens in a printing shop (I am referring, of course, to the old way of printing books with lead characters). Once the printing was done, the characters went back into their compartments so that they could be taken out again and arranged in a different order to compose another book. It is the same for human beings: the printers come – the angels of the four elements – and put together a human body using particles of earth, water, air, and fire. Then when that human being dies, everything is dispersed. After a while only the bones remain, and some time later even the bones disappear. Where have all these particles gone? They have returned to merge once more with the four elements of earth, water, air, and fire, whence they came... So where can all these men and women now be found, so that they may be resurrected in their physical bodies?

Think of all the brutes, all the murderers and tyrants that have inhabited the earth, of all those who were ill, gangrenous, or syphilitic. Imagine what a sight it would be if they were all resurrected... And consider just how many there would be; how many human beings have been born and have died over the millions of years humankind has existed. It is impossible to calculate. Where could we put them if they all came back? There would never be enough room on earth. Besides, we would have to destroy the whole of nature to recover all the particles of their bodies. I know, of course, that there are a few saints and prophets among them, but they are a minority lost in the midst of it all like a drop of water in the ocean. So I ask you, you who have a sense of aesthetics, what do you think of such a prospect? Charming, isn't it? To see all these people in the flesh, standing there waiting to be judged. Poor judges! My goodness, how sorry I feel for those poor celestial judges! How will they bear the stench? Because of course it will all have to be reconstituted. How can you judge someone if you do not know how they used to smell? It will be impossible to pronounce a verdict unless all the evidence is available, and I wonder how those great spirits will be able to bear such ugliness.

Poor Christians! And they rejoice at the idea that one fine day all those human beings will be resurrected: their uncles and aunts, their grandfathers... At the moment they are all just lying still and waiting. For millions of years they have been sleeping in their graves. What a school of laziness God invented! How patient he is, to keep all those people immobilized for so long without contributing anything to the cosmic economy. How can the Deity, who is so active, tolerate such inertia, he who is forever creating new heavens and a new earth, he who never rests? Some will say: 'But the Bible says that he rested on the seventh day.' Yes, but while he was apparently resting on the seventh day, he was in fact doing a different kind of work. The way Christians understand things always amazes me. They have reduced everything to human dimensions, and instead of man becoming like God, they have God behaving like a man. Incredible! Well I myself do not believe any of this.

Now, to get back to all those dead people whose bodies have been scattered in the four elements: how will they be reconstituted, since nature has made generations of human beings one after the other with the same materials? To be able to rebuild some, others would have to be destroyed. So you see, the resurrection of the dead as most Christians imagine it is implausible; it cannot stand up to the test of logic and common sense.

Let us suppose, for the sake of argument, that all those dead people have been resurrected, and now they have to be judged. Well, they have been in their graves for thousands and thousands of years, and are going to be judged on a life that lasted some eighty or a hundred years at most. Perhaps some even lived as long as Methuselah – nine hundred and sixty-nine years according to Genesis – but that is still very little in comparison with the centuries that have passed since they died. So they lived and worked for a very short time and then slept for a very long time. Actually, if they have to be judged, I think they would in fact be condemned for sleeping too much. Yes, because while they were asleep they were useless, and to be useless is the greatest sin. This would mean that they have all been judged even before being resurrected, so it woluld be pointless to summon them for judgement to be pronounced. It has already been done: they have slept too long!

Then there is another matter (I must say I find this idea of the last Judgement ridiculous): surely, instead of letting all these human beings sleep for thousands of years, they could have been given the opportunity to redeem themselves and make amends. But no, they are buried, and there they stay. Well, I find it unacceptable that people should be judged thousands of years after their death, without having had the possibility of making amends for their faults. No, the way I see it, this last Judgement is impossible. Or else it has to be understood differently.

Let us see how things work in society and in business, for instance. Every organization has a cashier, a treasurer, or a bursar. Suppose that the accounts were never checked, and that it was only thousands of years later that an inspector came along to examine the books and see what the treasurer had done with the money in his safe. Well, the treasurer would not have a care in the world! He would not care two hoots about a future inspection and judgement that were still thousands of years ahead. He would be far away by then. I am not exactly sure how these things work in the business world – whether accounts are audited on a yearly or a quarterly basis – but I do know that audits are carried out, and each time this is a kind of judgement. A judgement is made about the treasurer's work, about whether he has been honest, organized, and careful, and depending on the outcome, he keeps his job or he is fired. There is no question of waiting millions of years.

In the same way, if millions of years were allowed to pass before human beings were judged it would become far too complicated. Besides, it would even be useless for the education of these poor children of God, because they would have been allowed to accumulate so many debts and so many faults and crimes that it would be quite impossible for them to repair or improve anything. In actual fact there is a last Judgement for each and every one of us and it comes in different forms. When someone dies, it is a last judgement. The powers on high have decided that he has lived long enough, that his work is done and he is no longer needed here. So, off he goes; he has no choice. And when a person falls ill, that too is a judgement; he has been sentenced to confinement for a week or a month. Judges have examined the case and decided to send him to bed for a while to force him to get rid of certain impurities.

In order to help human beings, cosmic intelligence always has a few minor trials to give them, and that is the last judgement. Of course it is not absolutely the last. Let us say it is the last but one – in fact, it is always the last but one. Every time someone encounters illness, a set-back, or suffering of any kind, it means that the law has decided he has committed some fault. You see, in every judgement there is intelligence, love, and an educational aspect, whereas the last Judgement is stupid, implausible, and I cannot accept it because I know that everything God does is of immense intelligence and usefulness. Do not wait for a last Judgement, therefore, for we are constantly being judged without even being aware of it.

You must also realize that even death is not an absolute judgement either. Do not imagine that once you are dead you will remain in your grave, waiting and rotting away. No, your clothes – in other words, your body – will rot, but after a certain period of time, you yourself – that is, your spirit – will come back to earth and you will take on another body, for life goes on. Every new existence is the result of a judgement that has been pronounced on your previous existence. You will say: 'But then what is resurrection?' Resurrection is something altogether different from the idea the majority of Christians have of it.

First of all you must understand that a dead person will never rise to be judged, because there is no resurrection of the dead. The dead do not rise again; they have reached the end; their time is finished. It is the living who rise.[2] The souls that have left behind their clothes are alive. Yes, it is they who can rise, but not their physical bodies. Jesus himself said this: *'He is God not of the dead, but of the living…'* The body is already dead and will not rise again. It is the soul that rises. When? All this is

516

explained in the passage I have just read to you, but you have to know how to link things together in order to interpret it.

In this passage, Jesus also said: *'For when they rise from the dead, they neither marry nor are given in marriage, but are like angels in heaven.'* Where can human beings go in order to evolve to such a degree as to become angels? Not to their graves, that is certain. There is no evolution in the grave; you remain as you are. So it is not after thousands of years in their graves that human beings will rise like angels. How could they? And in any case, if they did become angels, why should they be judged? Angels are not judged. You must understand, therefore, that between death and resurrection there is period during which human beings can transform themselves and evolve. Yes, because they reincarnate. They will depart and return, depart and return many times over, and they will perfect themselves to such an extent that in the end they will become like angels. This is what resurrection is.

All human beings are thus predestined to resurrect one day and to become perfectly pure, like the angels. But this resurrection implies reincarnation. You cannot convince me that it is in their graves that human beings will become angels. No, never! They will leave their graves, they will reincarnate, they will learn, and they will purify themselves until they are perfect. Resurrection is this continual improvement which gradually leads them to perfection. All creatures will resurrect one day in this way. But not the dead. Only the living resurrect.

Listen and try to understand. What did Jesus mean when he said: *'Is not this the reason you are wrong, that you know neither the scriptures nor the power of God?'* What is the power of God he was talking about? The power of God is precisely this: to lead human beings to resurrection. The power of God is the power that transforms, that sublimates. Yes, but this power is not found in the grave. There is no resurrection in the grave, only dislocation, disintegration. God transforms only the living. Besides, elsewhere in the Gospels Jesus says: *'Let the dead bury their own dead; but as for you, go and proclaim the kingdom of God.'*

Reincarnation is not specifically mentioned in the passage I read earlier, but it is implied. If I ask: 'What happens to someone between the time he is buried and the moment when he is transformed into an angel?' no one can answer me. You have to admit that something must have happened for a person to achieve such a transformation, but you do not know exactly what. This is why the teachings of the Church are inadequate and incapable of establishing the kingdom of God on earth, because the kingdom of God cannot be achieved by lies or omissions. The Church must begin by revealing reincarnation. You will say: 'There is no mention of reincarnation in the Gospels.' Well, I have just shown you that reincarnation is clearly mentioned in certain places.

Jesus said: *'For when they rise from the dead, they neither marry nor are given in marriage...'* You married this woman or that man in one incarnation, and then in subsequent incarnations you married others. Could you find the husband or wife you had thousands of years ago, when you have had so many other spouses since? In any case, there would be no point in looking for them and finding them, because no one belongs to anyone else. This is not said explicitly here, but it is implicit. How many times has each person been married? And what rights would any one person have over another? Every man has had numerous wives, and every woman has had numerous husbands, and one day when they are tired of so many costly and appalling experiences, they will say: 'That's it, we don't want to marry in that way any more', and they will evolve so much in their conception of love that they will become angels.

What are angels like? What do they do? When two angels meet they merge with each other by radiating light and colour, and a truly extraordinary exchange of love takes place between them. Then they go their separate ways again and meet and embrace other angels in the same way. This is how angels have exchanges with each other, and they do not know what shame is. In the world of angels there are no wives waiting for their husbands with a rolling pin, muttering to themselves: 'He's not home yet. Who's he with this time? He'll see what's in store for him when he gets home!' The angels continually make exchanges of love with each other without lust or jealousy.

You see now what bliss awaits you when you become angels! Because I know very well that all men are burning with the desire to love all women and all women to love all men. And even if you say: 'No, no, that just isn't true. What an accusation!' I shall not believe you. Just give men and women a free rein for a while and you will soon see whether they are content with just one woman or one man. But given their current degree of evolution, they had better avoid multiplying their experiences, otherwise they will soon be ill or unbalanced. It is better to wait. I advise you to wait... to wait for a very long time. You have no idea of the joys God is preparing for you, but not yet, because given the way you are at the moment, things would not turn out very well. You must await transformation, resurrection. Only when you are like angels will you be able to come together to embrace and merge with each other without fear.

Now, how does this resurrection come about? Jesus said: *'I am the resurrection and the life.'* The fact that Jesus resurrected means that we too can accelerate the process of resurrection that will come one day for all humankind. Yes, all human beings will resurrect one day, but it will take a very long time. However, you can accelerate the process of resurrection if you wish, but to achieve this you must work to improve your thoughts, your feelings, and your actions. It is possible. Jesus resurrected; he did not wait for centuries to resurrect together with the whole of humanity. And he is not alone in having done this, for resurrection has always been taught in the initiatic temples, and many have already resurrected.

It is not necessary to die physically in order to resurrect. You do not need to be put in a grave first. To resurrect means to be freed from your old weaknesses, your old vices, and your old illnesses. This is resurrection. For a human being to resurrect, his cells must be perfectly pure and vibrate intensely. All those who live an intense spiritual life are getting ready to resurrect.

It may help you to understand the phenomenon of resurrection if I give you an example. Take the image of a seed: a seed that has been planted in the ground is just like a human being in his grave. When the angel of warmth comes, he caresses the seed and awakens it, saying: ' It's time to come out of your grave.' And then the life that lay buried there begins to stir. A tiny shoot divides the seed in two, pushes its way up through the soil, and grows into a magnificent tree. This is resurrection. But for resurrection to take place, the grave must first be opened, and only heat can open a grave – and by heat I mean love. Those who have a great deal of love in their hearts, a love free of self-interest, a spiritual love, open the graves of their cells.

Human beings have so many rotting, disintegrating cells in their bodies. If they only knew how many graves they are carrying around with them; thousands of tiny graves which must all be broken open. As long as your cells have not been brought back to life, they will remain inactive and you will never know what inner riches you possess. But once they have been awakened, once they have resurrected, your consciousness will expand and you will never be the same again. You will find that you feel and experience everything in another, more spiritual dimension. This renewal can only be achieved by means of heat and damp. Because damp – water – is the substance that serves as a vehicle for life. Water gives life, and heat – fire – gives impulse.

So here again we have an example of how the masculine and feminine principles work: they are both there to shake the seed from its slumber. Then the grave opens, and Christ, in other words, this tiny soul, this creature who appeared to be dead but who was really only sleeping, emerges alive. This phenomenon can be seen throughout nature. The image of the tomb opening and Jesus emerging, resurrecting, is a universal symbol; it is not restricted to Jesus or to Christians. A seed, any tiny seed, is also a tomb in which life lies buried until the angel of Spring comes to open it. How could the baby chick break out of the egg if the mother hen did not peck at the shell to open the tomb? And where does the custom of giving Easter eggs come from? From the fact that an egg symbolizes the beginning of life.

Let me illustrate this with yet another image, that of a butterfly.[3] What is a butterfly? It is a creature which has resurrected. It begins life as a caterpillar without grace or beauty. Then, one day, it weaves a cocoon and goes to sleep, and some time later a butterfly emerges. What went on while the chrysalis was asleep? The caterpillar was transformed into a butterfly because it had already triggered a certain number of processes which ended in this metamorphosis. Well, the same phenomena take place in human beings. At the moment they are still caterpillars, in other words creatures which are not very beautiful and which crawl along the ground and, above all, which eat the leaves of trees. They are pests, therefore, and the poor creatures are despised and persecuted until, one day, they turn into butterflies.

Nature has left messages and clues everywhere to teach us how our own resurrection can come about. What do you do when you meditate? You are like the chrysalis wrapped in its cocoon, preparing its own metamorphosis. If you have not yet become a butterfly it is because you have not yet worked enough. You go back to your prosaic life, like the caterpillar crawling along the ground eating leaves, and the next day you wrap yourself in your cocoon again, you spin a few more spiritual threads, and then day-to-day matters demand your attention again, and again you put off your spiritual work. The next day you work at it again, and the next, and the next, and so on, until you finally emerge from your cocoon as a butterfly. At this point you will no longer need to eat leaves, for you will feed on the nectar of flowers, in other words you will be nourished by all that is most subtle in the hearts and souls of all men and women. Yes, for every being possesses inwardly something delicious, a little nectar, and if you can feed on this nectar without damaging the flowers, you will be happy and will fly in the light.

Resurrection is possible, it is real. Many people have already resurrected, and one day everyone will do so. We only have to understand that this resurrection does not take place in the grave. Once you have been buried, that is the end, you will stay there – or rather, it is your body that will stay there and disintegrate. But you yourself have to come back to earth in order to resurrect, you have to learn to overcome your weaknesses, you have to wrap yourself in your cocoon like a chrysalis, in other words you have to stop feeding on selfish, self-interested thoughts and feelings. Indeed, the whole point of prayer and meditation is to learn to nourish yourself with

522

elements of a spiritual nature. People who do not understand this and who are interested only in pleasure and enjoyment, who spend all their time on mundane tasks and interests, neglect prayer and meditation, and that is a great pity because they are interrupting their work of transformation and hence their resurrection. It is meditation that transforms; I have often seen this. When someone is genuinely meditating, his face lights up. Every meditation must increase your inner light, and it is this light that helps to build your body of glory, thanks to which you will resurrect one day.

Those who have resurrected live a new life; they have different thoughts and different desires, their behaviour is different. Inwardly they are no longer the same, they no longer walk in the same direction, they have a different goal. Jesus said: *'I am the resurrection and the life.'* Why did he not simply say, 'I am the resurrection'? Why did he add 'life'? Is life different from resurrection? No. And when Jesus says: *'I am the resurrection and the life'*, it means that resurrection is simply a renewed form of life, a purer, more intense quality of life. And once you live this higher life, you resurrect.

Resurrection is nothing more than a certain quality of life, the life of a child of God. You do not need to wait hundreds of years to live this life. Christ is the resurrection and the life, so take Christ as your model, link with him, live the life he lived and you too will be resurrection and life. These are the new concepts I give to you, and these truths are the only ones that can bring you out of your graves. Yes, because at the moment you are still in your graves, and if you wait for the trumpets to sound before you come out, you may have to wait hundreds and thousands of years.

When Jesus said: *you know neither the scriptures nor the power of God*, this is the power he was referring to: that which is capable of transforming a caterpillar into a butterfly.

If you think a caterpillar is clever enough to make the beautiful colours of a butterfly all by itself, you are very much mistaken. No, it is the divine power acting within. We too have the power of God within us, and if we remember to put it to work within us every day, it will know what to do to make us luminous and powerful, it will know how to resurrect us.

So you see, the passage I read to you from the Gospel of St Mark gives us clear indications as to how Jesus understood resurrection. But there is another indication in the etymology of the word 'resurrection' in Russian and Bulgarian. In Bulgarian we say *vazkressenie* and in Russian *voskressenie*. Literally these words mean 'to descend from the cross'. And what is a cross?[4] The cross can be understood in the three worlds. I have already given several talks about the cross so I shall not go into it in any detail here. When you draw a two-dimensional cross you see that it is made up of six squares, and you can fold these squares to form a cube.

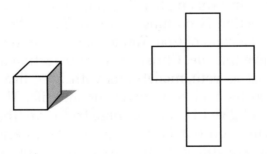

A cube symbolizes prison, matter, the number 4, the four states of matter – solid, liquid, gaseous, and igneous – corresponding to the four elements. To resurrect, therefore, means to be freed from this dependency, this slavery, this prison of matter that is the physical body, for the physical body is also a cross. You see what enlightenment this one word *vazkressenie* gives us. And to 'bear our cross' is to bear the difficulties of life, our physical and moral burdens.[5] The cross is heavy, and when a man comes down from the cross he is released from prison, he rises from the tomb, that is, from all that limits him inwardly, and he becomes free, free like a butterfly.

So resurrection is a real phenomenon, but as I say there is no such thing as the resurrection of the dead. Only the living resurrect, and it is those who are most alive who resurrect, those who live a very intense life, a highly divine life, a Christly life. Everyone will resurrect, some far more quickly than others, depending on whether they prepare themselves during their successive incarnations. In fact, those who make great efforts in this incarnation to become pure may not have to reincarnate again. Some great initiates no longer reincarnate. They leave this world and do not return in another body. Their spirit may return and make its home in other beings in order to help, instruct, and vivify them, but they do not take on another physical body.

If this passage from St Mark's Gospel is not understood in the way I have just interpreted it, resurrection and the last Judgement are totally incomprehensible. There cannot be a last Judgement such as people imagine, in which all the human beings who have ever lived rise from their graves to be judged. That is impossible, and as I have said, we are continually being judged. Every trial, every instance of suffering, every torment is proof already that we have been judged. Sentence has been passed, and we are paying. Once there is nothing left to pay, we will never suffer again.

Read this passage again and you will better understand what Jesus had in mind when he answered the Sadducees. You will have a clear understanding of God's plan and will see how it happens and how everyone can resurrect. The Church's interpretation of the resurrection lacks common sense and logic. It shows a God who is completely stupid, and its idea of the last Judgement also is quite absurd. So, do not worry, there will be no last Judgement. Yes, but remember that another last judgement awaits you, because you are being judged at every moment. If, for instance, you are bitten by a flea, that is a judgement. 'What?' I hear you ask, 'A flea-bite is a judgement?' Yes, if a flea bites you it is only after lengthy cogitation: it has found some impurities in your blood and wants to tell you that you must improve your way of life. If you purify your blood it will no longer attract fleas.

So many things in our everyday lives can help us understand the resurrection and the last Judgement. You meet a friend who is walking with a limp. He shows you his leg, which is severely bruised, and explains how he hurt himself. A few days later his leg is back to normal, the bruising gone. Well, everything I have just explained to you is summed up in this example. When you bruise yourself, some cells die. Then, some time later, the bruising clears up. Does this mean that the old cells have come back to life? No, it means that new cells have come to take their place. The old cells have been replaced by the new cells, which have cleared up the bruising. And once again your friend can walk and the pain has gone. This is the mechanism of resurrection.

This process recurs in the whole organism. Many people have cells that are already dead in their organisms, and they are not being replaced by new cells. Little by little, if the dead cells increase in number to the point of invading the entire organism, the individual dies. Others – and in particular young victims of fatal accidents – still have numerous living cells in their bodies when they die, and this is why doctors try to retrieve them for use in organ transplants. This is a fact: some of the living have so many dead bodies in their organism that they are already almost dead. They have too many rotting cells which they are unable to replace with new ones, while others die even though nearly all their cells are alive.

The same phenomenon occurs on the spiritual plane, but here it is not cells that are involved, but entities. Just as our physical body is made up of billions and billions of cells, our spiritual being also is composed of a multitude of entities. And here, too, it often happens that some of those entities die or that the individual is inhabited by dark and harmful entities, which must be replaced with pure, luminous ones. This replacement is resurrection. It is not definitive and it is not complete, but resurrection has already begun for some of you, and you must keep at it, continue this work of replacement, and then one day your resurrection will suddenly be complete. It will happen as St Paul says: *'in a moment, in the twinkling of an eye, at the last trumpet. For the trumpet will sound, and the dead will be raised imperishable, and we will be changed.'*

In reality, however, it is not exact to say that the resurrection happens in the twinkling of an eye. Or let us say that these words should be understood differently, and this is where chemistry can help us. Suppose you have some acid and pour a few drops of litmus into it. The liquid immediately turns red. You then pour an alkaline solution into it, drop by drop. At first nothing happens, but if you continue to pour, drop by drop, suddenly the red liquid turns blue. Well, symbolically this is also resurrection. The red changes to blue: the red is the Old Adam who resurrects as Christ, the blue of the heavens. You keep adding, drop by drop, until with the last drop everything is changed in the twinkling of an eye, and you resurrect. Your resurrection began long before, but there was no visible change until the very last second. What St Paul says is absolutely true, but it needs to be explained. Is this clear to you now? Resurrection does not happen all of a sudden. A great deal of work needs to be done first, and it is the last drop that transforms everything. Why do we have to wait for the last drop? That is a mystery even chemists cannot explain.

Many of you have already begun to resurrect, in that you have begun to replace certain selfish, dark, and violent entities within with entities that are intelligent, luminous, and full of love, but you complain that you see no change in yourself, that you still feel the same. Well, you need to be patient and wait for that last drop. Because that last drop is the 'trumpet'. No trumpet will ever raise the dead if the dead have not already done a great deal of work on themselves. A trumpet cannot raise one who is really dead. Try it: go to a cemetery and play your trumpet as hard as you like. No one will come out – unless it be some poor down-and-out who had settled there for the night and who appears from behind a gravestone all dishevelled, as if risen from the dead.

Physical resurrection? Physical death and resurrection? No, it is spiritual resurrection we are interested in, because there will be no physical resurrection. For those who have died it is all over. Those who are alive, however, those whose soul is alive... for them, yes, there will be a resurrection, for God is the God of the living.

Notes

1 See *Cosmic Balance – The Secret of Polarity*, Izvor 237, Chap. 17 (2): 'The Androgynes of Myth'.
2 See *Truth: Fruit of Wisdom and Love*, Izvor 234, Chap. 6: 'I am the Way, the Truth and the Life'.
3 See *La pédagogie initiatique*, Œuvres Complètes, t. 28, chap. VII : «La chenille et le papillon».
4 See *The Symbolic Language of Geometrical Figures*, Izvor 218, Chap. VI: 'The Cross'.
5 See *Le grain de sénevé*, Œuvres Complètes, t. 4, chap. IV : «Si quelqu'un veut venir après moi...»

Notes

1. See David ..., *The Birth of ...*, Chap. ...

2. See ..., ..., 1996, 124, Chap. 6 ..., ...
the Birth had the Law.

3. See ..., *Imaginary ...*, ..., Chap. ... trans-
lation, 1 ...

4. See ..., *Emotions of ...*, ..., Chap. 1, Chap. VI,
life ...

5. ..., *The ... Complete*, ..., 3 ..., 81 ... up, an
... explication.

4

The body of glory

That which is dead cannot be brought back to life; only that which is living can resurrect. You must be quite clear on this from now on. If one hears of those who have come back from the dead, it means that they only appeared to be dead; in reality they were in a coma. Those who are said to have been resuscitated were in fact not yet dead, even though they were thought to be because their heart had stopped beating.

Once the soul has left the body it is final; there is no point in trying to bring it back. Many stories that are quite untrue are told about this, stories invented by ignorant people or impostors. They tell of magicians who have brought the dead back to life. No, the truth is that these magicians call up earthly and subterranean entities by means of certain methods, and that they introduce these entities into the body of the dead person so that it moves again. It is not the dead person's spirit that comes back, but other entities. By means of certain rites, the magician entices these entities with elements that please them (blood and food) to enter the body and stay there a while. High initiates, however, have never been interested in bringing the dead back to life. Only necromancers claim that they can do this, while in fact, they do nothing more than attract other entities.

Even Jesus did not bring the dead back to life. You will say: 'But doesn't the Gospel say he did?' Yes, but these people were not really dead yet. 'And what about Lazarus? He had been dead for three days.' No, he was thought to have died, but in fact he was still alive. Indeed, did Jesus not say? *'Our friend Lazarus has fallen asleep, but I am going there to awaken him.'* And this in no way diminishes the merit of what Jesus did, because Lazarus would really have died if Jesus had not come to take him from the tomb. In fact, one might ask if what is said of Jesus' death, and therefore of his resurrection, is true? But I shall not go into this because I do not wish to trouble Christian consciences any more.

The dead do not rise. It is the living who rise again, the living who are sunk in lethargy like trees that 'die' in winter. And if we want to understand what true resurrection is, we have to look at the Gospel account of Jesus' transfiguration: *Six days later, Jesus took with him Peter and James and his brother John and led them up a high mountain, by themselves. And he was transfigured before them, and his face shone like the sun, and his clothes became dazzling white. Suddenly there appeared to them Moses and Elijah, talking with him. Then Peter said to Jesus, 'Lord, it is good for us to be here; if you wish, I will make three dwellings here, one for you, one for Moses, and one for Elijah.' While he was still speaking, suddenly a bright cloud overshadowed them, and from the cloud a voice said, 'This is my Son, the Beloved; with him I am well pleased; listen to him!' When the disciples heard this, they fell to the ground and were overcome by fear. But Jesus came and touched them, saying, 'Get up and do not be afraid.' And when they looked up, they saw no one except Jesus himself alone.*

The transfiguration of Jesus can only be explained as the manifestation of what spiritual tradition calls the body of glory. This manifestation can be so intense that a flood of light seems to surge from deep within the person and set fire to his body and even his clothes.

The seed of the body of glory lies in the etheric body – which is the double of the physical body[1] – and it is on this seed that we must work. How? With our thoughts, our feelings, our desires, all our psychic life, we can work transformations in the very heart of our cells. We are inhabited by billions of souls – our cells – and each and every one can resurrect. You may say that cells are not souls. The cells themselves, no, of course not, but each one houses a tiny soul which has been entrusted with a specific task. A cell of the eye is not a cell of the brain or of the liver. It is not simply a particle of matter which exists in a particular place in our organism. It is like a worker who knows what work it must do in the place in which it is located, because the correct functioning of the organism depends on its work. However, the 'consciousness' of these billions of cells is a reflection of our own consciousness. If, therefore, we live a disorderly existence, we weaken these souls, and they can no longer do their work properly. One after the other they cease to function and we go towards death, physical death as well as spiritual death.

The way in which biology and medicine understand human beings is not incorrect, of course, but it is incomplete, for they do not teach us to look upon our organism as a brotherhood of souls. And just as we can paralyse and annihilate all these kind creatures that work for us simply by behaving unreasonably, we can also bring them to life, regenerate them, and enlighten them by deciding to bring order and light into our life.

We cannot resurrect without the help of all our cells, because we are dependent on them. Thanks to the psychic and spiritual powers we possess, it is we who are in control, it is we who make the decisions. But if the cells of our limbs and organs are not capable of responding to the orders we give them, we are totally paralyzed. We are dependent on our cells, but at the same time it is up to us to facilitate their task, since we are a spiritual entity both conscious and free. The bond that exists between ourselves and all the souls that inhabit our organism is very difficult to explain, but it is there, and it is very strong. This is why we must reach the point where we animate, purify, enlighten, and spiritualize all the cells of our body.

Human beings have made great progress over thousands of years in that they have managed to animate a few cells of the brain, which think and reason, and they have come to understand many things thanks to these few souls. But that is still not enough. This understanding must be extended to all our organs. Only when we begin to understand things with the whole of our body, only when we feel them and vibrate in unison with them, do we truly understand them, and we can achieve this only by working on all those souls that dwell within us. The purpose of all spiritual exercises is to send light, life, and love to the entities within us in order to stimulate and inspire them. In this way they will begin to work better and better.

The mistake of human beings lies in their failure to sense the bond that binds them to all these inhabitants, and this lack of understanding paralyses and limits them. You will ask: 'How can we establish this bond with our cells? They will never understand.' And here again you are mistaken, because they too possess a form of intelligence. Just look at how your cells are able to repair themselves after you have hurt yourself. You need not do anything; after a few days the wound closes up and your skin is back to normal. Do you know how your cells manage to repair everything? No you don't, and neither do I. But *they* know. All these cells have a particular kind of intelligence which enables them to do different things. Their numbers include chemists, physicists, mechanics, biologists, doctors, philosophers, and more. One day science will discover all these wonders. In the meantime, however, it is up to us to work mentally to send light and love throughout our organism in order to regenerate it.

This work is possible, and it is made a great deal easier by the fact that the cells of our body are continually being renewed. After a certain time – this is generally said to be seven years – they are all replaced. New cells have succeeded the old. So why do human beings always make the same mistakes? Why do they cling to the same weaknesses? Why do they fall victim to the same illnesses? This would be inexplicable if it were not for the fact that when our organism attracts new materials from outside in order to replace those that have grown old and become worn out, one vital thing is not renewed, and that is the memory of the cells. Indeed, every new cell continues to work in exactly the same way as the one it has replaced.

We can compare this phenomenon to the way in which factories and businesses work. When the employees reach the age of retirement, they are replaced with younger people who are given the same work, with the same objectives and using the same methods. One might say that memory is being passed on from one worker to another. In the same way, because memory is passed on from one cell to another, a human being continues to make the same mistakes. The particles of his body can renew themselves as much as they like, but he stays the same because it does not occur to him to change the memory of his cells. The cells are new but they perform the same tasks in the same way. It is up to each one of us, therefore, to make improvements in our psychic life. In this way, not only shall we be acting on the material particles of our body on the physical plane, but we shall also be changing the memory of our cells, and our bad habits will gradually be replaced with new and better patterns of behaviour.[2] Our innermost memory is thus replaced, and it records new patterns.

It is said in initiatic science that every organ and every cell of every organ has an etheric double. Well, that is where memory is. All our cells, in particular those in the grey and white matter of the brain and the solar plexus, record our actions, our desires, our feelings, and our thoughts. These recordings are like patterns or moulds. Once recorded, everything must repeat itself. This is how a habit is formed, and in order to change a habit we must change the pattern and make a new recording by striving to act in accordance with the new goal we have set ourselves. To achieve this we need to be extremely vigilant. If we are not vigilant, we forget and the old pattern is activated again. The Scriptures say: *Discipline yourselves, keep alert. Like a roaring lion your adversary the devil prowls around, looking for someone to devour.*[3] Indeed, in this vigilance lies the secret of change, and henceforth we must learn to act and speak differently, and to nurture different thoughts and feelings in order to etch deep within us the patterns of the new life coming to us from celestial regions. If we get used to practising in this way, we shall gradually manage to change the old recordings, the old patterns.

In reality, those old patterns will never completely disappear, because nothing ever disappears in nature. Recordings cannot be erased; they remain in the archives, that is, in the subconscious. The only thing you can do is endeavour to replace bad habits by better ones. And when I say 'habits' I mean not only actions, but also feelings and thoughts, because in this area too we have bad habits like slippery slopes down which we let ourselves slide.

When, for whatever reason, people allow themselves to give a free rein to jealousy, hatred, lack of understanding, and so on, they are spreading putrid fumes, and the first to be affected by these fumes are those tiny beings within them, their own cells. And how are they going to feel, after maltreating their cells and setting them such a bad example? Too many people imagine they have done their duty when they have given other people a good impression of themselves, of their courage, self-control, and morality. Well let me tell you that it is not to others that you need to learn to set an example, but to yourself, to your own cells, because your cells are like children who need to be educated. What a charade! In front of others you seek to show yourself faultless, you express generosity and put on airs, but once you are alone with yourself, you abandon your good manners and give a free rein to all those bad thoughts and feelings. And then of course all your cells – who are watching your behaviour – receive a very bad example. Yes, because everything is recorded within, and your cells begin to think that they too can do as they please, and it becomes impossible to make them obey you.

I have so often told you that we must be examples.[4] But before we can set an example to others we must be an example to ourselves, to all this population of cells that inhabits us. They are in constant communication with us, and we cannot get away from them. The slightest deceit is recorded, imprinted on them, and some time later, inevitably, they imitate us. They say to themselves: 'Let's drink, eat, wreak havoc; our master is like us and we are like our master.' This is what human beings do not realize, that their cells follow their example. All a man's thoughts, desires, and actions influence his cells, and if he is dishonest, his cells also become dishonest and cunning, and it is he himself who will be the first to come to grief. Someone shuts himself away in his house, devising some dubious scheme or other, and thinking that no one can see him. Well, he is mistaken, because billions of eyes are watching him. His whole population of cells is there taking note and becoming exactly like their master. And then of course it is the master who begins to suffer, for whom things start to go wrong. And then he complains: 'But what is happening inside me? There's a revolution going on!' In fact, it is he who has taught his cells to behave like that.

All disorders within you are the result of the bad way you have educated your cells. You grumble as you sweep the floor, you knock over the chairs, you kick the door shut, you bang into the furniture. You are not aware of it, but these inharmonious movements are imprinted on your cells, and then they imitate you. When they move something they too give it a kick, and you shout: 'Ouch, what was that?' Well, some of your cells are simply kicking the furniture around; they are doing as you did.

So, if you have always given your cells a bad example, from now on you must give them the example of a better attitude, a better approach, a better way to behave. For your cells are watching, and they will take these changes into consideration. In this too they will imitate you. To begin with, of course, your new behaviour will not seem natural to you, but gradually it will become part of you, and you will feel supported and encouraged to continue in the same direction.

Let me repeat that it is to your cells you must first of all set an example, and do not wait until there are others there to watch you. Even when you are at home by yourself, try to achieve good things. Collect your thoughts and begin by going over the points you have not yet sorted out: 'Here I need to be more understanding or more patient; there I need to show myself less vulnerable; and there I need to show more trust,' and your cells, who see all your efforts, will take note and do likewise. And then you will see that gradually it will become less difficult to find the right frame of mind.

You know how pupils in a classroom sit quietly at their desks when the teacher is there, but as soon as he or she leaves the room, they begin to shout and argue with each other. And similarly with lions in a circus; when their master is there watching them, they are quiet and perform the tricks they are asked to do, but as soon as the lion-tamer leaves the enclosure or if he lets down his guard for just a moment, they go for each other and maybe even pounce on their master to tear him to pieces. Well, the cells of our organism do exactly the same: as long as we impose ourselves upon them with our control, our dignity, so long as we behave responsibly, they recognize and accept our authority and remain faithful to us. If not, they will take the first opportunity to betray us.

And I would go even further and say that when you set a good example for your cells, not only will you be supported, but thanks to the law of affinity, the new patterns you are recording within yourself put you in contact with the luminous regions of the invisible world who send you the purest energies and the most precious particles. It is therefore up to each one of you to attract the most subtle and most radiant elements from the cosmic ocean and form your body of glory with them, the body of immortality, the body of light.

We all carry this body of glory within us like a seed that we have to develop. How? Well, how does a mother form her child? A child is also a seed to begin with, but by eating, breathing, thinking about it, and loving it, she gives it the materials it needs in order to develop. It is she who forms her child, so she must be vigilant in her thoughts and feelings, so as to form it with all that is best in her. It is the same for the body of glory. We could say that the body of glory is the body – or dwelling or temple – that we build for the Christ-principle within us. When we experience a highly elevated state of consciousness, we attract luminous particles that contribute to the formation of our body of glory. This is how we help it to grow. It can develop only if it is given the best of ourselves, and if we nourish it with our flesh and blood, our fluid, our very life for a long time, one day it will begin to shine. The body of glory is made of materials that are pure light which neither rust nor tarnish. This is why it is immortal and works wonders, firstly within us and then outside of us.

Every human being can build their body of glory, on one condition, that they endeavour to outdo and surpass themselves in order to attract the purest and most luminous particles. As long as human beings remain on the level of ordinary consciousness, they attract elements, of course, but these elements serve to feed only their astral body. And then their astral body swells up, like that of the rich man in the parable, and prevents them from passing through the gateway to the kingdom of God. Something within us is constantly being fed by our thoughts and feelings, by the way we live, and it is up to us to choose what we want to feed: our lower bodies or our body of glory. The construction of the body of glory is a long-term undertaking, that is true, but you can all start today. By learning to bring order to your psychic life, by learning to purify and harmonize it, you elevate your level of consciousness and attract materials of the very highest quality.

This is what we do when we watch the sunrise every morning. In our minds, as we distance ourselves from the earth and connect with heaven, with the sun, we take a few very luminous particles to add them to our body of glory. But whether we are gazing at the sun, at the top of a mountain, in a church, or at home, the process is the same. We can always search for, find, and attract the best particles in order to build our body of glory, which becomes our own body. Then, the day we have to leave behind our physical body, which is no more than a wrapping, we go off into space with this luminous body that is the true temple of God.[5] It is in this body that we will live eternally. We will not die and we will regain all the powers we possessed in the distant past, while we were still close to God's

541

heart: animals will obey us, the spirits will serve us. Indeed, all the forces of the visible and invisible worlds are at the disposal of those who succeed in building their body of glory, because they have become true children of God. And it is in this body, not in the physical body, that God comes to dwell.

These truths are not new; they were already known in ancient initiations. The true teaching of Freemasonry for instance, which goes back thousands of years, teaches man to become the builder of his own spiritual temple by means of symbolic materials and tools which he must know and be able to use. One of the symbolic representations of this temple is the New Jerusalem referred to by St John in Revelations: a city of perfect dimensions, with foundations of precious stones, streets of pure gold, transparent as glass, and twelve gates of pearl.[6] I have already given you the interpretation of these twelve gates when I explained where they are located and what these pearls and precious materials really are. We saw that the New Jerusalem is not a city in the usual sense of the word, but a symbolic structure representing a human being, ourselves, the 'new man' with his twelve 'gates' of pearl which are the virtues. We also saw that God inhabits this new man as pure light, which banishes all darkness.

The New Jerusalem[7] is the body of glory, the temple that we must all build within ourselves using the tools and materials God has given us. Every disinterested, generous, sincere impulse, every spiritual emanation adds something to the construction of your inner temple, the new Jerusalem, your body of glory. And each time you are in touch with the truly beautiful, each time a masterpiece of art or of thought, or the contemplation of a beautiful view brings you into contact with the divine world and you feel that your whole being quivers and expands, remember to consecrate these few particles of pure joy emanating from you, so that they go to nourish your body of glory.

Happy are those who have understood that the time has come! Happy are those who work at building their temple, who have decided to bring the Creator into their inner temple! Happy and blessed are they, because they will see the glory of God!

You understand now, what true resurrection is. It is this intense life that enables man to build his body of glory. Resurrection is not the resurrection of the physical body after death. It concerns our body, yes, but the body concerned is the body of glory, that is, the physical body so purified and vivified by the spirit that when it disappears at the time of death, it makes way for a body of light. This work of purification is accomplished by human beings themselves during the course of their successive incarnations. You must not be misled into thinking that every poor wretch who has been buried will rise at the end of time in a body of light. This must be quite clear: contrary to what the Church teaches, the physical body will not resurrect at the end of time, and there is no need either to wait for the end of time before resurrecting in your luminous body. But it is up to each one of us to build our body of light, our body of resurrection, and it may even manifest itself during this life, as Jesus' transfiguration on the mountain proves.

The transfiguration of Jesus was the sudden bursting out of his spiritual body, his body of glory, on the physical plane, and the sight was unbearable, because it was no longer the physical light to which our eyes are accustomed, but spiritual light, which is the expression of a life so intense that it can strike us down. This is why it is said that the disciples fell to the ground. The moment had not yet come for Jesus to detach his body of glory from his physical body so as to inhabit it permanently, but he was already able to manifest it in all its glory.

A few people have been able to see the body of glory of certain initiates when they were in a state of rapture and ecstasy.

Their faces became radiant, and light emanated from the whole of their being. It is thanks to this body that initiates can travel in space and across mountains and penetrate even to the centre of the earth, because no material obstacle stands in its way. It can even help people from a distance. Yes, and even if an initiate's physical body is ill, he can continue to work and send help, for the physical body and the body of glory are two totally different realities. Even if an initiate is ill or dying, even if he is dead, his body of glory is still there, alive and radiant, and still able to touch creatures at a distance in order to instruct, advise, and console them and give them his blessing. Only the body of glory is immortal, because the elements that have gone into its construction are of incorruptible material and they do not disintegrate. This is why before leaving his disciples, Jesus said to them: *I am with you always, to the end of the age.'*

The ideal every true disciple seeks to attain is to build, in the depths of his physical body, the body that is known as the body of glory, the body of immortality, the body of Christ, which is the true body of resurrection. How did Jesus become the Christ? Long, long ago I asked him that question and he said: 'I have left a mark on earth, and that mark is indelible because I succeeded in building my body of glory. I loved God, I wanted to resemble him, and a multitude of beings and forces came to my assistance. I worked with only my thoughts and my love, but I was not alone; I called upon all the creatures of the celestial hierarchies and they came to replace the matter of my body with luminous and divine particles. They sanctified everything within me. My ideal was to resemble my heavenly Father, and I became like him. Now you must do as I did.'

This is what Jesus told me, and if you too love this high ideal, it will attract angels to you who will work to purify and transform you until all the matter of your being is illuminated by the spirit. To become like his heavenly Father, Jesus also had to have this high ideal, but it was not he who replaced every cell, every particle of his body. No human being is capable of that. There are other entities who are capable of changing the structure of matter, and we only have to invite them in. That is our work; as for them, they take on the other part of the work. When the man has deposited a seed into the woman's womb, it is not up to her to choose and organize the elements that will go to build the body of her child. How could she? There are billions of particles, and how could she arrange them correctly to form the limbs and the organs: the heart, the lungs, the brain, and so on? There are other entities who take charge of this, thousands and thousands of them. In the same way an initiate who is conscious that the seed of the body of Christ is within him sets certain processes in motion, directs them, and then all the powers of heaven and earth take charge of the rest. This too is what Jesus explained to me.

And now, ask Jesus this question: 'Should we be listening to our master, to what he tells us, to what he teaches us? Should we follow him?' His answer will be: 'Your master is my servant, he has learned a great deal from me, and he is passing this on to you. If you follow him you will advance on the path of evolution much more rapidly.'

May light and peace be with you!

Notes

1 See *«Au commencement était le Verbe»,* Œuvres Complètes, t. 9, chap. XIII : «Le corps de la résurrection».
2 See *Life Force,* C.W. 5, Chap. 2: 'Character and Temperament'.
3 See *The True Meaning of Christ's Teaching,* Izvor 215, Chap. 9: 'Watch and Pray'.
4 See *La pédagogie initiatique,* Œuvres Complètes, t. 27, chap. III : «Education et instruction - La puissance de l'exemple».
5 See *Creation: Artistic and Spiritual,* Izvor 223, Chap. 12: 'Building the Temple'; - *The Fruits of the Tree of Life – The Cabbalistic Tradition,* C.W. 32, Chap. 25: 'Building the Inner Sanctuary'.
6 See *The Book of Revelations: a Commentary,* Izvor 230, Chap. 17 'The Heavenly City'.
7 See *Les mystères de Iésod,* Œuvres Complètes, t. 7, p. 159-167.

Biblical references

They (demons) begged him not to order them to go back into the abyss – *Lk 8: 31, p. 302.*

'This is eternal life, that they may know you' – *Jn 17: 1-3, p. 442.*

'Those who love me will keep my word' – *Jn 14: 23, p. 300.*

'Those who want to save their life will lose it' – *Mk 8: 35, p. 341.*

To be born of water and the spirit – *Jn 3: 5, p. 501.*

Unclean spirit (man with) – *Mk 5: 2-10, p. 300.*

When Jesus heard this (John the Baptist beheaded) – *Mt 14: 13, p. 246.*

'Who do people say that the Son of Man is?' – *Mt 16: 13-15, p. 244.*

'Who sinned... that he was born blind?' – *Jn 9: 1-3, p. 245-246.*

'Why do the scribes say that Elijah must come?' – *Mt 17: 10-13, p. 246.*

'Wise men from the East came to Jerusalem' – *Mt 2: 1-14, p. 491-494.*

'You are gods' – *Ps 82: 6; Jn 10: 34, p. 16.*

'You have heard that it was said to those of ancient times' – *Mt 5: 21-46, p. 247.*

'You shall love the Lord your God' – *Mt 22: 37-39, p. 200, p. 447.*

'You will name him John' – *Lk 1: 13-17, p. 247.*

Index

Q

Quintessence, extracting the, *p. 316-322.*

R

Rebis, *p. 469.*
Recordings, new, *p. 224.*
Red and white, *p. 496.*
Reincarnation, *p. 15; p. 34; p. 219;*
  p. 225; p. 237; p. 244-268;
  p. 517-518; p. 525.
Religion, Solar, *p. 195.*
Renunciation, *p. 361-362.*
Resurrection
  - body (See Body of glory)
  - of the dead, *p. 510-514.*
  - of the living, *p. 516-528;*
    p. 532-533.

S

Sacrifice, *p. 248-250.*
  - of animals, *p. 339-341.* (See also
    Animals)
Seed, an image, *p. 166-167;*
    p. 180-186; p. 213-216;
    p. 520-521; p. 539-541.
Self, higher and lower, *p. 461-464.*
Senses, the five, *p. 445-446.*
Sensibility and sentimentality,
  p. 122-130.
Sephirotic Tree (See Tree of Life)
Serpent
  - in Genesis, *p. 32-33; p. 435-436.*
  - Kundalini, *p. 428-437.*
  - that eats its tail, *p. 454-455; p. 459.*
Shakti, *p. 435.*
Silence, *p. 112-119.*

Simeon, *p. 487-489.*
Sin, Original, *p. 12-14; p. 32-41;*
    p. 435-436.
Skin, *p. 380-381.*
Solar Plexus (See Plexus)
Solar religion (See Religion)
Solomon, Seal of, *p. 462.*
Spirits, Family, *p. 309-310; p. 494.*
Spring, a, *p. 129.*
Stable (Manger), *p. 491-496.*
Star (See Pentagram)
Strength of all strengths (See Emerald
    Tablet)
Subconscious/superconscious, *p. 425.*
Suffering, *p. 122-130.*
Sun
  - intermediary between human
    beings and God, *p. 194.*
  - image of perfection, *p. 105-108.*
  - spirit of Christ, *p. 196.*
  - sun and moon, *p. 469.*
  - sun, moon, and earth, Symbolism
    of, *p. 99.*
  - sun and Saturn, *p. 455.*
  - symbol of divine Trinity,
    p. 190-197.
  - symbol of human trinity,
    p. 190-196.
Sunrise
  - meditations at, *p. 186; p. 196-197;*
    p. 329-330; p. 464; p. 541-542.
Sympathetic nervous system,
  p. 399-402; p. 428-429.

T

Talmud, *p. 340.*
Telesma (See Emerald Tablet)
Temple, building the, *p. 541-543.*
Temptations, *p. 88-95.*

Books by Omraam Mikhaël Aïvanhov
(translated from the French)

By the same author:
(Translated from the French)

World Wide - Editor-Distributor

Editions PROSVETA S.A. - B.P. 12 - F- 83601 Fréjus Cedex (France)
Tel. (00 33) 04 94 19 33 33 - Fax (00 33) 04 94 19 33 34
Web: **www.prosveta.com**
e-mail: **international@prosveta.com**

Distributors

AUSTRALASIA
Australia - New Zealand - Hong Kong - Taïwan - Singapore
SURYOMA LTD - P.O. Box 2218 – Bowral – N.S.W. 2576 Australia
e-mail: info@suryoma.com – Tel. (61) 2 4872 3999 – fax (61) 2 4872 4022

AUSTRIA
HARMONIEQUELL VERSAND – A- 5302 Henndorf am Wallersee, Hof 37
Tel. / fax (43) 6214 7413 – e-mail: info@prosveta.at

BELGIUM & LUXEMBOURG
PROSVETA BENELUX – Liersesteenweg 154 B-2547 Lint
Tel (32) 3/455 41 75 – Fax 3/454 24 25 – e-mail: prosveta@skynet.be
N.V. MAKLU Somersstraat 13-15 – B-2000 Antwerpen
Tel. (32) 3/231 29 00 – Fax 3/233 26 59
VANDER S.A. – Av. des Volontaires 321 – B-1150 Bruxelles
Tel. (32) 27 62 98 04 – Fax 27 62 06 62

BULGARIA
SVETOGLED – Bd Saborny 16 A, appt 11 – 9000 Varna
e-mail: svetgled@revolta.com – Tel/Fax: (359) 52 23 98 02

CANADA
PROSVETA Inc. – 3950, Albert Mines – North Hatley (Qc), J0B 2C0
Tel. (819) 564-8212 – Fax. (819) 564-1823
in Canada, call toll free: 1-800-854-8212
e-mail: prosveta@prosveta-canada.com / www.prosveta-canada.com

COLUMBIA
PROSVETA – Calle 146 # 25-28 Apto 404 Int.2 – Bogotá
e-mail: kalagiya@tutopia.com

CYPRUS
THE SOLAR CIVILISATION BOOKSHOP – BOOKBINDING
73 D Kallipoleos Avenue - Lycavitos – P. O. Box 24947, 1355 – Nicosia
Tel / Fax 00357-2-377503

CZECH REPUBLIC
PROSVETA – Ant. Sovy 18, –České Budejovice 370 05
Tel / Fax: (420) 38-53 00 227 – e-mail: prosveta@iol.cz

GERMANY
PROSVETA Deutschland – Postfach 16 52 – 78616 Rottweil
Tel. (49) 741-46551 – Fax. (49) 741-46552 – e-mail: prosveta.de@t-online.de
EDIS GmbH, Mühlweg 2 – 82054 Sauerlach
Tel. (49) 8104-6677-0 – Fax.(49) 8104-6677-99

GREAT BRITAIN – IRELAND
PROSVETA – The Doves Nest, Duddleswell Uckfield, – East Sussex TN 22 3JJ
Tel. (44) (01825) 712988 - Fax (44) (01825) 713386
e-mail: prosveta@pavilion.co.uk

GREECE
PROSVETA – VAMVACAS INDUSTRIAL EQUIPEMENT
Moutsopoulou 103 – 18541 Piraeus

HAITI
PROSVETA – DÉPÔT – B.P. 115, Jacmel, Haiti (W.I.)
Tel./ Fax (509) 288-3319 – e-mail: uwbhaiti@citeweb.net

HOLLAND
STICHTING PROSVETA NEDERLAND
Zeestraat 50 – 2042 LC Zandvoort – e-mail: prosveta@worldonline.nl

ISRAEL
Zohar, P. B. 1046, Netanya 42110
e-mail: zohar@wanadoo.fr

ITALY
PROSVETA Coop. – Casella Postale – 06060 Moiano (PG)
Tel. (39) 075-8358498 – Fax 075-8359712
e-mail: prosveta@tin.it

NORWAY
PROSVETA NORDEN – Postboks 5101 – 1503 Moss
Tel. (47) 69 26 51 40 – Fax (47) 69 25 06 76
e-mail: prosveta Norden - prosnor@online.no

PORTUGAL & BRAZIL
EDIÇÕES PROSVETA – Rua Passos Manuel, n° 20 – 3e E, P 1150 – Lisboa
Tel. (351) (21) 354 07 64
PUBLICAÇÕES EUROPA-AMERICA Ltd
Est Lisboa-Sintra KM 14 – 2726 Mem Martins Codex
e-mail : prosvetapt@hotmail.com

ROMANIA
ANTAR – Str. N. Constantinescu 10 - Bloc 16A - sc A - Apt. 9,
Sector 1 – 71253 Bucarest
Tel. (40) 1 679 52 48 - Tel./ Fax (40) 1 231 37 19
e-mail : antared@pcnet.ro

RUSSIA
EDITIONS PROSVETA
Riazanski Prospekt 8a, office 407 – 109428 Moscou
Tel / Fax (7095) 232 08 79 – e-mail : prosveta@online.ru

SPAIN
ASOCIACIÓN PROSVETA ESPAÑOLA – C/ Ausias March n° 23 Ático
SP-08010 Barcelona – Tel (34) (3) 412 31 85 - Fax (34) (3) 302 13 72
aprosveta@prosveta.es

SWITZERLAND
PROSVETA Société Coopérative – CH - 1808 Les Monts-de-Corsier
Tel. (41) 21 921 92 18 – Fax. (41) 21 922 92 04
e-mail: prosveta@swissonline.ch

UNITED STATES
PROSVETA U.S.A. – P.O. Box 1176 – New Smyrna Beach, FL.32170-1176
Tel / Fax (386) 428-1465
e-mail: prosveta@prosveta-usa.com – web page: www.prosveta-usa.com

VENEZUELA
PROSVETA VENEZUELA C. A. – Calle Madrid
Quinta Monteserino – D. F. Las Mercedes – Caracas
Tel. (58) 0414 22 36 748 – e-mail : miguelclavijo@hotmail.com

PRINTED BY POLICROM S.A. -
08018 BARCELONA - SPAIN – MARCH 2002

Dêpot légal : mars 2002